Jean-6

FRANCE 1943-1945

# THE POLITICS OF LIBERATION SERIES

*General Editors: Geoffrey Warner and David W. Ellwood*

*Hilary Footitt and John Simmonds*

# FRANCE 1943-1945

*Leicester University Press*
*1988*

First published in 1988 by Leicester University Press
First published in the United States of America 1988 by
Holmes & Meier Publishers, Inc.

Designed by Douglas Martin
Phototypeset by Alan Sutton Publishing Limited, Gloucester
Printed in Great Britain by The Bath Press, Avon

*British Library Cataloguing in Publication Data*

Footitt, Hilary
France 1943–1945. – (The Politics of liberation series).
1. France, 1943–1945
I. Title   II. Simmonds, J.C. (John Christopher).   III. Series
944.081'6

ISBN 0–7185–1231–6

# Contents

# Illustrations

## Figures

## Plates

*(All photographs are reproduced by courtesy of the Trustees of the Imperial War Museum)*

Montgomery talking to fishermen in Port-en-Bessin, 10 June 1944

Bayeux: de Gaulle followed by a French crowd, 14 June 1944

Bayeux: Lt. Schmann, the voice of Free France from London, speaking to the crowd gathered to greet de Gaulle, 14 June 1944

The bakers of Bayeux apologize to their customers for a temporary halt in service, July 1944

Crosses of Lorraine on sale in Bayeux, indicating de Gaulle's popularity, July 1944

First British toops met by Capt. Gilles, President of the Calvados Departmental Liberation Committee, and M. Daure, the new prefect of Calvados, in the ruins of Caen, 9 July 1944

Bretteville L'Orgueilleuse: villagers discuss one of the first newspapers of the Liberation

Cherbourg: RAF officers looking at a German propaganda poster referring to the British occupation of Cherbourg from 1418 to 1480

De Gaulle with Leclerc at their first meeting at the Montparnasse HQ of the French Commander, 27 August 1944

Pro de Gaulle Parisians parading through the streets with banners, 26 August 1944

Col. Howley with Major Nunn and Pierre Mime, Secretary General of the French Ministry of Food, announcing the Allied plans for food distribution to Paris

A recruiting queue for the new French army: FFI line up to volunteer at a village near Caen, 15 August 1944

Beaumesnil (Eure): a Resistance chief questioning a woman accused of living with a German and passing information to the enemy

FFI members act as guides to Allied armoured cars in the reduction of Le Havre

The first Communist Party (PCF) meeting since 1940 at the Vélodrome d'Hiver in Paris, 9 September 1944

De Gaulle, Churchill and Eden, flanked by Duff Cooper and Bidault, taking the salute at the Armistice Day Parade on the Champs Elysée in Paris, 11 November 1944

# Acknowledgments

WE SHOULD LIKE to thank the French Government, the British Academy and the Twenty-Seven Foundation for their vital financial support, and the Cambridgeshire College of Arts and Technology for its consistent encouragement of the project. The staffs of the Public Record Office, the United States National Archives, the *Archives Nationales*, the *Institut d'Histoire du Temps Présent* and the Resistance Archive, formerly at Ivry, gave us invaluable help. Our thanks also go to the Editors of the series and the staff of Leicester University Press.

The book would never have been completed without the companionship and active encouragement of Diane Simmonds and Richard Footitt. For this we are deeply grateful.

Hilary Footitt
John Simmonds

# Editors' foreword

EARLY IN 1945, Josef Stalin enunciated the following proposition to a visiting delegation of Yugoslav communists: 'This war is not as in the past; whoever occupies a territory imposes on it his own social system. Everyone imposes his own system as far as his army has power to do so. It cannot be otherwise.' (Milovan Djilas, *Conversations with Stalin*). The purpose of the volumes in the Politics of Liberation series is to examine the liberation of Europe at the end of the Second World War in the light of this statement, which involves taking a new look at the link between international and national politics in both western and eastern Europe from the moment when the defeat of the Axis became apparent to that when the boundaries of the post-war political, economic and social systems were definitively established. The act of liberation from German occupation is seen as the focal point of this period, and the series sets out to examine the way in which the perceived national interests of the liberating powers — Britain, America and Russia — were translated into policies in the liberated countries, and the extent to which these policies were modified to take account of local forces and situations. In particular, while it has long been recognized that a key factor in the communization of eastern Europe was its liberation by the Red Army, the role played by Anglo-American forces in influencing developments in western Europe has received much less attention, and the series will aim to redress this balance.

Of necessity, each country is the subject of a separate volume in the series, but a common framework of enquiry unites them all. A number of areas have been defined as being of particular importance in each investigation: the nature of the country's political, economic and social system prior to enemy occupation during the Second World War and the impact of the occupation on this system; the nature, strength and long-term objectives of the Resistance movements in the country, its relationship to political forces from the pre-war era and to outside influences during the conflict; and the composition, strength and objectives of a government in exile or a well-defined alternative leadership abroad, if any, and the relationship of such a leadership with the host government. Examination has also to be made of the plans of the liberating power or powers with regard to the country, their attitudes towards the interests and activities of each other in the country, and the contrasts, if any, between their short-term and long-term objectives. The form of the liberation process itself, its speed and duration, the machinery used to regulate relations inside the country and the degree of intervention by the liberating powers in the country's process of reconstruction at its earliest stage all must be considered. Finally, the duration or otherwise of the political, economic and social arrangements which emerged at the time of liberation and the traces of the conflicts of that time remaining to the present day are critically examined.

Within this common approach, individual authors have nevertheless been left considerble scope to draw out specific features of each national situation; practical comparison is left to the reader. It is hoped that in this way questions will emerge which will take the comparative politics of the Second World War in Europe beyond the venerable problems of the 'origins of the Cold War', the 'development of European unity', or the 'rebirth of European democracy' round which they have revolved for so long. Much of the writing on resistance and liberation in the Anglo-Saxon world has so far tended to concentrate on the military as opposed to the political and economic aspects of the subject and while no one would want to deny the value of this kind of history it is clearly incomplete.

The sources for a series as envisaged are now plentiful. The German archives for the Second World War, which go into considerable detail concerning the politics, economics, etc., of occupied Europe have been available for research for some years. More recently, extensive British and American archives have been opened to scholarship. Nearly every European country has an institute for the study of its wartime resistance movement in which are to be found collections of primary documents, clandestine newspapers, oral testimony and other sources. While Russian archives are not of course open to unauthorized researchers from the West, the amount of Russian literature dealing with the role of the USSR in liberating eastern Europe and based upon these archives is now voluminous. Individual East European governments and communist parties have also published collections of documents and official histories of the subject. In addition, all the contributors to the series are familiar with the local historiography of the countries they treat and are thus able to take into consideration the influence of debates and analyses not normally accessible to the English-speaking reader.

G.W./D.W.E.

# Preface

The Liberation of metropolitan France is the central concern of this book, rather than the wider issue of the restoration of the French empire. The story of the Liberation of France is a paradoxical one. After the defeat of 1940, the French had a legally constituted regime which collaborated with the Germans. Unlike many other European countries, there was no official government in exile which could enter the country with the Allies and legitimately take over the reins of power. In this situation one might have expected to see at the Liberation either an interim period of direct Allied rule, or a French Resistance administration which had been placed in power by the Allies themselves. In the event, neither of these scenarios was realized. The regime which took over at the Liberation was firstly French, secondly unrecognized by the Allies, and thirdly independent.

The book views these events from two perspectives: that of the Allies, and that of the French. On the Allied side, the chief protagonists were the British and the Americans who were both actively involved in the 'D' Day operations. The Russians stayed very much in the wings, watching to see whether their Allies showed any signs of compromising with fascism before the final showdown in Germany. For the Anglo–American relationship, the Liberation of France was something of a test. The Allies started from different premises in their approach to France, and by the 'D' Day landings had still come to no agreement on either long-term policy aims in France, or short-term planning objectives.

The French on the other hand, despite the divergent claims of competing groups, and the severe communication problems between resisters in France, Algiers and London, had joined together and worked out extremely detailed plans for the political Liberation of their country. Before the Normandy landings there was a broad measure of agreement on long-term and short-term aims, and many interim administrative personnel were already nominated and in post.

The two planning systems, Allied and French, developed separately. When British and American troops landed on French soil not only was there no official agreement with the French, there was also no commonly agreed policy between the Allies on how to deal with the political future of France. As the Allied military liberated the first towns and villages they had had no official orders as to what they should put in the political vacuum left by the German retreat. This book pays a considerable amount of attention to what happened at this period 'on the ground', as Allied and French personnel faced each other and tackled the actual transfer of power, in the north and south of France and in the test case of the Liberation of the capital, Paris. It is our contention that it is in this phase of Allied–French relationships, the process of Liberation, that the foundations of what would be the new French regime were laid.

In this transfer of power 'on the ground' there was not one Liberation of France, but several. Everything depended on the balance of forces locally, the speed with which key Allied and French officials arrived, and the judgments made by those who witnessed the events. For some months after the Liberation of Paris, neither the Allies nor the French administration in the capital had political control of France. The country was a patchwork of competing local and regional power centres, coexisting with major concentrations of Allied troops.

In this situation the Allies failed to find any way of translating their massive military power into political control. They had no real alternative to the Gaullist provisional government established in Paris. They therefore watched this regime impose its own authority all over France, firstly rather suspiciously and grudgingly, and then with an increasing acceptance that its political objectives accorded well with Allied military and political interests. In considering the Liberation of France, one has the impression of two very distinct levels at work: the plans (or non-plans) of political and military leaders, and the often chaotic passing of power by usually quite junior Allied and French personnel. The diplomatic level lagged well behind the decisions made 'on the ground', on the roads and villages of France. In a very real sense, post-war France was built from the *communes* upwards, starting from Sainte-Mère Eglise in Normandy.

*Cambridge, September 1987*

# Abbreviations

| | |
|---|---|
| ACofS | Assistant Chief of Staff |
| ADCAO | Assistant Deputy Civil Affairs Officer |
| AEF | American Expeditionary Force |
| AFHQ | Allied Forces Headquarters |
| AGp | Army Group |
| AGWAR | Adjutant General, War Department (US) |
| AMGOT | Allied Military Government of Occupied Territory |
| 'ANVIL' | Codeword for the Allied invasion of southern France |
| 'ARGONAUT' | Codeword for the Conference at Malta and Yalta –Jan./Feb. 1945 |
| AS | *Armée Secrète* |
| AT(E) | Administration of Territories Committee (Europe) |
| BBC | British Broadcasting Corporation |
| BCRA | *Bureau Central des Recherches et d'Action* |
| BCRAM | *Bureau Central des Recherches et d'Action Militaire* |
| 'BIGOT' | Codeword for the special security procedure for OVERLORD |
| BIP | *Bureau d'Information et de Presse* |
| CA | Civil Affairs |
| CAS | *Comité d'Action Socialiste* |
| CAD | Civil Affairs Division |
| CAHQ | Civil Affairs Headquarters |
| CAO | Civil Affairs Officer |
| CCAC | Combined Civil Affairs Committee |
| CCAC/L | Combined Civil Affairs Committee (London) |
| CCS | Combined Chiefs of Staff |
| CDL | *Comités Départementaux de Libération* |
| CDLL | *Ceux de la Libération* |
| CDLR | *Ceux de la Résistance* |
| CFLN | *Comité Français de la Libération Nationale* |
| CFTC | *Confédération Française des Travailleurs Chrétiens* |
| CGE | *Comité Général d'Etudes* |
| CGT | *Confédération Générale du Travail* |
| CGTU | *Confédération Générale du Travail Unitaire* |

| | |
|---|---|
| CIC | Counterintelligence Corps |
| CinC | Commander in Chief |
| CLL | *Comités Locaux de Libération* |
| CMN | *Comité Militaire National* (of FTP) |
| CNF | *Comité National Français* |
| CNR | *Comité National de la Résistance* |
| COMAC | *Comité d'Action Militaire* |
| ComZ | Communications Zone |
| COSSAC | Chiefs of Staff, Supreme Allied Command |
| CofS | Chiefs of Staff |
| DCAO | Deputy Chief Civil Affairs Officer |
| DG | *Délégation Générale* |
| DGSS | *Direction Générale des Services Spéciaux* (De Gaulle) |
| DMN | *Délégué Militaire National* |
| DMZ | *Délégué Militaire de Zone* |
| 'DRAGOON' | Final codeword for Allied invasion of southern France, 15 Aug. 1944 |
| DSR/SM | *Direction de Service et de Renseignements et de Securité Militaire* (Giraud) |
| DST | *Direction de la Surveillance du Territoire* |
| EAC | European Advisory Commission |
| EACS | European Allied Contacts Section |
| ECAD | European Civil Affairs Division (US) |
| EM | *État Major* |
| EMF | *État Major Français* (Cochet) |
| EMN | *État Major National* (of FFI) |
| ETO | European Theatre of Operations |
| ETOUSA | European Theatre of Operations of the US Army |
| FEA | Foreign Economic Administration (US) |
| FFI | *Forces Françaises de l'Intérieur* |
| FFL | *Forces Françaises Libres* |
| FN | *Front National* |
| FO | Foreign Office |
| FTP (F) | *Francs-Tireurs et Partisans Français* |
| FUSA | First US Army |
| FUSAG | First US Army Group |
| G-1 | Personnel Division, War Department General Staff (US) |
| G-2 | Military Intelligence Division |
| G-3 | Operations Division |
| G-4 | Supply Division |
| G-5 | Civil Affairs Division |
| Gestapo | *Geheime Staatspolizei* |
| GF | *Groupes Francs* |

| GMR | *Groupes Mobiles de Réserve* |
| GPRF | *Gouvernement Provisoire de la République Française* |
| HMG | His Majesty's Government |
| JAG | Judge Advocate General (UK) |
| JC | *Jeunesse Communiste* |
| JCAC | Joint Civil Affairs Committee |
| JCS | Joint Chiefs of Staff |
| 'JEDBURGH' | Codename for secret actions teams to support Resistance groups |
| JIC | Joint Intelligence Committee (of British Cabinet) |
| LVF | *Légion des Volontaires Français (contre le Bolchevisme)* |
| MLF | *Mouvement pour la Libération Française* |
| MLN | *Mouvement de Libération Nationale* |
| MMLA | *Mission Militaire de Liaison Administrative* |
| MOI | *Main d'Oeuvre Immigrée* (section of PCF) |
| MP | *Milices Patriotiques* |
| MRP | *Mouvement Républicain Populaire* |
| MUR | *Mouvements Unis de Résistance* |
| NAP | *Noyautage des Administrations Publiques* |
| 'NEPTUNE' | Codename for military operations within OVERLORD |
| OCM | *Organisation Civile et Militaire* |
| OFRRO | Office of Foreign Relief and Rehabilitation Operations (US) |
| ORA | *Organisation de Résistance de l'Armée* |
| OS | *Organisations Spéciales* (of PCF, later FTP) |
| OSS | Office of Strategic Studies |
| 'OVERLORD' | Plan for the Allied invasion of north-western Europe: June 1944 |
| OWI | Office of War Information (US) |
| PCF | *Parti Communiste Français* |
| PPF | *Parti Populaire Français* (Doriot) |
| PRO | Public Record Office |
| PWD | Psychological Warfare Division |
| PWE | Political Warfare Executive |
| 'QUADRANT' | Codename for US/British Conference at Quebec, Aug. 1943 |
| R & A | Research and Analysis (Section of OSS) |
| RAF | Royal Air Force |
| 'RANKIN' | Codename of early plan for return of Allies to the continent in case of a German collapse |
| RNP | *Rassemblement National Populaire* |
| SAC | Supreme Allied Commander |

| | |
|---|---|
| SACMED | Supreme Allied Commander, Mediterranean Theatre |
| SCAEF | Supreme Commander Allied Expeditionary Force |
| SCAO | Senior Civil Affairs Officer |
| SD | *Sicherheitsdienst* |
| 'SEXTANT' | Codename for the international conference at Cairo, Nov.–Dec. 1943 |
| SFHQ | Special Forces Headquarters |
| SFIO | *Section Française de l'Internationale Ouvrière* (Socialists) |
| SHAEF | Supreme Headquarters, Allied Expeditionary Force |
| SI | Secret Intelligence (of OSS) |
| SIS | Secret Intelligence Service (British) |
| SMEA | *Service Militaire d'Études Administratives* |
| SNCF | *Société Nationale des Chemins de fer Français* |
| SO | Special Operations (Branch of OSS) |
| SOE | Special Operations Executive |
| SR | *Service de Renseignements* (French intelligence–2ème bureau) |
| SS | *Schutzstaffeln* ('Protection squads') |
| 'SUSSEX' | Codename of joint secret action teams behind enemy lines (Allied) |
| TODT | German construction organization |
| 'TORCH' | Codename for the Allied landings in North Africa, 1942 |
| 'TRIDENT' | Codename for US–British Conference, Washington 1943 |
| UD | *Union Départementale* (of trades unions) |
| UDSR | *Union Démocratique et Sociale de la Résistance* |
| UNRRA | United Nations Relief and Rehabilitation Adminstration |

# 1 The disintegration of the Republic

THE FRANCE that faced Liberation by the Allies in 1944 was deeply traumatized by the experience of 1940 and its aftermath. The actual defeat had been swift and devastatingly total.[1] With it came crashing down, not only the shaky edifice of the pre-war Third Republic, but also the whole network of relationships and value systems which underpinned that Republic. In the space of 11 days in May 1940 the Germans had reached the coast, cutting off British and French forces in the north from the remainder of the French forces and from Paris. The French government, with the new appointments of leading defeatists – General Weygand and Marshal Pétain – fled from Paris to Bordeaux.[2] Here, the group demanding an end to the fighting rapidly gained the ascendancy, and a new French government under Pétain called for an armistice with the Germans.[3] On many fronts French troops began laying down their arms even before the Armistice was signed. Pétain had agreed that the President of the Republic, the heads of the two Assemblies, the Cabinet, and possibly members of Parliament could leave Bordeaux for French territory in North Africa, thus preserving a government in exile. In the end, because of the stubbornness of the Marshal and the cunning of his advisers, only 29 deputies and one senator were aboard the ship, the *Massilia*, when it left for Casablanca, and these were subsequently arrested. Thus, instead of Republican continuity being preserved on French soil, the government and virtually all the politicians stayed in Bordeaux. The Armistice came into effect on 25 June 1940.

By the terms of the Armistice, France was divided and her army reduced. Two small zones, one in the far north which went under the German administration of Belgium, and the other in Alsace–Lorraine which went directly to the Reich, ceased to be French territory at all. In the north and north-east, two areas became special or 'reserved' zones of intense military occupation, and in addition to these there was the 'Occupied Zone' which covered the northern half of the country and the western coast. Here the French government was instructed to order all its administration to conform to German regulations and procedures and to 'collaborate faithfully with them'.[4] The French were directed to return all the population which fled from this zone and to

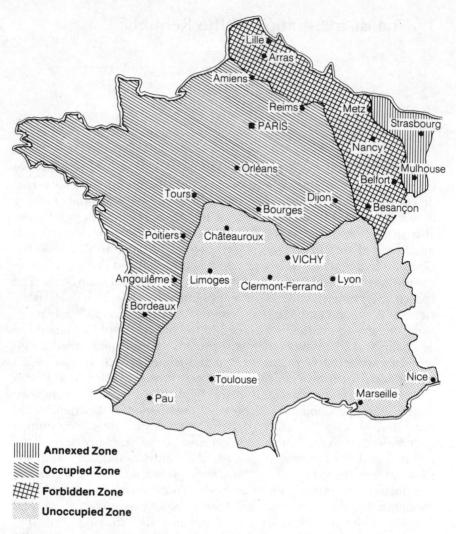

||||||| **Annexed Zone**

\\\\\ **Occupied Zone**

\#\#\# **Forbidden Zone**

      **Unoccupied Zone**

*Map 1*   France after the Armistice

leave all the economic resources of the areas where they were. The
German Military Administration of France set up its headquarters in
Paris, with five regional headquarters. Each prefecture had a *Feldkom-
mandantur* and each sub-prefecture, a *Kreiskommandantur*, but, whilst
the French government could still name its own regional administration, the occupiers had a veto on all appointments. In the Occupied
Zone, not only was the Third Republic dead, but French administration had ceased to exist for all practical purposes, and wherever a
French organization remained in existence, it was paralleled by a

German one. The Armistice allowed for the French government to
return to Paris, but it never did. Instead it moved to Vichy, so
assuming authority over the 'Unoccupied' zone in the centre, south
and south-east.

The army was reduced to 100,000 men (mimicking the Versailles
Treaty) and all military material was handed over to the Germans. The
navy was allowed to return and be demobilized in home ports, with
the German assurance that it would never be used by Germany to fight
her enemies. Transport, the economy, and particularly finance in the
Occupied Zone were taken over by the Germans, and the Vichy
government was obliged to pay for the cost of German occupation
troops. This turned into an open-ended commitment. French prisoners
of war were to stay in Germany and anyone continuing to fight on
behalf of France would be treated as irregulars – *'francs-tireurs'* – and
thus outside the protection of the Geneva Convention: a direct attempt
to dissuade any resistance.

An Armistice for the Pétain regime, now including Pierre Laval, was
a practical admission of the realities of the situation, and a great relief
to the mass of people. It was also an opportunity for a change of
regime.[5] As Paxton has pointed out, it would be wrong to blame the
death of the Third Republic solely on the machinations of Pierre Laval,
because a large number of parliamentarians were in favour of changing
the system that they blamed for the recent defeat and humiliation. The
British sinking of the French fleet at Mers-el-Kébir released the French
from final obligations to Britain and enabled Laval to launch his project
to overthrow the Third Republic. The Assembly got rid of the Constitution of 1875 on 9 July and on 10 July voted 'full powers . . . to
Marshal Pétain with authority to promulgate by one or more acts a new
constitution for the French state'. Counter proposals providing for the
Assembly to be consulted about further change, and maintaining the
Republic, even if power was given to Pétain, were swept away. The
Assembly voted by 569 to 80, with 17 abstentions, in favour of the
motion. Thus ended the old world of the Republic. There was uproar
and turmoil in the Assembly of the two chambers, but apart from the
30 detained in Algiers, there was no coercion on the members; they
voted enthusiastically or with a sense of resignation, not unwillingly.[6]

On the following day Pétain promulgated the first of his Constitutional Acts in which he declared: 'We, Philippe Pétain, Marshal of
France, assume the functions of Chief of State . . . '. The subsequent
Acts ended the Republic and transferred all the powers of the state to
Pétain. The Vichy regime was born. It immediately sought collaboration with the Germans through the Armistice negotiations, heads-
of-state contacts and the efforts of Laval, who was conducting his own
personal diplomacy via the German ambassador in Paris, Otto Abetz.

This new policy was symptomatic of the total change in the regime. The new government appeared to many as the revenge of the inter-war far right movements, wreaked upon the Popular Front Assembly. Yet although Ybarnégaray, a former right-wing leaguer, did become Minister for Youth and Health, members of the paramilitary right and their political successors failed to get posts at Vichy until later in its existence, and even then only a handful of less important ones. It was former Third Republican politicians like Laval and Flandin who held office under Vichy, and the early Pétain ministry was half composed of men who had served the Third Republic.

The distinguishing feature of the new Vichy regime, however, was its reliance on experts; non-political appointments. Admiral Darlan and a host of former top civil servants became ministers, including Baudouin, Bouthillier, Alibert, and Peyrouton. There were also ex-trades-unionists like Belin and representatives of the pre-war industrial elite like Pucheu and Lehideux. Nevertheless, later, as time went on and the situation became harsher, Laval surrounded himself with more right-wing cronies, and ex-leaguers of the 1930s made their appearance. If none of these were exactly 'new men', they represented a new combination and a set of ideas which were radically opposed to the consensus of the old Republic. If the Republic was destroyed by physical occupation in the north, it was no less dead in the south, killed constitutionally and ideologically by a 'new' network of men and ideas. In fact both were old and pernicious. These men wanted to turn the clock back in France to what they thought of as a traditional, hierarchical order, where church and family would supplant the destructive rationalism of the Great Revolution.

The whole of the underpinning political fabric of the Republic collapsed along with its institutions. The party system of the Third Republic and the individual parties themselves were destroyed by the events of 1939–40. If the British, still fighting on, looked for a Republican framework on which to build opposition to Vichy and the Germans, then they looked in vain. Party organizations, ideological and social movements did not survive the defeat intact.

The most substantial anti-fascist party, the French Communist Party (PCF), had been thrown into turmoil before the defeat by the Germano–Soviet Pact, signed on 23 August 1939. Communist Party attitudes from the defeat until the Allied invasion were complex and in some respects contradictory.[7] On the one hand, the PCF criticized the 'Capitalists of the City of London', asked its members to fraternize with ordinary working-class German soldiers and made a brief attempt to have the party newspaper, *L'Humanité*, produced by permission of the occupiers. On the other hand, there were condemnations of Vichy, calls to fight the 'oppressor', and demands for popular action to defend the rights of the working classes. Whilst it is true that the PCF showed no overt theoretical determination to resist, its line was at worst misleading and more often than not took the form of confused popular/mass rhetoric. Normal political activity was impossible, but there were important individual communists who took initiatives to start up resistance, whether they were sanctioned by the PCF or not. Although this might not amount to very much, the PCF was as actively opposed to the occupier as any other Third Republic group at this time, but communists remained a disorganized and hunted group.

The Socialist Party (SFIO) was in similar – if anything worse – disarray. In its Congress of Nantes in May 1939, the Party had produced a classic 'black and white' motion, declaring the absolute need to defend France, but opposing violence for the solution of any international disputes. On 2 September, however, the whole socialist group voted special war credits, and when the new Reynaud government was formed in March 1940 to prosecute the war more vigorously, six socialists were included. When Armistice was first mentioned at the Cabinet meeting on 12 June, the socialists opposed it to a man, but by 16 June in Bordeaux, socialist solidarity had fragmented. In the face of the crisis the Socialist Party began to break up, both ideologically and physically. There were no proper meetings of the party after it left Paris and most of its prominent men who were mayors decided that they should stay with their towns and constituents during those dangerous times.

The Radical Party – self-appointed guardian of the Republic, and yet its worst defender at moments of crisis – was similarly divided and destroyed by the events of 1939–40. It was indeed the Radical Party Speaker in the Assembly, Herriot, who called on the deputies to support Pétain, and the party overwhelmingly voted to give full powers to the Marshal. Some Radical Party leaders escaped in order to continue the fight against the invaders, and in the south radical resisters began to regroup in Toulouse and Lyon. However, many radical politicians simply returned to their towns and constituencies and waited out the crisis.

Men of the centre, and of the parliamentary right, often overwhelmed by events, drifted into support for Vichy, or, in the case of the extreme right, sought direct collaboration with the Germans. In all these groups there were notable men and women who rejected the prevailing view and moved into opposition, but they were something of an exception. The main hope for resistance to the invaders and Vichy had to be the parties of the left and centre-left, and these were manifestly unable to respond to the challenge.

Outside the political parties, the trades union movement was equally divided and destroyed by the defeat and its aftermath. Already weakened by the enmity within its ranks between socialists and communists, the *Confédération Générale du Travail* (CGT) seemed to drift through the last days of the war with their powers denied them in the 'union sacrée' patriotic agreements. The defeat and exodus, with industry and unions totally dislocated, crushed any attempt at resistance that might have been put up by industrial workers. So great was the atmosphere of disillusionment with traditional union activity, that some CGT leaders entered the Vichy Ministry of Labour, and others were prepared to edit journals which were little more than German propaganda.

The structure and substance of the Republic had disappeared. Unsurprisingly in this situation, resistance in France grew only slowly and sporadically. In the north, the presence of the Germans and their secret services made establishment of resistance groups very difficult, particularly in the border zones that were strictly policed by the military. But German occupation gave a focus to French patriotism, and the daily insults of Nazi dominance encouraged many ordinary people to refuse to accept the situation. In the south, free of German insignia, the population was slower to react against the Armistice and the defeat. They also had Marshal Pétain, whose traditional ideas appealed to many, whose French state appeared to be independent, and whose reassuring presence was said to mask a double game which he was playing to limit German incursions in French life.

Early resistance was spontaneous, like the demonstration of students at the Arc de Triomphe on Armistice Day 1940, and individual, like the *Conseils à l'occupé* written by the socialist Texcier on 14 July 1940, and the appeals for resistance signed by General Cochet and circulated in September of that year. Other members or former members of the armed forces intelligence began immediately to plan covert counter-intelligence and spying activities under the guise of legitimate Armistice army units. Captain Frenay, after his escape, acted outside the army in setting up his *Mouvement de la Libération Nationale* which, with the help of Berty Albrecht, published *Les Petites Ailes*, and developed into *Combat*. A right-wing officer, Loustaunau-Lacau, used his pre-war contacts to set up an espionage organization in the town of Vichy under the cover of an official aid committee for ex-servicemen, posing as a collaborator, whilst his assistant, Marie-Madeleine Fourcade, organized the clandestine *réseaux*. Employees of the *Musée de l'Homme*, including the director Rivet, Agnès Humbert at the *Musée des Arts et Traditions Populaires*, Cassou at the *Musée de L'Art Moderne*, established early propaganda and escape groups.

Individuals within pre-war organizations also took early resistance action. Communists, without party sanction and contrary to policy at that time, resisted in different parts of the country: Tillon in Bordeaux,

Guingouin in Limoges and Pastor in Marseilles. They often contacted anti-Nazi exiles in the party's *Main d'oeuvre immigrée* section who became the *Organisations Spéciales* and the nucleus of the *Francs-Tireurs et Partisans*. In Clermont-Ferrand, refugee members of the University of Strasbourg, led by de Menton, Teitgen, Courtin and Capitant, met to launch a Christian Democrat Resistance journal and in Lyon, d'Astier de la Vigerie and Lucie Aubrac printed *La Dernière Colonne*, later to become *Libération*. Avinin, Pinton, Clavier and Lévy organized *France-Liberté*, which published *Franc-Tireur*, and le Père Chaillet emerged from a large group of Catholic Democrats to found *Le Témoignage Chrétien*. In Paris there were a host of initiatives: the Trotskyists published *Vérités*, the CGT began to regroup, Pineau and Lacoste gathered their friends into *Libération-Nord*. Daniel Mayer circulated amongst militants and leaders in an attempt to recreate a clandestine Socialist Party, whilst members of many pre-war anti-Nazi organizations sought to re-establish contact with their friends.

From these small beginnings there developed, in the north, four major groups: *Libération-Nord*, *Ceux de la Libération*, *Ceux de la Résistance*, *L'Organisation Civile et Militaire*, and the newspaper, *La Voix du Nord*. In the south, *Libération*, *Franc-Tireur* and *Combat* were the major groups, and the communist-led *Front National* and *Francs-Tireurs et Partisans* were common to both zones, as was *Témoignage Chrétien*. Unifying groups from such different backgrounds, in such dispersed locations, with such a diversity of activity, and all prey to the close attentions of the Gestapo, was very difficult.

The British sabotage and intelligence agencies, SOE (Special Operations Executive) and SIS (Secret Intelligence Service), took time to establish themselves in France, and there was no clear idea in the early days as to what was actually happening. The British government, moreover, was cautious about dealing with clandestine groups in France. They would have preferred to treat with normally established and recognized political groupings opposed to Vichy and the Germans. The defeat had totally destroyed this possibility.

The Republic was dead, and there was no French government in exile to whom the British could accord diplomatic recognition. In the débâcle of June 1940 the only claim to represent a France which would continue fighting was made by a self-appointed candidate, General Charles de Gaulle, former Under Secretary of War, who had flown to London on 17 June with Churchill's liaison officer to the French government. Despite the resonant name, the General was virtually unknown in his own country. He spoke as an individual, and not as the official representative of the French government. Indeed he was to be court-martialled *in absentia* for desertion by the legitimate, Vichy, government of France.

The country's political structure had been destroyed by the defeat, a legally constituted regime was set to collaborate with the Germans, and there was no French government in exile. The combination of these factors left France in a very weak political position from which to negotiate its future with the Allies.

# 2 Preparations for the Liberation: the Allies

THE ATTITUDE of the Allies towards the political future of France was strongly conditioned by the different ways in which they perceived these events in 1940. The British, distressed to lose a major ally, instinctively sought to find a legitimate French administration with whom they could deal, and one which would be prepared to offer some resistance to the Germans. To begin with there was uncertainty as to where this would be found – within the Vichy regime itself, outside with General de Gaulle, or nowhere at all. Gradually, however, the British government took the view that the Gaullist organization was, in all but name, the 'real' government of France. His Majesty's Government's scenario for the Liberation thus became the establishment of this group in power on the grounds that it was popular with the Resistance, reasonably democratic and likely to install a 'normal' regime which would keep some control of the communists, and pursue a European policy supportive of British interests. Britain, geographically close to Europe, and, as it became clear, likely to be left with the major military and economic cost of policing a post-war settlement, was keen to ensure that the new French government would be a strong and sympathetic one.

The Americans, on the other hand, had not been belligerents at the time of the defeat of France and maintained relations with the legitimate government, Vichy. When the USA entered the war in December 1941, this open attitude towards the Pétain regime persisted, alongside a deep suspicion about the claims of Gaullism to speak for the French people. The American government approach to the political future of France was a good deal more pragmatic than that of the British: nothing should be agreed before the Liberation; the Allied military who entered France should, in the interim, keep control and hold the balance between competing French factions until elections could take place which would enable the people to choose the future regime themselves.

The USSR, entering the war on the Allied side in June 1941, recognized de Gaulle's committee as the representative of Fighting France in September 1942, over 12 months before the group was expanded to include members of the French Communist Party. Given their military difficulties in 1941–2, the Russians wished to support an organization which would prosecute the war against the Nazis without compromise, and no other French candidate existed. In the build-up to the Liberation, the USSR acted very much as a spectator to the preparations being made by the Americans and British. Their major fear was that the Allies would strike a deal favourable to the colla-borationist/Vichy elements in France, and their efforts were bent on attempting to ensure that decisions in the French sphere would be taken jointly by all three governments.

In the event, decisions on the political future of France were not made at all because the Allies chiefly concerned, the British and Americans, could come to no agreement. The differences in view,[1] and the stalemate which resulted forced the Allied military to take the initiative in political planning.

## Allied disagreements: recognition

CHURCHILL had been deeply discouraged by the defeatism of the Reynaud government in 1940, and was, by comparison, favourably impressed by the robust attitude of Reynaud's Under Secretary for Defence, General de Gaulle, who had made it clear that he thought the French should be continuing the fight against the Germans from the French empire. He encouraged de Gaulle to leave France for London on 17 June 1940, and took it upon himself to persuade individual Cabinet members of the wisdom of allowing the French General to broadcast on the BBC the following day. Given that no one as yet knew the terms of the Armistice, that the British were desperate to stop the French government handing ships and bases over to the Germans, and that de Gaulle had no status and no established popularity in France, the hesitations of the Cabinet, and the opposition of the Foreign Office – more disposed to deal with 'normal' governments than isolated individuals – were perfectly understandable. With the Armistice signed however, and the failure of the one attempt, aboard the *Massilia*, to transport members of a potential government in exile to North Africa, the War Cabinet could no longer deal openly with the regime in France, and declared itself ready to recognize a provisional French national committee, headed by de Gaulle. The actual scope of the recognition was limited by the fact that the General's call to continue the fight from the French empire had been met by an almost total negative response – only Catroux in Indo-China, and then be-latedly, would declare for him. On 28 June, therefore, the British recognized de Gaulle simply as, 'leader of all the Free French, wherever they may be'. Churchill continued to press for material aid for the group, and on 7 August the Prime Minister signed an

agreement with de Gaulle, giving British recognition to the Free
French, a headquarters in Carlton Gardens, some loaned finance, and
use of the BBC. De Gaulle's stock, however, did not improve when
Free French plans for an attack on Dakar turned out to be a disaster.[2]
Further difficulties over the 'Muselier affair', the Syrian campaign, and
the so-called 'rallying' to the Free French of islands off the coast of
Canada (Saint Pierre et Miquelon)[3] finally tried Churchill's patience
close to breaking point, and, by the end of 1941, he was, like other
members of the government, suspicious and wary of de Gaulle.

Contacts with Vichy had meanwhile never been completely abandoned, and the Foreign Office, at the end of 1940, was pursuing the
possibility of an 'understanding' on Vichy and British colonies in
return for a lifting of the British blockade of France.[4] With de Gaulle
unable to demonstrate widespread approval in France or the Empire,
and proving something of a liability in terms of the aggravation he
provoked, the British continued to support him as a symbol of French
Resistance, but as only one arm of a three-fold policy which included
help for all forms of Resistance in France, whether Gaullist or not.

In comparison with this three-sided policy, the attitude of the USA
before it entered the war in December 1941, was clearer. In practice the
USA could do little to strengthen the resolve of France to resist. The
Vichy regime appeared to the Americans to be the legitimate successor
to the Third Republic and they did not hesitate to recognize it.[5] To a
certain extent, the fact that a regime had been established at Vichy
which seemed to have some marginal independence from the Germans
was rather more than Roosevelt could have hoped for after the gloomy
first despatches of his ambassador in France. The Americans made
clear to Pétain that they admired him and were willing to offer him
support, but only on the condition that the French fleet did not fall into
German hands, that French North Africa and other colonies remained
under Vichy control, and that the regime afforded no aid to the
German war effort against Britain.[6] In support of this policy, the
American government was willing to give material aid to Vichy as a
means of assuaging its worst subsistence problems, so that it might
retain the loyalty of the people and be in a position to resist German
demands for greater collaboration.[7] Pétain's meeting with Hitler at
Montoire, and the collaborationist zeal of the Prime Minister, Laval,
gave the Americans pause for thought, and it was made clear to the
distinguished Admiral Leahy, who was sent as American ambassador
to Vichy, that he was to insist on a Vichy policy of non-collaboration as
a condition of American friendship. Information from French North
Africa added to the credibility of the policy since there appeared to be
substantial anti-German feeling among local Vichy circles. It was
rumoured that the military commander, Weygand, might still be

persuaded to join some kind of opposition to the Germans.[8] With the State Department strongly committed to Pétain, a policy of helping to 'resist at every point' was firmly established.[9]

In the light of this approach, Churchill's championship of the Free French and their leader did not impress the Americans. Leahy would have nothing to do with Gaullists who came to see him in Vichy, and indeed suggested that if the British got rid of de Gaulle it might well help to bring Pétain closer to Britain. The incidents which had weakened the Prime Minister's attachment to the General – the failure at Dakar, and the problems with Muselier, Syria and Saint Pierre et Miquelon (the last right on the American doorstep) did nothing to promote de Gaulle's reputation in the USA. Roosevelt's view was that he had recognized the regime at Vichy and would give no other recognition until France had been liberated, and the French people given a chance to express their own opinion.[10]

The policy of support for Pétain could however only continue as long as it appeared that the Marshal was in a position to oppose out-and-out collaborationists like Laval and Darlan. When Laval returned to power in April 1942, it became impossible to continue believing that Pétain was strong enough to resist German pressure. Leahy was instructed to return home for 'consultations', but the clear implication was that he would not return to France and that relations had broken down.[11] A small diplomatic staff was maintained in Vichy, but American attention turned to plans for the Allied invasion of North Africa and attempts to secure help for this operation from local French authorities and the Resistance. The USA wanted to involve a French leader who could call upon the local population, their own administration, the Resistance and especially military units to co-operate with the Allies during the landing. After his dismissal as military chief in North Africa, Weygand refused the American offer of this role, so the Americans turned to a French general in Algeria who had recently escaped from German captivity, General Giraud. The Gaullists were specifically excluded from this planning for security reasons, but also because of the deep distrust with which the President regarded de Gaulle. For Americans, the idea of Free Frenchmen being involved in the landings and, hence, being ready to fight Frenchmen from the regular army in Algeria seemed fraught with difficulties.[12]

Events in North Africa at the end of 1942 demonstrated an agnosticism in American views on dealing with French politics which was a clear hangover from this former 'help Vichy to resist' policy. When the Allies disembarked, the presence in Algiers of Admiral Darlan, former Vichy Prime Minister, put the status of the newly chosen General Giraud into some doubt. Before the landings Darlan had contacted the Americans with a view to changing sides, but had been rebuffed at that time. Now, as the man officially responsible for all French forces in North Africa, he was clearly in a key position to aid the Allies. An agreement between the American General Clark and Admiral Darlan was thus signed on 13 November 1942, formalizing the assistance which Darlan would provide, and giving him in return political leadership of freed North Africa, with Giraud as his military subordinate. The deal was greeted by a storm of protest from the Allied press in both countries, from the Resistance in metropolitan France, and from the Free French movement. In view of these reactions, it was perhaps fortunate for the Americans that Darlan was assassinated on Christmas Eve 1942, enabling the USA to appoint the less contentious Giraud in his place as High Commissioner for civil and military affairs.

The invasion of North Africa, and the events subsequent to this, was one of a series of factors which modified views within the British camp. The Foreign Office had become increasingly sceptical about the extent to which contacts with Vichy could be productive once Laval had returned to power.

Information from France, and in particular the evidence of the hostility with which the metropolitan Resistance had greeted the signing of the Clark–Darlan agreement and the apparent setting aside of the Gaullists, reinforced the growing Foreign Office opinion that it was misguided and dangerous to envisage the future of France without taking de Gaulle into account: 'De Gaulle is not like a quantity of gin which can be put back into a bottle'.[13]

The growing prestige of the Communist Party, whose organization had fully entered the Resistance after the German attack on the USSR in 1941, further inclined the Foreign Office to see advantages in supporting a clearly non-communist group like the Gaullists. By September 1943, the director of the French Region in the Foreign Office Political Intelligence Department was claiming that earlier divisions and doubts in the Region about the wisdom of supporting de Gaulle had now disappeared. It was vital to espouse the Gaullist cause if the Resistance were to be 'a valuable friend in the difficult period following liberation . . . The strength of de Gaulle depends entirely on how we treat him . . . The only possible people who could gain from our mistreatment of de Gaulle are the Communists.' The British Resident Minister in Algiers, the astute observer Harold Macmillan, echoed this view, pointing out that the General clearly felt he could handle the French Communist Party: 'He may prove a Kerensky, but I do not know who else will do any better'.[14]

Churchill, by contrast, was now more lukewarm about support for de Gaulle. Under increasing pressure from Roosevelt to align himself with American policy, and acutely aware of strategic considerations and British dependency upon the USA, the Prime Minister found himself in the awkward position of being pushed from one side by the Foreign Office, and from the other by the President. Churchill's difficulties continued when Roosevelt suggested that the imbroglio on French representation might be sorted out by inviting the four interested parties – himself, the Prime Minister, Giraud and de Gaulle – to come together at Casablanca in January 1943, so that a 'shot-gun wedding' could be effected between the two Frenchmen. De Gaulle's behaviour and his stubborn refusal to play the role assigned to him enraged the President and deeply embarrassed Churchill. The months following, in which de Gaulle and Giraud negotiated the formation of some kind of joint committee to represent French interests, provided a fertile ground for dispute between the Allies, with the Prime Minister again often caught in the middle.

The State Department was convinced that the British were actively supporting anti-American Gaullist propaganda, and the American chargé d'affaires in London, Matthews, suggested that the problem was really one of British jealousy over the Americans' leading role in North Africa.[15] By the time Churchill visited Washington in May 1943, American anti-Gaullism had reached new heights, with reports from Murphy, the American representative in Algiers, that the Gaullists in North Africa were becoming more confident and arrogant by the day. Although the Prime Minister sought to defend the British position – de Gaulle was clearly a symbol of Resistance and His Majesty's Government could not be expected to ditch him – he came under such pressure from the President and his officials that he wired back to the War Cabinet in London that serious damage to Anglo-American relations might be done if de Gaulle were not jettisoned: 'I ask my colleagues to consider urgently whether we should not now eliminate de Gaulle as a political force and face Parliament and France upon the issue'.

It is significant that the War Cabinet was united in a cogently argued refusal: if such a move were contemplated, the contribution of the Fighting French soldiers and navy would have to be reviewed, the influence on the Resistance would be considerable, as it would on other Allied governments and on British public opinion. In sum the War Cabinet considered that the American policy on France was fundamentally wrong and would never be understood in either Britain or France. Armed with this reply, Churchill stood firm against American pressure, but the buffer position in which he was placed was clearly uncomfortable.[16]

When the Giraud/de Gaulle negotiations finally gave birth to a French Committee of National Liberation (*Comité Français de Libération Nationale* – CFLN) on 3 June 1943, with the two men jointly sharing the presidency, it looked as though a welcome respite in the conflict might have arrived. Within a few days, however, it was evident that de Gaulle was manoeuvring to ensure his supremacy in the committee, and that Giraud was displaying, in the estimate of Murphy, the American representative in Algiers, extraordinary political naivety.[17] By the time the Allies met in Quebec in August 1943 for the Quadrant conference, de Gaulle had obtained full political control of the CFLN and the status of Giraud had been effectively diminished.[18]

By the middle of 1943, the difference of opinion between the Allies on the French question became of crucial importance as they prepared for the Liberation of France. There was no agreement on the need to recognize a particular French group or organization as the future administration of France before the Allied landing. The British (although the Prime Minister's own commitment to this wavered) now believed that the CFLN should be recognized as the future government of France. Eden pointed out to the Secretary of State, Hull, at Quebec that some form of recognition was vital, and that liberal opinion in general was in favour of recognition of the CFLN. Roosevelt maintained that the Allies' paramount concern should be for the democratic future of France. Nobody should, therefore, be recognized before the Liberation, and until elections had been held. In the intervening period, the Allies should hold the balance, probably by military administration, dealing with various French groups on a purely local basis.[19] Roosevelt told Churchill clearly in January 1943 that the role the American military had played in North Africa was the model to hold to in preparing for the Liberation of mainland France:

> I feel strongly that we have a military occupation in North Africa and as such our commanding general has complete charge of all matters civil as well as military. We must not let any of our French friends forget this for a moment. By the same token, I don't want any of them to think we are going to recognise anyone or any committee or any group as representing the French Government or the French Empire. The people of France will settle their own affairs when we have won this war. Until then we can deal with local Frenchmen on a local basis – wherever our armies occupy former French territory. And if these local officials won't play ball we will have to replace them.[20]

The Foreign Office was deeply suspicious of this American preference for dealing with whatever local authorities they chose, 'on the ground', on a purely local basis. When Foreign Office officials met State Department representatives in March 1943 they received the distinct impression that beneath the United States' desire to retain 'French territories in trust for the French people', there was, however much it might be denied, an intention to 'internationalize' parts of the French Empire, an intention which the British foresaw would be harder to implement if one central (Gaullist) authority was constituted.[21]

At least part of this sensitivity to French interests could be attributed to the general suspicions Britain harboured about USA intentions towards any imperial nation. Presidential statements on, for example, the future status of French territories like the Pacific Islands alarmed the Foreign Office a great deal: 'The next step might be to apply the same criterion to our own West Indian colonies.'[22]

Hand in hand with this fear of United States designs on the French Empire went the anxiety that planners might take advantage of a temporary period of military administration to foist an arbitrarily decided pattern of government on the French people, a ludicrous assumption, especially in the economic sphere: 'We and the Americans . . . decide what type of French economy best suits our interests and then proceed to impose it on the French people much as we imposed the mercantile system on the American colonies in the 18th century.'[23]

At the Quadrant Conference in August 1943, where the whole course of the war was reviewed, the stalemate on French recognition became public. No agreed joint statement could be produced. Instead two separate communiqués were issued. The British one recognized the CFLN as, 'administering those overseas territories which acknowledge its authority and as having assumed the functions of the former French National Committee in respect of territories in the Levant. His Majesty's Government in the United Kingdom also recognizes the committee as the body qualified to ensure the conduct of the French effort in the war within the framework of inter-Allied cooperation.' The American formula was predictably highly limited:

> The Government of the United States takes note, with sympathy, of the desire of the Committee to be regarded as the body qualified to ensure the administration and defence of French interests. The extent to which it may be possible to give effect to this desire must however be reserved for consideration in each case as it arises. On these understandings the Government of the United States recognizes the French Committee of Liberation as administering those French overseas territories which acknowledge its authority. This statement does not constitute recognition of a government of France or of the French Empire by the Government of the United States.[24]

## Allied disagreement: civil affairs

A YEAR before the Liberation, therefore, two seperate Allied policies for the future of France existed side by side. Unsurprisingly perhaps this same dualism was found in the agencies and organizations established to carry out the detailed planning for 'civil affairs' in Europe at the Liberation. In Britain, early planning had been the responsibility of the War Office. In June 1942 the War Office paper on 'Civil Administration in Occupied Areas' had foreseen the likelihood of two distinct phases in military operations – the first, when only a small amount of territory would be held and where the Commander-in-Chief would need to have complete control of administration, conducted by officers attached to his staff; and the second, when the occupied area would be larger, and where the balance of advantage would probably lie in the Commander-in-Chief handing over as much administrative control as possible to a specially constituted body. The paper accepted that routine administrative functions could be performed by the local authorities in the liberated territory, but suggested that it would be necessary to ensure that these authorities function 'within the framework of some form of emergency administration to be set up in agreement between the U.S., ourselves and for example in the case of France, the Free French movement'.[25] Whilst both phases as described implied a close Allied military control of administration, it was significant that the War Office alluded to the possibility of involving local authorities even during the first period by appointing some civil staff officers nominated by the relevant local body, in this case the Free French movement.

The Secretary of State for War set up an interdepartmental committee in late June 1942, the Administration of Territories (Europe) Committee (AT[E]), to consider the whole question of civil affairs in a broader framework. The committee was to be dominated by the War Office (the chairman was Sir Frederick Bovenschen, permanent Under Secretary at the War Office) although there was a representative of the Foreign Office, Orme Sargent, and of the Board of Trade, as well as the deputy Major-General in charge of administration, Home Forces. In addition, five US Army representatives and a representative of the US Embassy attended the committee. By the end of 1942 the AT(E) Committee reported that a civil affairs organization would be set up on the staff of the Supreme Allied Commander (SAC), with a parallel organization existing at British and American HQs. It further underlined the need for courses which would train personnel, 'for the work of administration and military government in areas of Europe'.[26] In fact a school for this purpose was created at Wimbledon in 1943, an extension of the training programme started at the Cambridge Intelligence Centre in 1941. In the meantime, a War Office section, MO11, expanded into a directorate in July 1943, concerned itself with establishing general ground rules for all liberated/invaded countries (largely based on the experience of British administration of occupied territories like British Somaliland, Cyrenaica and Tripolitania, with the addition of recent Italian experiences). The Foreign Office, it should be said, viewed this detailed planning by the War Office with some misgivings.

In the USA, by comparison, disagreements between civilian and military agencies about the control of civil affairs were more openly acrimonious and took longer to resolve.[27] The USA began planning in

January 1942 when the Provost Marshal General's Office was given charge of military government training and started to set up the Charlottesville school. Roosevelt himself was opposed to the military tackling civilian problems, and encouraged the claims of civilian agencies like the Office of Foreign Relief and Rehabilitations Operations (OFRRO) to control the planning process. In the event the War Department, with its Civil Affairs Division (CAD) set up under Hilldring in March 1943, won the day, and the following month War Department plans for civil affairs in Sicily went ahead to the almost total exclusion of agencies outside the department. The landings in Sicily in July 1943 and the prospect of landings in Italy in fact changed opinions very clearly in favour of a military solution to the civil affairs question. In November 1943, the President himself began to give way to the War Department view, and the latter, led by Stimson, built on this change of attitude, expanding its claim to civil affairs control from the initial post-battle phase to a much broader role in the post-Liberation period.

Thus far it was clear that civil affairs planning was being conducted separately by the British and Americans. As preparations for 'D' Day advanced it would be necessary to bring the two organizations together. In August 1943 therefore a civil affairs division was formed at the Chief of Staff, Supreme Allied Commander (COSSAC) in Norfolk House, London, under a British officer, Major-General Sir Roger Lumley. The division also inherited the so called 'country houses' which had been originally set up by the British to gather facts and examine problems connected with the administration of territories at the Liberation. As Donnison points out, the status of these 'country houses' was crucial in the internal debates on the nature of civil affairs which swept COSSAC and, after February 1944, the Supreme Headquarters Allied Expeditionary Force (SHAEF[28]). Under early British pressure, ideas of prolonged Allied Military Government of Occupied Territories (AMGOT) were abandoned by COSSAC, and the emphasis shifted away from regarding the 'country houses' as embryonic administrations to be transplanted to the occupied areas. Instead they were to be seen as linked to the general staff, with a mission to help the military commanders, and indeed the indigenous administration, to restore order, rather than to attempt to govern themselves. Civil affairs was thus viewed as a function of the military command and hence essentially mobile, moving with the army as it advanced, instead of the stationary and more permanent concept of separate 'country houses' left in the field as AMGOTs. The change of thinking was less influenced by political considerations than by the lessons drawn by members of COSSAC from the recent experiences of AMGOT in Italy. The debate within SHAEF was, however, by no means finished.

The doctrinal shifts of current which civil affairs joint planning withstood were clearly related to the general problem of trying to reconcile attitudes and policies which, as far as France was concerned, were totally opposed. Coles and Weinberg maintained that 'American civil affairs authorities did not start out with any hypernervous approach to Anglo–American relations, but became cautious only after receiving British proposals which from the American point of view were almost wholly on the wrong tack.'[29]

Certainly the USA became highly suspicious about the amount of quite detailed planning accomplished by British-based agencies like the AT(E) Committee, some time before American agencies had even begun to take an interest in civil affairs. They were worried by the suggestions from the London group on the likely duration of military responsibility, and by the British presumption that combined supply planning for north-west Europe should be based on the planning which had already been done by their own agencies. The American authorities were unwilling to allow Allied planning to be conducted largely in London, where their representatives would be subjected to the strong influence of an already well-established British planning system. Any planning system, however, would have to operate within the constraints of an agreed policy. On France this did not yet exist.

## Stalemate

WITH time running out and no agreement between the Allies on the political future of France, some effort would have to be made to provide the Supreme Commander with a directive on how he should handle civil affairs in the course of the military Liberation. A flurry of draft and counterdraft directives was exchanged in September and early October 1943. In a sense, the attempt to find one formula which would reflect the divergent American and British positions on France was swallowed up in the still-running dispute between the two as to which nation would control civil affairs planning for Europe. The submission and discussion of possible directives thus became part of a territorial struggle between the Allies, on the American side to ensure that planning was not concentrated on the well-established British controlled committee in London, and on the British side to oppose anything which would give real decision-making power to the joint Combined Civil Affairs Committee (CCAC) now established in Washington.

The first salvo in this particular struggle was fired at the beginning of September 1943 when the British agencies produced and circulated a draft directive to the SAC, embodying their views on the subject. The

SAC was to have supreme authority in the first phase of the Liberation, but administration should be conducted by the French, with the CFLN specifically given an advisory role. The SAC would hand over power as soon as military conditions allowed, and when there existed an appropriate civil body to whom power could be transferred.[30] The American reaction was to produce a counterdraft from the civil affairs division of the War Department, which they placed before the Washington Combined Civil Affairs Committee, thus bypassing both the London committee, and apparently their own representatives on it. The War Office instructed British representatives on the CCAC that they should on no account discuss the American draft, since this would give credence to the CCAC case to be considered the senior civil affairs planning committee.

In many ways this was a pity as far as the resolution of the French problem was concerned, since the American draft, revised by McCloy (War Department) and Dunn (State Department), represented a quite considerable advance in American thinking. Whilst the Allied versions still differed on the exact timing of the transfer of power to the French (the Americans insisting on the holding of elections as the key point) and on the importance to be accorded to the CLFN (the Americans still made a distinction between the French military whose advice SAC would seek, and the CFLN whose position was left undefined), the American draft did accept that SAC's authority would be for an initial period only. The suggestion of a lengthy AMGOT was now implicitly refuted in the agreement that there would be a (non-Vichy) French administration. These developments placed the Foreign Office on the horns of a dilemma. It wished fervently to capitalize on the apparent movement in American views, but was unable to discuss the American draft officially without supporting the USA's attempts to displace the centre of planning activity to Washington. In an attempt to circumvent the issue, the Foreign Office proposed that the Washington Embassy should try to set out a joint brief for the forthcoming Moscow Foreign Ministers' conference, based on those principles on which it now seemed, from the two drafts, there was agreement.[31] Whilst this was going on, the War Office in Britain became extremely distressed that matters which they regarded as a military responsibility should be discussed in this way by the Foreign Office and the State Department, to the exclusion of the War Office and War Department.[32] Relations between the Foreign Office and the War Office became stormy, with both sides lobbying the Prime Minister to support their respective cases. As part of their salvo, the Foreign Office circulated a long letter from Macmillan, criticizing the way in which the military were apparently seeking to produce highly detailed civil affairs plans. On the basis of his Italian experiences, these would be a 'sheer waste of time'. In his view, quasi-AMGOT principles would last no more than three weeks if applied in France, especially as, he claimed, three-quarters of the Americans in North Africa under the rank of colonel were opposed to the idea, and Eisenhower himself was changing his views.[33]

The argument in the British camp, however, was somewhat academic by the time the Foreign Ministers met in Moscow in late October 1943. It became clear at this meeting that whereas the Foreign Office had been aiming to use the draft directive to SAC as a means of broadening the discussion out into an eventual Allied agreement on political principles, Dunn for the State Department favoured doing no more than agreeing on a very basic framework for a directive, which could then be turned over to the Allied military who could fill in the details in the course of general planning.[34] Once more, the American representatives sought to avoid any attempt to resolve the French disagreement on a governmental or quasi-governmental level. Pragmatism was still the order of the day, with the political future of France at Liberation considered as a detail of interim military practice.

The British were disappointed and disturbed that this approach was still being advocated by the Americans, particularly as it was evident that the Russian Foreign Minister, Molotov, had discerned the difference of emphasis existing between his two colleagues. In this light, the Foreign Office felt the suggestion to refer the issue to the newly formed tripartite European Advisory Commission (EAC) was ill-judged, since the differences between the Anglo-Saxons would come out clearly in the open, potentially casting the USSR in the role of arbiter.[35] The Russians, viewing the arguments on the future of France from a distance, had been disturbed by signs which they detected – especially in the North African events – of Allied softness towards fascism. The sight of the two Western Allies producing agreements (on, for example, Italy) which were not sent for prior discussion with the USSR, angered Stalin, who was alert to anything which might indicate that the West was contemplating separate Armistice terms to discount the unconditional surrender which the Russians considered all important.[36] In this light they pressed for the question of France's political future to be decided by all three governments as a matter of high policy, before any detailed civil affairs planning was done. The USA was set on an entirely contrary course: the political future of France was a detail subsidiary to the more important task of continuing the successful prosecution of the war. Civil affairs considerations should not be allowed to interfere with the work of the armed forces. The British position – civil affairs planning geared to the belief that one indigenous group would assume power as soon as practicable – was poised, 'midway between these divergent points of view', a stance which would be, 'increasingly uncomfortable'.[37]

In the middle of November 1943, before the EAC could be involved, the War Cabinet pressed Churchill to bring up the issue of the counter-claims of the London and Washington committees when he met Roosevelt at the Teheran Conference in late November 1943. In fact the Prime Minister proved unwilling to tackle the question himself, and the task was left to Eden to try and persuade the Americans of the merits of the London Civil Affairs Committee as the centre of European planning. The response was still hostile, with McCloy pointing out that Washington had to retain at least nominal control of civil affairs, if public opinion in the USA was to be accommodated. In the end, as with the political policy and the directive, the only solution seemed to be to defer a decision, in this case until the SAC had been appointed.[38]

The situation was effectively a stalemate on planning for France. De Gaulle's growing domination of the CFLN at the expense of Giraud inclined neither the President nor the State Department to draw nearer to the British position. Churchill, already angry over events in Lebanon, was increasingly hostile to de Gaulle and shared Roosevelt's rage that the CFLN had arrested a number of ex-Vichy ministers, recently arrived in Algiers and expecting preferment from the Allies. At the end of 1943, the two Allied leaders were involved in a correspondence outdoing each other's condemnation of de Gaulle.[39] By December 1943 it appeared impossible to move on the French question, with all decisions in the American camp apparently having to be referred directly to the President, and Roosevelt ordering Hull to suspend future steps to plan for civil affairs in France: 'The thought that the occupation when it occurs should be wholly military is one to which I am increasingly inclined'.[40]

It would, however, be misleading to suggest that the Americans were totally united in intransigence. The monolithic anti-Gaullist attitude, which had begun to fray at the edges with the reassessment of observers in Algiers, became even less solid in the latter half of 1943. Most crucially for the future, Eisenhower's conviction that the Allies would have to talk to de Gaulle and the CFLN had strenghthened by the time he prepared to leave Algiers for Washington and thence London, where he would assume the post of SAC. In this respect, the General was still in advance of the Civil Affairs Division of the War Department which reprimanded him at length for assuming that de Gaulle was the *only* authority with whom the Allies could deal.[41]

Eisenhower's vital military perspective was supplemented by the reports being sent back by the American diplomatic representatives in Algiers. Murphy was urging in October 1943 that American policies should no longer be 'tied to the person of General Giraud'. Wilson, the newly appointed liaison with the CFLN had a long meeting with de Gaulle in November 1943, after which he informed the State Department that de Gaulle would be a major force in post-war France and that it would be sensible for the American Government to adapt its position to take account of this.[42] On 27 December 1943, Wilson and Macmillian met the French leader together and discussed an outline civil affairs agreement for France which gave a prominent role to the CFLN in the aftermath of the fighting.[43] In Washington, Bonbright, of the European Division of the State Department, who was particularly concerned with France, was already picking up the signals and urging a more pro-CFLN policy, on the grounds that a failure by the USA to recognize the French Committee would leave the CFLN to 'drift towards the Soviet Union'.[44]

Besides the reports of military and diplomatic representatives in Algiers, the findings of the United States Intelligence Services began to support the idea of a change in American policy towards France. Until the middle of 1943, the intelligence material had generally backed up Presidential/State Department official views. By late 1943, the emphasis had begun to change. Reports suggested that Giraud was not just at a disadvantage in relation to de Gaulle. In comparison, 'Giraudists hardly exist as a real political group and certainly not in resistance France'.[45] David Bruce, the head of the Office of Strategic Services (OSS) in Europe, explained that the Gaullist movement was democratic and moderate. If it irritated the Allies in discussions of sovereignty, this was because the 'serenely undefeated Anglo-Saxons' were unable to appreciate the French desire to regain their honour after a humiliating defeat.[46] OSS in Washington was less enthusiastic about the Gaullists, with reports of anti-American propaganda still flooding in, but intelligence from North Africa and metropolitan France was, by the end of 1943, emphatic that the CFLN and the Gaullists were there to stay, that they were democratic, relatively moderate, and best suited to dealing with any communist demands.[47] Thus the monolith of anti-Gaullism in the USA was much less solid at the end of 1943.

The President, however, remained unmoved. Before the Moscow Foreign Ministers' Conference in October 1943, Roosevelt had read Secretary of State Hull a new memo on civil affairs which not only repeated past principles, but stated that, to ensure freedom of choice after the Armistice, the SAC should, 'hold the scales even between all French political groups'.[48] Matthews, the new head of the European Division in the State Department, who had been very anti-Gaullist when he was chargé d'affaires in London, noted that Roosevelt was responding to British pressure to recognize the CFLN by moving back 'towards the idea of a wholly military occupation'.[49]

With 'D' Day only six months away, the Allies had still no agreed policy on France, nor any directive which could be given to the Supreme Commander. The military were still denied permission to open talks on civil affairs matters with the CFLN although Eisenhower had confronted Roosevelt on the issue during his short stay in Washington, and wrung from him the concession that talks could at least begin with the military wing of the CFLN on the practicalities of the landing and post-landing period.[50] Eisenhower had also briefed the War Department on the catalogue of burdens which the present attitude to civil affairs in France would impose on the SAC at the Liberation. Secretary of State Hull, however, whilst not unsympathetic to Eisenhower's case, still refused to distance himself from the President's anti-Gaullist stand.[51] At the root of Hull's intransigence, against the general advice now coming from his department, was President Roosevelt's continuing refusal to adopt a more conciliatory approach to the CFLN. As the weight of opinion in the American camp, particularly from the military, urged the need for an agreement or directive which accepted the reality of the situation, the President found himself (with Hull in attendance) increasingly isolated from his leading policy-makers on the French question. However, this did not diminish his determination. Throughout the winter and early spring of 1944, Roosevelt deliberately obstructed any attempt to develop a French policy more sympathetic to the interests of the CFLN.

In the middle of January 1944, for instance, McCloy produced a revised version of the original American draft directive, which represented another small step forward in American thinking.[52] The revised draft gave the CFLN an important and explicit role, forming the administration in the non-command areas and preparing the way for democratic elections. In effect the American War Department was now proposing *de facto* recognition of the CFLN through the medium of a draft directive to the SAC. The President insisted that the draft should contain safeguards against the CFLN imposing themselves on the French people. McCloy accordingly removed the reference to the CFLN arranging to set up elections, but left the rest of the draft directive intact.[53] Whilst the British attempted to get the provisions on the CFLN strengthened,[54] the President delayed making a decision on whether the revised document was satisfactory. By the end of February, McCloy and Stimson could still get no response from the President, who was clearly stonewalling on the question.[55] To the Prime Minister, Roosevelt explained that there was a great deal too much planning in detail, 'prophecies by prophets who cannot be infallible'.[56] When he did turn his attention to McCloy's draft, it was to eliminate systematically what he considered, 'political clauses', and, after renewed arguments with Stimson and McCloy, the President finally rejected the draft directive altogether, suggesting in its place a directive which he himself had written.[57] This paper gave the SAC responsibility for the whole of France, and allowed him to deal with anyone he personally chose, with the exception of Vichy. Section Three in particular would cause enormous offence to the French, since it implied that Eisenhower could establish his own French administration, and explicitly stated that he could talk to the CFLN, 'or any other group he might determine'.

The insulting tone of the President's draft directive succeeded in alienating almost all of his advisers, with the exception of the still loyal Hull. Halifax, at the British Embassy in Washington, reported that both the War and State Departments were 'increasingly perturbed' at the President's behaviour.[58] The European Division of the State Department had by this time moved closer towards the War Department's views on the future of France, leaving their Secretary of State virtually out on a limb. A reorganization of State Department Intelligence at the end of 1943 meant that the Research and Analysis Branch of the OSS in London passed reports directly to Washington from a wide variety of sources. Findings of joint OSS/SOE missions in the early part of 1944 pointed to the undeniable growth of Gaullist influence in metropolitan France. Thus, for example, a group in the Drôme, Isère and Savoie for the first five months of 1944 declared that: 'Politically de Gaulle is the only head the people look to. In many towns the Croix de Lorraine is marked up on 9 doors out of 10.'[59] The OSS 'Future of France' report, prepared for the State Department on 2 March 1944, confirmed that de Gaulle was the sole leader of the French Liberation movements, and that they were all determined to have a democratic 'Fourth Republic'.[60] By the end of May 1944 the, 'Civil Affairs Information Guide', drawn up by the OSS Research and Analysis Office in Washington, claimed that the Resistance was completely united on the view that 'the French Committee should function as the Provisional Government of France', and that 'some sort of Consultative Assembly should function beside the provisional government'.[61]

For the British agencies, one possibility to break the log jam would have been to persuade the Prime Minister to use his good personal relationship with the President in order to change Roosevelt's French policy. This Churchill was by no means willing to do. Just as the President had delayed giving his final rejection of the McCloy draft, so the Prime Minister found excuses not to raise the French question with Roosevelt. He told the persistent Eden that he shared the President's fears that the CFLN would import civil war behind Allied lines. Eden was reprimanded for always wanting to rush and do things, and Churchill quoted Talleyrand's famous, '*surtout pas trop de zèle*'.[62] By April the Prime Minister was still proving unwilling to tackle the President: Roosevelt was resting and he was loathe to disturb him; there were, with the strategic preparations for Operation Overlord, sound reasons to avoid quarrelling with the President – 'It was a very bad moment to ruffle the Americans'. As Churchill pointed out to the Dominions' Secretary, it would be a grave mistake to fall out with the President over small matters, and be seen as taking the side of Roosevelt's advisers in an internal American argument: 'I get a large number of very favourable and friendly decisions from him every week, and I do not want to spoil this process.'[63]

The only slight hope of a breakthrough was a more conciliatory speech on France made by Hull on 9 April 1944 in which he alluded to Frenchmen undertaking their own civil administration, and suggested that the USA was prepared to see the CFLN 'exercise . . . leadership to establish law and order'.[64] Although the Secretary of State claimed that his speech was nothing more than a reiteration of known American policy on France, it was evident that he had made a concession, albeit small, to the British point of view, under the pressure either of his own department, or of the clear indications that the Foreign Office was not prepared to give up the fight.[65] In private it was plain that Hull was still unwilling to do anything practical to advance the CFLN case for recognition.[66]

## The initiative passes to the military

By early May 1944 it was clear that there was no chance of getting an agreement on the draft directive to the SAC.[67] Eisenhower found himself preparing for the Liberation of France without any political agreement between the Allies on the recognition of the CFLN and without any agreed directive as to how he should behave in civil affairs. He had, of course, received a copy of the President's own draft directive – McCloy said that it was tucked away in Eisenhower's drawer, to be used if necessary as an unofficial guide.[68] Eisenhower's instinct was, however, to pursue a far more pro-CFLN line of planning for purely practical reasons. In January 1944, the SAC had pointed out that it was vital that he should begin planning with the metropolitan Resistance, eventually eliciting a telegram from the President which gave him permission to approach any French authorities for this purpose, including the CFLN.[69] Such an arrangement did not, however, deal with the crucial matter of how the Allied armies would handle civil affairs once they entered France.

In the absence of joint Allied policy on the political future of France, and with the landings drawing ever nearer, the military had been forced to plan on the basis of assumptions and educated guesses. The 21st Army Group, responsible for Allied landings, set up a civil affairs team on 5 November 1943 which had produced two drafts of a civil affairs plan for France by 8 March 1944. By 6 April it had held the first of a series of important conferences on the issue.

In all such planning the presumption was that the CFLN would be the French authorities with whom the Army would be negotiating, despite the fact that the planners had received no official orders that this was the case.[70] With Eisenhower's arrival in SHAEF, and the country houses returned to the General Staff, the emphasis of central military planning was definitively placed on civil affairs geared to military needs, rather than AMGOT civil administration. In the absence of agreed political guidance, SHAEF planners tended to work on the basis of the SAC's known views, hence SHAEF draft proclamation 6 alluded to effective civil administration by the French, and, on the Hull speech model, 'leadership' by the CFLN. Faced with the difficulties of producing a French handbook for the troops in the absence of political advice, civil affairs was urged to use Eisenhower's own policy of working through the French as much as possible.[71] On occasions, the uncertainty manifested itself in the production of duplicate draft proclamations, designed to express two essentially different policies on liberated France.[72]

The military were now desperate to resolve a situation which placed them in the front line of civil affairs, without providing the vital political instructions as to what they were expected to do. In early April McClure, from SHAEF G6, deplored the fact that the SAC might be placed in the position of taking all these political decisions himself on the ground (the Roosevelt directive) when he was above all responsible for the prosecution of a difficult military campaign.[73] Military talks with the CFLN would, in Eisenhower's opinion, hardly be enough. SHAEF required the full participation of the metropolitan Resistance in 'D' Day planning, and this could not be expected without the blessing of the CFLN. By the end of March 1944, the Supreme Commander was convinced that a civil affairs agreement with the CFLN was now vital. Within a few weeks he had communicated this to the Combined Chiefs of Staff, and told contacts in London – including SHAEF political representatives, Phillips (US) and Peake (GB) – that, although he still disliked de Gaulle, he would have to get an agreement with him: 'If you can't lick 'em, join 'em'.[74]

With military exigencies becoming more and more pressing, and no political resolution of the issue in sight, Eisenhower took the political initiative himself. To the surprise of the American political officer to SHAEF, the Supreme Commander authorized talks with the CFLN on general aspects of psychological warfare. A day later, preparatory military talks began with General Koenig (CFLN military delegate and Commander-in-Chief of all French forces of the Interior), at which it was agreed that Koenig might need to have civilian (political) advisers present at some of the future sessions.[75] Two days after these initial moves, Eisenhower asked for permission to extend military talks to civil talks, in order to 'arrive at working arrangements'. Roosevelt's reaction to this initiative was swift. A general order was issued that all conversations, working arrangements and agreements with the CFLN must be regarded as 'tentative', and that it should be remembered that Eisenhower was at liberty to consult others besides the CFLN.[76]

Eisenhower had thus been left at the end of April 1944 in the position of carrying on with his practical arrangements, without any political backing and with no assurance that those arrangements that were made would be considered politically binding. As the Foreign Office put it, he was operating on a strictly *'de facto . . . ad referendum'* basis.[77] However unofficial SAC's talks with the CFLN might be, they were nonetheless treating the Gaullist committee as the provisional government of France which it had just declared itself to be. The discussions indeed had broken down into five subcommittees to examine legal matters, fiscal questions, the problems of displaced persons, economic issues and security. Despite an Allied ban on French communications between London and Algiers, and the retaliatory action which this occasioned from the, by now, understandably sensitive French, the talks started, with subcommittees meeting and producing material.

A first draft civil affairs agreement, on the Belgian model, provided for a French delegate who would play the role of the Belgian military mission to SAC in the first phase, with the implicit assumption that such representation would, like the Belgian mission, be transformed at a later stage into the civilian government. Under this type of agreement, the CFLN's position would be virtually assured. Eisenhower was also prepared to accept the French proposal that the CFLN should issue Liberation currency, which went directly counter to stated American policy.[78] As Eden suggested in May 1944, all this was clearly out of line with present American policy on the CFLN, but if Eisenhower was able to 'put it over' the President, that was up to him. If the Foreign Office found the idea of these 'semi-official' talks rather distasteful, they were certainly not inclined to discourage the only opportunity currently on offer to break the deadlock.[79]

The actual position on the eve of 'D' Day was thus extremely muddled. There was no agreement between the Allies on what policy to pursue in France, and the CFLN had been accorded no official status. The SAC had received no agreed Allied directive as to how he was to handle civil affairs at the Liberation, and the unofficial presidential directive which he had been given was clearly judged to be inadequate, if not positively harmful to the situation. The only form of planning which existed was that done in an *ad hoc* way, without official political guidance, by the military themselves. The only point of contact for civil affairs planning with the CFLN was a series of unofficial talks which could have no real status in the absence of an Allied policy. The whole situation was unsatisfactory. As Eisenhower explained to the Combined Chiefs of Staff:

> The limitations under which we are operating in dealing with the French are becoming very embarrassing and are producing a situation which is potentially dangerous. We began our military discussions with the French representatives here in the belief that although we have no formal directive we understand the policies of our own governments well enough to be able to reach a working way with any French body or organization that can effectively assist us in the fight against Germany. For the present there is no such body represented here except the French Committee of National Liberation.[80]

# 3   Preparations for the Liberation: the French

FRENCH views on what should happen at the Liberation were, by comparison with those of the Allies in early 1944, clearer and more developed. By mid-1943, the internal Resistance had given its public allegiance to de Gaulle, and the General had set up the structure of what amounted to an alternative democratic government in exile, responding both to the implicit pressure of the Allies, and the explicit demands of French political parties to be represented officially in the Resistance. In addition, by early 1944, the French had a largely agreed policy on short-term and long-term plans at the Liberation. The administrative personnel who were, in theory, to take power in the interim, between the Allied Liberation and the arrival of a French provisional government, had been nominated to specific posts. The detailed plans which the French had developed before 'D' Day were dependent for their success on two largely unknown factors: the extent to which the group outside France would actually be able to control the behaviour of resisters within the country, and, most crucially, the willingness of the Allies to accept the policy and plans which had been made.

## The unification of the Resistance

THE FACT that Eisenhower could identify a French organization before 'D' Day which would be able to deliver effective military aid to the Allies at the Liberation indicated how far the Resistance had come since the 'débâcle' of June 1940. What had begun as the action of isolated individuals, operating in a vacuum without official structures, had developed into a number of separate groups. These groups were normally in desperate need of some link with the outside world to provide themselves with the money and weaponry which were vital if they were to achieve anything. Some groups forged direct links with the Allies, either the Americans or the British. Others were in contact with the Gaullist Free French. In each case the groups acted, with their sponsors, as independent units.

In September 1941, however, three of the groups in the south agreed to work as one organization militarily. News of this early military co-operation was brought to de Gaulle in London by Jean Moulin, a prefect from the Popular Front era, who had already distinguished himself by his refusal to work with the German authorities. The information arrived at a time when de Gaulle had, in fact, been considering abandoning any attempt to co-ordinate military action in France (which could be left to the Allies) in favour of concentrating on a political propaganda exercise.[1] Moulin's report of 25 October 1941 emphasized that de Gaulle would have to accept that military co-ordination was the top priority. According to Moulin, a failure to organize para-military formations would lead either to a proliferation of doomed actions by individuals, or to resisters being forced into the arms of the Communist Party (PCF) which had moved its formidable organization into the Resistance after the German attack on the USSR. Whatever its military efficiency at the Liberation, Moulin reasoned, a Resistance army would be of considerable help in preserving order during the transition from one regime to another.

Moulin was sent back to France in January 1942 as de Gaulle's personal representative, charged with the mission of getting the Resistance movements to declare their support for the Free French, co-ordinate their work, and ensure that the separate military organizations were placed under the command of de Gaulle. He was given considerable sums of money to distribute. A measure of the success of the Moulin mission was the fact that the leaders of the three main movements in the southern zone, Emmanuel d'Astier de la Vigerie (*Libération*), Jean-Pierre Lévy (*Franc-Tireur*) and Henri Frenay (*Combat*) officially declared for de Gaulle. D'Astier and Frenay went to London for discussions in September 1942. By the end of January 1943, the three movements had formed themselves into the *Mouvement Unis de la Résistance* (MUR, United Movements of the Resistance), and one unified *Armée Secrète* (Secret Army) had been created in the Vichy zone. Such an organization, whilst a remarkable achievement in itself, did not, however, mean in practice that all the Resisters involved were strongly pro-Gaullist, or that de Gaulle or his delegate were able to control the movements on the ground. Many resisters were *de facto* Gaullists, hoping that the General's name would serve to unite the Resistance and ultimately control the communists. Others were more sceptical, prepared to accept de Gaulle as a convenient symbol, but determined to maintain their independence and freedom of action. Very often American/British competition provided Resistance leaders with alternative sources of funding, provoking anxiety that movements directly sponsored by the Allies would be under their control rather than the Free French. Hence Moulin's concern when he discovered that Henri Frenay of the southern movement *Combat* was starting talks with the Allies (particularly Allen Dulles) in Switzerland:

'Whether one likes it or not, the fact of giving out sums of the order of several tens of millions of francs . . . is considered by the Americans as putting the movements under the orders of Giraud.'[2]

Thus far, de Gaulle's federation of the Resistance had been exclusively concerned with the Resistance movements, and these had developed outside the confines of the established political parties, divided and broken by the aftermath of the defeat. This was particularly so in the north of the country where the Passy/Brossolette mission (representing the Gaullist Committee in London and its secret service) was engaged in unifying groups around a conservative view which rejected the idea of a nationally united Resistance which would include political parties.

Gradually, however, the parties of the Left had reconstituted. The Communist Party had created two organizations which were to be dominated by its members, the *Front National* (FN) and a paramilitary wing, the *Francs-Tireurs et Partisans* (FTP). The Socialist Party's *Comité d'Action Socialiste* represented the re-emerging *Section Française de l'Internationale Ouvrière* (SFIO) but, unlike the communists, the party had taken the decision not to create its own separate Resistance movements and paramilitary formations, so that socialists could be found as individuals militating in most of the major movements. It was soon clear to the Socialist Party that this position would disadvantage them severely in relation to their traditional rivals, the PCF. If de Gaulle intended to continue building on a federation of Resistance movements, he would presumably have to accept the FN as part of this unit, which would leave the Communist Party fully represented in the decision-making of the Resistance, and the Socialist Party on the outside, without any effective voice. Faced with this organizational recognition of the Resistance movements, and fearing that the next stage would be to add PCF movements to the grouping, the socialists protested bitterly about the exclusion of political parties from the Resistance machinery that Moulin was building. In March 1943, the enormously respected leader of the socialists, Léon Blum, wrote to de Gaulle from captivity, urging him to see that a denial of the rights of political parties was tantamount to a denial of democracy: 'I beg you to realize clearly that the resistance organizations which have sprung up on French soil in response to your voice can, in no measure at all, be regarded as substitutes for political parties.'[3]

If the political parties were to be represented in any committee of the unified Resistance, a decision would have to be made on which parties could be included. If the movements of the Resistance and the parties of the Left were represented, then it was clear that the grouping would not be a fair reflection of national opinion. If, on the other hand, all the pre-war parties were included, as the socialists suggested, parties which had taken very little part in the Resistance would find themselves given a voice, alongside Resistance movements which had continued the fight against the Germans virtually alone. An important factor in the decision was the likely impact it would have on the Allies. Both the British and the Americans found it difficult to regard the Resistance movements as primarily representative of France, as they were led by men and women who were virtually unknown before the war, and who had no established political clienteles. As André Philip, then CFLN *Commissaire à l'Intérieur* (spokesman for home affairs) pointed out in the spring of 1943, the Gaullists desperately needed to appear as the representatives of 'legitimate' French political opinions:

> It is indispensable from the international point of view that we should be able to present ourselves as having the support of political groups who, as far as the British and Americans are concerned, seem to be the sole expression of French opposition.[4]

The events in North Africa at the end of 1942, and the subsequent jostling for power between de Gaulle and Giraud in the CFLN made it vital, from the Gaullist point of view, that some sort of proof should be afforded to the Allies that de Gaulle, and de Gaulle alone, enjoyed the support of democratic opinion in France.

On Moulin's second trip to France in March 1943, he was ordered to create a common organization of the Resistance which would include political parties and trades unions, a *Conseil National de la Résistance* (CNR, National Resistance Council). At the first meeting which Moulin chaired in Paris on 27 May 1943, there were eight representatives of Resistance movements (three for the non-communist left MUR; one for the northern *Organisation Civile et Militaire* (OCM) – conservative in tendency and containing members recruited in military circles; one for the socialist inclined *Libération-Nord*; one for *Ceux de la Résistance* from the Occupied Zone; one for *Ceux de la Libération* which existed in both zones; and one for the communist *Front National*), two delegates from trade union organizations, and six from political parties. The political parties included the Communist Party, the SFIO, the Christian Democrats, the Radical–Socialist Party, and two representatives from the parliamentary right, the *Alliance Démocratique* and the *Fédération Républicaine*. In an attempt to pacify the Resistance movements, who were generally most unhappy about the inclusion of parties in the Resistance Council, Moulin read a message from de Gaulle, stating that the presence of representatives of former political parties should not be interpreted as official sanction for the reconstitution of the parties as they had existed before the Armistice. De Gaulle himself, and several of his supporters from the early Free French days were, it should be said, equally suspicious about the consequences of increasing politicization of the Resistance, but the need to receive support from sources which would be accepted by the Allies as proof of the General's capacity to speak for France overcame residual ideological scruples.

The Resistance movements, however, were by no means reconciled to the re-emergence of political parties and decided almost immediately to create a rival to the CNR, a *Comité Central de la Résistance*, which would undertake to act as the real executive of the Resistance, without the unfortunate presence of representatives of political parties. In fact, the attempt was more theoretical than real, since the communist FN was unenthusiastic about an organization in which communists would be so evidently in the minority, and preferred to operate in the context of the CNR in which their actual representation was larger. Although the rival *Comité* set up a number of subcommittees in the latter half of 1943, it had been effectively outflanked by the CNR by the end of the year: indeed in December 1943 it was rather lamely insisting that these same subcommittees should remember to report back to the *Comité Central* rather than to any other body.[5] The CNR had thus become the representative forum of the metropolitan Resistance and, with its now strong political aspirations, was concerned not only to co-ordinate military action among the armed groups, through its *Comité d'Action Militaire* (COMAC), but also to prepare for the transfer of power at the Liberation, by overseeing the establishment of Liberation committees, and considering the names of candidates who might occupy administrative positions.

Ironically perhaps in view of de Gaulle's later and much publicized disdain for political parties, he had been instrumental in reintegrating parties into the 'official Resistance' and hence in ensuring them a position in post-Liberation France. Little wonder, therefore, that, as Moulin pointed out to his leader: 'the most fervent apostles of obedience towards you . . . are now . . . representatives of the former political parties, whether they're communist, socialist, radicals, popular democrats, national republicans.'[6] In return, de Gaulle received, by his own admission,[7] vital help in his campaign to convince the Allies of his credibility in comparison with that of General Giraud. In the following months, capitalizing on Giraud's absence from Algiers on a visit to the USA, de Gaulle had three decrees passed which effectively downgraded Giraud to military command. By October 1943 the CFLN had agreed that it would have only one president, appointed for one year and eligible for re-election, whilst the military commander would now be appointed by decree. The month before this de Gaulle had gone one stage further in producing democratic credentials by setting up a Consultative Assembly which was supposed to act as an embryonic Parliament to accompany the CFLN's role as government. Names of possible delegates were circulated, and agreed by the CNR. Once more, representatives of the political parties took their places alongside those of the Resistance movements. In total there were around 50 representatives of the latter, 20 for the political parties (in theory from among those who had not voted full powers to Pétain in July 1940), 12 communists who had been imprisoned in Algiers and subsequently released, 20 representatives of Resistance in the empire, and 10 local representatives from Algiers.

Members of the Resistance movements contended (and the polemic continues to this day) that the rebirth of political parties signalled in the establishment of the CNR and the Consultative Assembly effectively spelt the end of any hopes of a real change in French society after the war. Henri Frenay from *Combat* was particularly adamant that future revolution would be stifled:

> . . . this present reconstitution of political parties as they existed before the war, would be a grave error. The spiritual unity of the resistance would be threatened . . . these parties could only define themselves in relation to others by setting out party programmes. At the present time what could they possibly base these on except those principles which were found to be so inadequate in the recent trial we went through? And if they did do this, wouldn't it be the equivalent of reconstructing the former political structure, in other words, enclosing the coming revolution within strict limits, in a framework which is out of date?[8]

## The Communist Party (PCF)

IF, however, the representation in the CNR and the Consultative Assembly suggested that the pre-war political situation might be replicated, the potential balance of power between the parties was now very different. The structures of the conservative and radical–socialist parties had been virtually decimated, and they had no Resistance movements of their own which might serve as a political alibi for them at the Liberation. The Christian Democrats were playing an illustrious role in the Resistance (*Témoignage Chrétien*, for example) but were a minority, and had no organized political structures. The Socialist Party was still re-emerging organizationally, and had taken part in the Resistance on an individual rather than a party basis. Only the Communist Party (PCF) entered the Resistance with its own movement and paramilitary formation, and with its party structures reasonably healthy, if not entirely intact. This relative strength of the PCF was, as we have seen, a factor which preoccupied the Allies, since it was potentially a revolutionary party, whose scenario for the future of France might be very different from that of the British or the Americans, or indeed the rest of the Resistance and Free French. The PCF was a party of revolution which might now find itself in a unique position from which to change the course of events in France.

With the German invasion of the USSR in June 1941 the PCF had moved as a substantial organization into the ranks of the Resistance, taking with it a considerable experience of clandestine life and a readiness to take offensive action against individual members of the occupying forces – like the killing of a German naval officer at the Barbès-Rochechouart metro station in August 1941 – which represented an escalation of Resistance activity. In September 1942 the USSR had recognized de Gaulle's committee as the representative of Fighting France, and the PCF had sent a delegate (Grenier) to London in January 1943. The fact that the PCF had now lined up with the Resistance inevitably caused other political parties and movements to reassess their positions.

Relationships between the PCF (and its satellite organizations) and other Resistance groups were characterized by what Sweets calls 'far more contact than effective co-operation'.[9] This was somewhat ironic since the PCF, once completely committed to the Resistance, was, of all the Resistance groups, the one most constantly calling for unity of action. At the outset they had urged all patriots to join them in a *Front National* (FN) which indeed recruited a wide range of members from the far right to the far left. Its directing committee was clearly controlled by the PCF, but it was at pains to cultivate a non-political image, at times accepting ex-Vichyites into its ranks, and nominating conservative people to certain resistance posts. In northern France the FN rapidly became by far the most active movement. In southern France, the PCF had been slower to recreate its clandestine organization, and the FN was never in a position to seriously challenge the dominance of the MUR. When the MUR invited the FN to join it in the wider grouping of the *Comité Central*, the reply was emphatically negative. Despite its rhetoric, the PCF was not drawn to any form of unity which might remove the control of communist forces from the party.

The growing strength and apparent self-sufficiency of the communist organizations in the Resistance was a cause of concern to many. Passy, the head of the Gaullist secret service organization, the *Bureau Central de Renseignements et d'Action* (BCRA), was plainly worried by what he saw when he visited occupied France in early 1943. He reported that it was difficult to estimate the size of the communist armed forces (*Francs-Tireurs et Partisans*, FTP) precisely because they kept their troops separate from other groups, but he treated the PCF claim to have no more than 1500 men in Paris at that time with some scepticism. A similar unease about the party among Resistance movements was reported at the beginning of 1944, with calls for the CFLN to assert its central authority as a means of counterbalancing PCF influence, and warnings that the party was making every effort to stimulate the development of local Liberation committees which it intended to dominate with its own nominees.[10] The underlying fear, whether explicitly stated or not, was that the PCF was preparing to seize power at the Liberation. Later historians have supported this contention, Kriegel, for example, arguing that the party had 'a direct strategy of the conquest of power'. According to this thesis, the PCF attempted to infiltrate and control the Resistance and Liberation organizations at every level, with the objective of seizing power by the classic Leninist system of parallel powers which overcome and replace the normally established units. Rieber has claimed that the sheer number of communists on the different key organizations of the domestic Resistance (the CNR, COMAC, the Parisian Liberation Committee) indicates the communist intention to dominate the Liberation and political aftermath.[11] The reverse side of this thesis is provided by PCF accusations of the CFLN's persistent anti-communism: the communist groups were not being adequately armed, information on suggested administrators for the Liberation was given to non-communist members of the CNR only, and so on. The Communist Party indeed reported to the CNR that there was a definite attempt to marginalize the communists in the nomination of future administrators for liberated France: 'It seems to us that what they want, in Paris and Algiers, is to keep the communists on one side – communists are good for fighting and getting themselves killed, but they're not desirable as candidates for administrative posts.'[12]

Evidence on the intentions of the PCF is difficult to find. The archives of the party's secretariat, political bureau and central committee are unavailable to the historian and, even if they were accessible, are unlikely to show anything that would be politically sensitive to the PCF. The problem is thus one of assessing PCF intentions on the evidence that is now currently available. As Kedward has pointed out, there are severe limitations in the approach of much non-communist historical analysis to such evidence:

> the accepted procedures of free-thinking historical research are seen as irrelevant when communist history is involved. Communist evidence, facts and interpretations, held to originate in political dogma and not in the realities of history, are believed to be suspect if not worthless as documentation. From this springs the dubious practice of preferring evidence about communists to evidence from communists.[13]

The problems in this latter procedure are illustrated by the contradictory messages on the Communist Party which the CFLN were giving to the Allies, where the evidence retailed was designed to produce a particular effect on the listener which would be useful for the CFLN cause. Thus Laroque, head of the French military planning group, *Service Militaire d'Études Administratives* (SMEA), was asked by the chief of the Wimbledon civil affairs school to give an appreciation of the future prospects of political parties in France. He implicitly

reassured civil affairs that the communists would present no trouble to
the Allied military by stressing that the PCF had limited its action to the
purely military, and was unlikely to be as important as the Socialist
Party after the war. De Gaulle on the other hand, in conversation with
Macmillan, played up the communist menace to indicate how important it was for the CFLN to establish itself speedily in France with
Allied help: 'to prevent difficulties and even civil war in France . . . An
interval would be dangerous and would only give an opportunity for
the Communist Party to seize power.'[14]

These difficulties in making an assessment of PCF intentions are
compounded by the fact that the PCF at this period can hardly be
considered to be as monolithic as at other stages of its history. As
Agulhon[15] has pointed out, the PCF was as subject to the communication problems which the war situation imposed as other groups
and parties. As with other organizations, the communist leadership
was geographically scattered: Thorez was in the USSR, Grenier was in
London and then later in Algiers; Marty, Bonte, Fajon and Billoux were
in Algiers; Duclos, Frachon and Tillon operated in metropolitan
France, the latter often in the provinces, and the former mainly in
Paris.

Thorez in fact told Garreau, the CFLN representative in Moscow, in
January 1944 that: 'the undoubted desire of his party was not only to
support the Committee [i.e. the CFLN], but also to participate in its
governmental responsibilites, during the period of Liberation as well
as at the stage of reconstruction'. Garreau's report emphasized that
Thorez had made it clear that the PCF had absolutely no intention of
taking power either immediately or after the Liberation.[16] Other
leading communist personalities involved – Duclos, Tollet, Hervé,
Chaintron and Pannequin – have consistently denied, in memoirs and
later interviews, that there was any covert plot to take power. Most
admit that the party's hope in 1944 was that its presence during the
Resistance would ensure that it obtained considerable influence at the
Liberation.[17] In other words, that it would indeed accede to power
after the Liberation, but via legitimate democratic means, the ballot-
box. The desire, therefore, was to ensure that PCF activities in the
Resistance would produce a mass following for the post-Liberation
days. It was vital that the party should not give an impression of being
revolutionary, which might well scare off potential supporters who
could otherwise have been attracted by the party's Resistance record.
Hence the tone of PCF publications, like the PCF programme, publicized by Grenier in 1943, which was so unremarkable – sustained
patriotic note, no reference to class war, working-class solidarity or
Moscow – that the Foreign Office described it as containing: 'nothing
. . . that even a moderate Socialist could not accept'.[18] When a

representative of the Socialist Party had talks with members of the PCF central committee about the possibility of joint political action, it was evident that the communists were most reluctant to do anything which might give the present struggle an 'aura of class'. At a CNR discussion on the status of 'trusts' (a traditional left-wing bogey) after the war, the PCF delegate refused to vote on the motion on the grounds that it might divide the Resistance. The communists had indeed impressed upon the socialists that any action they took together must not be directed against the bosses: 'there *are* patriotic bosses. No need to fight against them at the minute.'[19]

More significantly perhaps, the party's internal publications tended to strike the same legitimate Republican note. The internal and semi-confidential party journal, *La Vie du Parti*, designed to brief local leaders on central committee policies and deal with organization, put a considerable emphasis at this period on control and the importance of leadership in the future. The main theme appeared to be the need to construct a large and disciplined organization, adapted to the mobilization of a mass following. From February 1944 onwards, recruitment on a mass scale was demanded – '*promotion de la Libér-ation*'[20] – which anticipated the return of normality and open political activity. In so far as the political future was envisaged by the PCF, therefore, it was seen in terms of creating an election-orientated organization, which would be able to translate wartime gains into post-war parliamentary power. In general, as Michel[21] pointed out, before the Liberation, the communists were activist as far as fighting was concerned, and '*attentiste*' in politics, preferring to emphasize the immediate problems of winning the war, and expelling the Germans, rather than longer term considerations of the political/economic/social policies to be adopted in post-war France. In the words of Thorez's May 1944 broadcast from the USSR, 'The hour of armed insurrection for the Liberation of France is about to strike. Everything must be subordinated to this sacred duty. This is no time for discussions about the future French regime. The people will see to this, as soon as they are free again.'[22]

Such political '*attentisme*' did not, however, stop the PCF from using its Resistance activism to help create a mass movement or following which it hoped would be translated into power through the ballot-box after the Liberation. The party was thus extremely concerned with those political preparations for the Liberation which were likely to have a material effect on its standing after the war: hence PCF interest in the nature of local and national elections in the post-war period, their worry about the form and duration of interim assemblies and their concern about the projected distribution of power between locally chosen bodies and government administrators.

## Political preparations for the Liberation: a new Republic?

AS THE war advanced, and the Free French and internal Resistance adopted more unified structures, thoughts turned increasingly to what should happen at the Liberation. The problem was not a shortage of ideas – the old joke went, 'Everyone's got their own political constitution'[23] – but rather how these ideas could be reconciled and brought together.

Initially at least Resistance groups within France were more conscious of the watershed effect of the defeat of 1940 than were Resisters outside. The Free French judicial committee, set up to consider legal institutions for the post-Liberation period, produced early plans which still sought to respect the institutional apparatus of 1940: at the Liberation a government committee of war would be nominated by the President in office on 16 June 1940. If he could not be found in the liberated area, the committee would be ratified by the Presidents of the Senate and National Assembly. Only if this failed would the President of the French National Committee (de Gaulle) establish the committee of war by decree. In comparison, the metropolitan Resistance was deeply marked from the outset with a desire for a complete change in the post-war world, a 'revolution' of some sort, although the actual content given to the word varied enormously from a wish for reforms in general, pragmatic institutional alterations and moderate reformism, through to a political and social revolution which would change France completely and have implications for the rest of Europe. The desire for change, for a total renovation of France, was closely linked to the insistent call for a complete change in personnel in the new regime. Publications of the metropolitan Resistance gave considerable and increasing weight to the need to punish the traitors and collaborators and ensure that they never again assumed positions of prominence in liberated France. The CNR emphasized the urgency of this '*épuration*' (purge) by placing it as a preamble to its March 1944 programme of measures to be applied at the Liberation.

Within this general acceptance of change and renovation, approaches towards general planning for post-Liberation France varied enormously, according to the emphasis of the group concerned. Some took a legalist approach, intending to create a new France by establishing a stable Republic which could never repeat the disasters of the pre-war French system. Mirkine-Guétzevitch[24] has produced a useful typology of these plans under five principal headings: proposals that envisaged a total return to the constitution of 1875, and hence to the Third Republic; those which envisaged a return to the Third Republic, but provided for an element of constitutional revision; schemes that advocated the end of the Third Republic and the parliamentary regime itself, and its replacement by an American-type presidential regime; plans strongly influenced by the Communist Party, and generally presented as a variant on the Convention model, prefiguring the future 'peoples' democracies' of Bulgaria, Poland, Romania, and Hungary; and finally a rather more hybrid set of plans which proposed a democracy based on a parliamentary regime, but one which had been modified and 'rationalized', in comparison with its predecessor. Other approaches were more overtly political in their aims, seeking to produce a new society in which economic and social relationships had been profoundly altered. The CNR programme, for example, called for nationalization of the principal means of production, and of insurance companies and banks. There should be worker-participation in industry, wage improvements, the re-establishment of a strong trade union organization, social security and pension coverage, and the extension of political and economic rights to the colonies.

At the end of 1943, with the Liberation fast approaching, these differences of opinion about the political future of France emerged into the open. The question of what regime should be established as soon as the country was liberated was of crucial importance. When the Consultative Assembly debated the issues in January and March 1944 there was, on the surface, considerable unanimity. All the draft plans (prepared by the CFLN, the Socialist Party, the Communist Party and the Assembly Committee) agreed that as soon as a substantial portion of metropolitan French territory had been liberated, the CFLN and the Consultative Assembly should establish themselves on French soil. At the earliest moment after the Liberation of the whole of France, general elections should be held by universal adult suffrage – including women – for a constituent assembly. All provided for some means by which a provisional assembly would bridge the gap between the complete Liberation of France, and the time when, after the return of prisoners and deportees, general elections could be held.[25] Three questions, however, were hotly disputed. First, there was an argument about exactly how the period between the arrival in France and the holding of elections – crucial to the re-establishment of political power and supremacy – would be handled. Both the CFLN and communist plans envisaged the holding of immediate local elections. In the CFLN scheme electors would register to vote by producing ration cards. Under the PCF plan elections would take the form of public meetings in each town and village, with the audience indicating their views by a show of hands. The third suggestion, strongly supported by the socialists, was that elections should be deferred until 80 per cent of registered male electors in each *commune* had returned. In the interim, councils elected in the last pre-war elections (1935) would be re-established. Those which had remained in office after July 1940, and hence potentially implemented German/Vichy policy, would be temporarily replaced by 'special delegations'. The CFLN plan for immediate elections based on the ration-card was attacked on all sides as impractical, and laying itself open to large-scale abuse and falsification. The communist suggestion was treated with considerable hostility by non-communist members of the Assembly. With the PCF strength in the Resistance and their organizational ability, it was evident that the party stood to gain enormously, in comparison with its pre-war performance, from elections held in this informal way at the moment of Liberation. The socialist plan on the other hand sought to minimize the PCF lead in the Resistance by delaying elections and by placing parties like the SFIO, which had polled well in 1935, in an advantageous local position from which to organize for the future. The communists, understandably, therefore bitterly attacked the socialist proposal.

The law (*ordonnance*) of 21 April 1944 which finally emerged accepted the socialist approach which had clearly found majority favour in the Assembly: 1935 elected councils, appropriately purged, would assume power until the holding of local elections, although it was agreed that those which had to be reconstituted (because inquorate after purging) would be set up after the prefect had taken the advice of the relevant Liberation committee. In effect this solution was tantamount to recognizing the right of the 'old men' of the Third Republic, albeit after pre-selection, to assume a key place in post-war reconstruction. The beneficiaries would undoubtedly be the non-communist political parties, in particular the socialists and the rump of the Radical Party.

The second question on which clear differences emerged was that of votes for women. In the March 1944 debates there was agreement that women should be given the vote to elect a constituent assembly, but a difference of opinion on whether it was good to give them the vote earlier. As far as women voting in the first elections which would be held in liberated France – local elections – there was, in fact, a great deal of hostility beneath the ritual compliments about women's role in the Resistance. The Chairman of the Assembly's committee pointed out that the committee had unanimously agreed that women should not be permitted to vote in the first elections because there were practical difficulties in ensuring that names were entered for the first time on the electoral register and also because, in the likely absence of many men still in prisoner of war camps, there was a danger that universal male suffrage would be actually replaced by universal female suffrage. It was evident that some of the arguments which had persuaded political parties before the war against the advisability of giving the vote to women – the likelihood that women might be influenced by conservative sections of the population, in particular the Church – still prevailed. Grenier from the PCF, however, proposed an amendment allowing women the right to vote in the first elections to be held in liberated France, and the motion was passed by 51 votes to 16, with the PCF and the socialists largely voting for, and the Radical Party against. In a sense, the diminished position of the Radical Party in the Consultative Assembly, compared with its dominance of the assemblies of the Third Republic, ensured that the block vote against female suffrage was lifted, although the manner of its lifting was, given the circumstances, remarkably grudging.

The third issue concerned the nature of the Assembly which would be set up before elections for a constituent assembly could take place. The CFLN, in the January 1944 debates, had proposed that this interim assembly be chosen by indirect election, based on departmental assemblies, and that it should stay in office for between six and twelve months. The reactions of the CNR and several individual sections of the metropolitan Resistance had been bitter on this subject: 'the CNR . . . considers that such an assembly would not have the willpower to renovate the country, it would be totally devoid of authentic representativeness and of authority over the country'. If the CFLN plan provided for an assembly which would have the minimum democratic credentials with which to control the executive, the communist plan, envisaging three stages, took care to limit both the size and duration of the interregnum assembly: a constant total of 100 members, sitting for no more than six months. The PCF evidently feared that the sort of relatively ineffectual parliament proposed by the CFLN, with a probably low communist participation, might well be transformed into a permanent assembly. The earlier the elections were held, the more likely it was that the PCF might benefit from the positions it had won in the Resistance. The Assembly committee, with strong socialist participation, suggested a much larger assembly than the one envisaged by the PCF – 353 members, drawn from the Resistance and the pre-war local councils – which would sit for up to one year after its establishment. The communist position throughout the debates was that the question of electing an interim assembly should not be decided until the return to France, a view which naturally aroused the suspicions of other representatives who could envisage the PCF taking political advantage of a situation which had not been clearly regulated in advance. In the event, the solution retained by the 21 April *ordonnance* was initial enlargement of the Consultative Assembly, followed by direct elections, followed by elections to a constituent assembly within a year of the full Liberation of the country.

In this complex and very public debate on the future administration of France, the decisions taken had served to close off certain possibilities and options. To begin with, PCF attempts to profit electorally at the moment of Liberation from their likely build-up of local power had been short-circuited. Then the influence of the 'new men' of the metropolitan Resistance had been decisively curtailed in the emphasis placed on the maintenance of pre-war local councils. Thirdly, the delay in local elections, and in the election of a constituent assembly, effectively gave the executive a considerable breathing space in which to establish itself before it would become truly accountable to the people of France.

## Political preparations for the Liberation: the transfer of power

FROM the CFLN point of view, some of the problems which might arise when power was transferred at the Liberation were starkly illustrated by the experience in September 1943 when Corsica had been liberated by French forces. A *Commissariat à l'Intérieur* paper underlined the key issues which would have to be addressed.[26] In Corsica, Committees of the FN which had grown up outside the instructions of the *Commissariat à l'Intérieur*, had taken power at *commune* and departmental level. Clearly organizations of the Communist Party, these had initially claimed to be the sole authority. At least as disturbing to the *Commissariat*, however, was the fact that the French military commander had established a military territorial organization, with powers apparently deriving from the 'state of siege' law, which could potentially have given him wide powers to control the civilian prefect. The paper alluded to the way in which the French military had sought, in the early days of the Liberation of Corsica, to limit the powers which the *Commissariat* had wanted to give the prefect, and to attempt to bring the Resistance under military control. The situation had been resolved, the paper claimed, by the prefect establishing his authority with the FN committees, recognizing them only on a *de facto* and temporary basis, and by the CFLN taking immediate action to recoup for the civilian representatives some of the powers taken away from them by the 'state of siege' measures. Armed with this, the civilian authorities had set about an immediate organization of municipal councils in order to 'avoid the problem of an over-active section of the Resistance giving an inaccurate picture of the views of the general population'. The twin dangers that the Corsican experience signalled were clearly those likely to arise from the military authorities and from so called 'unrepresentative' groups, which might not recognize the CFLN.

The *Commissariat à l'Intérieur* concluded that they must set up an administrative organization for the Liberation well in advance: prefects and regional prefects, *Commissaires de la République*, nominated and in position before the actual Liberation. In addition, the CFLN and the *Commissaires* would clearly have to agree and adopt a series of measures to be taken at the Liberation which should have been communicated to the relevant local officials in plenty of time. As far as the Allied dimension was concerned, the events in Corsica underlined the need to organize liaison missions which would induce the Allied military authority to accept the civil measures taken. Certain officers of the liaison mission should receive delegated powers from the CFLN and they should all be given the instructions passed to the civilian French authorities, although modified for their use. The keynote of the conclusions was immediacy. The military should be controlled by limiting its powers and the orders it received, and the revolutionary impulses of certain sections of the Resistance should be submerged by the speedy creation of local Liberation Committees on a very broad basis. The embryonic civil administration should be established by the next moon – in case there was to be an October 1943 landing – a liaison mission must be set up in Britain, and the basic decrees and instructions to the civilian powers should be written and adopted immediately.

The two pillars of the civilian administration which the CFLN were proposing to set up were then the *Commissaires de la République* and the local committees of Liberation. The relationship between these two, and the choice of personnel, would be of crucial importance to the future administration of France. Significantly, whereas the arguments over the new regime had been brought fully out into the open in the Consultative Assembly, the planning for the immediate takeover of power was a good deal more hermetic and less responsive to consultation. In between the two series of sessions of the Consultative Assembly at which the projects for setting up civilian administration were discussed, the CFLN passed an *ordonnance* (14 March), 'concerning the exercise of civil and military powers in metropolitan territory during the Liberation period'.[27] Although passed on 14 March, the *ordonnance* was not in fact published until 1 April, after the Assembly had finished its debates and was no longer sitting. The *ordonnance* provided for a delegate of the CFLN who would be appointed to exercise, in liberated territory, the whole of the ruling and administrative powers vested in the CFLN and its commissioners until such time as the CFLN was in a position to take power directly itself. The delegate would have administrative and technical support, including an officer representing the service departments and the High Command, and given the job of liaising with the Allied High Command. The liberated territories would be divided into two zones – a forward zone and a rear or inner zone. In all zones, the delegate of the CFLN would be called on to restore civil and military administration and set economic activity in motion. In the forward zone these responsibilities would be assumed by the military delegate, in the inner zone by *Commissaires de la République*, acting under the modified state of siege measures.

Looked at from the point of view of those who had spent some considerable time discussing the nature of future civil administration in France, the *ordonnance* was at best worrying, and at worst profoundly disturbing. It made no reference to the role of local authorities which the Assembly had been considering and defining since the beginning of 1944. In addition, the committees of Liberation, which were to have an advisory function in the constitutional text, as well as a vital consultative role in the replacement of former municipalities, were not mentioned at all. The six communist members of the Assembly wrote a letter of protest to the Assembly President, Félix Gouin, claiming that the CFLN *ordonnance* was: 'contrary to the spirit of the debates in the Assembly on the organization and administration of France.' In the terms of the text they warned the CFLN delegates would be given exorbitant powers for an unlimited time to establish government of their choice, and to virtually control the Resistance paramilitary organizations. As Fajon expressed it: 'the *ordonnance* of 14 March gives to one or two people very considerable powers, and sets up in liberated territory a real French "AMGOT" brought in entirely from the outside to the people of our country who have not even been consulted'.[28] Le Troquer, who had been appointed the 'disembarkation' delegate under the terms of the new *ordonnance*, attempted to answer the criticism in an 18 April interview, underlining the fact that it was inconceivable that any CFLN delegate would not co-ordinate his action with that of resisters and the CNR. To this extent, he claimed, the *ordonnance* of 14 March and the constitutional discussions in the Assembly were complementary.[29]

The confidential instructions issued to the *Commissaires de la République* by the CFLN, however, made this a difficult argument to sustain. The emphasis was on the strictly administrative role that they should assume throughout, and on the necessity for the *Commissaires* to keep the committees of Liberation under tight control. The *Commissaires* were given the task of replacing the Vichy prefects with new nominees or, in their absence, with temporary appointments. In addition the *Commissaires* were to oversee the general purge of the administration. As far as the relationship with the *Comités Départementaux de Libération* (CDL's Departmental Liberation Committees) were concerned, the *Commissaires* were instructed that they were the representatives of the government, and the CDL the representative of local Resistance, 'the true emanation (on the day of the Liberation) of the mass of French patriots'. The text recognized that it was extremely difficult to give generalized advice about Resistance in France, since it varied so much from area to area. However the *Commissaires* were told that the former Occupied Zone was 'less politically nervous' than the departments in the south. In either case: 'you must never appear . . . as the representatives of a particular faction'. In areas where there was clear unity, the *Commissaires* should try and enhance the standing of the CDL, which should be a faithful reflection of the character of the department. The instructions made clear that the *Commissaire* was not allowed to choose the members of the CDL but could use his influence to ensure that those who 'deserved to be there' joined the CDL. The instructions were categoric on the purely advisory role which the CDL must have as soon as the *Commissaire* had assumed office.

> You will not accept any decision-making *Directoire* which could undermine your own power. There cannot be, especially in these troubled times, two heads. You represent the government to the people, and not the people to the government . . . You will forget that you have belonged to a party or a particular movement, because you will have become for your region those who look after the permanent interests of the Nation.[30]

Clearly the CFLN intended to place administrators on whom it could rely in positions of immediate authority, over the heads of any framework, like committees of Liberation, which had sprung directly from the Resistance. Arguably, the Resistance had been consulted in the choice of these 'super-Prefects' who were given far-reaching powers at the Liberation. The *Commissaires* were, in fact, chosen by a committee (*Commission des Désignations*) chaired by Debré, a career civil servant. The committee, although discussing candidates with the metropolitan Resistance, was very much under the direct control of the CFLN representative, Laffon.[31] Groups in the more politicized southern zone seemed more inclined to criticize the basis of designation than those in the north. Some, for example, considered that *Commissaires* should be chosen either completely from within the Resistance groups or else wholly from people outside. For some people technical competence for the job was less important than the individual's Resistance record: 'Let's have confidence in the people . . . they will be able to pick out the elites who can assume technical responsibilities, when the time comes'. Others felt technical ability was far more essential than a spotless resistance record, and Closon (sent over by the CFLN, and given the task of setting up CDLs) suggested that this second thesis was possibly becoming more attractive to Resistance organizations: 'As the months and years go by, the Resistance tends to become institutionalized. Gradually a sort of "central administration" spirit is created with the serious dangers that that inevitably brings.'[32]

It was clear that the men who eventually emerged from this process of selection were generally taken from the ranks of the professional administrators – 14 of those 18 nominated at the Liberation had already been in politics or administration before the war. Their origins and background were typical of pre-war senior adminstrators: Foulon lists eight as coming from the liberal professions, six as former civil servants, and three ex-parliamentarians.[33] Only one, Yves Farge (at Lyons), who had been in the directing committee of the FN, could be said to have any links with the PCF, although Raymond Aubrac (Marseilles) was reckoned to be sympathetic to the communist left. On the whole the men chosen, whilst generally having close ties with the region and the local Resistance, were people who could be expected to adopt the apolitical administrative persona demanded by the CFLN and ensure that the local Liberation committees did not step out of the CFLN concept of their role.

The original view of the committees of Liberation, held for example by Resistance movements in the south in the summer of 1943, was very different from that of the CFLN. The CDLs would be representatives of the Resistance, and would take control of the insurrection during the Liberation period. From this would follow a key post-Liberation role: 'it is . . . perfectly legitimate and politically necessary that, at least for a certain time, the authority of the government be delegated at every echelon to the same men who will direct the insurrection, that is, the current leaders of the Resistance'. Closon, for the CFLN, was strongly opposed to this view: 'I cannot believe that the insurrection, if it takes place, can be directed by a sort of local soviet, which would be, in the absence of any control, the representative of the central power.' In his opinion the insurrection would largely be a matter of transferring powers, and the important thing was to ensure that a representative of the central authority was on hand to take over straight away. If this happened, and he already had evidence from three large departments that the nominated prefects intended going to their areas immediately on 'D' day, the CDL would assume a purely advisory role.[34]

In the south, where regional Resistance structures were strong, Resistance leaders demanded that they should set up regional Liberation committees as well as the departmental one favoured by the CFLN. The MUR again pressed the claim of Resistance movements to be strongly represented in the committees, rather than the feared political parties. The political parties in the south understandably demanded the right to nominate their own members. On the whole it was thus in the southern zone where the CFLN's views of the role of committees came under the most direct challenge before the Liberation. Closon for the CFLN believed that from the point of view of a future central power it was vital for the CDL members to speak with the authority of a party or trade union mandate otherwise there could develop an: 'open opposition, dividing the Resistance forces at the very moment when we must unite our efforts'. The participation of trade unionists was, he claimed, of particular importance for the Liberation: 'it will be very useful for the prefects to be able to call on the support . . . of trade-union representatives each time they have any difficulties'.[35]

If, however, the CFLN representative was perturbed at the attitude of the southern movements towards the formation of CDLs, he was equally worried by the Communist Party's *'attentiste'* approach. In the north where the party was strong through the FN, the PCF professed some reluctance to get involved in the establishment of CDLs. As Villon, FN leader in the north, explained to Closon: 'It's useless to prepare in minute detail for the takeover of power. You must have confidence in the people who will, when the time is ripe, choose . . . the personnel to fill the administrative and political posts. It is possible that there will be a certain amount of uncertainty at that moment, but we just have to accept that.' The party clearly considered that in the north at least it could benefit from a period of chaos to establish its own forces in key positions. Closon on the other hand saw the danger for the CFLN in a situation where order could be maintained by 'people other than us'.[36]

The way in which Paris fitted into this framework was obviously of great importance. In fact the communists, lead by André Tollet, had taken the initiative by proposing that a Parisian committee of Liberation (CPL) should be set up, and had circumvented both the Gaullist representative and the other members of the Resistance, by announcing its establishment as a *fait accompli*, with 18 signatures, six of which were communist or quasi-communist, whilst the other signatories had not actually been consulted. The CFLN delegates, in particular Sereulles, reacted sharply to this, claiming that since Paris was so important, it would be more appropriate to put it under some kind of CNR control, in preference to having a Parisian committee. Closon, who had not attended what was apparently a very angry meeting, reported that he felt this approach was misguided. It had to be accepted that Paris was communist:

> We can't hope to get the help of the Communists if we eliminate them from the Paris scene. We know the methods of our comrades, and we realise that it's better to give them an official position than to leave them to create in the shadow organisations which will spread disorder . . . If, as is likely, the Communists pursue, at least up to the Liberation, their present policy, they will not demand an excessive number of seats in an officially created committee, for which we will be able to choose one of our own men as chairman.[37]

The CLFN's policy, therefore, was to seek to oversee the establishment of committees of Liberation, to ensure that all groups were represented and that no one political tendency (in particular the PCF) gained control. In addition, their powers were to be carefully contained within the realm of consultative action, with the 'apolitical' *Commiss-aires de la République* taking the major decisions on behalf of the central administration, the CFLN.

Given the general orientation of CFLN policies, it was unsurprising that the question of how government departments should be run before the return of the CFLN to France was treated as very much of a 'reserved domaine' by CFLN officials. *Ceux de la Libération, Ceux de la Résistance* and the *Organisation Civile et Militaire* (OCM) complained to the then *Commissaire à l'Intérieur*, d'Astier de la Vigerie, in late 1943 that they had learnt quite by chance of proposed interim administrators, without having had a chance to comment on them through the CNR, the *Comité Central* or the *Commission des Désignations*. The reply was categoric: no such people could be chosen at the moment, and if it became necessary to proceed to a choice, the CFLN alone would decide who should fill the posts.[38] By the beginning of 1944, the issue was still highly sensitive. D'Astier, for the *Commissariat* of the Interior, suggested to de Gaulle in January that they must hasten to take a decision: 'Clearly only measures like these can avoid the risk of essential functions being occupied by unqualified people, put in office by irresponsible groups . . . also, only these measures can ensure that the Allies have no pretext for intervening in our central administration.' D'Astier's proposal was that a provisional general secretary for the principal ministries should be designated at the choice of the CNR who, he pointed out, were making insistent demands to nominate provisional administrators. De Gaulle, who had, like d'Astier himself, been opposed to any suggestion of provisional administrators who might set up ministries as rivals to the CFLN, rallied to the compromise of temporary general secretaries, but insisted that they should be designated by the Gaullist representative in France, and not by the CNR. The issue provoked long discussions in the CNR *bureau*, and it was not until 15 February 1944 that the CFLN managed to get agreement on its view: 'The desire of the *Délégation* is to submit for CFLN approval only the names of technicians, to the exclusion of political men. If you accept one political nominee, all the parties will propose their own candidates. In January the PCF wanted Justice, War and Education. The Socialists then asked for Agriculture and Finance.'[39] In fact, the final list of provisional administrators for government departments included the name of only one communist, Marcel Willard at the Justice Ministry.

The effect of these long drawn-out negotiations on the process by which power would be transferred to the French civilian administration at the Liberation was to reduce the probability of the internal

Resistance forces being able to take political initiatives at the crucial
time. In particular, the influence of the left-wing forces of the Resistance, and especially the Communist Party, was, at least in theory,
short-circuited. Arguably, the plans which had been established for the
Liberation reinforced the political authority of the CFLN and set out to
achieve a return to non-Resistance political 'normality', with land-
marks like prefects and political parties, not dissimilar to that of the
pre-war period.

## The eve of Liberation

THE ability of the CFLN to direct events on the ground at the
Liberation depended on the extent to which the Gaullists had been able
to establish structures which could control the situation at 'D' Day. The
links which the CFLN developed with the Resistance before this time
were thus of vital importance. The civilian link with the internal
Resistance was provided by a *délégué général* (general delegate). The
first of these had been the charismatic Jean Moulin who, despite
considerable difficulties, had managed to achieve some kind of early
unification of the Resistance, imposing his own personality over those
of often antagonistic and independent Resistance leaders.

Moulin's brief had been extremely wide. As *délégué général* he had
been head of a staff of some 40 people, including an information and
press bureau, and the planning organization of the metropolitan
Resistance, the *Comité Général d'Études* (CGE). He had been responsible
for distributing funds to the Resistance movements and controlling the
liaison organization with London, through which information was
received and transmitted. In addition, he had acted as the chairman of
the MUR's steering group, and as the first chairman of the newly
formed National Resistance Council (CNR). His tragic capture and
death in June 1943 understandably threw the question of CFLN
representation in France into confusion.

To begin with it was difficult to find a person suitable to take on such
a mammoth task, particularly since Moulin had had no time to groom
anyone for his succession. In the event, no likely candidate could be
found, and the post was initially split, on a temporary basis, between a
delegate for the northern zone, Claude Bouchinet-Serreulles, and one
for the south, Jacques Bingen. It was agreed that no one could combine
the job of *délégué général* and chairman of the CNR, so the latter post
was given to a man who came directly from the metropolitan Resistance, Georges Bidault, a Catholic who had been a militant in *Combat*
and then subsequently in the FN. Serreulles and Bingen, working with
a second generation of Resistance leaders who were generally less
aggressive in their independence than Frenay and d'Astier de la

Vigerie had been, tended to see their role as one of assisting and working with the movements, rather than forcing them to toe the line. In this period the Gaullist representatives in the civilian delegation seemed to speak increasingly with the same voice as the Resistance movements. This rather surprising identification, which had not occurred during Moulin's time, was undoubtedly helped by the relative isolation in which the civilian representatives in France worked. From the time of Moulin's capture in June 1943 until the appointment of Alexandre Parodi as *délégué général* in March 1944, there was a stream of telegrams and messages from the CFLN representatives complaining at the failure of Algiers and London to keep them informed about what was happening: 'You're taking two months to take a decision that we've asked you to take, and then you make the decision on facts that you had right at the beginning, and which are three-quarters of the time out-of-date: this failure to reply may well compromise the authority of the government and have serious repercussions.'[40]

It was clear then on the eve of Liberation that the political control of de Gaulle's committee over the development of events in France was a good deal more notional than real. The CFLN representatives were not in a position to play a firm executive role, and the existence of the CNR, as a separate entity from the delegation, provided a parallel centre of political decision-making and initiative, in which the Resistance movements, and in particular the parties of the left, had a considerable voice. Serreulles himself described the situation at the end of 1943 as one of potential anarchy.[41]

From the point of view of the actual transfer of power on the ground, the attitudes and relative strengths of the armed forces of the Resistance were crucial. As the likelihood of a 'D' Day invasion grew closer, CFLN representatives turned their attention towards the task of fusing the separate groups involved into a coherent military organization which would accept orders from a central control. There were several distinct paramilitary groups in metropolitan France, and their conceptions of what constituted military action and discipline were often wildly different. In the north and the south the major Resistance movements had theoretically combined their paramilitary groups in an *Armée Secrète* (Secret Army), headed by a career army officer. De Gaulle's view on the organization of a Resistance army was strongly conventional. It could only operate effectively if integrated into a tightly disciplined Fighting French unit, with a clear and disciplined chain of command. Like any other army it should be separated from political activity, and de Gaulle issued directives demanding a partitioning between the military and political wings of Resistance movements. His directives met with considerable local hostility, both because it was evident that the external Resistance was seeking to impose an outside framework on groups which had already evolved their own methods of working, and because it was genuinely difficult in the context of 1943–4 resistance to separate the two functions.

A similar argument developed over the strategy which the *Armée Secrète* should adopt. Gaullists envisaged that the Resistance army would spend its time preparing methodically for 'D' Day in the framework of detailed plans worked out with the Allies. The communist paramilitary formation, the *Francs-Tireurs et Partisans* (FTP), rejected the principle of keeping their troops waiting for 'D' Day, in what they described as 'underground barracks'. Until the Liberation, they claimed, Resistance troops should be encouraged to build themselves up for the ultimate fight by taking a series of preliminary actions which would act as a kind of training, as well as bringing in more members: '. . . for a locomotive to pull away, it is good to put it "under pressure" for a time!'[42] The merit of this strategy would be to transform the movements into mass organizations, based on the participation of ordinary members of the working class. Gleefully quoting back de Gaulle's own line on national Liberation being intimately linked to national insurrection, the party suggested that Liberation through an insurrection by the people would ensure that the French themselves (rather than the Allies) chose their own government. The FN added for good measure that evidence from Yugoslavia indicated that Churchill himself set more store by a Tito who would fight straight away rather than a Michailovitch who would not.[43] Non-communist members of the Resistance were deeply troubled by this philosophy which seemed designed at least to ensure that the PCF secured key positions for itself at the Liberation, and possibly to stimulate a national uprising which would lead to revolution. With the growth of more groups which would clearly not be fitted into an overall army framework before 'D' Day – the *maquis* Resistance, largely made up of men who had refused to go as forced labour to Germany – de Gaulle saw the danger of allowing a situation to develop in which the non-communist Resistance was kept 'under orders', waiting for action, whilst communist and left-wing movements prepared separately for insurrection. His directive to the *Armée Secrète* leader in May 1943 thus accepted the principle of immediate action before the Liberation.

The CFLN still attempted, however, to establish a command structure which would give it some control of the internal Resistance troops. A national *délégué militaire*, Chaban-Delmas, was appointed, and under him, military delegates for the north and south, with a lower tier of regional military delegates. The idea was that the delegates would help distribute money to the paramilitary groups, give out weapons, and agree particular operations in which the arms and money should be used. The effectiveness of the structure depended on the Gaullist military delegates receiving an adequate stock of weapons which would enable them to have some platform from which to direct operations. In the latter part of 1943, with the British Bomber Command still committed to a strategic bombing offensive, and hostile to SOE's attempts to divert aircraft to the task of dropping arms for Resistance groups, supplies to the Resistance were becoming progressively rarer. Gaullist delegates pointed out at the end of November 1943 that no weapons had been received in France since September, although 8000 militants had been briefed for two consecutive months to expect a weapons drop. Such delays, provoking angry questions in the Consultative Assembly in Algiers and personal appeals to Churchill from d'Astier de la Vigerie, did little to strengthen the position of the CFLN military liaison structure in France.[44] As Bourgès-Maunoury, military delegate for the southern zone, reported in January 1944: 'Our authority is based on charm; money is circulating outside our power; armaments don't come when we order them; we are perpetually facing odious political difficulties.'[45]

In addition to these problems of credibility, the external Resistance was likely to face the situation of parallel chains of command operating at the Liberation. The Gaullist blueprint for action was that the united paramilitary movement of metropolitan France would be transformed at 'D' Day into the *Forces Françaises de l'Intérieur* (FFI, French Forces of the Interior) under a commander nominated by de Gaulle – General Koenig in London, General Cochet in Algiers – who would be subordinate to the SAC. Resistance activity would thus be incorporated into an army structure which would be an integral part of the combined Allied operation. The CFLN desire to keep some control of what would happen in France at Liberation accorded well here with the concerns of the Allied military. The Gaullist Secret Service, the *Bureau Central de Renseignements et d'Action* (BCRA), which had close dealings with the Allies through the activities of SOE, noted that the Allies sometimes demonstrated 'a certain reserve' when faced with the problem of arming and deploying the Resistance: 'It was feared that well-armed and well-organised forces of the French Resistance could become a political instrument of some leaders, thus hindering the free expression of the national will.'[46] As 'D' Day grew nearer, this general unease about the likely reliability of such unconventional troops crystallized into a desire to be assured that the French had a definite chain of command to the metropolitan Resistance, which could be used with confidence by the Allied military. General d'Astier de la Vigerie, the head of the French military planning organization, *Bloc Planning*, found that General Montgomery had only one major question to ask him: was there an adequate command structure so that an order given to the Resistance would be efficiently executed?[47]

Whilst the CFLN could reply that such a structure had indeed been established, the fact was that these lines of command were muddied by the existence of a separate military command under the Resistance. The CNR had set up a military committee, *Comité d'Action Militaire* (COMAC), which also claimed to have authority over all the metropolitan paramilitary groups. De Gaulle attempted to limit their role to that of inspection, control and co-ordination, on the grounds that they did not have the technical capability to assume a direct command role. To the extent that COMAC was not integrated into the Allied military command, this was of course correct, but the fact remained that COMAC was based in France, whereas Koenig, the commander of the FFI, was still in London. The diarchy continued to exist, despite categoric assertions from Koenig that COMAC could not be given the command of the FFI in any circumstances. The *délégué militaire national*, Chaban-Delmas, reported that there were considerable difficulties on the ground because of the parallel command structures. In the heat of the military operations, regional military delegates were still trying to clarify the overlapping responsibilities.[48]

Thus, although the CLFN had made detailed plans for the Liberation which tended to limit the role of left-wing parties and Resistance groups, and aim at the re-establishment of political 'normality', the actual situation on the ground in metropolitan France, with a parallel political and military command structure, carried the potential for a very different scenario from that envisaged by the CLFN. In a sense the decision-makers within the Gaullist Committee were always rather isolated from the arguments in metropolitan France which had produced these competing centres of power. Emmanuel d'Astier de la Vigerie, a former leader of the left-wing *Libération* Resistance movement, found the atmosphere of the CFLN, once he was appointed *Commissaire à l'Intérieur* in November 1943, slightly unreal:

I have grasped the fact that, in this strange Government . . ., the Council of Ministers has three facets: the administration, the executive and the legislative. The administration is rarely in question; when things go too badly there are always sufficiently good reasons, a plenitude of weighty excuses: the war, the Allies, the atmospheric conditions. The executive . . . is dealt with in a smaller committee by *Symbole* [de Gaulle] and two or three of the interested executives . . . As for the legislative, it takes up about four fifths of the sessions . . . this assembly of improvised legislators makes only hypothetical laws.[49]

The key question was the extent to which the hypothetical laws and the political decisions taken by de Gaulle and his small executive would be implemented in the chaos of the Liberation.

One important means by which the Gaullists could seek to influence events to their advantage before the Liberation was through their secret service organization, the BCRA, which had major control of transmissions into and out of France. By early 1944 the organization had fought off an attempt by the secret service attached to the Army of Africa (and thus dominated by Giraudists) to gain control of the apparatus, and was clearly dominated by Gaullists. Its leader, Passy, was, like de Gaulle himself, somewhat sceptical about the likely military efficacy of a Resistance movement which was not incorporated in a tightly defined structure and which appeared as: 'an abundance of desires to do good, of courageous thoughts, exalted imaginations expressed through disorderly acts without real effectiveness'.[50] The BCRA's overall ethos was strongly anti-communist and it took considerable interest in the supposed activities of the communist Resistance, analysing copies of their clandestine press and Vichy police reports on left-wing groups which came their way, and often passing on selected information from these to their British and American colleagues.[51] Other elements within the CFLN regarded them with some suspicion, in particular the *Commissariat à l'Intérieur* which had mounted an unsuccessful attack on the *Bureau* in the summer of 1942 in an attempt to wrest from them the all-important control of operations in France. Relations between the Interior and the BCRA worsened still further after the appointment of d'Astier de la Vigerie, whom the BCRA considered to be a fellow-traveller of the Communist Party and, therefore, unable to be trusted with any confidential Resistance information.

In metropolitan France, groups which were on the Left and sometimes even in the political centre, viewed the power of the BCRA with misgiving. This was particularly the case when it became clear that the organization had sent a special mission to one group about which the Resistance had grave political doubts, and had provided it, much to the embarrassment of the CLFN military delegate, with its own separate radio link. The organization concerned, the *Organisation de Résistance de l'Armée* (Resistance of the Army organization, ORA), was, as its name suggests, made up of officers from the remnants of the Armistice Army which had finally been disbanded in November 1942. It was conservative in philosophy, and represented, for many members of the metropolitan Resistance, a continuation of the old officer hierarchy which had shown itself to be, both before and during the de Gaulle/ Giraud struggle in North Africa, Vichyite and opposed to any of the major changes which the internal Resistance espoused. For left-wing Resistance, the apparent endorsement by the BCRA made it appear likely that the new army which would emerge from the Liberation would be traditional in structure and led by a traditional (and in many cases compromised) elite. Whilst on the one hand the BCRA was establishing its direct links with ORA, the CNR was demanding that ORA's leader, General Revers, should take a clear anti-Vichy stand before there was any question of incorporating his movement into the Liberation FFI.[52]

In comparison with this undoubtedly special treatment given to ORA by the BCRA, the Communist Party complained that it was being kept deliberately short of arms and weapons. Through the FN and via their representatives in the Consultative Assembly, the PCF kept up a barrage of complaints about discrimination in supplies in the early part of 1944.[53] De Gaulle's addition of two communists – Grenier and Billoux – as ministers in the CFLN in April 1944 did not noticeably assuage the complaints from metropolitan France. Grenier, as *Commissaire à l'Air*, was to be involved in an acrimonious argument, whose polemic would spill out over the post-war years, about the failure to drop adequate amounts of weaponry to *maquis* groups in the Vercors. [54] Comparative fugures on arms drops are, at this distance of time, difficult to establish, but what cannot be doubted is that the BCRA was deeply anti-communist, and that it operated in this vital domain of contact with the Resistance in a highly independent way, with little accountability, even by the relatively free executive standards of the CFLN.

In this fluid pre-Liberation situation where carefully laid political plans might well be pre-empted by the progress of fighting on the ground, and where mutual suspicions within the internal Resistance, and between Algiers and France, were often strong, the great unknown in France was the policy which the liberating Allies were going to adopt. Rumours abounded. In April 1944 there were reports of an Anglo-Saxon military mission meeting senior French civil servants to assess what measures should be taken to feed the population at the Liberation, all without the apparent knowledge of the CFLN. In May 1944 another Allied mission was said to have arrived in Paris with the task of purging the Hôtel de Ville and the prefectures, ready for the takeover of power at the Liberation. Beside these rumours went reports, especially worrying at a time when the French Resistance was desperately short of weaponry, that the British were continuing to arrange arms supplies for their own Resistance groups, and were indeed deciding, independently of the French authorities, which particular *maquis* group were worth supporting and which were not.[55]

If there were quite profound differences of opinion between Frenchmen as to what should actually happen politically at the Liberation, there was understandable unanimity on the view that the future of France should be determined by the French themselves rather than the Allies:

It is vital that the Allied Commander in Chief is not allowed to take the initiative in the measures to be taken at the Liberation . . . we must affirm the right of the French people to participate as allies and as citizens of a sovereign state in the liberation of their country.[56]

## French planning and the Allies

FRENCHMEN involved in the political planning for Liberation were working in what amounted to total darkness as regards Allied intentions. The work of the Free French *Commission du Débarquement* (Landings' Committee) had ground to a halt in early 1943 when it became clear that any further progress on instructions to French Liaison Officers, for example, were dependent on discussion with the Allies, who were unwilling, given the disagreement on policy which existed, to confront the French. In September 1943 the CLFN had sought to clarify the position of the British and Americans by submitting a draft agreement which was designed to lay the ghost of AMGOT once and for all. The French scheme divided liberated territory into three zones (combat, militarized and interior) which would be agreed between the SAC, the French Commander-in-Chief, and the civilian delegate of the French Committee. The Allied Command had the power to initiate police measures etc., only in the combat zone. The automatic resumption of French sovereignty was assumed, and the CFLN was effectively given authority through their delegate who had 'powers of regulation and administration'.[57] The French draft stayed unanswered on the table and, as the months passed, the implications of the silence with which it had been greeted provoked increasing anxiety within the French camp. A specialist committee like the *Commission du Débarquement* found it almost impossible in late 1943 to make any reasonable assessment of Allied views, and was driven to piecing together British and American presumed intentions from the evidence of an exegesis of public statements by ministers and officials. By the end of 1943 Viénot, the French representative in London, reported that there was total stalemate on the question of some kind of political agreement between the Allies and the CFLN on the French draft, and that the only way forward would be on technical matters.[58]

A vital channel of information, in the absence of a direct response, was the material gleaned by the French from their link in London with the civil affairs team established in SHAEF. De Gaulle had sent de Boislambert from Algiers in August 1943 to set up two agencies specifically designed to work with the Allied military, the *Service Militaire d'Études Administratives* (SMEA), headed by Pierre Laroque, and the *Mission Militaire de Liaisons Administratives* (MMLA), led by de Boislambert himself. These replaced the moribund *État Major Français* (EMF) of General Cochet which de Gaulle had left in London in early 1943, but which had achieved relatively little in terms of liaison with the Allies both because of the Allies' own uncertainties, and because of its failure to get the support of the BCRA, and, if the bitter Cochet were to be believed, of de Gaulle himself.[59] The SMEA and the MMLA were soon reporting on the current Allied position as it appeared to French officers who were sent on training courses at the civil affairs school at Wimbledon. Laroque carefully analysed reports made so that clues to Allied intentions on civil affairs policy could be divined. On the whole it appeared in late 1943/early 1944 as if the British were dropping AMGOT from their vocabulary, and the general tenor of the teaching seemed to indicate that an agreement with the CFLN was expected to provide the legal framework for any provisional Allied administration. The impression of French officers attending the courses was that the British were slightly embarrassed over the whole question of using French Liaison Officers: 'The British indeed seem to realize that the likelihood of an AMGOT is more and more remote, and that they must therefore consider using their civil affairs organization in a different way.' The picture was not, however, entirely hopeful from the French point of view, since, at the beginning, American officers who came to Wimbledon were clearly far less certain of the attitude they were supposed to adopt to French Liaison Officers, symbolically perhaps eating apart from the others, and mentioning decisions that had to be taken at a 'higher level'. Laroque was also perturbed that the legal basis on which the Wimbledon courses were premised seemed to be that of the Hague convention, unsuitable for France since it was designed for enemy countries. He urged that the French ensure its substitution by a 'state of siege' framework, and the *Commission du Débarquement* certainly took steps to investigate the implications of such a framework which might be suitable if operated within the bounds observed by the Allies in 1918 and 1939.[60]

A touchstone of the development of Allied attitudes was increasingly felt to be British and American interpretations of the role of French Liaison Officers at the Liberation. Captain de Rothschild, in what was regarded as a key report in January 1944 from the Wimbledon course he had attended, thought that the British view was to: 'impose the minimum administration via their Civil Affairs branch for the minimum time'.[61] No clear line was emerging about how the British envisaged the transfer of power to local authorities, and de Rothschild pointed out that the Allied civil affairs operation was of such a massive scale – 3000 British, slightly more American – that the French could never match it in the field. The French objective, therefore, would have to be to use their Liaison Officers, presently considered by the British as interpreters, as essential political elements in each civil affairs HQ, to ensure that civil affairs on the ground kept well away from interference in French administration.

On American views, there was always considerable uncertainty. On the whole reports suggested that the American army had very little idea of the precise role of French Liaison Officers. A French officer who went on a course with the 5th Infantry Division reported that the problem, particularly in the lower ranks, was probably that the American Army had been training for several years for an invasion, without being able to recreate the actual situation of Liberation, where an indigenous population would present particular and evident difficulties. Certainly the SMEA accepted that Allied conceptions of civil affairs depended upon the person one was speaking to and oscillated between the extreme form adopted by some Americans where French Liaison officers were subordinates whose job was to foster American intervention in administrative and economic life, and the more acceptable British formula where French officers were advisers who could sort out delicate administrative difficulties.[62] In a sense, the SMEA and MMLA could do little more than interpret the signs of Allied activity and try and relate them to possible Allied intentions: thus Laroque discovered that civil affairs were being reorganized, and speculated on whether this might indicate the final death of AMGOT. At times, the information gained by the London organizations provided a spur to French preparations, revealing gaps in current French planning, like the relative slowness in supplying instructions on the preparation of currency, stamps and ration cards.[63]

If, however, the lack of a political response from the Allies forced French agencies to put considerable emphasis on the role that their Liaison Officers would have to play in forestalling possible Allied AMGOT plans on the ground, the CFLN were firmly convinced of the need to keep these same Liaison Officers strictly subordinated to civilian representatives. Advisers to the *Commissariat à l'Intérieur* indicated that there would be some danger for the French in mixed civil affairs organizations where French specialists could easily find themselves subordinate to Allied officers, rather than part of the administrative liaison team under CFLN orders. By early April 1944 this point had been incorporated into SMEA's notes on the employment of Liaison Officers: 'These French officers will be with a group or Allied detachment, but not explicitly incorporated into one. We must above all avoid even the appearance of a mixed AMGOT.'[64] The whole objective of French Liaison Officers had to be to encourage a mobile conception of civil affairs, since the more sedentary Allied civil affairs became, the more likely it was to establish itself as a quasi-permanent force on French territory.

Thus as 'D' day grew closer, French preparations for the Liberation had been conducted in a complete vacuum, the Allied political intentions and civil affairs plans guessed at, but largely unknown. In the absence of an agreed Allied policy, the military had been forced to take the initiative, so that decisions on the political future of France were now likely to be taken 'on the ground' by military commanders during the actual Liberation. This the CFLN planners implicitly recognized in accepting that their own planning would require 'a great deal of empiricism'. The advantage that the French had was that they had established the structure of an interim civilian administration which would be ready to step into power in each area, as soon as it was liberated. Much would depend on the speed with which this personnel could arrive at relevant centres, their political astuteness and above all the attitude which the Allies would take to affirmations of French sovereignty.

As 'D' Day approached, the two separate planning systems – Allied and French – joined only by the 'unofficial' talks Eisenhower had initiated, met head on in the tense build-up to Operation 'Overlord' in London. Inevitably the result was aggravation and stalemate on the diplomatic level.

# 4 The Allies, the French, and the beginnings of Liberation

WHILST negotiations between the Allies and the French on recognition for the CFLN and for a civil affairs agreement were stymied at the inter-governmental level, at the lower levels in each government contacts were maintained and discussions continued on a host of topics. For the French, without recognition or a civil affairs agreement, these negotiations on individual topics were vital to their future interest.

Questions like the use of individual French units in the post landings phase, although of minor significance for Eisenhower, were very important for the CFLN because they would validate its claim that Frenchmen were liberating France, and demonstrate the physical existence of a French Army, within which de Gaulle wished to integrate the armed members of the Resistance.

Unfortunately, British experience with the French prior to the North African landings and the Italian campaign made them wary of the apparent lapses in their security. In the vital build-up to the Normandy landings, the British thought it wise, therefore, to impose a cipher ban on French communications between London and Algiers. This ban, which was implemented on 17 April 1944, dramatically reduced the ability of the French in London to maintain communications with the proto-government in Algiers. It infuriated the French, and in particular de Gaulle, who thought that it was an indication that the French were not trusted and that they were being excluded from the Liberation of their own country. Against this background of indecision, confusion and growing tension, relatively minor matters assumed major significance and bedevilled Allied/French relations. One of the more important of these was currency. It was essential for the Allied forces to have recognized purchasing power when they landed in France, to be able to control currency circulation and to have sufficient currency to prevent problems. The British supported French demands for 'new' francs to be printed. The Americans had 'yellow seal' dollars which they had already used in North Africa, but they were willing to compromise on a 'military franc'.[1] Eventually in January 1944, a compromise was worked out by which the Americans would print notes called 'supplemental francs' which would not imply any military authority, but which would be issued by SAC and distributed under his authority. The notes were to have the words *'Liberté, Égalité, Fraternité'* on one side, and a French flag with the words *'République Française'* on the other. Roosevelt, however, rejected *'République Française'* because it implied that the Allies wished France to be a republic, when it might choose some other form of government. He proposed the words *'la France'*. Morgenthau, the Secretary of the Treasury, Stimson and McCloy each tried to argue for the original form of words, but all they could retain on the reverse side was the flag.[2]

By April 1944, no agreement had been reached. SHAEF was willing to accept the new compromise, with the proviso that a proclamation from the SAC would make it legal tender. The French resisted, and Eisenhower, in an attempt to resolve the problem, suggested to Koenig that he ask for French authority to issue the American supplemental francs. Hilldring, for the Civil Affairs Division (CAD) and the War Department, protested that the American government could not allow this.[3] By May no decision had been made, and SHAEF prepared two currency proclamations – one for a French signature and one for Eisenhower's. The British Foreign Office was exasperated with the American attitude – 'as usual taking their cue from the President' – but they were powerless and could only hope that the CFLN were not too offended by supplemental francs, which, given the date, were inevitably going to be distributed in France.[4]

A similar issue which worried the French was that of Liaison Officers. Here, once again, the Allies looked upon the use of French Liaison Officers as a simple matter: to ensure efficiency and a quiet rear area for the battle regiments. But for the CFLN these men would be representatives of the new French administration and would need to have a position separate from the Allied units to indicate their independence and legitimacy. They would liaise on behalf of the French administration with the Allied authorities and, as with the currency problem, they would indicate the presence of a new regime and one which had some continuity with past French regimes. The Eisenhower – Koenig talks included the number, nature and use of the Liaison Officers – by June 1944 there were 187 French Liaison Officers in training in Britain, ready for the 'D' Day landings, as well as 53 French Liaison Officers in training in North Africa.[5] Despite the deteriorating Allied/French relations, SHAEF managed to secure the continuation of the training programme and the availability of 180 officers.[6] The French, angered by Allied intransigence, began to talk of the Liaison Officers being unavailable if they could not represent what they considered was the provisional government of France. Army commanders, and Montgomery in particular, were convinced that it was vital to have such officers and declared that they should be appointed whether or not there was an agreement.[7] The French wanted to restrict Liaison Officers to frontline units to avoid their becoming involved in any kind of more stable, 'mixed AMGOT' administration: they should help establish the initial French administration in liberated territories, stimulate resistance and ensure tactical liaison with Allied troops. This would in effect put the Allied command in third place. General Whiteley, of G3 SHAEF, disliked the French views and was concerned that the Liaison Officers should play a normal military role, disarming the Resistance behind Allied lines, rather than promoting or co-ordinating it. The British warned of the difficulties which would arise between the Allies if the French Liaison Officers went as civil administrators.[8] Even at this late date differing views on the role and functions of French Liaison Officers persisted and this difference was to become crucial as the landings approached.

## Confusion on the eve of the landings, May–June 1944

KOENIG, the CFLN representative and head of the FFI, had found the uncertain nature of the 'official, semi-official' talks with the Allies embarrassing and declared that the ban on communications was a final insuperable barrier to co-operation. It was no surprise, therefore, that the Eisenhower–Koenig talks broke down on 4 May. Eden wanted the British to allow Koenig to return to Algiers and come back with the experts he needed to continue talking, but Churchill immediately scotched the idea on the grounds of security.[9] Massigli, CFLN Commissioner for Foreign Affairs, asked that le Troquer, the disembarkation delegate, should be allowed to report back to Algiers after a few days in England. The Joint Intelligence Committee of the Cabinet (JIC) suggested a special cipher for Koenig, with British censors. None of these suggestions for breaking the impasse was sanctioned. Pressure from Algiers on the Allied governments to ease their communications ban was duplicated by that from Eisenhower who was horrified at the breakdown in talks. He proposed to tell Koenig the name of the country to be invaded and the month of the invasion, as a means of regaining his confidence and co-operation. This presumably worked because he later reported that conversations had resumed unofficially and that he had hopes they would lead to a more substantial understanding. But the Supreme Commander was very unhappy about the situation and complained to the Combined Chiefs of Staff that he was operating under impossible conditions.[10]

Eisenhower finally proposed that de Gaulle and a group of French experts should be invited to London from Algiers, and he was supported by SHAEF. The Foreign Office persuaded Churchill to telegraph the President on the question, and progress then depended on his reply. Eisenhower was not immediately worried about French *military* co-operation, because the Leclerc Division would not come on to the battlefield until 'D' Day + 90, but he was very keen to get the fullest co-operation from the domestic Resistance, whom he rated highly as a disruptive force.[11] Roosevelt's agreement to the invitation for de Gaulle to come to London in May appeared to ease the situation, but was accompanied by a note warning Eisenhower that, whilst he could have authority to talk to the CFLN representatives on a 'military level', he must do nothing which might even hint at recognition:[12] the President's resolve was still firm.

On 16 May Koenig reported to Grasset of SHAEF G5 that he had been instructed not to talk about anything but strictly military affairs, and news broke on the same day that the Consultative Assembly proposed changing the title CFLN to the *Gouvernement Provisoire de la République Française* (GPRF). The Foreign Office thought this was the opportunity to recognize the *de facto* status of the GPRF whilst stressing the word 'provisional', which might be acceptable to the Americans, but Churchill disliked this French presumption[13] and assumed the President would not recognize the new title. Talks in London were yet again at a stalemate. Koenig would not accept a cipher with British censors; de Gaulle wanted full restoration of communications; the British would not let GPRF representatives return to Algiers; Churchill, fearing the President's reaction to the GPRF, would not budge; and the military – apart from Eisenhower and Bedell Smith – were against lifting the communications ban.[14]

Roosevelt's reaction to the announcement of the GPRF was predictably bad, and Churchill, having got his agreement to invite de Gaulle to London for 'D' Day, revised it so that it would be sent after the landings had started. The Foreign Office managed to countermand this rather insulting invitation and, from 19 May onwards, efforts were concentrated on getting the General to accept the invitation and arrive in London before 'D' Day. Duff Cooper, British representative to the CFLN, who had originated the idea, invited de Gaulle provisionally and then reinforced it with assurances over liberty of communication and honoured-guest status on 27 May. To facilitate matters Viénot, the CFLN representative in London, was allowed restricted access to confidential ciphered communication. De Gaulle accepted the invitation with some warmth, although later reports from the USA made him fear that he was about to be used to support the Supreme Commander, that Roosevelt was no nearer recognition – despite the Hull speech – and that Koenig would be totally controlled by Eisenhower.[15]

The Foreign Office had meanwhile prompted Churchill to ask the

Americans to send a representative – Stettinius perhaps – to negotiate with de Gaulle and the British when the French leader arrived in London. This was seen as a means of starting up discussions again without involving the highest level veto, but Roosevelt would not send such a representative. His view was that, once the landings had started, Eisenhower would be in charge and the exigencies of war would force the French to co-operate, leaving recognition until much later after the Liberation and a subsequent election. The State Department was much less sanguine about the situation in London and thought that the British would open talks with the French Committee and then face Washington with a *fait accompli*. This would probably be at odds with American policy, but if the Americans rejected it, they would be accused of being unreasonable, obstructive and anti-Gaullist.[16] American representatives on SHAEF also took the same line, prophesying that GPRF anti-American sentiment might cause trouble in the rear areas of the Allied forces. The American government, however, still refused to address the French authorities as the 'GPRF' in any documents, which made material coming from joint military and civilian bodies very difficult to produce. Eisenhower's draft broadcast proclamation maintained references to the French Committee, but these were finally erased after Roosevelt intervened through the US Joint Chiefs of Staff.[17]

De Gaulle arrived in Britain at 6.00 a.m. on 4 June 1944 at Northolt and went to see Churchill in his train headquarters at Droyton near Portsmouth. The morning talks went well and it was not until the end of lunch, when Churchill introduced the question of recognition and de Gaulle's visit to the USA, that the atmosphere deteriorated. De Gaulle angrily recited all the rejections of his recognition proposals since the previous September, rehearsed all the recent slights to French honour and declared that he was not there for his candidacy as leader of the GPRF to be endorsed by Roosevelt. He specifically attacked the Allies for their handling of the currency question : 'I have just learned . . . that despite our warnings, the troops and services about to land are provided with so-called French currency, issued by foreign powers, which the government of the Republic refuses to recognize and which, according to the orders of the inter-allied command, will have compulsory circulation on French territory.'[18] De Gaulle said that if Eisenhower proclaimed the notes to be legal tender, he would return to Algiers. The whole concept of an Allied landing in co-operation with the GPRF would collapse and no civil affairs agreement would be made.

The GPRF in Algiers were similarly outraged: they reserved the authority to issue franc notes and declared that no nation had treated a friendly country in such a way. De Gaulle thought the currency was 'counterfeit'. Roosevelt telegraphed to Churchill that he was entirely of the same view as the Prime Minister: de Gaulle was trying to use the issue to 'stampede' the Allies into recognition: 'Personally I do not think the currency situation referred to in your cable is as critical as it might first appear nor do I feel that it is essential from the point of view of acceptability of the supplemental currency that de Gaulle make any statement of support with respect to such currency.'[19] The State Department thought that de Gaulle might be persuaded to issue a 'unilateral' statement validating the currency, but assumed that he would want to use the words 'provisional government of the French Republic', which Roosevelt would probably reject. As an alternative, they suggested some form of joint Allied governmental statement. The Foreign Office rejected this because it could say very little on currency without angering the French even further.[20] By this time, the Foreign Office had come to the conclusion that nothing could be done on an inter-governmental level, and nothing *was* done.

On the afternoon of 4 June de Gaulle went with Churchill and Eden to Eisenhower's headquarters where he became engrossed in the landing plans, but was furious again when the Supreme Commander told him that he would broadcast a proclamation to France on the day of the invasion. De Gaulle thoroughly disapproved of the draft that he was given, because it appeared that Eisenhower was to 'take charge of our country', and because it made no mention – apart from the Military Mission – of any French authority, let alone the GPRF. Eisenhower allowed that it might be altered at de Gaulle's suggestion, but the next morning de Gaulle sensed more betrayal when he found that his amendments were too late. The proclamation had already been printed and the attack was to start that night.[21]

The next blow for de Gaulle was on 5 June, when Peake told him that Eisenhower would broadcast his message first, followed by the King of Norway, the Queen of the Netherlands, the Grand Duchess of Luxembourg, the Belgian Prime Minister and then de Gaulle. Although in terms of strict protocol this was correct, it was the last straw. He refused to accept last place in the order, saying that he preferred to broadcast at some other time. In the afternoon Churchill was told, erroneously, that de Gaulle would not broadcast at all and was in high dudgeon when he attended a Cabinet meeting at 6.30 p.m. Here, Eden dropped another bombshell: de Gaulle had told Koenig that he would not allow the Liaison Officers to land with Allied troops, because he had no civil affairs agreement with the Allied governments. It was quite possibly spite at not having been allowed to edit Eisenhower's broadcast, or broadcast independently himself.

There was general agreement among Ministers that this action on the part of General de Gaulle was far more serious than his refusal to broadcast.
The Prime Minister said that if General de Gaulle refused to agree to Liaison

> Officers proceeding with Operation 'Overlord' it would not be possible for us to have any further discussions with General de Gaulle on civil or military matters. It might even be necessary to indicate that an aeroplane would be ready to take him back to Algiers forthwith.[22]

Viénot rushed between the Foreign Office, de Gaulle and Churchill, trying to moderate and calm tempers, but was insulted and harangued at every turn. Finally, it was clear that de Gaulle would broadcast later on 6 June, but would not sanction the 120 Liaison Officers leaving for France, and at 1.30 a.m. Churchill sent for Morton: 'Go and tell Bedell Smith to put de Gaulle in a plane and send him back to Algiers – in chains if necessary. He must not be allowed to re-enter France.'[23] By dawn Eden had managed to suppress an order to that effect, and later in the morning de Gaulle duly recorded his message to the French people. He refused to show his script to Duff Cooper or Peake for the very good reason that he referred to himself and the GPRF as 'le gouvernement de la France'. The British could still have confiscated the disc, but Eden let it be broadcast, although he expected another tirade from Churchill and criticism from the USA.[24] It was not until the next afternoon, 6 June, that de Gaulle agreed to Duff Cooper's request that he release at least some of the Liaison Officers. As Duff Cooper reported:

> I saw de Gaulle at three o'clock. I pointed out to him that in his own interests he ought to agree to the officers going, as otherwise it would be said of him that he had refused to help us in the battle itself. He would not accept the logic of this argument but eventually said that to please *me* he would agree to send at least some officers if not all.[25]

De Gaulle insisted that his reason for refusing the departure of the Liaison Officers was that they had been designated as administrative Liaison Officers in the original French document of September 1943 and had been trained as such, which was not how the Allies intended to use them.[26] Eventually 20 of the originally agreed 120 for the first wave actually went to France, although they arrived a little late. The Foreign Office had some sympathy for de Gaulle's point of view,[27] but most commentators noted the damage he had done to his relations with the Allied governments. Cadogan declared: 'That puts the lid on. We always start by putting ourselves in the wrong and then de Gaulle puts himself *more* in the wrong. He deserves to lose the rubber.'[28] Churchill had no sympathy since de Gaulle had also objected to the Allied supplemental francs being declared legal tender by proclamation from SAC. Reviewing the situation at the War Cabinet meeting on 7 June, the Prime Minister said that de Gaulle's actions had caused President Roosevelt to have the worst opinion of the French leader and that recent events had led him to share that opinion. It was clear to him that de Gaulle was more concerned about personal ambition than the future of France and that whilst he, Churchill, and Britain, 'had stood by him through many crises,' they had now to consider their friendship with the USA as paramount.[29]

On the American side, Grasset for SHAEF was furious and Matthews, adding a gloss to Stettinius's final report on his State Department mission to Britain, said: 'There could hardly be a worse time for letting political bickering interfere with the struggle for the Liberation of France'.[30] Isaiah Berlin, who headed the political survey section of the British Embassy in Washington and wrote weekly reports for the Foreign Office and the Ministry of Information, noted on 18 June that the 'tide in favour of French recognition has been checked by the news of de Gaulle's cancellation of the Liaison Officers'.[31] Hull, according to Stimson, was beside himself with rage and although he, Stimson, was angry at de Gaulle's actions, he still pleaded the case of the GPRF, but got nowhere with the newly intransigent Secretary of State.[32] Leahy, Chief of Staff to the President, was similarly outraged, and during a party on the Secretary of the Navy's yacht, joined with Forrestal in a savage attack on the Gaullists, running through 'the whole history of despicable French behaviour'.[33]

Even more than the currency affair, the refusal to send Liaison Officers with the Allied forces on the Normandy landings soured Franco-American relations and provided a very bad basis for the visit of de Gaulle to the USA in early July. At a moment when most American opinion was swinging, however reluctantly, towards acceptance of the GPRF, and when early battlefield reports indicated indigenous support for de Gaulle, this incident wrecked the faint possibility of early recognition for the provisional government.

What was remarkable throughout this turbulent visit of de Gaulle to London was that the Foreign Office managed to keep alive the idea of talks. Eden played down the violent disagreements of the 4 June meetings in his despatches and, in the afternoon and evening of 5 June, he and Duff Cooper made strenuous efforts to calm Churchill by getting the truth on de Gaulle's broadcast threat, whilst negotiating with Viénot to persuade de Gaulle to adopt a more reasonable position on Liaison Officers and currency. On 6 June a relay of advisers worked on the two intransigent principals. De Gaulle finally agreed that Viénot could certainly stay and talk after he had returned to Algiers, but this was hardly a concession since Viénot had always been available for talks, even if cut off from North Africa by the cipher ban. Nevertheless Eden persuaded Churchill that this was the basis for talks and thus it was that, despite his tirade in the 7 June Cabinet, Churchill outlined the framework of future negotiations with the representatives of the GPRF and hopefully the American government.[34] There were, however, still difficult periods, when Churchill threatened once again to send de Gaulle back to Algiers, and when Eden and Churchill had a 'shouting match until 2 a.m.' because the Prime Minister would not allow talks with Viénot. Eden suggested a 'less spectacular' set of negotiations through the committee that had sorted out civil affairs with other exiled governments, presided over by the Judge Advocate General (JAG). Two days after this suggestion – on 14 June – Churchill finally acceded, the Foreign Office drafted a model agreement for discussion and 19 June was agreed with Viénot as the date for convening the 'Official Committee' under JAG.[35]

Throughout these hectic days of 'D' Day squabbling, talks were kept alive and, after the relief of the successful assault, continued in a positive, detailed fashion, albeit at a level one removed from the heads of state.

Despite the arguments and apparent stalemate, the Allies, by making de Gaulle part of the landings' public relations exercise, accorded him political status, and a measure of control over the actions of French administrative personnel. Unfortunately for the Allied military, the Liberation had begun and GPRF representatives were establishing themselves before there was any agreement on recognition of a French government.

## The landings, June 1944

AWAY from the deliberations of the 'officials' in London and the 'politicking' of the national leaders, the initiative in civil affairs was already passing to military and civilian personnel on the ground. The overall civil affairs context and the recognition debate, as seen from the Allied Normandy bridgehead, were exceedingly confused, yet military commanders were faced with immediate practical decisions, large and small. Thus the landings proved to be both the first test of civil affairs planning, and the experience which was to give substance to its sketchy outlines. In many cases it remade policy entirely and in others it set precedents that were to be followed throughout France.

21st Army Group and the US 1st Army had gone ahead with civil affairs planning and, on the eve of embarkation, civil affairs officers, right down to the smallest 'C' and 'D' groups (mobile front line civil affairs units), were issued with up-to-date briefings to supplement the SHAEF Civil Affairs Handbook for their intended areas. All the material stressed the overall control of the Supreme Commander, but urged that the maximum possible amount of civil affairs activity be left to the French. The standing operations and administration instructions for civil affairs insisted that there would be no military government, but, remembering the landings in North Africa, the 2nd British Army suggested that if the local authorities were unco-operative, the local military commander should assume powers similar to those that French officers had under the 'state of siege' laws.[36] Orders issued with regard to the Resistance indicated that, while 'civilians with guns' were not allowed in the combat zone, the FFI, under General Koenig, were to be regarded as regular forces of the GPRF and thus legitimate bearers of arms.[37] Every civil affairs officer commanding a group had explicit instructions on how to co-operate with the local civil and military authorities. Whilst Eisenhower's address to his troops on the eve of the landings stressed the operation's importance as the first step in the Liberation of Europe from Nazi domination, some commanders reminded their men that they were landing on Allied, friendly soil and that it was their job to see that the 'tricolore' flew again in France. Eisenhower had wanted to make a direct reference to the CFLN (GPRF), saying that he would 'look to them for leadership', but it had been expunged from the final draft.[38]

Political guidance given for each civil affairs area had an appendix in the form of a 'white list', indicating Resisters and other loyal personalities, and a 'black list', indicating collaborators and people under suspicion. The appendix warned officers not to assume that local personalities who were in jail at the time the Allies arrived were necessarily on the 'white list'. The briefing document went into great detail politically and socially, even indicating the addresses of pre-war brothels: 3, rue de la Cuvée, in the case of Bayeux.[39] The overall effect of all the instructions was that Allied officers should give authority to representatives of the provisional government or the Resistance wherever they could.

Reports from civil affairs officers who accompanied the landings were not very encouraging about the reaction of the local population. The first civil affairs units, which were established in Courselles on 7 June and in Ouistreham, Reviers and Cresserons on 8 June, reported that, 'at first sight it is impossible to differentiate between pro-Nazis, Vichy or patriotic Frenchmen'.[40] Major Kerr-Smiley, C.O. of the 202 C.A. Detachment which moved into Bayeux on 7 June, following hard on the front, noted that the detachment had arrested five collaborators, but did not make any political comment. The detachment simply began its work alongside the existing Vichy mayor and subprefect, and an order from Eisenhower on 9 June confirmed their established practice of issuing proclamations and orders through the French authorities on the ground.[41] Early reports were full of practical action to restore public services, ensure relief and supply, and bring about public order. The major features of these reports was their surprise at finding a relatively wealthy, undisturbed and well-fed countryside, when they had clearly expected to find a ravaged country, suffering the privations of Nazi oppression. The population appeared to be 'luke warm' about their

Liberation and to have been quite contented under German occupation.[42] The American 1st Army, which rapidly established civil affairs groups at Sainte-Mère Eglise, Carentan and Isigny, reported similar calm and co-operation, with little sign of any political preference among the population. The occasional German counter attack – as that on Carentan – disturbed the work of civil affairs units, and there were reports of women sniping at Allied soldiers in Bayeux, but they turned out to be wildly exaggerated, if true at all. In general the civil affairs units encountered very few difficulties. The remaining Vichy officials seemed willing to put up and endorse Allied proclamations, and it was only where the Germans had completely evacuated the population that the advancing civil affairs units had to post their own orders.[43]

Allied command was very keen to know what the reaction to their landings would be, and to try and avoid the mistakes of North Africa and Italy. Several observation missions were sent as soon as the bridgehead had been consolidated. Early reconnaissance by senior civil affairs officers found that this area of France was little interested in Resistance activity, that it was traditionally conservative, quite Pétainist and thus not enthusiastic about de Gaulle. It was ready, however, to support him as the only possible leader for France at that time. Ellias, of 21st Army Group Civil Affairs Main Headquarters, reported that the attitude of the people could best be summed up in the words of one mayor who said: 'We had been waiting for him [de Gaulle] and were he to come to France as recognized head of a provisional government, all would rally to him.'[44]

De Gaulle finally arrived in France about 2.00 p.m. on the afternoon of 14 June at Courselles, and went directly to visit Montgomery at his headquarters, whilst sending Coulet ahead to establish the presence of the GPRF as a civil administration in Bayeux. Montgomery thought that de Gaulle's reception in France was poor, but the fact that the leader of Free France had chain-smoked during the whole of his time in Montgomery's caravan had probably not endeared him to the British Commander. De Gaulle described his appearance in Bayeux as prompting 'an extraordinary emotion', and the French who accompanied him agreed that he was given an ecstatic welcome.[45] He addressed the people of Bayeux in the main square and referred to himself as the 'President of the provisional government of France'. More importantly, he oversaw the installation of Coulet as *Commissaire de la République* and representative of the GPRF. Coulet was appointed to this post by de Gaulle on 12 June, when it had become apparent that the previously agreed nominee, Bourdeau de Fontenay, could not get through the lines. Coulet clearly understood the significance of his post in Bayeux and saw his installation as a brilliantly audacious piece of pragmatism by de Gaulle, who had established a French administration despite the lack of Allied agreement. He immediately dismissed the mayor and the Vichy subprefect, Rochat. Although appreciating the efficient and co-operative manner in which the latter had dealt with the Allies, he preferred to appoint the provisional government nominee, Triboulet.[46] The civil affairs organization of 21st Army Group found out about it only when Lewis (SCAO of 21st Army Group) met de Chevigné (GPRF Military Delegate) by his broken-down car on the road to Bayeux.

De Gaulle, having established Coulet, disappeared on a quick visit to the village of Isigny in the American sector to make his presence felt. The British, who had expected him to return directly to his ship, imagined that he had 'bolted' and thought momentarily of putting restraints on him, but the affair turned out to be a storm in a tea cup and he turned up later that evening. Returning to England, he was well aware of the importance of the day's work and told supporters that the provisional government was now an accomplished fact which the Allies would accept without protest.[47]

The installation of a new administration did not please Lewis because he found that the new Gaullist nominees were much less efficient and amenable than their predecessors: 'The new authorities are determined to assert French sovereignty. They give the impression of being intensely suspicious of civil affairs, and unwilling to afford more than a grudging recognition of our existence.' This judgment was the outcome of the first meeting between Coulet and Lewis on 16 June when Lewis said he would provisionally accept the presence of the French group until he had further orders from his superiors, and Coulet replied that whether or not Lewis accepted it, his presence was a fact that no instruction from an Allied government could alter. He added, with emphasis, that he had been sent by the provisional government of France to re-establish French administration and maintain French sovereignty.[48] On 18 June there was the first of a regular series of meetings between Coulet and representatives of the Allied Civil Affairs Headquarters. At this point, in the absence of an Allied agreement, decisions had to be taken on the ground and the 21st Army Group and US First Army Group command decided to recognize Coulet and his team as the *de facto* administration of the part of France that had been liberated, in line with the final SHAEF civil affairs instructions, but more particularly following the policy laid down in 21st Army Group Civil Affairs Technical Instruction 14.[49] Whilst he was not very complimentary about the local Gaullist officials in Bayeux, Lewis was very much more impressed with Coulet at the 18 June meeting and Coulet reciprocated this feeling. From that point onwards relations were relatively good, despite the occasional disturbance over the currency question and Liaison Officers.

Earlier on 12 June the news had broken that the Liaison Officers de Gaulle finally agreed to send to France would not be taking supplemental francs with them and would not necessarily accept these francs as legal tender when they arrived.[50] This sent Churchill into a fury, and prompted Roosevelt to demand an immediate proclamation that Eisenhower alone should authorize the notes – the last thing the Foreign Office wanted at that stage. Roosevelt telegraphed to Churchill: 'It seems clear that Prima Donnas do not change their spots'.[51] The French however appeared adamant – Koenig told Grasset that he could hardly expect French Liaison Officers, as representatives of the provisional government, to use francs which were rejected by the government and which would be unacceptable to the French people.[52] He also objected to the BBC calling French Liaison Officers, 'civil affairs officers', because it implied that they were just adjuncts to the Anglo-Saxon military machine.[53] In the end de Gaulle was mollified by his trip to France and agreed, upon return, to release more Liaison Officers. After talks between Koenig, de Boislambert (head of MMLA) and Biddle of EACS, a further 30 officers accompained echelons of the 21st Army Group, but EACS still thought that the French were trying to extract every advantage they could from holding back the Liaison Officers, who were desperately needed.[54] Although the French Liaison Officers were designated to accompany Allied army units, they still saw their role as representing the French administration to the Allied military, and there were reports that they tried to minimize the functions and importance of Allied civil affairs activities so as to protect French sovereignty and French administrators.[55]

In the early days of the Normandy landings, supplemental francs were in practice accepted throughout the area. There was some evidence of discontent on the French side – they would have to go to 'Monsieur G5' when they needed funds – but the 'francs' were widely accepted. Indeed Coulet issued an order to all bank managers on 18 June, instructing them to accept supplemental francs but to keep separate account of them, presumably for redemption at the end of the war. He also ordered the population to accept them. In the early days of the landings, the banks had few transactions, yet the amount of supplemental money on deposit soon grew, particularly for the payment of taxes. The careful Normans did not really trust the Allied money any more than they had trusted German military currency, and sought to shift the question of its value and redemption to the government by paying their taxes with it. Coulet could see a problem developing here and frantically telegraphed Koenig for instructions. Eventually, in the absence of instructions, and given that there was no civil affairs agreement, Coulet notified 21st Army Group Civil Affairs HQ on 27 June that he would have to tell the bank managers not to accept supplemental francs for the payment of taxes.[56] The civil affairs officers at 21st Army Group were horrified and tried to get him to change his mind, or at least delay. At a subsequent meeting with Lewis (Senior Civil Affairs Officer, SCAO 21st Army Group), the two sides struck an agreement by which Coulet withdrew his notice to the bank managers in return for a promise that the supplemental currency would be redeemed in Bank of France notes at the end of the war. The parties kept the agreement secret so that it would not appear as if civil affairs were admitting the weakness of supplemental francs, and so that Coulet and his group would not appear to be questioning their validity.[57] This agreement did not, however, ensure that all bank managers accepted the francs willingly and reissued them. It was also noticeable from the Allied viewpoint that Coulet's subsequent telegrams on the subject were much less precise and that he always refused to endorse the francs openly.[58]

The episode of the supplemental currency angered Roosevelt and it upset Churchill who exaggeratedly reported to Eden that Bedell Smith thought Eisenhower would throw Coulet out of France as a result of his attitude. Holmes of SHAEF G5, on the other hand, was concerned that the British had agreed to redeem all supplemental francs which came into banks before close of business on 30 June, which might, despite the limited nature of the agreement, set a precedent.[59] When SHAEF finally got a full picture of the currency problem in Normandy, they arranged that Koenig should order Coulet to accept supplemental francs for all purposes, including taxes. Coulet, defending nascent French authority in the liberated areas, was unhappy with this command and continued to insist on separate accounts for supplemental francs. By the first days of July, however, those in the field, like Lewis, and those at governmental level, like Eden, declared the currency crisis to be over.[60] For the French, currency was more than a matter of utility, so it was always likely to provoke dispute. Whether the French denunciation of supplemental francs was pique, principle, or disruptive tactics, it certainly caused a crisis. What could have been a relatively unimportant issue became, for want of a civil affairs agreement or recognition, a crucial touchstone of co-operation. An unstable compromise was achieved, which avoided an open conflict, but was unsatisfactory for all parties. This situation allowed many small incidents to become magnified in significance and disturb French–Allied compaign co-operation. Thus the fact that a poster appeared in Cherbourg in the first week of July declaring supplemental francs to be legal tender, signed 'the mayor' and dated 19 June – eight days before the Liberation of the town – became a matter of bitter dispute over the question of GPRF authority and French sovereignty. What was an unfortunate American blunder became, as a result of the unresolved general question, a major row. And the only one in an otherwise remarkably smooth liberation of the town.

Eden and Lewis may have thought that the currency issue was settled, but it continued to appear in the negotiations, throughout July and into August, which were concerned with the larger issues of civil affairs and recognition. It became muddled with questions surrounding the payment for supplies, the use of captured booty and civil materials, the aid system to be set up after the war, and the legal problems surrounding French government holdings in foreign and domestic banks. As far as the invasion forces were concerned, currency was no longer a problem, but at the governmental level it became one of the myriad of details that prevented agreement on civil affairs.

In the liberated area, however, practical co-operation was developing. On 19 July Coulet issued an order to all the mayors in the liberated areas, in the name of the GPRF, instructing them to co-operate with civil affairs officers and the Allied authorities, which pleased Lewis.[61] The establishment of such a relationship cemented the authority of the Regional Commissioner and his team, which had in any case begun to fill the vacuum left by the lack of an agreement. The representatives of Allied civil affairs did not know how to deal with the French representatives, nor what authority to ascribe to them, but had general instructions to co-operate with local French authorities and, more importantly, no orders to limit or deny their authority.

The early reports, from the smallest civil affairs detachment to the most senior civil affairs officer at army group headquarters, displayed a number of common features. Firstly, there was the sheer weight of practical work and the confusion, resulting not only from the fighting, but also from the presence of so many units operating in the same area. Then there was the constant attempt by civil affairs officers to work through the existing officials – Vichy if necessary – for the posting of proclamations, the distribution and collection of supplies, control of refugees and conserving of bank reserves, the repair of broken services and the recruitment of labour. All of this implied recognition of the French by Allied military as the practical administration in villages and towns. The meetings and negotiations with Coulet and de Chevigné – the GPRF Regional Military Delegate – went further towards recognition since they not only implied, but also demonstrated the willingness of the army headquarters to accept these nominees as the French administration for whole regions.

By the end of June, although Caen had not fallen, the Allies had secured a large bridgehead from the estuary of the Orne to the west coast of the Cotentin peninsula, at Port Bail, including the first big town, Cherbourg, taken on 27 June. This gave senior civil affairs officers the chance to make a more broadly based reconnaissance, and there were several reports at the end of the month. Maginnis (US War Department), who had been in Carentan since 12 June, and Capt. de Pury, on a visit to the US Zone, noted that no one knew what authority to ascribe to Coulet and his declarations, but neither of them questioned his or the other GPRF representatives' right to issue decrees.[62] Most reports mentioned that the people of the area were traditionally conservative, but whilst the American civil affairs officers tended to estimate de Gaulle's popularity as only 50 per cent (and some said that Normandy would have preferred Giraud to de Gaulle), the British reports spoke of enthusiastic support for de Gaulle.[63] Captain de Pury (CA 1st US Army) reported that Captain Howley, the CO of the A1A1 Civil Affairs Detachment of the 1st Regiment (US VII Corps), 'went out of his way to make the French feel it was their show; from the moment he entered Cherbourg'.[64] De Pury repeated his earlier suggestion that Louis Marin (pre-war leader of the moderate conservatives and a native of Lorraine) should be allowed to tour the area, but he acknowledged that the majority wanted the GPRF even if it did have a 'Popular Front tail'. He also reported that the pre-war radical politician, Lemoigne, looked an obvious candidate for the post of subprefect, but that Coulet instead appointed a conservative, Levandier, which showed his sensitivity to the politics of the region. Given that the head of the Resistance in Cherbourg turned out to be the largest wholesale grocer in the town, and that he introduced civil affairs officers to 'a number of solid citizens', they had few fears about the actions of the left. Indeed the only problems that the civil affairs officers had were drunkenness among French citizens and Allied troops alike, and the security of released Todt workers (civil construction workers, often from German-conquered territories), who were either Ukrainian Russians or the 'dregs of Marseilles and Paris'. Again, the civil affairs detachment in Cherbourg seemed to concern itself with the recruitment of labour, salvaging of war material, organization of transport and many other tasks that would naturally seem the province of the army service corps, whilst Frenchmen got on with the restoration of local administration.[65] Colonel Marcus, who was specifically sent by Hilldring, the CAD Director in the US War Department, to observe the reaction of the liberated population to de Gaulle and the political state of France in general, reported on 7 July that the 'Normands are not politically minded'. He noted the lack of enthusiasm for de Gaulle, which he said was partly because of local confusion. The population knew that Roosevelt did not support de Gaulle, but they could see that the army clearly did.[66]

It is clear that different approaches were taken by different British and American units. While Maginnis, in Carentan, noted the arrival of Gaullist administration causing confusion and difficulties, the OSS reported that civil affairs and the GPRF, together with Colonel Kingstone and Colonel Usher of the civil affairs detachments, were planning the joint civil administration of Caen, to begin from the moment of its Liberation.[67] Coulet appointed Daure, the ex-rector of the University of Caen and his brother-in-law, as the future prefect of Calvados, although he was still trapped behind German lines.[68] When the 201, 208 and 209 Civil Affairs Detachments finally moved into Caen, they found the acting mayor, Poirier, and the Vichy Prefect, Caucaud, were still in post, but they immediately allotted transport to the dishevelled Daure, who had presented himself, and was sent off to Bayeux to get instructions from Coulet. On 11 July, only two days after the last German troops were dislodged from the outskirts of the city, Colonel Usher, leading the civil affairs units, decided to give full control to the French.[69] The British were not simply allowing the French to take up civil administration, they were helping the representatives of the GPRF to assume local power. Lewis, Senior Civil Affairs Officer with the 21st Army Group, who was not enthusiastic about his first contacts with GPRF delegates, reported at the end of July that in Caen, 'French co-operation was wholehearted and enthusiastic. The bearing of the French authorities and people under fire was beyond praise.'[70] The presence of Coulet, and prior planning by the two sides, ensured close and effective co-operation, despite enormous problems and the death of Colonel Usher soon after Liberation. Also the Allied authorities were pleased to endorse proclamations issued by Coulet and Daure, giving them direct credence as the legitimate French administration.

During the period of the landings and the establishment of the bridgehead, the attitude of Allied officers 'on the ground' had evolved in a way which greatly favoured de Gaulle and the GPRF. At the beginning, the Allies were willing to work with Vichy officials and administrators whom they found *in situ*, whilst not knowing what status to accord representatives of the GPRF. Then they were willing to tolerate Coulet and his nominees because they were established and active. Eventually, they supported him with some enthusiasm and tacitly aided the establishment of a French presence in the towns they liberated. There were teething troubles in Allied–French relations at the town and village level, but nothing that seriously disturbed the rear areas. Indeed, given the novelty of the situation and the lack of overall agreements, it was remarkable how well the two sides co-operated.

## Civil affairs in France, July to mid-August

BY THE middle of August, the original beach-head had been extended inland, with the taking of St Lô on 18 July and the final capture of Caen

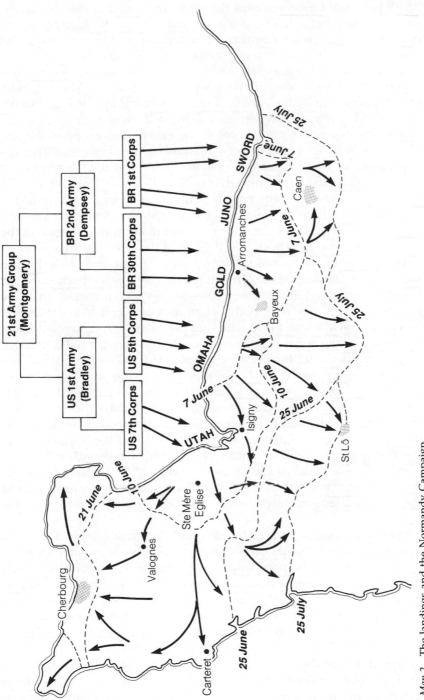

*Map 2*   The landings and the Normandy Campaign

on 19 July. The Canadians and British were pinned in the area to the south of Caen, but in the west the Americans broke through, with five divisions going further westward into Brittany and the rest swinging south and east in a long sweep behind the frontline German forces, going towards the Seine. The new German commander, Kluge, was ordered by Hitler to counter attack westwards, towards Mortain, with the idea of cutting off the Americans in the Cotentin peninsula, but (by the second week in August) found himself almost surrounded as Patton's sweep nearly cut him off in the Falaise pocket. By 18 August the Allies held an area between Nantes on the Loire estuary, the approaches to Tours, Chartres (close to Paris), and the Channel coast near the Seine estuary. There were 27 civil affairs units in the US Military Zone and 30 in the British Zone, sending in a vast amount of detailed information to their respective superiors, including political information. The Allies were still very keen to know the reaction of the French, once the first shock and delight of the landings were over.

The overall impression of the larger area was still one of a calm and moderate political opinion. On 8 July the Intelligence Section of the SHAEF Psychological Warfare Division (PWD), reported that the farmers seemed to admire both Pétain and de Gaulle[71] and Holmes, lunching with Mack on 1 July, said that people in Normandy had asked him whether the Allies could be persuaded to give Giraud a position which accorded with his prestige.[72] But SHAEF G5 reported that any hesitancy in supporting the GPRF was because the population in this area did not like its 'radical' elements.[73] The people of Cherbourg, apart from 'the small group of politically conscious', were still not expressing any political preferences, and by the second week in July, de Pury, reporting on Bayeux and Caen, said that the populations of the first town, liberated a month before, and the second, still in the frontline, were equally indifferent to politics.[74] By the middle of the month, civil affairs reports noted that the lack of partisanship might be the result of a long-nurtured union by political groups in the face of the enemy.[75]

These rather vague and confused reports began to narrow down into a clear impression that de Gaulle and the GPRF were broadly accepted by the majority of the population. Even the US 1st Army CA reports commented that, whilst de Gaulle was not personally very popular, the elements of the GPRF administration were widely accepted.[76] The French Country Unit of SHAEF noted on 22 July that the acceptance by the USA and Britain of the GPRF as the *de facto* government of France had given its representatives much greater authority than that which they had when they arrived, and it stated quite bluntly that 'the unchallenged position of de Gaulle and of the "Provisional Government" in all territories liberated by Allied or French forces is undoubtedly in great part responsible for the gradual acceptance, first by Great Britain and then by the United States, of Algiers desiderata concerning the administration of metropolitan France'.[77] The Foreign Office reported its satisfaction with the calm state of liberated France and the complete adherence of the population to de Gaulle, which, given the conservative nature of Normandy, did not surprise British commentators.[78]

Recognition of the GPRF representatives was so widespread and immediate that de Pury saw their assumption of authority in Cherbourg as perfectly normal, despite the fact that earlier he had been very worried about a possible erosion of Eisenhower's authority and a challenge to American policy.[79] The emergence of a regular Liberation press, the *Presse Cherbourgeoise*, the *Renaissance du Bessin* and the single sheet *Libération*, helped by the Political Warfare Division and the Civil Affairs Unit, was carefully watched as the first sign of political revival, but turned out to be thoroughly friendly to the Allies and very patriotic. The reorganization of the main union, the *Confédération Générale du Travail* (CGT) in late July amongst the 'very active dockers' was reported as having greatly helped civil affairs units in their clearing and restoration of the docks. A group of repatriated prisoners demanded that the red flag should fly alongside the Union Jack and the Stars and Stripes, which caused a small incident, but these signs of political revival were unlikely to disturb the good opinion of the Allies.[80] A meeting of G5 branch chiefs at the beginning of August, examining French reactions, found that the citizens were calm, everything was running very smoothly and there were no political developments of any note.[81] In fact, when the first post-Liberation poster by the Socialist Party appeared in Cherbourg, the PWD hailed it as 'the re-establishment of free speech'.[82] Reports on the Liberation of Rennes and the surrounding areas mention regrettable incidents of attacks on collaborators and mistakes by the civil affairs units who, in one case, opposed a mayor chosen by the Resistance, until they found that the majority of the population supported him. They noted that 'Recognition of his [de Gaulle's] administration as the only possible government [for France] is widespread . . . Church officials are expressing themselves as pro-Ally and pro-Resistance; their enthusiasm for the Liberation is clouded over only by their dislike and fear of Russia.' They added that 'French politics are essentially non-clerical'.[83] By the middle of August, Scully, Prather, Awtry, and Krevener of the US 12th Army Group CA reported that the Liberation of Laval had gone very smoothly, that the new prefect, Duperier, was in full control and that politically there were no problems. The SHAEF French Country Unit, commenting at the same time on the Vienne, noted that Resistance was unified, with a joint – rather than a single party –

programme and that 'There seems no question of a rival to the Provisional Government of de Gaulle.' To round off these impressions, the 'First General Report' of the 21st Army Group Civil Affairs praised the actions of the GPRF and of its nominees, noted the transitory problem of currency, but reported favourably on their sensitivity to the conservative opinions of the Normands.[84]

The more friendly attitude of the Allied civil affairs officers towards Coulet, de Chevigné, his military counterpart, and their subordinates, was also very noticeable in the middle of July and beginning of August. The Allies were still hazy about the precise position of the French administration, but Grasset thought that whatever their status was the relationship with them had to be accepted and made to work for the benefit of the SAC.[85] Eisenhower thought that the GPRF officials were far too worried about the question of sovereignty, which was understandable, but which was not an excuse for them to limit or minimize the functions of the civil affairs officers.[86] The Liberation of Cherbourg changed opinions about the French administration. Reports noted its efficiency, its dispassionate political stance and its co-operative manner.[87] Lewis on 9 July talked of relations with the French authorities 'improving daily',[88] and this despite the aggravations of the currency question which was not settled in Normandy until 4 August – if then. Similarly the relatively calm Liberation of the devastated city of Caen helped to boost Coulet's prestige and, although there were reports of him going behind the backs of civil affairs officers, most comments emphasized the efficiency of the administrators and Coulet's increasingly co-operative attitude. By the end of July reports were coming through SHAEF that the French legal system was working again in some areas; that the police, after some early problems, were now operating effectively to ensure public safety; that French administrators were getting to grips with the supply and refugee problems, and that the conferences between French authorities and the Allied representatives were increasingly cordial and effective.[89] The planning for the Liberation of Rouen went very smoothly, as did the Liberation itself, and the establishment of Coulet as Regional Commissioner. There was genuine admiration for the French administrators from Allied commentators as August progressed and as the French coped with both the large new areas of territory that had been liberated and the preparations for the move on Paris, all with a very small staff.[90]

As far as the Allied civil affairs side of the relationship was concerned the first impressions were that civil affairs officers were doing (as Captain Langelon reported) 'a damned good job', although 'handicapped from the standpoint of language, since relatively few officers can use French with any facility'.[91] De Pury found on 29 July that in Cherbourg, 'Many officers [of CA detachments] did not seem to grasp the fact that the French have a government of their own', but said that nevertheless their performance in Cherbourg was remarkable.[92] By the end of July, a revised SHAEF directive on civil affairs predicted the establishment of Forward and Interior Zones, with certain military areas and lines of communication within these. The Interior Zone was to be the responsibility of the French and, even in the Forward Zone, civil affairs officers were ordered to work through the French authorities. Officers were instructed to be scrupulous in not favouring one political group or another, but repeatedly exhorted to give the French control of legal and law enforcement duties.[93]

The problems that persisted were all physical, technical or military, in the widest sense: preventing people moving around and clogging up the roads, feeding refugees, housing bomb victims and providing water and sanitation. The drunken behaviour of American servicemen, the unruliness of German Construction (TODT) workers, whom the local population thought should be severely treated, and the spread of venereal disease after the closing of the police-regulated brothels, dominated the reports of the time. Once Liberation had been established in an area for a few days there were worrying reports of reprisals against collaborators. The French on the other hand thought that the Allies were not tough enough with collaborators. Also in this post-Liberation period there was a lot of wild celebrating by youngsters, driving around and firing off guns, but this posed no real threat to law and order because it did not last long and was soon controlled by the French police. There was not one single report of a political action or manoeuvre by the Resistance.[94] This calmed the fears of SHAEF and the Allied governments when, in the middle of August, attention turned to the landings in the south of France, and preparations for the Liberation of Paris.

The Liberation of this larger, post-beachhead area was significant for a number of reasons, given the Allied view of French politics on the eve of the landings. Events had vindicated the British view that the French would co-operate, that de Gaulle was popular and that there was no alternative in practical terms to the GPRF as the governing authority of France. They had also fulfilled British hopes of a piecemeal practical recognition to accompany 'official level' talks going on in London. Furthermore, several large towns with potentially difficult political problems had been liberated relatively peacefully. Another stage in the practical recognition of the GPRF and de Gaulle had been reached with the installation of their nominees, Coulet and de Chevigné, as Regional Commissioner and Regional Military Delegate in Rouen. In addition several cities (Cherbourg, Rennes, Laval and Rouen) had been liberated where there had existed – in varying states of organization – local Liberation committees, which, rather than take revolutionary action, had co-operated fully with the Allies and the GPRF representative. Another test of acceptability had been passed by the provisional government, and this cemented their position as 'the French authorities'.

## *The Allies and the French Resistance, 1944*

DURING 1944 the Allies had become increasingly concerned firstly about whether the Resistance would co-operate within Operation 'Overlord' and secondly how the Resistance – and particularly the communists – would act in the immediate and longer term post-Liberation period. Allied planning with regard to the Resistance came fairly late in the day and displayed the usual divisions of opinion between the Anglo-Saxon authorities. The hesitations of the American administration were over-ridden by the enthusiasm of Eisenhower and SHAEF for Resistance involvement. By the pre-landings period, secret services and armed forces planners were taking full account of the Resistance, although not certain about how to use them.[95]

The OSS/SI and British SIS (the intelligence units) had not co-ordinated their intelligence gathering system – as had OSS/SO and SOE (the action units) – but the OSS Research and Analysis Branch still obtained documents from their French contacts in BCRA Special Forces HQ missions and their own SI agents, so they were quite well informed about France. Their considered opinion was that the bulk of the Resistance was in favour of the GPRF, de Gaulle and the Allied plans for landing. Resisters were keen to eliminate the 'Quisling element' and wanted a Consultative Assembly to work alongside the GPRF in a liberated France. Their report on the Resistance at the end of May said that it was co-operative and predominantly left wing, and they urged a massive programme of arming Resistance groups.[96] The reports from the Normandy landing area in June showed that there had been little Resistance in the area and, where it did exist, it had been useful and co-operative, particularly in the case of Cherbourg. The OSS view of the Resistance was vindicated and the American government began to receive glowing reports of their exploits. Writing to Marshall on 12 July, Donovan, the Head of OSS, could say, 'All factions are united against the Germans and that unity creates a strong base for a stable, democratic France, with little danger of civil war or extremist control.'[97]

One of the main sources of information on the French Communist Party (PCF) for the Americans seemed to be its intelligence agents in Spain and North Africa. The military attachés in Madrid – Stephens, Solberg and Sharp – were convinced that the PCF was going to launch some kind of coup during the Liberation. They forwarded very exaggerated reports of communist Resistance numbers, retailed French Vichy police reports about the Moscow control of French communists, spread the flimsiest stories of communist 'killer groups' and presented quite mild PCF policy documents as revolutionary tracts.[98] Whenever the OSS reported on the communists from Algiers, or from Washington, they were much more measured. A report by agent Joseph R. Starr, with comments by David Rockefeller, on 27 June 1944, noted that: 'they do not seem to be using the Resistance as a method of furthering partisan ends. Whatever may be the ultimate aims of the communist leaders it appears that the movement is for the time being thoroughly nationalist and patriotic.'[99] Indeed Donovan, the Director of OSS, reported that they were not as strong in the CFLN (two out of 21) as their popular support warranted. The OSS in Algiers put it even more clearly when they reported that, as the invasion of France approached, the PCF had two choices: either to submerge themselves in the general effort, or to take independent action, and that they had plainly taken the former course.[100] Fears that the PCF might try to dominate the CNR, cause an insurrection in Paris, or disrupt events in Algiers, were exaggerated, declared the OSS, and there was no evidence of their ill-intentions.[101] Donovan, in his memo to Marshall on the Resistance, stated that: 'they owe their influence not to their communism but to their record in the Resistance . . . They are not planning a putsch.'[102]

By the end of July, part of 93 'JEDBURGH' missions and 52 'SUSSEX' missions had been flown into France as an element of the overall SHAEF strategy to stimulate and co-ordinate Resistance in conjunction with the Normandy landings. The SUSSEX missions were made up of two main teams, either of a Briton (SIS) and a Frenchman (Brissex Missions), or an American and a Frenchman (Ossex Missions). Although the very first was originally sent to work with the major French trade union in Paris (the CGT) they were thenceforth exclusively devoted to military intelligence and were supposed to avoid contact with the established Resistance groups. The JEDBURGH teams were three-man outfits of British (SOE), American (OSS) and French (BCRA), who parachuted to Resistance groups behind the German lines. What they found in many parts of France in July was a generalized support for the GPRF. By the time of the landings they were required to report on politics and were often sent to clarify a confused political situation. Most teams, like CHLOROFORME, which had been despatched to sort out political divisions in the Resistance of the Drôme, found no political differences, and saw a well-organized Resistance which was solidly behind de Gaulle. Others, like the STEADY/ex-GLOVER mission to the Haute-Marne and Langres plateau, reported that 'the political situation was obscure when I landed in France. It was still obscure when I left.' Many of the JEDBURGH groups found that the Communist Paramilitary Group (FTP) were acting independently and none too co-operatively. The DODGE report for Valence, the Drôme and Isère said that: 'The FTP impressed me as being an indisciplined lot. In great part they consisted of Italian communists and Spanish Republicans; a disorderly and ruffianly crew of brigands.' In fact some JEDBURGH team leaders found it necessary to exert discipline on the FTP and JEDHAROLD leader, Major Whitby, cut off all arms supplies to the FTP until they recognised the GPRF nominee, Chaumette (AS), as prefect of the region. But several instances of the FTP stealing arms and supplies did not add up to an insurrection, much less a civil war in the making, and the reports made no mention of any communist political ambition. As JEDHARRY reported: 'All the time I was in the Morvain, I had very little evidence of the so-called "communist plot"; the only scare stories came from died-in-the-wool reactionaires.' But in many cases of conflict or confusion the JEDBURGH team stepped in to adjudicate or resolve a dispute, and always in favour of the GPRF nominee or a moderate. JEDHUGH in Indre and Isère often sorted out squabbles between the leaders of the FTP, AS and ORA, which was done by simply saying, 'we have orders from London', and Legrand (from the team) was eventually appointed military delegate of Indre-et-Loire by Koenig. Lt Henquet, the American member of a JEDBURGH team in Blois, sorted out a local problem by taking the step of appointing a Resister called Valin to head the local FFI where the provisional government nominee, Matron, was under suspicion.[103] Indeed Koenig complained to Bedell Smith that the 'Special Forces' detachment (JEDBURGHS) were controlling the Resistance without his being consulted, despite the fact that he was Commander-in-Chief of the FFI.[104]

Allied misgivings about the political ambitions and insurrectionary motives of the Resistance were allayed by the modest reaction of the domestic Resistance, such as it was, in the landings area and by reports from elsewhere on effective and militarily valuable actions by Resisters. The expected uprisings in the centre, south and east, at the moment of the landings, had not materialized, and although there had been confusion about whether to call for all-out Resistance or for a staged uprising (leading to one or two major tragedies), it had not produced civil war or anarchy. The flood of intelligence from the OSS and British missions in France had served to calm the two governments for, even where there were disturbances, they were put into the perspective of general calm. Also, from these reports, it appeared as if the French Communist Party and its FTP military affiliate had not made any attempt to seize power, even at a local level. The FTP might have guarded their independence too vigorously and indulged in some unruly military behaviour, but they were susceptible to discipline and not a serious problem.

As an augury for the southern landings, the news of June and July from Resistance France was very reassuring, and it encouraged the Allies to place more reliance on local forces and French local administration when they began the landings in the south.

## Allied attitudes in the post-landings period

ON THE diplomatic level, attitudes lagged well behind the *fait accompli* of the Liberation. The aftermath of the 'D' Day acrimony in fact distracted the Allies from consideration of the civil affairs and political repercussions of the events in Normandy. Roosevelt was predictably horrified by de Gaulle's irresponsible behaviour.[105] He nevertheless allowed Eisenhower to negotiate with representatives of the CFLN on practical matters.[106] The British[107] and the US War Department sought to capitalize on this apparent change of heart, but Hull and Roosevelt were, in truth, as firm as ever against recognition.[108]

Once the President learnt that de Gaulle had not simply visited France to fly the flag, but had left behind him a skeleton administration, his opposition to the GPRF burst into public view. At a press conference on 23 June Roosevelt declared that de Gaulle had been wrong and precipitate to appoint prefects and subprefects in the area so far liberated and that there would have to be a much larger area of liberated territory before any civilian, let alone Gaullist, administration could be contemplated.[109] Roosevelt still thought that de Gaulle was 'a narrow-minded French zealot with too much ambition for his own good and some rather dubious views on democracy.'[110] He found himself, however, in a difficult position when de Gaulle finally accepted his invitation to visit the USA. Roosevelt had hoped that if he could get de Gaulle to Washington he could persuade him to moderate his position, but he above all did not want de Gaulle's visit to imply the recognition which he had publicly refused. To avoid a *fait accompli* between the British and Free French, Roosevelt had to welcome de Gaulle's forthcoming visit, only three days after publicly castigating him.[111]

Churchill remained angry with de Gaulle about the latter's behaviour in London and telegrammed Roosevelt, declaring that, if de Gaulle did not arrange for three or four commissioners to stand by ready to go to France, the British would send him back to Algiers.[112] What Churchill did not fully realize was that de Gaulle's dearest wish was to take representatives of the GPRF to France from Britain, not as some kind of super Liaison Officers, but as a practical expression of GPRF authority. Churchill had been pleased with his own visit to the landing area on 12 June, but was worried about letting de Gaulle 'muddy the pools', saying that the General only wanted to 'get cheap cheers in Bayeux, and to make a harangue in which he will represent himself as the future President of the French Republic'. De Gaulle, he said, was a 'wrongheaded, ambitious and detestable anglophobe'.[113] On 13 June, the day before de Gaulle's proposed visit to France, Churchill was still threatening that there was time to cancel if he did not start to behave better. On 14 July Churchill and the Cabinet came in for a roasting from the House of Commons for the British failure to recognize the GPRF, and thus, when de Gaulle wrote a eulogistic letter to the Prime Minister on the eve of his return to Algiers, he got a very cold and formal reply from Churchill.[114] Such was Churchill's displeasure that he circulated a very anti-French report from Rex North of the *Sunday Pictorial* to the Cabinet. It declared that six out of ten people in Normandy distrusted and detested the Allies and half of them had collaborated with the Germans. Two days later, on 22 June, his wife sent him a cutting from the *Times* with the note: 'M. Coulet, de Gaulle's nominee, doesn't seem so very intransigent', but it failed to moderate his anger.[115]

The Foreign Office had hoped the landings would be a spur to negotiations for recognition. They had connived at the presumption of authority in de Gaulle's broadcast and then found themselves embarrassed by his behaviour in London, but were still convinced that there was no alternative French leader. Thus they pressed for him to be allowed to visit France as early as possible and, although momentarily shaken by reports of his apparent disappearance, they regarded the visit, when it was over, as a success. They also began to try and distance themselves from Washington's hardened attitude to the events of 4–6 June and declared that they would not share the blame for a policy with which they disagreed.[116] Cadogan urged Eden to dissociate the British from Roosevelt's statements on currency, and the suspicion grew in London that the State Department were indulging in underhand tactics to wreck talks.[117] On the one hand the Foreign Office was giving support to the recognition negotiations under the auspices of the Judge Advocate General (JAG), and on the other hand, they supported the actions of SHAEF whose various divisions were working out their own practical arrangements with the French. Eden had found de Gaulle almost affable on 16 June after the latter's return from France, and he continued to urge Churchill to press Roosevelt for a change of heart. Being closer to the battlefield, the British looked increasingly to the developing situation in France for an answer.

SHAEF, however, had planned on the assumption that there would be some sort of recognition, or a civil affairs agreement with the French – and probably the GPRF – before the landings. Their emphasis in civil affairs was on giving as much responsibility to the local French authorities as they could, so they were always liable to give credence to any commissioners, prefects or subprefects that were installed in France. In the early days of the landings and during rapid advances, this often meant unfortunate dealings with Vichy officials, but it also meant recogniton of the GPRF appointees. In the first days after the establishment of Coulet and de Chevigné, SHAEF did not know what level of recognition to accord them, nor how to deal with them, but Bedell Smith's advice from SAC, and Peake's advice from the British side, pushed them towards recognition. Peake, British Political Officer at SHAEF, was conscious of the problems, was surprised that Coulet's first proclamation in the name of the provisional government had not prompted a 'military explosion', and made strenuous efforts to ensure that the political news which might come after the fall of Cherbourg was dealt with by more experienced hands than those in the SHAEF Press Department, so that they might avoid, 'all sorts of trouble both in parliament and with the public generally'.[118]

SHAEF meanwhile kept a close scrutiny on the French. They questioned Koenig, Commander-in-Chief of French forces, on 12 June about the role of the 20 Liaison Officers present in France and whether they would accept 'supplemental francs', but got little satisfaction. Biddle, ex-US Attorney General, produced a paper for SHAEF entitled *Reinstatement of French Administration* which accepted the French decrees on commissioners, prefects, Liberation committees and local councils, almost to the letter.[119] Finally, Grassett, Biddle's superior at EACS, met Koenig, together with Holmes of SHAEF G5, and asked what line of authority Coulet had to the Allies. Koenig said that, in lieu of a full French administration, Coulet and de Chevigné were both responsible to him, and he to Eisenhower, and that he was willing to state that in writing. This only meant that the chain of authority led back to Eisenhower until such time as a national civilian delegate was appointed by the GPRF, and Col. Dostert's analysis of the situation came to the conclusion that 'Thro' the appointment of these two officers, the GPRF . . . has in a *de facto* sense extended its jurisdiction over metropolitan France'.[120] Holmes for the American side in SHAEF G5 was not happy about the outcome and reported to Washington that de Gaulle was bent on full authority.[121]

In the early days of the landings American Civil Affairs officers were less co-operative with the GPRF nominees than the British, but by the time Cherbourg fell they had changed their attitudes, and Halifax, in conversation with Dunn, pointed out that, by the last week in June, the GPRF was being allowed to appoint civil administrators in each liberated area and that this was actually in line with Eisenhower's instructions. He suggested that Eisenhower should be allowed to recognize the GPRF as the 'provisional authority' since this in practice was already happening. Halifax said that, unless some kind of agreement was made, the GPRF would 'inadvertently step into the position of authority'.[122]

Churchill and Roosevelt were both isolated in their renewed intransigence against de Gaulle, although in the American case some of the State Department hierarchy again supported their leader. The British Foreign Office was hoping that either discussions in the JAGs Committee or – more likely – the development of practical recognition in France would bring a solution. They were prepared to wait while the SAC and SHAEF moved towards full negotiations with Coulet and de Chevigné, presaging negotiations with the GPRF as a single authority. But the American members of SHAEF – Holmes, Dunn and the rest – were in a particular dilemma, because, while Roosevelt's telegram to Eisenhower allowed them to go some way towards such negotiations, the President's memo of March strictly forbade them from the logical consequences of these talks. Yet they could do nothing to stop the development of the practical relationship which each day legitimized de Gaulle and the GPRF. Their problem was that they had no overall agreements on civil affairs or recognition with which they could halt or deflect French initiative taken on the ground. This meant that they came up against a series of *faits accomplis* on the French side which were difficult to dispute and almost impossible to reverse.

## The Official Committee of the Judge Advocate General: civil affairs planning in July 1944

THE achievement of the Foreign Office in salvaging Anglo–French talks – even at a secondary level – from the wreckage of the de Gaulle visit to London and the subsequent confusion following the landings came to fulfilment when the Cabinet decided to allow talks to take place officially under the auspices of the official committee of the Judge Advocate General (JAG). This committee had worked out civil affairs agreements for Belgium, Norway and the Netherlands, and the Foreign Office used a modified version of the Belgian agreement as a draft. This and the French document had many points of agreement, but there was one important difference : the French desire to have control over information and propaganda. A second problem was that, throughout the French document, powers currently attributed to the Supreme Allied Commander (SAC) were implicitly attributed to the GPRF, and in many articles the French document made French officers the primary actors in any situation. Lastly, there was the French insistence on the 'zone concept' from their original paper of September 1943. Their argument was that Belgium was a small country, likely to be totally in the battle zone and then totally liberated, but that France was liable to be liberated in stages and that interim arrangements had to be made.[123]

The five British members, led by Sir Henry McGeagh, tried to keep the draft as close to the British/Belgian model as possible on the grounds that the Americans knew and accepted it, but the French declared that this deprived the representatives of the French Committee in France of much of their authority, giving it to the SAC. This was not acceptable, nor was the JAG committee's insistence on referring to the provisional government as the 'CFLN.' Viénot claimed that French willingness to allow Eisenhower to determine when a 'Zone of the Interior' could be handed to the French was a concession. He was probably relying on the pro-GPRF attitude of Eisenhower, rather than risking the delaying tactics of Roosevelt and Churchill.[124] Eventually agreement was reached on the six main articles dealing with the respective powers of the SAC and the French authorities, based on a division of France into 'Forward' and 'Interior' zones. Currency was still a difficult issue, but all the other economic and legal articles were close to agreement by 24 June. The committee even managed to get round the problem of what to call the French by deciding to finalize the agreement with an exchange of notes between the Secretary of State and Viénot,[125] rather than governments.

The British were delighted with this progress. The Americans, however, were very wary of what was going on. Holmes from SHAEF warned that the 'British will go as far as they think the US will allow and then try to sell the agreement to the USA'.[126] He noted that even Bovenschen from the War Office and the AT (E) seemed to have been ignored by the JAG committee. Eden, he believed, thought the French had genuinely moderated their view and that there was a great deal of public pressure in Britain for recognition. When Holmes finally saw the draft agreement on 27 June he thought it was good, but not as good as the old McCloy document, which would have given less authority to the French.[127] Roosevelt told the Prime Minister: 'I hope you will not make any agreements with the Committee prior to giving me an opportunity to comment thereon. I should not like to be faced with a *fait accompli* when de Gaulle arrives in Washington'.[128] Churchill was quick to placate the President, saying the talks were only at the level of officials, that they had to be ratified by the Foreign Secretary and himself, and that His Majesty's Government would consult the President before making any such agreement public. Warnings from McCloy that the President would not change easily, and from Halifax, that presenting cut and dried documents was apt to create American resistance, made the Foreign Office think long and hard about the way to 'sell' the draft to the Americans. The consensus was that a cable from Churchill would probably be the best approach.[129] Churchill refused and suggested the government tell the House of Commons that an 'official level' agreement had been sent to the Americans and that the British would consider it at a governmental level when they heard from the Americans at such a level.[130]

The agreement was sent to the USA immediately after its initialling by Viénot and McGeagh on 30 June, and Halifax was briefed by the Foreign Office to point out the 'American' parts of it in forthcoming talks on 4 July. By this time the GPRF had ratified the document with one or two provisos about the mutual aid, booty, and the judicial articles.[131] The 'selling campaign' did not go well. At a press conference on 8 July, Roosevelt cast doubts on the document and its concessions to the French. Churchill commented that 'this quite confirms my view that we had better wait and see what actually happens in America before attempting a 14th July demonstration'.[132] There Churchill referred to de Gaulle's visit to the USA which was soon to overtake consideration of the JAG agreement, and cause yet another delay.

## De Gaulle's visit to the USA

THE reasons for Roosevelt wanting de Gaulle to visit the USA in the first place are difficult to understand. Lippmann, doyen of Washington political commentators, told the British Embassy that the President wanted an end to the Franco–American animosity so that he could go to the coming elections with a good diplomatic record. The Embassy agreed, declaring that this would help to wash away the 'earlier stains of appeasement and opportunism',[133] but they were worried about the possibility of a sudden volte–face by the President which would leave Britain out in the cold and make it appear that it was the British who had been holding up recognition all along. The visit, which started on 6 July, went very well. The General appeared to be in a 'mellow mood', and Roosevelt at a state luncheon declared that, 'There are no great problems between the French and the Americans, or between General de Gaulle and myself'.[134] Roosevelt told de Gaulle of American plans for a string of bases around the world which would ensure peace, and mentioned his intention of installing them on French territory such as Dakar. De Gaulle, ignoring this, replied that the future security of Europe was more important and that bases on the Rhine against Germany would be more to the point. De Gaulle did claim American agreement that the GPRF should in future issue French currency, saying that Roosevelt told him it 'was not a question he had ever gone into very deeply'. He had clearly expunged the President's bad opinion of him.[135] Isaiah Berlin reported that the visit had been very successful, and that only Leahy, of all the people the General met, remained opposed to him. In fact Leahy records that de Gaulle made a good impression on him and that his reservations were confined to the members of the provisional government.[136] Leahy, indeed, sent Roosevelt a telegram indicating his change of heart over de Gaulle and recommending that the USA recognize de Gaulle's government in some way. Roosevelt replied that he was prepared to sign some form of recognition as long as it included the provisos that complete authority was reserved for Eisenhower and that the French be given the opportunity to make a free choice of their own government.[137]

At his press conference of 11 July, Roosevelt announced the *de facto* recognition of the GPRF, although he still insisted on calling it by its former title:

> The United States has decided to accept General de Gaulle's French Committee of National Liberation as the working authority for civilian administration in the liberated areas of France.[138]

The statement, which Roosevelt based on the text of a Franco-American agreement made during the talks, preserved the points he insisted on, but seemed to make them secondary to the declaration of recognition. Thus, whilst Roosevelt thought that he had convinced de Gaulle to fall in line with the American view on the need for democratic government in France, and got his general agreement to the American concept of world security, the French interpreted the agreement in a very different way. They saw the *de facto* recognition as *de jure* recognition. They ignored American views on the break up of the French empire and the placing of American bases in former French territory.[139]

The British were initially both confused and angry at the sudden change of direction in Washington. On 11 July the Foreign Office was unsure whether the President's statement actually meant *de facto* recognition, but on the following day, Eden replied to a question from Irene Ward in the House of Commons that it amounted to *de facto* recognition, but nothing more. Eden then used the President's statement to try and persuade Churchill to demand immediate recognition of the GPRF on the grounds that Britain had loyally stood by the American non-recognition viewpoint, whilst themselves preferring recognition, and that now they felt free to demand it in full. It appeared to the British that earlier Foreign Office warnings about an American flanking manoeuvre which would suddenly recognize the

GPRF and make it appear that British intervention was the stumbling block were justified by the events. Churchill was upset that, after all his efforts with this question, the President had suddenly changed his mind without consulting the British, making the Prime Minister appear to be the real opponent of French recognition. As a means of stealing a march back from the Americans, Churchill suggested on 18 July that the British should begin using the title 'provisional government of the French Republic' when referring to the CFLN. Eden, however, thought it unwise to antagonize the USA, although he determined to 'keep a close watch and see that the Americans do not again get ahead of us'.[140]

Whatever the different Allied governments thought of the statement, its public impact was considerable. Opinion in America swung as rapidly towards de Gaulle as it had swung away from him in June. In North Africa, his position in the provisional government was immensely strengthened. On a more practical plane, the Allied planners and commanders were encouraged to soften their resistance to French intervention in civil affairs. D'Astier's and le Troquer's visits to France were both allowed as a result of the President's statement, because they could no longer be seen as attempted *coups de main*.[141]

The negotiations on recognition and civil affairs that had started with the JAG Committee were now at inter-governmental level, but becoming more complex as time went on. The British were sticking by the final JAG/Viénot draft; the French had changes to propose on aid, supply, booty and the legal system, and the Americans had their own redrafting of the JAG proposals, designed to stress the overall authority of the SAC and the need for elections.[142] The Cabinet, at the instigation of the Foreign Office, decided that this was the moment to urge full recognition on the President, and the Prime Minister telegraphed him with congratulations on the success of de Gaulle's visit. He expressed satisfaction that the British/French draft was a working basis for the Americans, said he was sympathetic to the American amendments, but hoped that they would be careful of 'French susceptibilities'. In other words he did not want the first five points of the American draft to give the impression that Eisenhower had complete authority over the GPRF.[143] Presidential intransigence was also under renewed attack from the War Department, because Eisenhower was becoming frantic for a settlement, firstly to save his staff the valuable time now spent negotiating with Koenig and the rest, and secondly so that an agreement could be signed before a large section of France was liberated. Hilldring (CAD) and his deputies pressed the President and the American negotiators to give way on details so as to speed the process, but the whole affair dragged on until the end of July.[144]

Whilst the immediate impact of de Gaulle's visit to the USA was considerable, its long-term effects were less dramatic. The French remained suspicious of American motives, seeing their plans for world security as little more than plans for American domination, and worrying about an American military presence in the French empire. De Gaulle was much less enthusiastic about his visit than the British, for example, expected. The Americans did not rush forward with the logical consequence of the visit: full recognition. Roosevelt was not prepared to see de Gaulle, and more particularly the group of men who made up the GPRF, assuming power under Allied auspices when Paris was liberated. He stood firmly behind the two major provisos in the Franco–American agreement which enshrined the minimum demands of American policy: complete authority reserved for Eisenhower, and the opportunity for the French to choose their own government. None of this improved conditions for the Allied civil affairs officers of the proposed southern landings. It left a vacuum of political authority which representatives of the GPRF and local Liberation committees could exploit.

## The landings in the south, August 1944

THE actual organization of civil affairs for the south was never as large or as methodical as that for Normandy. The landing was originally planned to be much smaller: three assault divisions and three follow-up divisions. The civil affairs officers and other planners of the Combined Allied Command for the Mediterranean (AFHQ) in the south, waited to take their cue from SHAEF. They had the difficult Italian campaign during the planning period of early 1944 and there was uncertainty about whether the landings would indeed take place.[145] A landing in the south had first been mooted at the QUAD-RANT, Quebec, Conference, in August 1943, and was taken up at the Cairo Conference. It was expected that Allied progress in Italy (to the Pisa–Rimini line) would release equipment and troops for the Normandy landings and provide the two divisions to chase and harrass the retreating German forces in the south. In December 1943 at the Tehran Conference, the plan was expanded into a full-blown attempt to roll up the German forces from the rear and drive to the Rhine. The Allied attack at Monte Casino on 12 January was held up and the Anzio landing faltered long enough for Kesselring to improvise a furious counter attack. AFHQ sent a warning on 22 February that Allied forces in Italy should be strengthened and the southern French landings put aside.[146] The Combined Chiefs of Staff replied that it had been decided to give Italy priority over southern France. This coincided with the British strategy of an attack towards the Ljubljana gap, Austria and southern Germany, to which Eisenhower was entirely opposed. On 1 March Patch was appointed Commander of the US 7th Army in preparation for landings in southern France, and de Gaulle, who had taken over military control from Giraud, insisted that they go ahead with what he called 'the battle for France'. The British stalled, but the Americans won by refusing to reinforce the Italian armies, and Wilson (Commander in Chief of AFHQ) was ready to start planning for the southern landings on 7 June. Slow progress in Italy caused him to call for the scrapping of the landings plan as late as 19 June[147] and in this he was still supported by Churchill. Eisenhower simply over-ruled them.

Against this immensely complicated background, it is not surprising that the civil affairs planning for the southern landings was confused and dislocated. The planners of AFHQ found that most of their efforts went into the Italian AMGOT and that for France, apart from the 'on-off' disruption, they also had to wait upon developments in London and Washington over questions of recognition and planning responsibility. On 8 January 1944 AFHQ sent the 7th Army an Interim Directive for civil affairs in the Southern Zone which emanated from the Combined Chiefs of Staff. Section 5 of the document declared that:

> military government will not be established in France. Civil administration in all areas will normally be conducted and controlled by the French authorities.[148]

Throughout the directive the phrase 'French authorities' was used and the appendix made it clear that this was done intentionally, to cover any French group or individual that the civil affairs units might wish to contact. But the appendix went on to say:

> Excluding, of course, Vichy, the Committee National is, at present, the only French authority in the field with which we can do business.[149]

Clearly the AFHQ did not want planners to approach France in the same way that they were planning for Italy, and were realistic enough to see that, with a large French military contingent involved in the campaign, co-operation with the CFLN would be essential. On 19 January, the military government section of the AFHQ ordered Col. H. S. Gerry to join the southern French Landings planning group in Algiers – set up in December 1943 and called 'Force 163' – to start civil affairs planning for the coming invasion. By March he had acquired a small group of planning officers and had set up a training school.[150] But none of this solved the problem of whether civil affairs could be planned on the basis of CFLN recognition.

The invasion itself remained in doubt. Furthermore there were difficulties in AFHQ as a whole which spread into the civil affairs section. The British frequently left the words 'provisional government' in French documents that they translated, symptomatic of their much friendlier attitude to the CFLN and de Gaulle. This caused problems in inter-Allied agencies such as the Political Warfare Bureau and the civil affairs section, where American officers could not lend their names to anything carrying appellations of this sort.[151]

The final decision to go ahead with ANVIL was taken on 1 July when it was renamed DRAGOON, although Churchill again tried to scupper the plan in the last two weeks of July. The civil affairs planners still had, as Coles and Weinberg commented, 'no organised unit, no table of organisation, no equipment and no Civil Affairs manual'.[152] The planning group became the Civil Affairs Section of the 7th Army, and 1678 Civil Affairs Regiment was created to solve the organizational problem, with 90 officers and 250 men. A civil affairs headquarters was established, ready to land immediately after the landings and direct civil affairs on a regional basis.

The whole emphasis in the south, where Resistance was thought to be strong, was on passing administrative power to the French wherever and whenever possible. As a result, at the time of the landings, Civil Affairs Section of the 7th Army had only 594 personnel for a projected 31 Departments, whereas in the north, 3600 men had finally been detailed to administer 18 departments.[153] The Americans were suspicious of the French in North Africa and on this matter, they were joined by the British who, although heartily endorsing the policy of French responsibility, were concerned that Cochet, the military delegate in the south (there was no civil delegate designated at that time), had no power and could not guarantee co-operation since he was out of favour with the Gaullists.[154] Meetings had begun with Cochet after an AFHQ authorization on 5 May, and the G5 group of AFHQ met Cochet and his staff from 14 June. The French side offered 73 officers and 167 men as Liaison Officers, who were originally attached to army units, but by August the French decided that these men would be attached to local authorities, such as Prefects and mayors. This followed the breakdown of talks, after the cipher problem,[155] and reflected Koenig's announcement in London that the French Liaison Officers would be available for transfer to army units when a Civil Affairs agreement was signed. The talks with Cochet went on until 21 July – some 43 meetings – and junior military from each side continued discussions after that, but the outburst by de Gaulle when he withdrew 120 Liaison Officers from the Normandy landings almost destroyed the tentative agreements made in Algiers. This desperate situation was not helped by the fact that the Allied side could still provide no guidance for the southern civil affairs planners, even after the Normandy landings. On 6 August, nine days before the southern landings, G5 of AFHQ complained that:

> No final directive to SACMED concerning the administration of Civil Affairs in Southern France has yet been received. The relationship with the French at the working level has been excellent. A definite agreement providing for the administration of Civil Affairs and the issuance of currency is, however, urgently needed now.[156]

However unfinished civil affairs planning for the south was by the time of the landings, there was a basic structure and an overall policy which differed markedly from that in the north. AFHQ had delegated much more responsibility for civil affairs to the Commanding General of the 7th Army – on 28 July it had given him complete responsibility for civil affairs in the south – than SHAEF had given its commanders. The 7th Army, in turn, gave the French much more authority than SHAEF was willing to do in the north. Also, the independent Civil Affairs Headquarters, which was to establish itself directly after the landings, was in a position to implement the transfer of authority to the French.[157]

Allied intelligence for the southern landings was remarkably wide ranging and detailed. The respective units of the British and Americans – SOE, SIS and OSS – were all established in Algiers by February 1943, and had begun active work immediately. There were problems resulting from the old clash between the British SOE and SIS over which group should deal with the OSS on which matter, because the OSS included both direct action (SOE) and secret intelligence (SIS) within one organization. An agreement between Donovan (OSS) and Menzies (SIS) that any operation with SIS implications would first be cleared though a joint SIS/OSS committee in London threatened to ruin the excellent co-operation between SOE and OSS in North Africa, but the local SIS detachment ignored the agreement and work went ahead with few problems. The dispute between the regular *Service de Renseignements* section of the *Deuxième Bureau* and the BCRA also threatened to disturb operations, but this virtually disappeared when the rival organizations were merged in October 1943.[158] This intelligence work intensified when AFHQ invited representatives to join Force 163 on 10 January 1944, subsequently with a Special Project Operations Centre on 1 May and a Special Force unit no.4 attached to the 7th Army, both of which were to stimulate and co-ordinate Resistance activity. Between January and July hundreds of agents were sent into southern France and thousands of reports came back, mainly concentrating on military objectives. In early August, however, a series of missions were sent into the south with, as a subsidiary task, orders to report back on the political situation. All these groups were also told to state that, whilst they were Allied special operations units, they were under the general aegis of Koenig and the French Military High Command.[159]

Reports from these teams in early August 1944 stressed the good fighting potential of the Resistance in the south, but they also noted that there were political divisions of a serious nature between the FTP and the FFI and between the communists and others. It was reported, for example, that Guingouin in the Haute-Vienne 'showed definite communistic tendencies', and was interested in the political attitude of the Allies and the missions they might drop.[160] But it was also noted that 'he never allowed any political consideration to interfere with the military plans which we made in common'.[161] The OSS reported 'a chaotic and dangerous political fracas' in the Toulouse area in early August[162] with communists and socialists vying for political advantage; but they also noted that the British led 'HILAIRE' team were negotiating between them, although they did not always approve of HILAIRE'S decisions.[163] By the time of the landings, Allied groups were in touch with, and often co-ordinating, local Resistance groups, Liberation committees and CFLN representatives, where those had been designated. The basis was laid for a rapid handing over of authority to the French once the liberating armies moved through the south.

The landings themselves, apart from one mishap, were a remarkable success, and by the evening of 15 August, most of the Allies' major objectives had been taken, some exceeded, and all the initial civil affairs officers landed. The following day Civil Affairs HQ had been established in Sainte-Maxime, corps civil affairs command posts had been set up, and the G5 section of the 7th Army under Col. Gerry had come ashore.[164] The C.A.O.s attached to each US Division, including the 7th Airborne Division, were the men who ran into the problems involved with the southern landings. The very first to touch ground, Lieutenant Welsh with the 1st Airborne Task Force, had to appoint the pre-war mayor of Le Muy to his old job, because there was no Resistance representative, no French Liaison Officer and no Vichy mayor in post.[165] But most of the civil affairs officers found that the biggest problem was keeping up with the rapid initial advance of the armies. Many towns were by-passed and left for the CAHQ to deal with. The weakness of German forces in the south, the surprise of the Allied attack and poor initial German response favoured a very fast Allied advance in the first weeks of the operation.

Another factor was that the local Resistance liberated many towns – Draguignan, St Raphaël, Fréjus and St Tropez for example – in advance of the Allied armies. In many places the Resistance was organized, with a Liberation committee, a nominee for Mayor and an FFI Commander.[166] Lt. Commander G. G. Schroeder (the Chief of the Naval Section of JICANA), reporting to the Military Intelligence Division of the War Department on the political situation in southern

France on 19 August, noted that there was very little friction between the Resistance groups in his command post town of St Raphaël. Administration was in the hands of the French and was as efficient as the conditions would allow. The only disturbance was 'the shaving of the heads of girls who had lived with Germans [which] was done in a spirit of fun and cheerfulness'.[167] Schroeder reported 'excitement' in Draguignan and some shooting, but declared that the political situation in Aix-en-Provence was very stable. He was worried about the continued separate identity of the communist FTP, but thought that the arrival of a nominated military commander of the FFI for the Sixth Region would sort things out. He further reported that the population of Aix had no feelings one way or the other about de Gaulle.[168] A general report of 23 August on the whole of the south of France substantiated what Schroeder had said. In most towns of the liberated area, a French Liaison Officer had been present at the appointment of the mayor or had ratified a Resistance nomination, thus assuring a relatively smooth transfer of authority. 'The real force behind all administration at the moment is the Resistance movement', the report continued.[169] 'The CAOs with Third Division have covered 13 towns including St Tropez, Cogelin, Collobriers and Ramatuelle. In each town the Resistance Group was well organized and, although no French Administrative Liaison Officer was available, public officials were confirmed by local representatives of the *Comité Départemental de Libération*. These towns under their new mayor and Resistance Groups are well-organized and it is believed they will be efficiently run.'[170]

Even in the turbulent conditions of Draguignan, the civil affairs officer was able to report on 21 August that Departmental administration was, 'as firmly established as is possible', and he left to undertake other work.[171] The French Regional Commissioner, Aubrac, was installed as the Commissioner for the south in the same town in August and a representative of the GPRF Col. Lavilleon (Chief of Staff for the *Délégué National, Zone/Sud*) reported that he had appointed or confirmed mayors in the area and that Vidal was now in post as temporary prefect for the Var at Draguignan.[172] Within eight days of the landings, in a Department like the Var, the skeleton of regional, departmental, and local administration in French hands existed and was beginning to function. But there were many instances of political problems, involving young members of the FFI, and the CA Report for southern France noted that, 'the danger of possible civilian disorders has been brought officially to the attention of Colonel Lavilleon'.[173] The majority of reports in this early period concerned the squabbles between FTP and FFI which were often conciliated by SOE/OSS officers. The real problems for civil affairs officers were the shortages of food, lack of French Liaison Officers, communications and public safety violations (including those committed by American troops in Aix-en-Provence).[174]

Whilst the communist influence was strong in such improbable places as Cannes, Nice, Grasse and St Tropez, and in more predictable towns like Draguignan, the Allies were more concerned with the major towns of the south where they expected political problems: Limoges, Marseilles, Toulouse and Montpellier. The case of Limoges, the first of these to be liberated, was potentially the most dangerous. The strength of the communist-led Resistance under Guingouin was likely to run into the traditional socialist and radical predominance from the pre-war period. For some time before the probable liberation of the town, Staunton of SOE, Vignier (French) and Brown (OSS) had been negotiating on the means to be adopted for the liberation of the town. The Allied representatives had managed to persuade Guingouin that, given the strong German garrison, it was best to negotiate their surrender or withdrawal, rather than stage a hopeless although heroic attack. On 21 August the Allied representatives – Staunton, Vignier, Brown and Guéry (FFI) – negotiated the garrison's surrender with its commander, General Gleiniger. Unfortunately the Germans fought among themselves, the Gestapo arrested the commander and there were those among the defenders who fought on, causing some Resistance casualties. Captain Stoll, however, surrendered the main force and Limoges was taken without a bloody battle which might have resulted in the breakdown of law and order.[175] Captain Fraser reported that the SOE/OSS representatives present set up an Allied HQ at 2, rue Louvier-Jalanais, and he worked in close co-operation with Guingouin and his team for the rest of his stay. He also noted that members of the Allied forces did a great deal to calm the atmosphere and keep the peace between FTP and FFI.[176] Guiet, an American member of the same, stated that:

> The political situation at the time of our arrival and departure from the field was the same. There was no political outburst at all during our stay; only consciousness that France should be freed before starting politics again.[177]

'Marseilles', declared the CA History of operations in southern France, 'with a population which included the dregs of six continents, the flotsam of many races – provided the first real test of CAHQ's effectiveness.'[178] The Allies entered the town on 24 August and its German garrison surrendered on 28 August, 'although most of the city had been in Allied hands for several days, more as a result of the spontaneous rising of the population, led by well-directed FFI action, than by direct Allied intervention'.[179] The advance detachment of the 2678 CA Regiment, under Colonel Parkman, reached Marseilles on 24 August and he presented himself to the *Commissaire Régional de la*

*République*, Aubrac, who had already arrived at the Prefecture.[180] He noted that: 'The Resistance elements seem to be in control of the departmental and municipal governments and appear to be working well with M. Aubrac.'[181] Major General Montsabert, the military governor of Marseilles, expressed concern about the number of young people with guns roaming the streets, and issued a 'state of siege' order disarming all civilians, but this seemed to worry Parkman very little. His main concerns were labour to clear the port, and supplies for an already under-nourished city. To this end, he and the Civil Affairs Headquarters immediately began negotiating with the French authorities, ascribing to them full authority over the town. By 27 August it was reported that civilian life was returning to normal, and on 30 August AFHQ G5 noted that: 'local government was functioning efficiently. M. Aubrac had made arrangments with the CCAO for semi-weekly conferences to discuss civil affairs problems and finally the large number of young men and armed FFI youths scouring the city in commandeered cars had almost vanished.'[182]

For Allied civil affairs officers, the first two weeks of the operation had been a great success, with the French taking over their responsibilities in the liberated areas often before Allied troops arrived. They worked well, and there appeared to be few problems in the political sphere. There were wild celebrations, revenge taking, fights between French and Allied troops, supply problems and labour shortages, but administration, even in rowdy towns like Toulon, Cannes, and Nice, was stable. In only one case before September did a CFLN appointee appear to be in jeopardy: 'Evidently fearing communist influence, the prefect of Avignon asked to have a CAO in that city for a brief time to observe.'[183] In many ways the Allied civil affairs administrators were very fortunate, as one of their number, Major L. Van Dusen, commented: 'If the French had failed to take over their responsibilities, we would have been in the soup. As it was, they proved capable and we encountered no unsurmountable difficulties.'[184]

It was the speed of the advance, and the relatively small number of civil affairs officers, which caused the Allies problems. The civil affairs officers with each Division moved so rapidly that they got out of touch with the Corps, and they had to leave many towns behind without any civil affairs presence. The result of this was a plan on 18 August, rushed into operation a week later, that the CAHQ would take care of all the major towns left behind the advancing combat troops. Unfortunately, despite reinforcements of five enlisted men, the CAHQ had very few personnel (only nine officers) and they were all diverted to Marseilles, Nice and Cannes when they were liberated. Rather than have a headquarters with nobody in attendance for days on end, it was moved from Sainte-Maxime to Marseilles. Civil affairs troubles did not end there. The civil affairs regimental structure provided reasonable communications within the 7th Army (when division could contact corps) but very poor ones with AFHQ, which had overall responsibility in the G5 field. Also the CAHQ tended to work independently of everyone. As a result, the Allied civil affairs detachments were obliged to hand over responsibility to the CFLN/Resistance administration, accord them full responsibility, and end up working as liaison channels from the French administrators to the various 7th Army field commanders. As Donnison has so succinctly put it: 'It was intended by SHAEF that civil affairs administration within liberated territories should, wherever possible, be indirect. In the south it became so indirect that it really ceased to be administration at all.'[185]

# 5   The Liberation of Paris

THE DRAMA of the landings and battles from June to August 1944 had diverted public attention from the more subtle questions of recognition and sovereignty. The landings themselves had facilitated the establishment of the GPRF representatives in France, giving a measure of authority to the provisional government and providing a demonstration of the French claim to be able to govern themselves. This, and the military's satisfaction with the situation, dissolved any lingering desires on the Allied side for the establishment of an AMGOT. Negotiations had struggled forward and, by the latter part of August 1944, there was an agreement on civil affairs and a surprise *de facto* recognition. By this time the agreements were almost irrelevant. There had been civil affairs co-operation for over two months. *De facto* recognition, when it came, only acknowledged a situation which already existed in France. These painful and fruitless hesitations were a substitute for any positive Allied policy on the re-establishment of democratic structures in an independent France. Since the Allies had no agreed policy, they had nothing to put in the way of an *ad hoc* assumption of power by the French when areas were freed – and by predominantly Gaullist administrators. As the Allied armies drew close to Paris, this *ad hoc* system was about to swallow up the national capital and seat of government, a much more significant prize than any of the regional centres thus far liberated.

The Liberation of Paris was a crucial test case of Gaullist planning, communist/left-wing revolutionary potential, and Allied intentions. In Paris, the Resistance was, by August 1944, both strong and largely dominated by the Left. Here, Resistance pretensions to conduct an armed insurrection and to lay the foundations for a post-Liberation legitimacy based on a popular mandate would be particularly strong. The GPRF, and especially de Gaulle, feared that a premature uprising by the Resistance in the capital would lead to a bloodbath, chaos, or a left-wing coup, before Gaullist representatives had had the opportunity to install themselves. The Allies, already outflanked by the *fait accompli* of the northern and southern landings, had so far deliberately stood aside from the events in Paris for strategic reasons. By the time they agreed to change their strategy and head for Paris, they were too late to affect the transfer of power which had been determined. In the rapidly developing situation before the Allies marched on Paris, two things stand out with particular clarity. Firstly, the Communist Party appeared to act, not to seize power in a coup but rather to manoeuvre itself into the strongest possible position from which it could fight elections in a future Republic, as a Jacobin, patriotic party. Secondly, although the Communist Party was to be instrumental in hastening the uprising, the seizure of buildings and the street fighting actually led, not to the establishment of soviets, but to the placing of GPRF representatives in key positions of power.

## The French perspective

THE political situation of the Resistance in Paris was peculiarly complex because the capital had its own Liberation committee (CPL), three regional FFI commands, the National Resistance committee (CNR), and the CNR military committee (COMAC). In addition to this, the GPRF was represented by its civilian *délégué général* (Parodi), and his military counterpart, Chaban-Delmas. The political complexion of the Resistance bodies in Paris was crucial in the arguments which separated them from the GPRF representatives.

The executive committee of the Parisian Liberation committee (CPL) was led by Tollet, a member of the French Communist Party (PCF) and Parisian chief of the trade union, the *Confédération Générale du Travail* (CGT). It also included Carrel, representing the PCF-dominated *Front National* (FN), Marrane, a long serving member of the PCF in Paris, and Obadia, representing the *Union des Syndicats*. Hamon of *Ceux de la Résistance* (CDLR) was the most prominent non-communist and he was generally supported by Mme Lefaucheux for *L'Organisation Civile et Militaire* (OCM) and Deniau for *Libération–Nord*. During the days just before Liberation, meetings of the executive committee (*Bureau*) were attended by as many as three representatives of the *Délégation* and decisions were rarely taken by an outright vote.

The CNR by August 1944, was also composed of many different strands in the French Resistance and in French politics. The communists in it were balanced by conservatives like Laniel (*Alliance Démocratique*) and Debû-Bridel (*Fédération Républicaine*). There were many centrists or uncommitted members, like Blocq-Mascart (OCM), Tessier of the Catholic Trades Union (CFTC), Lecompte-Boinet (CDLR), Mutter, *Ceux de la Libération* (CDLL), Degliame of *Combat* and Bastid, a radical. Finally, there were socialists like Mayer, Laurent and his replacement, Ribière, who put up stern opposition to overtly communist plans. The *Bureau* of the CNR – its executive committee – did appear to be communist dominated, since Bidault (a Christian Democrat) and Blocq-Mascart, *Organisation Civile et Militaire*, were outnumbered by Saillant (CGT) and Copeau and Villon of the PCF. In fact it transpired that Saillant was still partly loyal to the non-communist Jouhaux-faction of the pre-war CGT and thus not an automatic supporter of the PCF line. Copeau, whilst he often agreed with communist sentiment in the CNR, was not uniformly pro-communist, and his appointment to a prospective post in the GPRF Ministry of the Interior gave him a second loyalty in August 1944.

COMAC, the military wing of the CNR, similarly seemed under the control of the PCF, given that Villon was its President, Kriegel-Valrimont (MUR) was a communist and de Vogüé, despite an aristocratic lineage, was a left-wing sympathizer. COMAC in its efforts to command the Resistance forces of the Paris region and shape the insurrection, was in close contact with the FFI through its regional commander, Rol-Tanguy (FTP), who was sympathetic to the PCF line, and his deputy, Gallois ('Cocteau'). They in turn delegated to de Marguerite, for the Seine region, and he to his subordinates in east and west Paris. The fact that this whole FFI structure was primarily answerable to the Commander-in-Chief of the French forces, General Koenig, and to his headquarters, appeared somewhat theoretical to the armed Resisters of Paris, about to do battle with the Germans. Thus relations with Koenig's national representative – the *Délégué Militaire National* – Chaban-Delmas, his deputy for the northern region, Ely, and the two regional *délégués militaires*, Sonneville and Rondenay, were always strained and often contentious. The domestic Resistance forces thought that they had earned the right to drive out the Germans with their own tactics, including an insurrection. The GPRF representatives, however, were concerned about the long-term effects of such disruption.

In much the same way, there was a dispute in general terms between the CNR and the GPRF representatives. The local committees wanted an armed and popular uprising as the logical end to their years of work and sacrifice, to restore Parisian and French honour and to guarantee democracy for the victors. But de Gaulle's representatives feared that an insurrection could lead to such turmoil that it would be impossible to set up a French administration in the capital, leaving a vacuum for the Allies to fill, even at this late stage, with an AMGOT. Thus there was a struggle for posts, for control of events and a search for levers of authority by the different French bodies in Paris right up to the early days of August 1944. For the GPRF, the Parisian Liberation Committee should be subordinate to the prefect and regional commissioner, and the local Resistance to the FFI. The nominees of the GPRF should be installed in Paris as everywhere else in France. But Paris was not just another region of France. It had a turbulent history and was important as the seat of French national government.

From the beginning the Gaullists and the PCF, seeing the vital importance of Paris, had argued over the choice of administrators for the capital. In the pre-Liberation phase at least, the will of the GPRF prevailed. The *Comité Général d'Etudes* (CGE) and the planners in Algiers decided that the local government of Paris should be in the hands of two traditional figures: the prefect of the Seine Department and the prefect of police (an arrangement that successive governments had thought was judicious, given the radical transformation of Parisian local government during the 1871 Commune). Luizet was chosen as prefect of police and, with his experience in Corsica, was clearly qualified for the post, although the PCF disliked his appointment. Much more controversial was the appointment of Flouret – a pre-war political administrator – as prefect of the Seine. Tollet expressed the feeling of the left-dominated CPL that: 'As for the prefects, it [the CPL] would like to see them nominated with the assent of representatives from the population as a whole. To do this they must be men with a proven Resistance record.'[1] The *Délégation* representatives assured the CPL that, 'every guarantee and precaution had been taken with their appointment.'[2] At the 31st meeting of the CPL in July, Tollet read a letter from the Paris Regional Committee of the PCF which proposed that Marrane – a former president of the *Conseil Général* of the Seine and mayor of Ivry – be designated as Prefect. Parodi, *délégué général*, apparently attending the CPL bureau for the first time, regretted that it had not been consulted over the case of Flouret, but insisted that the appointment of a prefect for Paris was the prerogative of the government at Algiers.[3]

Basically the PCF had challenged too late in the day.[4] Even if the communists had moved earlier, it is unlikely that the GPRF would have changed its mind. Parodi took a strictly practical view: 'It is essential, given the situation, to keep Flouret, who, after all, is already here and has been underground for the past three months.'[5] This argument over the appointment of the prefect of the Seine was a clear warning for the GPRF. They had, however, managed to impose their will, an indication that, whilst the Parisian Resistance might have the guns, this would not automatically translate into political power at the moment of Liberation.

The PCF were also too late in raising the question of the structure of municipal government at the time of the coming Liberation. The *ordonnances* of early 1944 had clearly subordinated the local and departmental Liberation committees to the regional commissioners and prefects: to act as consultative assemblies, representing the range of local Resistance and political movements. During the same period, however, the CNR developed a concept of the CDL's as 'the soul of a Department',[6] which gave them the moral right to direct and initiate the liberating insurrection, and determine the installation of the new local administrations and public order bodies.[7] This to some observers, looked like the beginning of a movement towards French soviets, but the CNR instructions did insist on the need to support and amalgamate with the FFI, and establish representatives of the central authority (GPRF) and the new administration.[8] By the time of the Liberation there were 40 Local Liberation committees in Paris and its suburbs, enthusiastically insurrectionist and mainly influenced by left-wing movements.

The *Comité Parisien de Libération* certainly saw itself as 'an emanation of the people',[9] and adhered to the CNR definition of their role.[10] Its authority came from the fact that it represented: 'The old guard of fighters, with all its potential and all the authority conferred on it by its role in the struggle for Liberation.'[11] In addition it took the PCF insurrectionist view, quoting de Gaulle's own 18 April 1942 dictum that, 'national liberation cannot be separated from national insurrection.'[12]

The fact that the left-wing of the Resistance, represented in the CNR, COMAC, and the CPL, were pushing for the organization of a mass uprising led to speculation about their motives. De Jonchay, a member of Koenig's staff wrote to him on 1 August 1944 to report a conversation with Malleret-Joinville (Chief of *Etat Major National* of FFI) in which he declared that the communists wanted a Resistance movement independent of any Allied influence, even that transmitted via de Gaulle and Koenig.[13] Laffon, on the other hand, who was one of the men charged with the task of finding post-Liberation administrators, thought that the communists would settle for the Republic since they had a stake in it.[14] De Gaulle himself was seriously worried by the possibility of a communist takeover, but, as we have seen, this concern was often expressed to his American contacts during discussions about the amount of support he wanted for the GPRF. There was hardly an issue of the clandestine *L'Humanité* which did not carry a call for mass insurrection in August 1944, and the vigour of communist and FTP attacks increased, despite the successes of the Gestapo in Paris during June and July.

In the post-war period commentators have been divided on what the communists were attempting in Paris. Collins and Lapierre for example give the impression that the PCF was bent on a seizure of power and that Rol-Tanguy (FFI Regional Commander) was ruthlessly pursuing a street battle with the Germans as a vehicle upon which to launch a revolution. M. R. D. Foot came to the conclusion that, 'The

Communists had relied on a mass rising in Paris to provide an irresistible revolutionary impetus, which could transform the face of France and which their experienced men on the spot would have every opportunity to direct.'[15] Rol himself, however, had insisted that he was only carrying out the orders of COMAC, who had declared as early as 24 May 1944 that all FFI forces should take part in 'mass Resistance actions of an insurrectional character'.[16] Tollet, President of the CPL, called it the first act for many citizens in the patriotic fight for freedom, and Agulhon pointed out later that 'the language of national unity [used in PCF documents] is undoubtedly its main characteristic; it is the central theme of the Communist message during the summer.'[17]

The prelude and stimulus to the uprisings which became the Liberation of Paris were the strikes and protests of the Paris unions. Tollet has said that rather than a concerted plot, the decision to have strikes in July was taken by individual unions, although there was co-ordination for the national holiday on 14 July. The Parisian strikes in August, however, and particularly those on the 10 and 17 July, were organized by an inter-syndical committee. Again Tollet has stressed the patriotic – rather than revolutionary – nature of the workers' actions, and this is borne out in tracts distributed in the name of Benoît Frachon, Secretary General of the CGT: 'in Paris today, the inspiration of our ancestors of 1792 is in the air. Paris, ravaged for four years, has started to make its torturers pay for their crimes.'[18] Rather than plotting a revolt, the union leadership was urging its members to organize the 'normal' types of syndical action more relevant to peacetime: 'The essential task at present for union militants, is the organization of legal meetings in every factory and in every union.'[19] This emphasis on a normal pattern of meetings and protest can also be found in the public demands for action made by the PCF. The headlines in *L'Humanité* might be urging the party's clandestine members to prepare for the mass uprising, but in more practical and immediate terms action was expressed as patriotic duty:

> Patriotic duty, at a time when the enemy is trying to remedy its lack of manpower by maintaining their mobility, is to disorganize communications, sabotage the railway, derail trains, blow up bridges, to strike with increasing force against rail communication.[20]

This tract went on to describe a whole series of actions, from killing *miliciens* to sabotaging production, each one being headed 'patriotic duty'. An instruction in June 1944 from the Central Committee to its regional and functional divisions declared that the PCF must rouse the French people:

> They must show the world that we are a great people, inspired by liberty, whose sons are fighting in Italy and in Soviet skies, with a valour to which the Allies have

paid tribute, a great people who, to take their share of the victory, do not recoil from their share of the fighting, a courageous people who want to find, through the fight for their liberty, their independence and greatness.[21]

The Parisian regional organizations of the PCF also issued instructions to their members in June 1944 on their conception of the role of the local Liberation committees during the 'period of national insurrection'. The committees should take charge of the fight against the Germans and take the initiative in solving the social and economic problems of the immediate post-Liberation period. They should also designate the new provisional municipal authorities, taking account of the record of patriots during the Resistance, the nature of the 1939 councils and the wishes of the masses. This appeared to be a call for populist, left-wing government, but the appeal was based, according to party leaders, on the need to promote the best patriots.[22]

When, in May 1944, the Central Committee of the PCF addressed the question of the preparation and conduct of the 'national insurrection,' the argument put forward was that by action, men and women could avoid death at the hands of the Nazis, and the tract ended with exhortations to rally round the CNR and the GPRF.[23] By 6 August the central direction of the party in Paris was concentrating on recruitment to the FTP and *Milices Patriotiques*, armed attacks on Germans, and preparation of a general strike. There was a call for Resisters to replace collaborationist local authorities with ones which had 'the confidence of the masses', but only so that they could establish 'republican order'.[24] Kriegel has called the PCF policy: 'the conquest of power from within'[25], which implies the infiltration of the Resistance to dominate government later during the new period of republican normality. In this context, it was in the PCF's interests to avoid promoting armed anarchy, which would undermine the strategy and bring them into conflict with Allied and Gaullist forces. Tillon has stated that on 5 August he had a message from Duclos – senior PCF secretary in France – which dissociated the PCF from responsibility for starting the insurrection. He says he learned later that the PCF leader in exile, Thorez, had, at the behest of Stalin, ordered Duclos to prevent the PCF starting the insurrection. Duclos did not reply to his note of 8 August and so the initiative was taken to launch a call for insurrection on 10 August.[26] Hervé, whilst believing that the PCF 'betrayed the revolution' in 1944, agrees with Elleinstein that a seizure of power was impossible, given the close proximity of overwhelming numbers of Allied troops.[27] In his well-publicized address to the Parisians – 'Forward People of Paris' – Thorez called upon the working classes of Paris to sabotage work for the Germans, to protest about the lack of food and to prepare themselves for the coming struggle, but he did not urge them to revolutionary action, only to, 'take their place in the preparation and direction of the national insurrection.'[28]

The policy of mass insurrection had been taken up by the CNR, its military committee, COMAC, and the CPL, but proved to be one of the most thorny issues dividing them from the French authorities in Algiers and London. Kriegel-Valrimont says that the dispute as to whether the control of Resistance action at the time of the Liberation should lie in London or Paris came to a head at the beginning of May 1944 and continued until the Germans had left the French capital.[29] Ely, Koenig's representative and deputy to the National Military Delegate of the GPRF for the northern zone, reported to the COMAC meeting of 1 May 1944 that there was to be a new unifying committee in London which was to control Resistance action and take away the centralizing function of COMAC. This committee – *Comité d'Action en France* (COMIDAC) – recognized the need for insurrection, but feared the disorder that it might generate, and as a result hoped to limit it to certain areas. When its directive to the internal Resistance was issued on 16 May, it had no reference to insurrection at all.[30] On 22 May 1944, COMAC in Paris repudiated this purely military idea, declared itself to be in favour of mass action, and totally opposed to the decentralization of the armed Resistance. For COMAC, their control of the Resistance was essential to the concept of mass insurrection and, in order number nine of 24 May 1944, they sent all FFI units instructions for the insurrection: 'Thus you can provide our people with the opportunity to take up the insurrection, inseparable, according to General de Gaulle, from national liberation'.[31] The announcement in June that the FFI would be integrated into the regular army changed very little for the Parisian Resistance and the same was true of the repeated calls from London to co-ordinate actions with Allied advances. On the other hand, the two telegrams that COMAC received from Koenig on 14 June telling them that no more arms would be parachuted into France until the August moon did stir them into angry reaction.[32] They also rejected the thesis developed by Chaban-Delmas, the National Military Delegate of the GPRF, that insurrection was the legitimate work of the Resistance to weaken and harry the Germans, but that once Allied forces were on the immediate battlefield, all efforts should turn to support for regular troops. National independence and pride could only be restored through the involvement of large numbers in a popular insurrection.

Throughout June Chaban was attacked by the other members of COMAC for trying to defuse the insurrection, although he did occasionally defend the Resistance military organization when Koenig sent his more peremptory telegrams.[33] The divisions grew worse between London and COMAC. Chaban and Ely (Military Delegate for the north), armed with telgrams from London, stoutly defended the GPRF position, but even the announcement that Eisenhower had accepted the FFI as part of the Allied forces did not persuade COMAC to relinquish control of the FFI, particularly around Paris. At each turn COMAC was confirmed in this role by the CNR.[34] It was also supported, at a remove, by the CPL, who, at their 34th meeting, took it upon themselves to 'prepare, direct and push forward' the popular insurrection.[35] Just as the plans of the CPL were hardening, however, the resolve of COMAC began to weaken. Although at a meeting on 14 August it was stated that their positions had been accepted by Koenig, COMAC had in fact modified their aims and issued a command that: 'General Koenig's orders for the implementation of Allied strategic plans will be carried out as a priority by the FFI.'[36] Indeed it might have been the case that by August 1944 the FFI themselves were becoming worried by the problems which might be caused by the onset of unco-ordinated and anarchistic popular insurrection.[37]

The same concern was shared by the GPRF and de Gaulle. With Parodi reporting growing disquiet about the nature of the administration and action of the Resistance in Paris, de Gaulle telegrammed him on 31 July 1944, to stiffen his stand against the left on the CNR, COMAC and CPL. De Gaulle reminded Parodi that the Liberation of Paris might be delayed and that: 'Every initiative must be encouraged on the strict condition that its sole aim is to destroy the enemy and that it doesn't create a situation which might harm the authority of the government and as a consequence, national unity.'[38] He told Parodi that, as the representative of the provisional government, his instructions must carry precedence, although the GPRF attached great importance to the consultative role of the CNR and CDLs. De Gaulle recognized Parodi's problems but exhorted him:

> Always speak loud and clear in the name of the state. The numerous manifestations and actions of our glorious Resistance are the means by which the nation fights for its salvation. The state is above all these manifestations and actions.[39]

At the beginning of August, Parodi reported that the CPL had accepted that the *Garde Républicaine* and the *Gendarmerie* would occupy the public buildings under the orders of the GPRF but that the question of who actually directed action for the Liberation of Paris was still being debated.[40] Chaban-Delmas had said that the question of insurrection in early August was not a difficulty, only its timing,[41] but in fact the struggle for control of the insurrection and thus perhaps the leadership of post-Liberation municipal government was still unresolved. Parodi wanted strong and clear instructions from the GPRF so that he could end the debate. Feeling that his communications with London (BCRA) were not good or that he was not fully understood, he sent Chaban-

Delmas to London in early August with the message that the Allies must hasten towards Paris; he could not delay a premature and problematic insurrection. On 11 August, Parodi demanded a text from the GPRF that would define his powers between the beginning of an insurrection and the arrival of de Gaulle in Paris, particularly in the case of an attempt to reconvene the National Assembly.[42] Word of Laval's attempt to re-establish the 1940 Assembly by bringing its president, Herriot, to Paris on the morning of 13 August had already reached the *délégué général*. Meanwhile, Chaban in London was pleading with the Allies to move rapidly on Paris and avoid a premature uprising, turning into another Warsaw ghetto.[43]

The warning was particularly apposite in view of the escalation in trade union activity in Paris. Trades unions had re-emerged at a national level in Spring 1943, but many internal disputes between ideological groups remained. In Paris the *Union Départementale* (UD) was established in the summer of 1943, based on the remaining communist union leaders, since most of the socialist unionists had either collaborated or were inactive. Eleven major unions belonged to the UD of which the leading three, rail, engineering and building, were traditional communist strongholds. Each of the unions had their own headquarters and technical facilities for propaganda etc. This remarkable organization was in place and operational by the early weeks of 1944 and its propaganda began to reiterate, with greater and greater emphasis, the need to prepare for a general strike.[44] On 20 June the UD of the CGT organized a committee to plan for a general strike leading to Liberation and this set about the establishment of similar committees for the 'inter-branches' level in each factory or major enterprise. Instructions for these *Comités de Préparation à la grève générale* emphasized the need to involve the widest section of the population, to mobilize, based on a factory organization, and to ensure food, water and medical supplies. The strike committee's final call was to stop production for the Germans.[45] Small strikes, protests and sabotage began to multiply all round the Paris Basin in late June and early July.[46]

The people of Paris were becoming impatient to be rid of the Germans, and the beginnings of industrial disruption heightened tension and expectations. As the German forces began to withdraw under Allied military pressure, a delicate situation developed in which Resistance leaders and militants began to get the impression that the forces on each side were starting to balance out, when in fact the Germans still had formidable power. The Resistance seemed to be on the brink of an insurrection which the GPRF representatives feared would be disastrous. The Paris Resistance sought to catch the emotional wave and be carried on to an uprising, whilst the GPRF

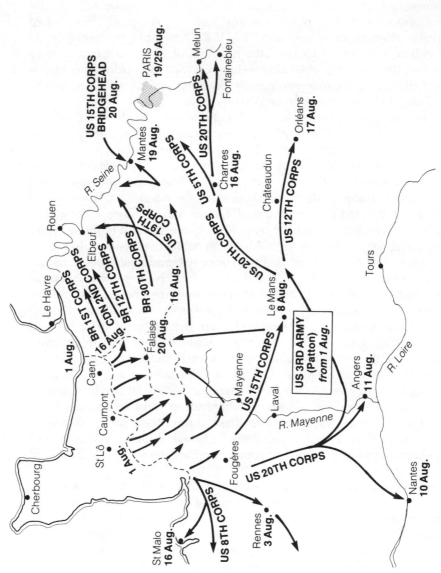

*Map 3*   The advance on Paris

representatives worked to slow and delay the movement. While these crucial events were happening in Paris, the Allies were still struggling to get political recognition and a civil affairs agreement with the prototype government which was soon to arrive in the capital.

## Allied plans for the Liberation of Paris

THE PROSPECT of liberating Paris was an entirely different matter from the Liberation of the other areas. Apart from its practical significance as an administrative and communications centre, it had a key emotional/ symbolic value, since the group who established themselves in the capital would have the tacit loyalty – as the legitimate administration – of a large section of the French people. Whilst the French in Algiers, London and France eagerly awaited the Liberation of their capital, Allied authorities viewed the progress of the battle front towards Paris with mixed emotions, none of them particularly sanguine. Their reservations were strategic, administrative and political: they were afraid that the Liberation of Paris might turn into a bloody street battle, followed by a vengeful uprising, a collapse of law and order, and political skirmishing for the starving, devastated city. The Allied High Command wanted to delay taking Paris until the first week in September at the earliest and hoped that the Germans defending it would have withdrawn or been dramatically weakened by that time. Events however overtook them and forced their hand.

For Eisenhower, Paris was a problem that he would rather have avoided because of its potentially wasting military value. From its very earliest plans, SHAEF had decided that Paris would be a difficult city to capture because of its urban structure, well suited to defensive street fighting. It could easily absorb inordinate numbers of troops that were needed elsewhere to continue rolling back the broad front. Also, the Allies could hardly bomb German defenders into submission without destroying the city and that would cause a rift between them and the French which might seriously affect the war effort. The destruction of Caen had caused some adverse comment, and even the relatively limited destruction of Paris during the street fighting would elicit much harsher criticism of Allied tactics. In addition, Eisenhower wanted to save the fuel and ammunition that an attack on Paris would eat up, particularly as one of the major problems he had faced after the breakout from the beach-head had been a constant shortage of fuel and its restraining effect upon the Allied advance. The Allied command felt that, once inside Paris, the armies would be very difficult to withdraw and that a large numbers of troops would be 'lost' to the battle front for several weeks.[47] Bradley, the Commander of the recently formed 12th

Army Group, and Patton, the fearsome commander of US Third Army, which was operating in the Paris area, agreed whole-heartedly with this plan.[48] Their aim was to pass west and east of the city, hopefully leaving a large German army bottled up in the capital, which would be taken when that army had been seriously weakened physically and mentally by the actions of the Resistance.

Despite the opinions of numerous French and Allied experts, the military command still feared the possibility of a revolutionary uprising in a starving Paris: 'It [the Allied High Command] suspected that at the moment of the departure of the Germans, a centre of disorder might be created in the Paris region, which would be prejudicial to the subsequent orderly development of operations.'[49] The civil affairs Handbook for France expressed a similar sentiment, declaring that the city had become the stronghold of collaborationism, which had attracted the scum of the population: 'on the other hand the communist leaders, partly no doubt because of their equivocal policy in the first two years of the war, do not appear to have welded the Paris working class into the outstandingly powerful instrument of resistance which the strength of the pre-war communist vote might have suggested.'[50] But it still described Paris as a deeply divided city of intransigent politics, which would be troublesome to administer. In the Foreign Office, Speaight thought it quite natural that the PCF should be the largest group on the *Comité Parisien de Libération* (CPL), but Mack thought that the 'situation in Paris will present many difficulties', and Harvey hoped that, in such an event, the British and the Americans would seek to interfere.[51] The Foreign Office was firmly against fulfilling Koenig's request for 40,000 sten guns to be dropped to the Resistance in the Paris area, despite the fact that Churchill had announced Britain's determination to help the Resistance to the limit of its resources, because, as Peake said to Mack, 'there will always be a temptation to put them to mischievous uses should political passions be inflamed when the war is over'.[52] Politically then, Paris for the Allies was an unknown quantity and a problem, compounded by the generally uncertain status of the provisional French government which would soon be taking up residence. All in all it was a danger spot.

For the Allied civil affairs authorities, involved in detailed planning, the potential supply problems of Paris were becoming a nightmare. The longer the Liberation could be postponed, the better chance they would have to marshal their units from other areas, build up stocks of supplies and organize transport. Allied planning for the Liberation at a practical level was going ahead, but it was predicated on the idea that the capital would not be liberated until the first week of September at the earliest. Events outran the civil affairs planners as much as the military. From the end of July when SHAEF G5 began planning for the relief of Paris, problems immediately began to appear. Firstly, moving large amounts of food from Britain would seriously deplete stocks for British domestic consumption.[53] To leave Paris unfed would be politically unacceptable and possibly dangerous, but to starve Britain at a crucial stage of the war was also unthinkable, and so supplies from the USA were hurried across the Atlantic in an attempt to meet the situation. Coulet, the GPRF regional delegate, was working well with civil affairs planners, stockpiling food for the Liberation of Paris, but it was clear that the French did not have the technical capacity to move and distribute the supplies. Secondly, civil affairs groups would have to find transport from hard-pressed Allied sources.[54] By 10 August, the Liberation, which had been expected in early or mid-September, was obviously only a week or so away and SHAEF G5 increased its personnel and its efforts to bring forward the supply plans, but the problem of transport remained unsolved.[55] Added to this was the fact that the Allies had failed to recruit sufficient labour for the job, and were thinking of bringing men from distant liberated regions for the Paris supply task.[56] The actual plan for relief was only sent from SHAEF via the 12th Army group to First and Third Armies and the Communications Zone commanders on 22 August, three days before the Liberation.

On the political side of the question, SHAEF found itself without any clear conception of what might happen and Grasset of G5, in early August, mused that he expected the CFLN (*sic*) to establish itself in France once an Interior Zone had been established, although the agreement on zones had not then been signed.[57] By the first week in August, experienced civil affairs units were being pulled out of Normandy, Brittany and some other quieter rural areas, to be replaced by lines of communication teams. Colonel Howley and the A1A1 Detachment of civil affairs, which had been so successful in the restoration of Cherbourg to normality, calm and French administration, were withdrawn, strengthened and readied to go into Paris.[58] Howley had command of 23 civil affairs units that were earmarked for the capital. When these units were concentrated at Sées, prior to entry into the city, there were 24: 2 'A' (headquarters) level, 2 'C' level and 20 'D' level (smaller) detachments ready to move into the individual *arrondissements*. Meanwhile, events in the city itself outran Allied attempts to avoid Paris or plan for its relief on an Anglo-Saxon time scale. The domestic Resistance, after four years of waiting and suffering, was impatient to have its day of glory, a chance at last to fight back against the Germans.

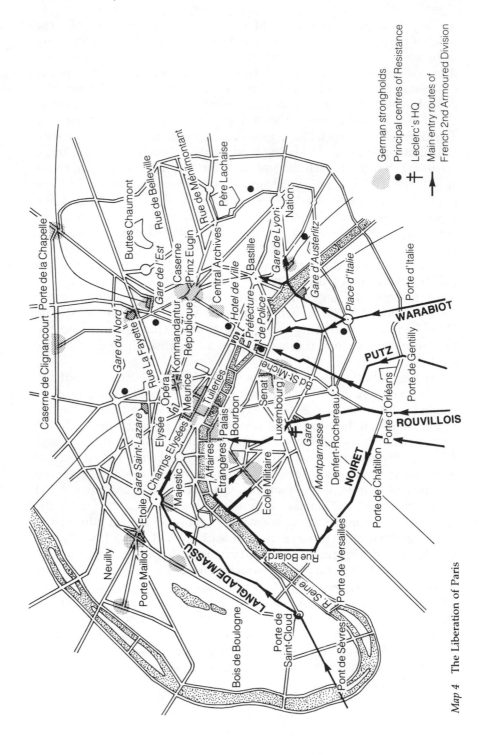

*Map 4*   The Liberation of Paris

## The insurrection in Paris

THE DAY OF 14 July 1944 was marked by serious disturbances. The CNR launched an appeal entitled *Le 14 Juillet de Combat*, demanding demonstrations of patriotic fervour,[59] and this was taken up by the CPL. It was the *Union Départementale des Syndicats* (UD), however, which organized the most important actions, with strikes and demonstrations in Suresnes, the 20th *arrondissement*, Ivry, Vitry, Villeneuve-Saint-Georges and Puteaux, around Paris. There were also demonstrations on the Champs Elysées, at Les Halles, Maubert-Mutualité, Convention, Faubourg Saint-Antoine and a number of other *arrondissements*. The main strikes and demonstrations were organized by the leaders of the UD and the FTP, and most numerous among those arrested were railway-workers from Ivry, Choisy and Villeneuve-Saint-Georges. The railwaymen's union immediately began a campaign to get their colleagues released that led to a series of strikes and demonstrations, which progressively paralysed rail transport around the capital and increased the tension felt by occupier and occupied alike. There were other factors which contributed to the heightening of tension: the advance of the battle front, which by 13 August could be heard from the outer suburbs of the capital, and the shower of Resistance propaganda tracts.[60] More importantly, the Germans began to organize the withdrawal of their administration from the major public buildings on 9 August. A convoy of civilians left at 5.30 a.m. on 10 August from the Gare de l'Est. Papers were being burnt in all the major German administrations on 11 August and finally the French collaborationist newspapers and radio personnel began to move out on 15 August. It would be trade union action, and strangely enough, that of the police, which would escalate the already tense situation.

Tillon, who had moved the command centre – *Comité Militaire National* (CMN) – of the FTP to Paris on 24 July, was aware of the growing signs of a coming battle. On 8 August he learnt from Raphaël, his liaison with Duclos, that the PCF Secretariat meeting to decide on the date to start the insurrection in Paris had been indefinitely delayed. He had already written to Rol of the Paris FFI, saying that they should co-ordinate action as soon as possible to 'open the gates of Paris for the Allies', and now he sent a letter to Duclos declaring his intention to ask the CMN of the FTP to start the insurrection without delay. Thus it was that on 10 August the CMN of the FTP issued a poster entitled *'En Avant pour la Bataille de Paris'*, urging its members to action. The poster called for disruption of enemy communications, attacks on the occupiers, cessation of work and a 'levée en masse', but it also demanded co-operation with Allied forces and discipline:

Through the *Milices Patriotiques*, under the control and authority of the Liberation

Committees, replace the treasonable law of the enemy with the French legal system of the Provisional Republican Government.[61]

Unbeknown to Tillon, the CGT had been moving towards its own insurrectionary action. The railwaymen's protests over their imprisoned colleagues had resulted in a list of demands delivered to the directors of the railway, the SNCF, on 5 August, and special delegates of the UD concentrated their efforts in raising the level of militancy at key railway installations: Noisy-le-Sec, les Batignolles, Montrouge, Juvisy, Villeneuve-Saint-Georges, Chelles and La Chapelle. Finally, on 10 August – the same day as the FTP poster – the CGT put out its call for a general strike of the railway workers, and this, despite many difficulties, caused serious disruption on lines in the north and east of Paris. This was followed by instructions to the 'inter-branch' organizations to begin preparing for their own industries to strike. The call was for a mass mobilization outside the confines of the Resistance, to gather up all those former unionists who had taken an *'attentiste'* attitude during the war. In pursuit of this, the militants were urged to hold 'legal' meetings. This implied working within the Vichy labour charter rules to get men behind a list of demands which would lead to limited action.[62] What worried the unionists was that there were thousands in the Paris area who, in July 1944, were still working for the Germans, and in formerly well-unionized plants. Clearly the idea of a revolutionary strike was far from their calculations. Since the management had declared a holiday in many factories in July to calm the situation, union organizers had to go to workers' homes to get them involved. Although there were 250 engineering factories in the Paris region, dominated by their popular committees, a tract addressed to the *'métallos'* on 13 July complained that thousands of them were still working for the Germans.[63]

The next stage of the insurrection was action by the Paris police who declared for a strike on 15 August. The increasing unwillingness of the French police – particularly in working-class areas of the city – to take action against anti-German demonstrations had persuaded the German authorities to disarm them, highlighting their insecure position between occupier and Resistance. In fact, the police had three well-developed Resistance organizations, one of which, *Front National de la Police*, had persuaded the *Comité de Libération de La Police Parisienne* to call a strike on 15 August. Lefranc, the left-wing leader of the *Front National de la Police*, in conjunction with André Carrel, who represented the *Front National* on the CPL and was in charge of its military commission, led the call for a police strike, and, after a meeting of the police Resistance organizations with Rol-Tanguy, they achieved a joint call for a strike.[64] The UD of the CGT, the *Front National* and the PCF wished to maintain the proletarian nature of the strike, but they had considered the possibility of calling out the police. Already, it had been agreed that the majority of those guarding the public buildings during the insurrection would be police and that they, as men with arms training, would be very important during the military conflict. On 13 August the Committee of the *Front National de la Police* heard that the Germans had disarmed the *Gardiens de la Paix* in Asnières and Saint-Denis, two left-wing working-class suburbs. The *Front National* committee decided that, given the threat to all police posed by this German policy, they must strike on 15 August. Lamboley of *Police et Patrie* agreed that his organization would also strike and print strike posters, but Ribière (Revel) of *Libération-Nord*, which was the parent movement of *Police et Patrie*, counselled waiting for the CNR call to arms. On 14 August the three police groups met for the first time, set up a Liberation committee, but could not decide on a strike. *Front National* were in favour, *Police et Patrie* were against and *Honneur de la Police* (Bayet) wavered. The *Front National* had invited Rol-Tanguy to the meeting, and since he did not share the reservations of Tollet and Carrel (of the unions) towards the police, he was able to win them over. The recently appointed director of the municipal police, Hennequin, tried to appeal to the policemen's sense of duty to stay at their posts, but the police Liberation committee announced that anyone remaining at their post would be dismissed after the Liberation. Thus the strike was almost total.

Hennequin issued an order saying that the police could report for duty in civil clothes to explain away the non-appearance of uniforms on the street, but from 7.a.m. on 15 August, there were almost no policemen on the streets of Paris. Partly as a result of this, attacks by the FTP and other Resistance groups against *milice* barracks and isolated German patrols began to multiply. On 16 August the post office workers struck to a man and the rail strike was almost general. Other strikes developed, but their value was rather as mobilizers of street crowds than destroyers of German production. By July 1944 the work-force in Paris was only a fraction of its pre-war size, and pro-German production was very limited.[65] On 17 August *Radio-Paris* failed to come on the air, and Jean-Hérold Paquis, the best-known collaborationist radio voice in France, left in a convoy of fascist collaborators for Nancy. In his last broadcast on the evening of 16 August Paquis declared that the Allied landings in the south had failed in the face of ferocious resistance from German defenders, but the silence from the *Radio-Journal* programme was mute testimony to Allied success.

The end of German control signalled the end of Vichy rule. On 13 August Laval brought Herriot, the former President of the Assembly, to Paris for discussions with Otto Abetz, the German Ambassador, with a view to recalling the 1939 Assembly and handing over power to it with a semblance of legality. The talks were held in the Hôtel de Ville, under the auspices of the right-wing President of the Municipal Council, Pierre Tattinger, but the German SS Chief in Paris, Oberg, and the SD Chief, Nosek, were against the move. Abetz contacted Himmler, but he ordered the re-arrest of Herriot. So, on 17 August, with Resisters waiting outside the Hôtel de Ville in a vain attempt to seize Herriot, and after approaches from Tattinger to the FFI on the one hand and von Chlotitz on the other, the attempt to forestall the Resistance failed. On 17 August there were also demonstrations at Saint Paul and the Hôtel de Ville, where a delegation demanding food was received by the municipal authorities.[66]

The military wing of the Resistance was aware of the changing situation and on 15 August Rol-Tanguy, on behalf of the Ile-de-France FFI, issued a call to the police, Republican Guard, *Gendarmerie*, *Gardes Mobiles*, GMR, and prison guards, urging them to join the FFI and fight the Germans. On 16 August, Defresne, Chief of Staff of the FFI, issued the order for occupation and defence of public buildings (general order number 8) and harassment of German vehicles (no order number). But he also issued an order to commanders of local FFI instructing them to enrol all Resisters into the FFI, to have nothing to do with uncontrolled acts, to denounce self-appointed leaders and ensure organized action.[67]

Parodi, on behalf of the GPRF, was urging caution on the Resistance movements and called on the BCRA in London to support him with appeals for calm.[68] COMAC, meeting on 16 August, also heard from Parodi about the need to control the action that had started so as not to provoke harsh German reprisals, but learnt that Koenig had agreed to delegate command of the FFI to them for the insurrection. COMAC however was not restrained by this responsibility and (in its order number 4) called for people to begin action immediately rather than wait until the Allies were within 50 kilometres.[69] Chaban-Delmas, the *Délégué Militaire* of the GPRF, arrived back in Paris on the night of 16 August with instructions from de Gaulle to slow down Resistance action, no encouragement from the British over an early Liberation, and confirmation from Patton, whom he saw at his HQ, that there was no hope of the Americans entering Paris before the first days of September. But Chaban was too late for the meeting of COMAC. On 17 August, all the organizations of the Resistance were meeting and in touch with each other.

The *Comité Parisien de Libération* (CPL) met in the morning with Rol-Tanguy (Chief of FFI) and decided to wait for the decision of the CNR on the timing of the insurrection. The CNR was meeting at the same time and, whereas the *bureau* of the CPL in Ivry was balanced in its view, the CNR was in favour of announcing the insurrection. Parodi for the GPRF argued against haste. Villon (PCF) was vigorously in favour, and Bidault declared that the CNR could not delay or halt a movement which had already gained momentum.[70] On the same day the 20 regional leaders of the FTP met at Champigny – almost without security precautions – and launched an appeal, in liaison with the FFI, for a rising.[71]

Thus it was that on 18 August several posters appeared which exhorted the population to insurrection. Firstly, there was a poster from the CGT and the Catholic trades union (CFTC) calling for a general strike by all workers.[72] Then there was a poster from Rol Tanguy, in the names of the FFI and the *Milices Patriotiques*, calling for a general mobilization of all Resistance forces.[73] There was a poster from the CPL, dated 17 August, declaring that the hour had arrived to chase the invader out of Paris, which included a reference to a similar call by the CNR, and there was a poster from the PCF calling for the national insurrection.[74] The *Bureau* of the CPL had yet to decide on its position and it was not until the afternoon of 18 August that Tollet, Carrel and Rigal, on the left, won out against Hamon (CDLR) and committed the CPL to the insurrectionary poster it had already issued.[75] Parodi had got the agreement of the CNR to meet daily from 18 August onwards and monitor events, by which means he hoped to influence and even control the rate of development of the insurrection.[76] But the call for insurrection had now been made. Chaban telegraphed Koenig with a long report on the situation in which he pleaded for an early intervention by the Allies. If this was impossible, he asked for clear instructions and a firm warning to the population on the BBC that the Allies would not be in Paris until early September, so that they could avoid another Warsaw.[77] Parodi, on the other hand, reported that the population was eager for action and that it would be a humiliation for the Parisians if the Germans left Paris, rather than the Resistance fighting for it. He also reported that an agreement had been reached for 'a scenario which would include the proclamation of the Republic at the Hôtel de Ville and the public acclamation of the Provisional Government and of General de Gaulle'.[78]

Finally there was the FTP order for a general mobilization, which Tillon put out from the CMN of the FTP. He later felt that he had been abandoned by the PCF during the first two weeks of August and had been obliged to act because of the growing number of unco-ordinated FTP attacks on Germans and collaborators.[79] By the evening of 18 August, the FTP had seized the *mairies* in Montreuil, les Lilas, Bondy and Pierrefitte, and 100 companies of FTP organized by René Camphin, were roaming the streets, threatening other suburbs.

The common feature of the appeals was that they saw the Liberation of Paris, the re-establishment of the Republic and the defeat of the occupiers as the work of the people, validated by the idea of insurrection, and given authority because it emanated from the ordinary masses. As the CNR poster said: 'The Republic will be proclaimed in the presence of the people of Paris'.[80] After all the arguments, it was trade union action, and ironically the police, who set events in motion, outside the authority of the GPRF representatives.

## The seizure of buildings

THE CIVILIAN *délégation*, representing the GPRF, found it impossible to prevent, or even slow down, the launching of the uprising, but it could make sure that the posters and other material distributed to mobilize the crowd were textually pro-Gaullist and pro-Republican. They could also begin work within the rising to get the GPRF nominees for key posts into office. The proponents of a popular uprising found themselves taking over buildings for the use of provisional government nominees and guarding them after the installation of these new adminstrators. In this context one of the last acts of 18 August was the most decisive: it involved seizing a government building, establishing a French provisional government presence and marking the start of a new regime. Yves Bayet, a leader of *Honneur de la Police*, learned from Parodi that the CNR and CPL would make the insurrection 'official' on the next day and so, on his own initiative, he launched the occupation of the prefecture of police, a plan already prepared by the joint Liberation committee. He sent the order to the chief of his own organization, Fournet, on whom he could rely. The order was very simple: 'Assemble 2000 men tomorrow morning at 7 o'clock in the immediate vicinity of the prefecture of police'.[81] Pierre of the *Front National de la Police* was ready for action, as were his colleagues in other *Front National* organizations, and Lamboley of *Police et Patrie*. Fournet, the third police union leader, called for an assembly of police the next morning, at 7 a.m., on the Place du Parvis of the Notre-Dame, directly outside the prefecture, rather than in streets near the building, hidden and dispersed.

When the three leaders of the police Resistance arrived at the prefecture early next morning, there was a large crowd of police in civilian clothes, which forced its way inside the prefecture, past a startled sentry, and took control of the building without a shot being fired. The insurrection in Paris had begun in earnest, but it was led, as on 15 August, by the forces of order, whose natural discipline and hierarchy, together with a non-leftist majority in their organization, meant that their aim was the establishment of a new French authority, not revolution. The prefecture was in the hands of the Resistance by 8 a.m. All the Vichy personnel had been arrested by 9 a.m. Bayet arrived shortly after that to declare that he took possession of the prefecture in the name of the provisional government of France, and at 11 a.m. Luizet, the GPRF nominee for prefect of police, arrived to take command. The police in the building, with the habit of obedience to superiors, accepted him immediately and there was never any question of any other group taking control of this first important edifice. The GPRF was thus present at the beginning of the real insurrection and its representative was obeyed.

On the same morning, but unaware of what was going on in the prefecture, the *Bureau* of the CNR and the *Bureau* of the CPL met in two separate rooms at 41, rue de Bellechasse to discuss the order for an insurrection. The posters of the previous day had called for mobilization, a general strike and harrassment of the enemy, but the national insurrection had yet to be 'officially' announced. The CPL met first and naturally called for insurrection in line with its position at previous meetings,[82] but the CNR was the more important body, representing as it did the totality of the domestic Resistance, and here there was the possibility of opposition to the insurrection. Although Parodi had been told of the GPRF order from London to slow down the Resistance action in Paris, he agreed to the declaration of the CNR in favour of insurrection. In the first place, communications with London were very poor and he felt that messages coming to him via intermediaries who had been travelling for days, did not take account of the rapid changes in the situation on 17 and 18 August. Also, by the time of the CNR meeting, the CPL had issued its order and news had come of the occupation of the prefecture. Parodi had been bicycling to meetings in different quarters of the city and had seen the signs of growing popular defiance of the occupiers. Paris, he thought was ready to erupt:

> the insurrection, from the moment that it appeared possible, was the normal outcome of all the propaganda effort, the organizational effort, of all the struggle which had been accomplished and directed by the Resistance in the previous four years. All that effort, the death of our comrades, all that had obviously been done for something other than that we should fold our arms at the moment when the fight became possible. Consequently, I have the strong feeling that when the CPL proposed the insurrection it was right in line with the Resistance. What it asked us to do conformed with every action of the Resistance up to that time. To tell the truth, if I had been opposed at that time to the decision of the CPL, I think I would have immediately lost all scope for action and all authority over the Resistance and thus any possibility of controlling events. I thought that one of my responsibilities was to sustain the unity of the French Resistance until the very end, right until the arrival in Paris of General de Gaulle. Otherwise we ran the very great risk at that time of smashing the Resistance, if there had been a deep split on the question of insurrection.[83]

Parodi saw the call for insurrection as a natural outcome of the Resistance and something which, even if he opposed it, would take place anyway. If he did oppose it, he calculated that he would lose any future influence he might have over the course of the action and also lose his authority as representative of the GPRF, which would make it difficult to carry out his mission of establishing the Republican Commissioners in their ministries. Thus it was that the CNR put out its *'Appel à l'insurrection'* of 19 August which declared that the hour of the national insurrection had arrived:

> Maintaining discipline, deaf to provocation, in a complete union of all patriots, the French people will rise up to fight and to triumph, following the orders of the Provisional Government of the Republic, presided over by General de Gaulle and acting in its name in the area of invasion.[84]

Parodi's diplomacy and realism had helped to produce a crucial document which, although probably not read in any detail by the insurgents, ensured the primacy of the GPRF as the ultimate arbiters of the insurrectionary outcome. This meant that, for the time being at least, the political initiative still rested with Parodi and the representatives of the GPRF, then collecting in Paris. On a more practical level, Rol Tanguy issued the general order for insurrection for the FFI for the Ile-de-France Region,[85] without waiting for the outcome of the two important meetings in the rue de Bellechasse. Independently of them all, Tillon and the CMN of the FTP met on the same morning and issued its own call for action, envisaging the formation of assault companies which would carry the attack to the Germans, as well as groups to guard bridges and assure the Allied routes into Paris.[86]

Rol Tanguy, alerted to the occupation of the prefecture, went there on his way from the headquarters in Montrouge to his new command post in the 19th *arrondissement*, so as to assert his overall control of armed Resistance as the FFI chief for the region. By the time Rol had organized his subordinates and returned to the prefecture, he found the new prefect of police installed in the office of his Vichy predecessor. There was no formal agreement on the division of respective powers, but the prefect tacitly agreed to Rol's overall command, whilst the FFI chief made no attempt to interfere with the control Luizet had established in the prefecture.

Luizet, Rol and Bayet then went to meet Parodi and together they composed a proclamation, which was issued with Parodi's 'signature' as representative of the GPRF, and began with the words 'RÉPUBLIQUE FRANÇAISE'. It declared that all forces in the Paris region – including the police Resisters – were integral parts of the FFI and thus came under the command of Rol Tanguy as Regional Chief. It called on all men between the ages of 18 and 50 to mobilize under the FFI, to arm themselves at the expense of the Germans and to attempt all types of action, ending with the call: 'People of France, everyone to the fight! Open the Paris road to the victorious Allied armies! Long live de Gaulle! Long live the Republic! Long live France!'[87]

Rol Tanguy had met Parodi and Luizet for the first time and appeared to have gained ascendancy over the other two in the control of Resistance action. Yet there had been the semblance of Republican formality. The mobilization was called by the new Republican government and the prospective head of state's name had appeared at the bottom of the document. Rol had overall command, but Luizet (or his deputy) remained in control of the most important action thus far.

But 19 August also saw a number of other Resistance actions which more directly affected the transfer of political power from the remains of the Vichy regime to the representatives of the provisional government. Parodi had reported to London on the day before, that the *Délégation Générale* strategy for the occupation of public buildings was complete and that the CPL had agreed to the dispositions of police, *Garde Républicaine*, FFI, and *Milices Patriotiques* to take over various buildings. All of this would fall under the control of the two prefects, once they had been installed. The actual organization of the ministries and public buildings had been drawn up in an internal Resistance *Noyautage des Administrations Publiques* (NAP) plan of April–May 1944. This gave NAP cells in the major ministries the task of weeding out collaborators and facilitating the installation of the new *Secrétaires Généraux de la République* (the provisional general secretaries/ ministers). By July 1944, Evelyne Garnier, the general secretary of NAP, had put NAP representatives in each ministry in touch with the relevant GRPF – designated provisional general secretary so that a smooth hand-over of power was assured.[88] Parodi's plan was for an orderly assumption of control by those elements designated for each building, after which each provisional general secretary would be fetched by a bodyguard to take up his office.

In the heat of the moment such plans did not always work and some buildings were liberated spontaneously. The Elysée Palace of the President was seized by a group of the *gardes* (the public buildings security corps) from Penthièvre, and the Matignon Palace (the Prime Minister's residence) by a group who formerly made up Laval's bodyguard. Mutter, GPRF Commissioner for the Colonies, Miné, for Supply, and Lecompte-Boinet at Public Works, simply moved into their respective buildings without opposition. Guingebert for Information also took over Henriot's old ministry without trouble, but Willard, seeking entrance to the Ministry of Justice in the Place Vendôme, had to pass large numbers of Germans moving out of hotels in the vicinity and was more discreet. The presence of a Resistance group already in the building helped the arrival of the new team, and served to make it appear that nothing untoward was happening.

By the evening of 19 August 1944 several important ministries had been occupied by the GPRF nominees and other buildings were in the hands of the Resistance. But not all these buildings were subject to Parodi's plan, because an agent of the SOE was parachuted into France in July for the specific task of seizing the Ministry of the Interior, Place Beauvau, and holding it 'in the Gaullist interest', which he did.[89] The Gaullist interest, or rather the influence of the GPRF, was the first to make itself felt in Paris, although on 19 August very few people even knew about the occupation of the ministries. Whatever the immediate practical impact of these new secretaries, however, once they were installed, there was no possibility of any other group seizing public buildings and using them to establish an alternative authority. GPRF authority had been established, if only in isolated buildings.

The other main public buildings – telephone exchanges, generating stations, post offices, banks, radio stations, newspapers, factories and so on – had been the subject of a detailed plan, drawn up on 17 and 18 August by Colonel de Margueritte (Lizé), the Commander of the FFI for the Seine. Much of this plan was carried out on 19 August, and many other major factories, depots and installations were seized by Resistance groups within them.[90] But in some cases, as with the strikes in the public utilities, it was the Parisians rather than the Germans who were inconvenienced, so an instruction was issued for such installations to be guarded against destruction rather than brought to a halt. Thus it was that some of the most vigorous proponents of popular uprising found themselves guarding buildings to ensure the orderly transmission of republican power.

The occupation of the *mairies* was, by comparison, a very disorderly affair and in some areas provided the images of communist revolution so feared by the non-communist members of the GPRF. In Joinville, Alfortville, Rosny and Neuilly-sur-Marne the communists gained control of local government because they were the first to move. In Le Perreux, the MLN were quickest, and in Saint-Maur, a CGT group replaced a communist group which had broken an agreement. In the city itself, most of the occupations went off without any fighting or disturbance. The local Liberation committee would present itself at the *mairie* and the Vichy administration would concede to it, and in some cases, as in the 19th *arrondissement*, stay to help the new administrators. In the 18th *arrondissement*, the new administration was almost exclusively communist, but then the Resistance in the area and the local Liberation committee were also overwhelmingly communist. In the 17th *arrondissement* some young Resisters got into the *mairie* on the night of 18 August and by 19 August had taken over the building with

Montgomery talking to fishermen in Port-en-Bessin, 10 June 1944

Bayeux: de Gaulle followed by a French crowd, 14 June 1944

Bayeux: Lt. Schmann, the voice of Free France from London, speaking to the crowd gathered to greet de Gaulle, 14 June 1944

## AVIS | NOTICE

Par arrêté préfec-toral, la fabrication totale et la vente de la pâtisserie sont inter-dites jusqu'à nouvel ordre. | By order of the Prefect the making and selling of pastry is forbidden till new orders.

Les pâtissiers de Bayeux s'excusent auprès de leur aimable clientèle de ne pouvoir continuer à la satisfaire momentanément.

The Bakers of Bayeux apologize to their customers for a temporary halt in service, July 1944

Crosses of Lorraine on sale in Bayeux, indicating de Gaulle's popularity, July 1944

*First British troops met by Capt. Gilles, President of the Calvados Departmental Liberation Committee, and M. Daure, the new prefect of Calvados, in the ruins of Caen, 9 July 1944*

*Bretteville L'Orgueilleuse: villagers discuss one of the first newpapers of the Liberation, 19 July 1944*

*Cherbourg: RAF officers looking at a German propaganda poster referring to the British occupation of Cherbourg from 1418 to 1480: 'Murderers always return to the scene of their crime' (July 1944)*

*De Gaulle with Leclerc at their first meeting at the Montparnasse HQ of the French Commander, 27 August 1944*

*Pro de Gaulle Parisians parading through the streets with banners, 26 August 1944*

Col. Howley with Major Nunn (right) and Pierre Mime, Secretary General of the French Ministry of Food (left), announcing the Allied plans for food distribution to Paris, over the radio on 26 August 1944

A recruiting queue for the new French army: FFI line up to volunteer at a village near Caen, 15 August 1944

*Beaumesnil (Eure): a Resistance chief questioning a woman accused of living with a German and passing information to the enemy, 30 August 1944*

*FFI members act as guides to Allied armoured cars in the reduction of Le Havre, 12 September 1944*

The first Communist Party (PCF) meeting since 1940 at the Vélodrome d'Hiver in Paris, 9 September 1944. The slogan is 'Thorez must return' (to Paris from Moscow)

De Gaulle, Churchill and Eden, flanked by Duff Cooper and Bidault, taking the salute at the Armistice Day parade on the Champs Elysées in Paris, 11 November 1944

a riotous party of patriotic celebration, interspersed with the shaving of prostitutes' heads and the arrest of suspected collaborators. By the afternoon the nominated local Liberation committee took control, but it was incomplete and all it could do was give a lavish distribution of food for the few coupons that remained. In the 1st *arrondissement* the Germans took charge of an empty *mairie* building during the day and then retreated from it after a small skirmish with the FFI. But in the 20th *arrondissement*, the Resistance was driven out of the *mairie*, and in Neuilly their defeat almost turned into a mass execution, before the Vichy mayor intervened to prevent it. In other areas the local public buildings were either still being used by the occupiers or left abandonned by fleeing Vichyite officials, some the target of sniping, and some, caught between the fire of the two sides, roaming backwards and forwards, seeking both to fight and to avoid each other. The CPL was supposed to be in charge of the seizures of *mairies*, but on 19 August it had no control over the spontaneous actions of local groups, and this Liberation was a matter of local initiative.

The most complete set of seizures was that of the press offices and printing works by the clandestine journals. The flight of the collaborationist press left some buildings free for occupation on the evening of 18 August, such as that of *Je Suis Partout*, occupied by the *Mouvement Républicain de Libération* (later *Mouvement Républicain Populaire*, MPR). Resisters in the collaborationist *Paris-Soir* tired to organize the return of the pre-war owners, but there was a confusion of attempts to seize it by different groups. Finally, by the morning of the 20 August the various clandestine papers were installed in the offices and printing shops allocated to them by the NAP plan, in conjunction with the BIP (the press organization of the CNR).

Seen from the German point of view, the situation had decayed through protest and strike into street fighting and finally into a sporadic and fitful insurrection. There was no logical pattern to the sequence of events and there appeared to be no overall plan, nor any controlling body. The provisional government's civil and military representatives were caught in the middle of this chaos and had a set of their own problems. Communications with London were bad, but the GPRF insisted on their attempting to slow or halt the insurrection, whilst they had few means of demonstrating that this was impossible. They had established their presence, but they could not control the uprising and they feared losing the co-operation of the local Resistance. They were, however, establishing the first crucial centres of a future provisional administration, and if the fighting left enough of the normal governmental structure for them to use in the coming weeks, then any autonomous efforts at political control by the Resistance would be overcome.

## The truce

RUMOURS of a communist plot, the knowledge that the Allies would not be moving immediately on Paris, and the fear of consequent general bloodshed and disorder, made the partisans of caution in the provisional government group of the internal Resistance attempt to apply the brakes. The plight of those who had seized and were defending the prefecture of police – the first Resistance stronghold – was dire. If they were not to be wiped out, some kind of ceasefire had to be arranged. On the German side this coincided with the desire of the military to extricate their troops from the trap that was being laid for them by the Allies. To do this, they wanted calm in Paris, and the German military Commander, von Choltitz, was persuaded that his reputation would not be enhanced by the bloody destruction of the French capital. Thus the two antagonists moved hesitantly towards a short truce, which was extended, but quickly broke down, having never been fully observed by either side. The confusion and chaos of events added to an almost total absence of intelligence on the Resistance side, made it difficult to hold meetings, give coherent orders and control armed forces. Just as revolution was almost physically impossible, so was a careful, staged uprising in co-ordination with the Allied advance.

During the afternoon of 19 August the street fighting intensified, the news of arms and material shortage was bad for the Resistance and opinions about the sudden outbreak of armed action began to change. In the first place, reports were coming into the various Resistance headquarters of German counter attacks in the suburbs. Secondly, German attacks on the prefecture began to look serious for the poorly armed defenders there. In the afternoon, Parodi received a visit from an unknown Colonel, Claude Ollivier (Jade Amicol), who declared himself to be the head of the 'intelligence service' in France, carrying a message from the Allies to the effect that they would not alter their plans. Bluntly he told Parodi that the Resistance was at the mercy of the Germans.[91] At the prefecture the Resistance occupiers were faced with a German tank firing at the door leading from the Parvis Notre-Dame, and only five hours' ammunition with which to hold out. General Dassault, military adviser of the FTP, suggested that the prefecture should be evacuated, and Parodi eventually gave way, writing an order for evacuation which Hamon (on the *Bureau* of the CPL) undertook to deliver. Hamon never reached the prefecture – stopped by intense gunfire – and, although they received the order by telephone from several sources, the defenders of the prefecture were unwilling to relinquish it and dubious about the practicality of doing so. Raoul Nordling, the Swedish Consul, had been in contact, directly and via intermediaries, with Von Choltitz for some days. He had arranged the release of French political prisoners and hostages on 18 and 19 August and on the morning of 19 August had gone to the prefecture. In the afternoon he received an anonymous telephone call from the prefecture saying that the defenders had only an hour or so of ammunition left and begging him to do something. He went to see Von Choltitz, and proposed a truce so that the injured could be evacuated, a truce fixed for 8.55 p.m. to 9.50 p.m. Hamon, on learning of the truce, made his way back to the prefecture and, after a series of telephone calls between him and Nordling, the truce was extended to the rest of the night. Von Choltitz was persuaded that it was in his best interests to accede and have a quiet night to regroup his forces. The Germans' main concern at that time was to maintain calm in Paris so that retreating German troops could pass through the city unmolested. It is doubtful whether he responded to the romantic blandishments of Tattinger and Nordling concerning the beauties of the city. He undertook a more calculated view of his own strength and of the disruptive potential of the Resistance.

During the night of 19 August, Luizet, Bayet, Pré – Parodi's subordinate – and Ribière of the CNR, visited the prefecture and were all in favour of extending the truce beyond its new 6 a.m. deadline. The same night in the prefecture, a small group gathered with the intention of occupying the Hôtel de Ville. It had been agreed by the major Resistance committees that at some point during the insurrection the CPL would formally take charge of the Hôtel de Ville and establish a new administration for Paris. It was, however, Hamon who, around midnight on 19 August, took the initiative to occupy the Hôtel de Ville the next morning. Hamon had declared that he did this so that if there were further negotiations for extending the truce, or if the truce broke down, the Resistance would be in charge of the main symbol of Republicanism in the capital. He further claimed the right to take this action as the only member of the CPL who was at the centre of the insurrection and understood the gravity of the action.[92] There have been criticisms that he did not contact his colleagues in the CPL, and that he tried to forestall the communists by seizing the Hôtel de Ville. But it had been agreed by all parties that the CPL would take control of the building and Hamon did that on their behalf. Hamon and his group, the Bayets – father and son – Ribière for the CNR and Pré for the *Délégation* of the GPRF, together with a group of FFI, gained entry to the Hôtel de Ville before 8 a.m. There had been three groups of FFI in the Hôtel de Ville on 19 August, but none had established itself, and it was the third of them, Stéphane (Worms) of the FFI, mandated by Rol, who returned the next day and was charged by Hamon, in the name of the CPL, with the defence of the building. Hamon and his group, reinforced with Besse, a member of the PCF, from the Union of *Syndicats* – supposedly representing the communist point of view – went on to a meeting that had been arranged with Nordling during the night. He assured Nordling that he spoke for the communists, although he had not consulted them, and the two negotiators drafted a proclamation calling for a continuation of the truce.[93]

From here Hamon went to a meeting of the *Bureau* of the CNR to get ratification of the truce. Whether this was one of the daily meetings of the CNR, agreed upon on 18 August, or whether it was a special meeting called by Bidault is far from clear. Of the 16 members of the CNR, apart from Bidault, only five were present. Since this was a meeting of the *Bureau* of the CNR, Tessier and Ribière, who were only members of the committee, were technically observers and should not have had a vote, whilst Saillant, the CGT member of the *Bureau*, was not present. None of the five representatives of political movements was there, nor were the delegates of CDLR, CDLL, *Libération Nord*, *Libération*, *Combat* or the CGT. But the meeting did include Tollet and Hamon from the CPL, Parodi, Pré and Chaban-Delmas from the *Délégation* and General Dassault of the FTP. This crucial meeting was not representative, but then few of the meetings of the CNR and the CPL had been fully attended and this was an emergency meeting called for a very important decision, at very short notice, in difficult conditions. The meeting was opened by Parodi who argued in favour of the truce on the basis that the Germans had massive forces which they could use against the Resistance, and that the truce was a recognition by the German command that the Resistance had liberated Paris. Hamon introduced his text and General Dassault argued that accepting it did not prevent the Resistance from fighting the German army in the suburbs. Villon of *Front National* argued against the truce, but suggested that the Resistance should abandon its occupation of public buildings and return to guerilla tactics: the insurrection of the people should not be betrayed. Blocq-Masquart of *Organisation Civile et Militaire* (OCM) was in favour of the truce to save civilian casualities. Avinin of *Franc-Tireur* was in favour, with conditions, and Bidault, the chairman, summed up by saying that it was a German recognition of the Resistance victory, a result which went beyond what they could have hoped for. In the vote, Bidault, Blocq-Masquart, Tessier, Avinin and Ribière were in favour of the truce. Only Villon was against. The others did not have a vote in the CNR, but Tollet indicated his opposition and Hamon his support.[94] Hamon, Pré and Chaban-Delmas went to see Nordling and submitted the text, minus the name of the CPL, since Tollet had objected, and it was then slightly modified by Choltitz to emphasize the need for calm. It was this text which was announced by loudspeaker cars towards midday on 20 August to the people of Paris.

The meeting of the CNR *Bureau* was clearly not satisfactory in terms of membership, so Bidault called for a plenary meeting of the CNR during the afternoon. At this meeting Villon argued vigorously that a truce would shift the site of reprisals to the working-class suburbs of Paris, and that Allied policy was one of unconditional surrender, which the truce violated. The task of the Resistance was to fight the Germans, he said, not to protect the occupation of a few buildings. He was strongly supported by his communist allies. Since Parodi was absent, however, the CNR decided not to take a decision, but to meet again on the following morning.[95] Villon and his supporters thought that this meant that the truce was not in force, but the earlier 'little truce' of 19 August had continued into the morning of 20 August, and the loudspeaker vans had spread the news of the extended truce before the CNR meeting in the afternoon of 20 August had ended. There was much confusion as to what decisions had been taken, and who had ratified what, but in effect the truce was established and a text announced to the population in the afternoon!

> By virtue of the promises made by the German High Command to leave public buildings occupied by the French in their hands and to treat French prisoners in accordance with the laws of war, the Provisional Government of the French Republic and the National Council of the Resistance orders you to hold your fire against the occupier until the total evacuation of Paris. The population is requested to remain perfectly calm. Do not go out onto the streets.[96]

It appeared for the moment that the partisans of caution and delay had won the day. Parodi, who had been swept away by the enthusiasm of 19 August, but who had several messages from London counselling delay, Pré, Hamon and Chaban-Delmas, all of whom wanted a calming of the situation, had assured GPRF occupation of the major buildings and a halt in the street battle in order to consolidate that control. The possibility that they were acting against an expected communist seizure of power exists, but by the afternoon of 20 August – apart from exaggerated reports from one or two *mairies* – there was little evidence of a communist plot. There was, however, the clear possibility of German reaction via reprisals or bombing, and there was equally the uncertainty that a bloody and prolonged street battle might create a chaotic situation which could destroy the fragile existence of GPRF representatives in the capital, and open the way for an Allied administration of a damaged and disrupted Paris.

The FFI, whose actions the truce most directly affected, saw the cessation of hostilities in a very different light. Fighting was still taking place in the 13th *arrondissement* around Place d'Italie, Avenue des Gobelins and Place de l'Hôpital, perhaps because this was a left-wing *commune*, and perhaps because Colonel Fabien had his FTP headquarters in the local *mairie*. In the 19th *arrondissement*, near the Gare du Nord, in the 18th towards the Porte de Clignancourt, and in the student quarter of the Left Bank, where the violent clashes of the previous day were carried on, fighting continued in a sporadic fashion. There were outbreaks of violence in the suburbs, where it engendered a carnival atmosphere. Rol-Tanguy, from his underground headquarters beneath the Lion de Belfort, near the Denfert-Rochereau station, was organizing the spread of fighting in accord with the order of general attack that he had issued the day before. When he heard that Chaban-Delmas had visited Colonel de Margueritte (Lizé) late on 19 August, as *Délégué Militaire National* representing the GPRF, and told him to stop fighting in line with the truce agreement, he ordered the resumption of hostilities immediately:

> I have learnt of the approach made to you by the National Military Delegate (DMN). This intervention is in flagrant contradiction with the general orders I have recently given and with the general order of 19th August 1944. I insist that these orders, which demand the intensification of the guerilla war and in particular constant and co-ordinated patrols of the FFI in your department, are executed without delay.[97]

This order at 7.40 a.m. on 20 August had been preceded by a protest to COMAC about the interference of Chaban-Delmas and praise for the actions of Lizé. To reinforce his order to Lizé, Rol-Tanguy sent a general order to all FFI commanders in the Paris region, at 4.45 p.m. 'No counter-manding official order has been issued by me, ordering a ceasefire. As a result, whilst the Germans remain in Paris, the order is to fight them.'[98] His subordinate for the Seine Department, Lizé, reacted firmly to these directions. At 10.15 a.m. he ordered an all-out attack, and later he declared that any order for a truce given out over loudspeakers was not valid until backed by a written order. At 2.15 p.m. he issued a firm directive to continue the fight:

> Following the unacceptable hesitations of certain unit commanders, the colonel commanding the Department of the Seine finds himself obliged to remind all his subordinates that orders concerning the continuation of the all-out struggle are still in operation, that no truce has been concluded and that only he can decide on a suspension of the fight and thereto informs his subordinates.
> You are similarly reminded that any dealings with the enemy are considered, under military law, as an act of high treason and, as such, punishable by death. This penalty will, if necessary, be ruthlessly applied. The Colonel expects that all his officers and men will, in these difficult circumstances, prove to have the discipline and fighting spirit which alone will ensure our success.[99]

Given the dispersed nature of the fighting, the difficulties of communication and the excitement of the people involved, it was impossible to bring about a cessation of fighting in the streets. Given the attitude of the two most important FFI commanders in Paris, who had equated the truce with treason, there was clearly very little chance that it would become complete by the end of 20 August. The CPL itself put off a decision on the truce question until the day after.[100] The other major influence in the Paris street fighting – the FTP – had no intention of putting up its arms. Tillon toured the 'hot spots', as he had done every afternoon since the insurrection had broken out, encouraging his men in their fight.[101]

The representatives of the GPRF in Paris might have been concerned about the poor response to the truce, especially in the suburbs, and the possibility of bloody chaos ruining their plans, but they were consolidating their positions in Paris. On 20 August Laffon, the Provisional Secretary General of the Interior, moved into the Ministry of the Interior – presumably still occupied by the SOE – along with his deputy, Ribière, who represented the Interior Committee of the CNR and the *Délégation* of the GPRF. The installation of the Provisional Secretary of the Interior was very important in that it signalled the establishment of GPRF control over the forces of law and order. In the morning the new prefect, Flouret, had gained entrance to the Hôtel de Ville, and, instead of a clash with the left-wing members of the CPL who had opposed his appointment, he began working alongside a CPL delegation. Monik of the Ministry of Finance, Courtois at the Ministry of the Economy, Professor Milliez at Health, to be followed the next day by Valléry-Radot, Professor Wallon at Education, and Colonel Duc as interim representative at the Ministry of War, were all established in their buildings during 20 August. Whilst they had little means of influencing events in the immediate term, their very occupation of the buildings at such an early stage of the insurrection reduced the possibility of conflicting authority when the Germans left.

The *Délégué Général* on the other hand was absent from the CNR meeting in the afternoon and out of touch with his *Commissaires*: he had been arrested. Setting out with his sister, Pré and Laffon to tour the city and observe the state of the truce in the early afternoon, he was arrested, eventually taken to see Choltitz and then released around 6 p.m. By the end of the day, the Resistance was split, the *Délégation* in favour of a truce, the CNR and CPL divided and unable to take a decision, and the FFI, COMAC and FTP against the truce and ignoring it. But behind this chaos, the local Liberation committees were establishing themselves in the *mairies*. The prefecture and Hôtel de Ville were still in Resistance hands and the ministries were rapidly being occupied by their GPRF nominees.

The confusion of Resistance action continued into the next day. The CPL issued a call for the struggle to continue: 'Now more than ever everyone into the fight'.[102] The *Front National* put out a statement declaring that the truce was a German trick and ended with the bloodcurdling cry, 'Not one Boche must leave the Paris region alive'.[103] But the FFI was still out of step. In the morning of 21 August Parodi met the prefect of police, Luizet, Chaban-Delmas, the Délégué Général, Kriegel-Valrimont, Rol and Lizé of the FFI to discuss the truce, but came to no conclusion. After Rol left the meeting, declaring that he would not allow the Germans safe routes of retreat through Paris and would fight as vigorously as he could, the others persuaded Lizé to issue an order allowing the Germans such 'open' routes. Rol, learning of this, ordered Lizé to issue a statement that the truce had been broken, that the fight continued and that his men should 'cover Paris with barricades'.[104]

The meeting of the CNR at 5 p.m. was a heated affair which opened with Parodi (*Délégation* GPRF) and Bidault (CNR) outlining the history of the truce and the reasons for past decisions. They, and those who had voted for the truce, were roundly condemned as traitors by Villion and Gillot (PCF). The previous meetings of the CNR they characterized as improper and the CNR were invited to denounce the 'fake' truce declaration of the previous day. Saillant introduced the text already issued that morning by the CPL. Chaban defended the truce by concentrating on the practical difficulties for the Resistance and the fact that he represented the wishes of Koenig. Finally, the CNR adopted the CPL text against the truce, with the proviso that it was not published until the next day at 4 p.m. The truce then was definitely broken but Parodi had gained a little more vital time,[105] during which the Matignon Palace (Prime Minister's residence) was taken over by GPRF representatives.

On 22 August, the order for insurrection, signed by Parodi, was posted and all the other Resistance authorities issued their own exhortations. Rol for the FFI declared 'Paris fights' and took up the *mot d'ordre* of the FTP, '*Chacun son Boche!*'[106] As Tillon has said in his memoirs: 'The 22nd was to be the great day of the barricades'.[107] But whilst the proponents of all-out attack now appeared to have gained the ascendancy, Parodi, in the afternoon, held the first meeting of all the *Secrétaires Généraux* present in Paris at the Matignon Palace: in effect the first Cabinet meeting of the interim government. Alongside the confusion of the truce, therefore, an interim government had been established in Paris, and a government composed of GPRF nominees.

The first Cabinet meeting in the Matignon was concerned with the matters of immediate moment rather than the establishment of a new governmental system and implementation of a new policy. Parodi warned his provisional secretaries not to take up their posts in ministries which were vulnerable to attack, but for most of them it was already too late, and they ignored his order to evacuate vulnerable buildings. The problem of food was discussed, difficulties caused by the FFI and its demands were examined, and a call made for the unions to lift their strike so that vital supplies of coal and oil could be moved into the city. One of the main topics to be considered was the control of the Liberation press by the Secretary for Information. He declared that he could not censor the press, so that for example, an article attacking Nordling had been published without his knowledge. He also declared that henceforth the Liberation press was free to go ahead and publish from its new locales without hindrance from the new administration. Chaban intervened to transmit a message from de Gaulle and Koenig to the Resistance, saying they must proceed with the utmost caution and ensure the security of the major personnel of the new administration. He said that it was possible that the Allies would change their plan to bypass Paris, but that it would have to go to the highest Allied authority and that would take time. What the liberators of Paris must do was give the Allies time to change their tactics and then come to the aid of Paris, otherwise the Resistance would be crushed.[108]

More significantly for the men at the meeting, it was decided that Resistance papers of the next day should carry full explanations of the relationships between the Resistance, the new authority in Paris, and the provisional government in Algiers. It was also suggested that the names of the prefects, *Délégation*, and the new secretaries be given to the BBC for broadcast to the French population as a whole. The interim government had little control over the events in Paris, but they were establishing their identity as the legitimate authority for the immediate post-Liberation period.

On 23 August fighting was widespread in Paris even before the agreed end of the truce at 4 p.m. Choltitz's reaction to this was to put more heavily armed patrols on the streets and one of them, in attacking the Grand Palais, set fire to it: a grim warning for the Resistance. The situation of the FFI was precarious and Rol issued an order appealing to all FFI units in the Paris region, and those behind Allied lines, to come to the aid of the beleaguered city.[109] One or two of the more vulnerable ministries were evacuated, but the majority remained *in situ*. On 24 August, the fighting continued with ferocity and the position of the FFI deteriorated, but they were not forced to abandon any important public buildings. One sidelight to the fighting was that on 24 August Luizet telephoned Lizé and told him that the police forces, by order of the GPRF, had reverted to the control of the prefect of police and could no longer be considered members of the FFI in the Department of the Seine under Lizé. This meant that the single most important armed group of Resisters had left the control of Lizé and Rol, and the single most important centre of Resistance, practically and symbolically, had come under the authority of the new administration. Lizé and Rol were naturally furious, but there was little they could do.[110]

A note dropped from a scout plane at 5 p.m. that day, close to the prefecture of police, gave the defenders renewed hope. Leclerc's message was short but important: 'Hang on – we're coming'.[111] By 9.22 p.m. a small unit of the 2nd French Army under Captain Dronne had arrived in front of the Hôtel de Ville, and, although it was only a token force from one of the three columns moving forward under Leclerc, it was positive proof that Allied plans for the Liberation of Paris had been advanced and that Paris would be freed rather than bypassed.

Up to the very last moment, the Allies had acted as spectators of the events unfolding in Paris. Eisenhower's decision to change the original plan was a late one, based primarily on military, rather than political intelligence. On 21 August, for example, Eden reported to the Prime Minister that during his two-day trip to France both Eisenhower and Montgomery had impressed on him their determination to stick to their plans.[112] He also claimed that de Gaulle had accepted this, but it is clear from de Gaulle's actions and his memoirs that he had not agreed, and took much more notice of the increasingly dire warnings coming from Parodi than did the Allies. Churchill, who normally left the control of military affairs in the hands of Eisenhower, was disturbed by the news reaching him from Paris.[113]

The news of the insurrection was taken very seriously by de Gaulle and the provisional government who mobilized all their forces to persuade the Allies to change and head straight to Paris. Parodi's telegram of 18 August, demanding that the commander of the FFI, Koenig, go to the Allied High Command to hasten the occupation of Paris, arrived in London on 20 August, but Koenig got no change of heart from the SAC. Massigli, GPRF diplomatic representative in London, went to see Eden, and on 22 August told him that, although the representatives of the provisional government had tried to 'hold them back', the communists had provoked an uprising in Paris which was liable to cause chaos. It was imperative, said Massigli, that the Allies move to occupy Paris as soon as possible and supply guns, now that the truce had broken down. Eden told Massigli that it was his impression that de Gaulle had accepted the logic of the Allied plans but been offered help with arms, which was supported by Churchill.[114] Ismay, on behalf of the War Cabinet, approached Churchill on the same day, pointing out that the military situation in Paris could deteriorate rapidly, causing the Allies many problems in the following weeks, and urging that action should be taken.[115]

On 20 August de Gaulle returned to France and in the evening received a full report on the uprising in Paris from Koenig. The next day he had other reports, amongst them one from Leclerc (Commander in Chief of the French 2nd Division), who deplored the Allied failure to close the Falaise gap, criticized the very slow progress of the armies and demanded that de Gaulle intervene so that the French armoured division could move on Paris. On the evening of 20 August De Gaulle had failed to persuade Eisenhower, but the next day he had reiterated his arguments in a letter, urging the SAC to attack. He threatened that if Eisenhower did not change his mind then he, de Gaulle, would have to withdraw the French 2nd Armoured Division from the Allied Command structure and send it to Paris on his own responsibility.[116] On 22 August, General Redman, as a liaison officer with the FFI and French military, went to see Eisenhower to urge the move on Paris and arrived at Supreme HQ at the same time as de Gaulle's letter, which prompted Eisenhower to tell Bedell Smith that he 'might be compelled to go into Paris'.[117]

It was on this day, 22 August 1944, that Commandant Cocteau (Gallois), direct from the fighting in Paris, arrived at Eisenhower's headquarters as the representative of Rol (the Chief of Paris FFI). Cocteau had started from Paris in the evening of 20 August when Rol-Tanguy, although opposed to the continuation of the truce, realized that a bloodbath might ensue and decided to send an appeal for immediate Allied intervention. On 21 August Cocteau reached Patton's headquarters and was treated with some respect, once his credentials, as subordinate to the Paris commander of the FFI, had been verified. Bradley told him that the Allied Command could not change such massive plans at a moment's notice, and that their objective was Berlin: Paris was incidental. Cocteau requested that he be allowed to contact Leclerc and, after a long night drive, arrived at Bradley's HQ, which was also Leclerc's. There he had an interview with General Sibert, 12th Army Group's intelligence officer, before Sibert went with Bradley to see Eisenhower. It was at this latter meeting that Eisenhower finally gave way to the pressure of the previous days and agreed to move immediately towards Paris.[118] News of the situation in Paris, said Eisenhower, had convinced him of the necessity for an attack. Cocteau, representing Rol and straight from the fighting in the capital, carried more conviction than other entreaties and possibly convinced the Allied command that speed was essential, on the basis of hard military intelligence.[119] After further pressure Bradley decided that Leclerc should be reinforced with the US 4th Division. This was not a political decision, but a result of military intelligence that indicated that an early arrival by strong American forces could forestall the destruction of Paris and disrupt the retreat by the 26th and 27th Panzer Divisions through the city. This intelligence also indicated that a swift advance, avoiding certain strong points, would meet little serious German resistance, and that whilst the German chaos persisted, the Allies should take advantage of it.

## De Gaulle establishes himself and the nucleus of a provisional government

THUS IT WAS that after two days of rapid progress, an advanced guard of French troops reached the Hôtel de Ville on the evening of 24 August. By means of the radio stations which were now in Resistance hands, the whole of Paris knew of the arrival within the hour. On the previous evening, de Gaulle in Rambouillet sent a message to the prefect of police telling him that he would be in Paris on the next day, that he would go to 'the centre' and that he, Parodi and Luizet would arrange everything.[120] De Gaulle's aim was to reach Paris as quickly as possible after the Allied troops had entered, to forestall any possibility that the Allies might, despite the agreements so far reached, set up a low-level AMGOT.

Meanwhile at 4 p.m. on 25 August Von Choltitz, having surrendered to Billotte at the Hotel Meurice, was taken to the prefecture of police, where he and Leclerc signed the document of surrender. From here he went to the Gare Montparnasse, Leclerc's HQ, where he signed the order for German forces in Paris to cease fighting. At both these meetings Rol and Kriegel-Valrimont protested that the Parisian FFI and Resistance were not represented on any of the documents of surrender. Chaban-Delmas supported Rol's contention that he should sign on behalf of the Parisian FFI and the text of the surrender was amended. At 4.30 p.m. de Gaulle arrived at the Gare Montparnasse where he received a situation report from Leclerc and went on to establish himself in his old office in the Ministry of Defence, which he had left on 10 June 1940. In his memoirs de Gaulle said that nothing had changed in the building except that now the state did not exist and he would have to set about rebuilding it. His very presence in the ministry was a demonstration of his assertion that the Republic had never ceased to exist, that Vichy was an illegal regime and that the GPRF was a natural continuation of the true French state, with all the Republican legitimacy that this implied.[121] In his memoirs, he clearly records his annoyance with the fact that Rol had been allowed to add his signature to the surrender, and he spoke harshly to Leclerc of his giving way to Resistance pressure over the matter.[122]

Parodi, Chaban and Luizet, all arriving shortly after at the Ministry of War, convinced de Gaulle that he should be seen in Paris as soon as possible. The General arrived at the prefecture of police at 6.30 p.m. and was then persuaded to go to the Hôtel de Ville to meet the prefect and the CPL. There he was greeted by Tollet, on behalf of the CPL, by Bidault, on behalf of the CNR, and by the prefect, Flouret. After emotional speeches of welcome, Bidault invited de Gaulle to proclaim the Republic to the crowd waiting below. De Gaulle replied that the

Republic had never ceased to exist. Bidault was thus obliged to hold on to the prepared declaration of the CNR. Instead of a proclamation which mentioned the heroism of the people as the motive force of the Liberation and the charter of the CNR as its inspiration, and which did not mention de Gaulle, the speech from the window of the Hôtel de Ville by de Gaulle was a nationalistic, patriotic and emotional evocation of France, and a reminder of the need for the fight to go on. The CNR/CPL delegation had avoided going to the prefecture of police to await de Gaulle and made him come to their headquarters, but he had, in a short radio interview and the speech from the window, made it clear that authority rested with the GPRF, its ministers and himself, not in the Hôtel de Ville.

The radio in Paris was the vital means by which the existence of a new authority would be made known and the arrival of de Gaulle in the city confirmed this. It incessantly announced the march down the Champs-Elysées, which was to take place the next day, and invited the citizens of Paris to celebrate the city's Liberation. When de Gaulle walked down the great avenue at 3 p.m. the next day, followed a pace behind by the leaders of the *Délégation*, the CNR, the CPL, the FFI and the Resistance groups, his progress was relayed across France and the crowds were huge. His visit to the cathedral of Notre-Dame for a service celebrating the deliverance of Paris was also reported on the radio, as was his calm and brave demeanour when firing broke out, both in front of and inside the cathedral.[123]

Out of these events grew the instant legend of the fearless leader, and the new identity of the future provisional leader of France. The incidents of 26 August, more than any Gaullist propaganda or skilful tactics, helped to establish the authority of the new provisional administration. The celebrations though had caused their own problems. In the first place, General Gerow, commanding officer of the US 5th Corps, had ordered his subordinate, Leclerc, to move his troops to the north of Paris in pursuit of the fleeing Germans, but de Gaulle ordered Leclerc to place his troops along the route of the parade, and it was this order that was obeyed. Gerow looked upon such behaviour as insubordination, to match a previous incident when the Leclerc division had gone too far ahead of the Americans on the approach to Paris.[124] The second problem was that the Resistance would not accept Cardinal Suhard, the Archbishop of Paris, as the celebrant of the mass in his own cathedral of Notre-Dame. In previous months he had met the German Commander of Paris inside his church, celebrated a mass for the death of the collaborator Henriot, welcomed Pétain to the cathedral portals, and held a mass for the dead of the Allied bombing. In the latter it was true that he had made veiled criticisms of the occupiers and the collaborators, but this was not sufficient to save his reputation. As a result, he was prevented from officiating at the mass, and indeed there was no mass, only a singing of the Magnificat. Despite these problems, de Gaulle was the focus of attention, praise and new-found loyalties.

De Gaulle's establishment of his own group of administrators in Paris was paralleled by his careful, if distant, handling of the Resistance groups and authorities. Having somewhat snubbed the CNR on 25 and 26 August, he wrote to Bidault on 27 August, praising the domestic Resistance and outlining his view of their future contribution to French administration:

> I think I can tell you that the wish of the government is that the men who make up the National Resistance Council will become, in accordance with the spirit of the decree promulgated on 22 April 1944, on the basis of advice and suggestions from the council itself, the nucleus of the Consultative Assembly sitting in a liberated France which should help the Government with its provisional objectives, notably the preparation of the first meeting of the National Constituent Assembly. I shall be very keen to keep in close contact with the assembly of the Council.[125]

De Gaulle declined an invitation to attend the CNR meeting of that day, but invited them to meet him at his headquarters in the Ministry of War, where he outlined the need for the Resistance to integrate politically and militarily into the new state.[126] From then began the daily meeting of the *Conseil des Ministres* at 14, rue Saint-Dominique by which de Gaulle started organizing the government of the country. Many of the ministers from Algiers arrived in Paris on 2 September and the first meeting of *Secrétaires Généraux* with ministers took place on that evening, symbolically uniting the just-recognized GPRF with the provisional administrators. Finally, on 10 September, he announced the new government. The CNR at its meeting of 8 September had declared that none of its members would individually accept portfolios in the proposed new government, so that collectively they could persuade de Gaulle of the need for a strong united CNR presence in his administration. Villon and Saillant refused offers, but Bidault broke ranks and accepted. The National Resistance Council were to hold fewer and fewer meetings (those held were increasingly spent supporting the CPL and its travails[127]) and their influence on events rapidly diminished, leaving the nucleus of the GPRF administration unchallenged at the national level.

The military problem was more pressing because it was more immediately dangerous, but de Gaulle took action to head off the trouble that might arise from confusion of command or an attempt by the Resistance to establish its own peacetime military organization. On 27 August the GPRF in Paris announced the appointment of Koenig as military commander of the city, and he posted a notice declaring that he assumed command of all armed forces in the capital. He also called for the FFI to show their discipline, having shown their fighting worth. On 28 August de Gaulle issued an order to integrate the armed Resistance into the army.[128] This order also dissolved the command chain of the FFI in the Paris region and handed its functions to Koenig as military governor. The CNR and COMAC replied by denouncing the order and denying its reasoning.[129] Villon of the PCF refused a post in de Gaulle's government on the grounds that he was betraying the FFI,[130] which de Gaulle denied[131]. This was only the beginning of the absorption of the armed Resistance into the regular forces, but crucially it took control of armed men out of the hands of COMAC and the local FFI command.

The CPL was also ignored by de Gaulle and the new administrators. In the early days of the Liberation, from 24 August, the CPL seemed to follow events rather than shape them. The continued presence of German snipers, the sudden influx of Allied military, the hunt for collaborators, and the chaos of all aspects of city life left the CPL impotently viewing events from the sidelines.[132] The CPL criticized the prefect for not doing more, and demanded that they should have a monitoring role on his actions, because in the early days he had not consulted them. The CPL also proposed the establishment of an armed *milice* as their own police force. The new government rejected it and the CPL replied that the new administration did not trust the people.[133] The advice of the new Ministry of the Interior was that the GPRF should cut the ground from under the CPL by making vigorous attempts at purging the system of collaborators and announcing strong economic measures as an earnest of their determination for a 'renovation' of France.[134] The plan of the CPL to set up 'new' municipalities in line with the Algiers CFLN *ordonnance* of 21 April was looked upon with some suspicion by the Allies and de Gaulle, but it altered the make-up of the *communes* very little from the provisional administrations that took over in the first days of the Liberation. The reformation of the *Conseil Municipal* for Paris and the *Conseil Général* for the Seine was proposed on the basis of a strong Resistance representation. For the municipality there were to be 21 members of the Resistance, 40 of the pre-1940 council, 20 representatives of the *arrondissements* and 7 'personalities' (mainly religious). The Resistance representatives would reflect the left-wing majority in the local Resistance committees – the right-wing and centre councillors of pre-1940 had largely left the city and the *arrondissement* Liberation committees were also predominantly left-wing. The *Conseil Général* was to be made up of the 88 municipal councillors, 21 representatives of the Resistance and 50 pre-1939 councillors, once again a strong presence of the Left.[135] The demands for new municipal councils, first made on 28 August, had received no reply when they were reiterated by Tollet and

Marrane on 4 September, but the CPL was already caught up in the massive problem of supply and the complex question of purging the various municipal administrations.[136] They were still without a response by 25 September although lists of nominees were almost complete.[137]

De Gaulle's aim had been to get to Paris as soon as he possibly could to establish the presence of a national GPRF leadership in the capital. Units of the French army had been prominent in the Liberation of the city. GPRF nominees had seized the ministries. The Resistance had fought under the banner of the FFI and their proclamations had remained true to Republican legality. But de Gaulle needed the symbolic effect of public approval for him as head of the new provisional French state. He was also wary of the left-wing in the Resistance, and the possibility of temporary disorder leading to a breakdown of those fragile remnants of the administration which he needed for control of the capital, and later of the country. To establish himself he used public display with media coverage and early contact with those officials already in place. He also distanced himself from the domestic Resistance, making it clear that his authority came from the GPRF in Algiers and the Consultative Assembly, rather than the armed Resisters in Paris, of whatever persuasion. But the armed Resisters would not simply disappear and the tension of the struggle persisted with the vengeance and celebration that followed Liberation. Thus de Gaulle's position, greatly enhanced by his public appearances and his private strategy, was still physically threatened. His main task was to reduce the power and influence of the local Resistance organizations, which he set about, whilst requesting Allied protection for the dangerous period before his authority was fully established.

## Allied views on the Liberation of Paris

FEARS OF an insurrection and complete breakdown in law and order clouded the Allied attitude to an otherwise desirable political and propaganda victory. In addition to their strategic and tactical reservations, the Allied military had thought that Paris might produce a political clash, into which they would be unwillingly drawn, further hindering the advance. Civil affairs arrangements were not ready for an early Liberation, so that when they were obliged by events to make a direct march on the city, many Allied authorities expected the worst. For these reasons they were anxious to know what happened in the first few days of the Liberation and rushed their many representatives into Paris to report back on the situation. These reports were generally very complimentary to the French and reassuring about public order. Their impressions undoubtedly ensured that the Allies made no attempt to control or restrict de Gaulle and the GPRF. Although the underlying fear of disruption remained to some extent, most Allied observers declared by early September that public order and the authority of the GPRF were established.

On 26 August, de Gaulle telegrammed SHAEF and told Eisenhower that it was imperative that he leave the Leclerc Division in Paris to maintain order. On that day the fighting had moved to the northern and north-eastern suburbs of the city and Leclerc had set up his command HQ at the Porte de la Chapelle, with the strong possibility of a German counter attack on the three Allied armies – Leclerc's 2nd Division, the US 4th Infantry Division and the US 15th Corps, which had not managed to forge a coherent line of attack north of the city. Eisenhower and Bedell Smith visited the city on 26 and 27 August, partly to receive the adulation of the crowds, partly to confirm physically their support for de Gaulle, and partly to sort out the squabble between Gerow and Leclerc. Eisenhower smoothed over the dispute between commanders and discussed the problems of order with de Gaulle. He agreed, apparently at de Gaulle's request, that the Leclerc division could stay in Paris, and an American division would march through the centre to show the support of the Allies for de Gaulle and their potential power against trouble-makers.[138] But Eisenhower reported back to Washington that there was no challenge to de Gaulle's authority and that all groups seemed to be animated by a desire for unity. He did note one or two potential trouble spots, including the delayed plans for a Council of Ministers, which were being held up by Resistance demands, and the roaming bands of FFI, but he declared that everything was really under the control of the GPRF representatives.[139] De Gaulle also asked for an early transfer of government personnel to Paris, which Eisenhower agreed to, but which started a long wrangle about how many personnel the Allies could transport and how quickly they could do it. The French ignored SHAEF plans for these transfers, brought the first 30 government members on the cruiser *Jean Bart* and demanded the movement of a further 3000. This caused a great deal of consternation in SHAEF, hard-pressed as it was for transport.[140]

Allied civil authorities tried to recover from what had been a chaotic chain of events before the Liberation, particularly as regards the media, where they had clearly been caught out. On 10 August, for example, the Political Warfare Executive (PWE) had issued an intelligence directive which stressed the good work and co-operation of the Resistance, but made no mention at all of Paris.[141] The French Service of the BBC, better informed of the situation in Paris, did begin to prepare for the Liberation with a broadcast of the 'Advice for Paris and the Major Cities', written by de Gaulle on 12 August and broadcast on

17 August.[142] On 15 August, during an interview with men of Leclerc's division, the impatience to move on Paris became evident and André Gillois sent a special message that evening to the policemen of Paris not to leave for Nancy in the general retreat, but to hide and be ready for action during the coming Liberation. On the following night, Gillois addressed Parisians directly and declared that for Von Choltitz and the German occupiers of Paris, the hour of French revenge was at hand. He warned Parisians, however, not to act precipitately and give the Germans an excuse to massacre prisoners.[143]

Even on this Service, references to Paris in the days preceding the Liberation were few. Koenig's official statement for 17 August contained no mention of Paris. Pierre Bourdan, broadcasting on 18 August made a long report on the Leclerc Division and their advanced position in the Allied attack, but apart from saying that their ambition was Paris, other references to the city were omitted. On 19 August Koenig's nightly military report surveyed all the fighting in France, but ignored Paris, and even Waldeck Rochet, the PCF representative in London and an ex-deputy for the Seine Department, failed to mention the existence of an insurrection.[144] Parodi telegraphed from Paris that the people of the city were disappointed not to hear any mention of their success on the broadcasts from London.[145] The directive of the PWE was clearly still in force. On 17 August a central directive was issued by the PWE on the situation in Paris. It reported that as a result of frequent power cuts it was very difficult to listen to the radio in Paris and that there were very few battery sets in the city, but it did not mention the threat of insurrection. On the same day a meeting of the French directive of the PWE, including Buckmaster (for the French Forces High Command, EMFFI), Kerr (for the OSS) and Mayoux, Boris and Diamant-Berger (for the GPRF)[146] – all of whom must have known about the growing turmoil in Paris – made no reference to the insurrection. On 20 August, SHAEF G5, in its weekly guidance to the Psychological Warfare Department, warned Parisians that food would be short, that travel restrictions would remain and encouraged everyone with the news that Vichy recognized its defeat. But again nothing on the capital.[147] The news that the Allies would announce the text of a joint civil affairs statement on 22 August came at a time when it was about to be outdistanced by events, and yet it was not linked to these events by the media. The statement included the declaration that, 'General Eisenhower has been authorized to deal with the French authorities at Algiers as the *de facto* authority in France so long as they continue to receive the support of the majority of Frenchmen who are fighting for the defeat of Germany and the Liberation of France.'[148] This may have encouraged Eisenhower to look favourably on the entreaties of de Gaulle, Cocteau and so on, but it only regularized a situation that had existed for some time and was soon to be superseded by the arrival of GPRF leadership in Paris.

The competition amongst news media to be the first to announce the Liberation of Paris led the BBC to declare it liberated on the evening of 23 August and quite suddenly break the PWE embargo. This very much angered the Allies and the SAC in particular, who held a press conference the next day to deny it. It was discovered that the announcement had somehow eluded the radio censors who should have stopped it.[149] Unfortunately, the error was compounded the next day by the King who sent a telegram of congratulations to de Gaulle.[150] On 24 August the PWE and Office of War Information (OWI) issued special guidance for the Liberation of Paris, which declared that it had already been achieved: 'The manner of her liberation by the FFI gives thrilling proof that Paris, despite the oppression and hardship of a four year occupation by the enemy, had lost none of its *élan*.'[151] It also laid great emphasis on the fact that Paris was only one element of the Allied strategic plan which meant that the fighting would go on until the unconditional surrender of Germany. A central directive from the PWE on the same day confirmed the insurrection and the sudden change of direction, but neither document mentioned the possibility of a provisional French government in Paris within days.[152] What is interesting about these directives for the Allied media is that, having not mentioned the insurrection, they now suddenly declared Paris liberated and retailed the French version of a city freed by its own people, rather than by Allied military forces.

Meanwhile Allied civil affairs teams had entered Paris and were beginning to report back. The A1A1 civil affairs team assigned to Paris was concentrated at Sées ready for the entry to Paris, with 2 'A', 2 'C' and 20 'D' type detachments. It was alerted for movement on 23 August and arrived in the Tuileries Gardens on 26 August, a headquarters being established by Lt. Col. Howley at 7, Place Vendôme. The 'D' size detachments were dispersed one to each *arrondissement*. One 'C' detachment went to Sceaux and one to Saint-Denis. Howley had several problems of command from the moment he entered Paris. Firstly, Gunn (G5 of the 1st Army) said that he should not allow his men to begin work until the new military commander for Paris, Koenig, invited them to do so. Howley contacted Koenig and got the invitation, but then he fell foul of General Rogers (Commander of the Communications Zone which was to include Paris) who thought he should control civil affairs, whereas Howley was sure *he* should.[153] At the same time representatives of many different Allied units reached Paris and began reporting back on what they found and setting up their own agencies. One of the first, Col. Ryan of 12th Army Group G5, claimed that the Parisians had given de Gaulle an enthusiastic welcome.[154] Major Younger, reporting to the Foreign Office, and described as 'on the intelligence side of SHAEF', agreed with this assessment. He witnessed the events in the Champs-Elysées and at Notre-Dame on 26 August, said the shooting was harmless because it was 'the *maquis* who shot into the roof in order to give vent to their feelings', and thought the reply by American troops was much more dangerous because it was aimed lower. Whilst Younger noted that de Gaulle was very popular, he prophesied something close to a civil war because of the undisciplined nature of armed Resisters.

The communists, according to Younger, were nationalistic, but feeling entitled to 'a big say in the government of France'. 'The French bourgeoisie', he reported, 'are very nervous. They waylay British and American officers, invite them to their houses and fill them up with champagne. They take the opportunity to point out that although they may have had to do business with the Germans and even work in offices with Germans they have been in no sense collaborationist.' Younger indicated surprisingly few reprisals and a good attitude towards the British, but suggested that American lack of tact would soon make them unpopular.[155] This report circulated round the British Foreign Office and confirmed its predilection for de Gaulle. Eden incidentally thought the offers of champagne might cause serious trouble. The civil affairs report from Howley gave further substance to de Gaulle's popularity, and although he echoed the warnings of disruption, he also noted many early achievements.[156]

Holman told the Foreign Office on 5 September that he had seen Koenig, who was very satisfied with the public order situation, but who paradoxically did not want to press for a Zone of the Interior, hinting at future disturbances. Luizet told him that the fact the police had started the insurrection against the Germans had taken the wind out of the communists' sails. The FFI, he said, had been a source of trouble, but the situation was under control from the start because of the police intervention. Since the Liberation a special Commissioner had been appointed for each *arrondissement*, who would see that Resisters were drafted into the army, and disarmed or arrested if they had broken the law. It would, however, have to be carefully handled, as would the purge of the police. He suggested that a gift of cigarettes from His Majesty's Government to the Paris police would go a long way to help morale! Events, said Holman, had outrun the civil affairs arrangements made by the Allies, but everything was quite calm.[157]

Major Palfrey, on the other hand, who interviewed the new prefect on 27 August, was asked by Flouret if he could arrange for the civil affairs organizations to help reorganize the police. He thought that wholesale arrests by the FFI demonstrated that they were better armed and more powerful than the police, which was very disturbing, because they had usurped, to some extent, the authority of the police. SHAEF also noted the existence of de Gaulle's skeleton administration in Paris and commented that those *Secrétaires Généraux* who had been contacted by SHAEF representatives were, 'competent, sound and reliable'.[158] The SHAEF general survey confirmed that de Gaulle's popularity was being maintained in the early days of the Liberation, but noted that, whilst the PCF was the best-organized political group in the Resistance, its leadership had been decimated by German reprisals. The Liaison Officers from SHAEF to de Gaulle, Col. Archdale and Major Levy, reported that by 31 August, de Gaulle's provisional government had been established in Paris, with six provisional ministers already in the city. They supported the setting up of a full provisional government, 'to give the French some concept of a central authority in control of things,' and urged the transport of the 47 members of the GPRF arriving on the *Jeanne d'Arc* from Algiers.[159] They argued that the greater sense of stability given to the population of Paris would decrease the chance of factional troubles and avoid the need for special security forces. Scowden reported from Paris to Hilldring, of CAD that 'The people are very happy. They received the Americans with open arms and General Koenig, the Governor, has things well in hand. In fact yesterday I talked to Col. Stearns who had just come back from an interview with Koenig, and he thought the situation was in good shape.[160]

At the end of the first week in liberated Paris, SHAEF drew together its information in a major report on the situation. It noted that the civil affairs detachments were in place and working well and that the French at the local level were doing their utmost to 'demonstrate the capacity of the French for governing themselves'.[161] Civil administration had greatly improved in the few days since the entry of the Allies and there were no critical problems, nor any expected. The fact that de Gaulle had taken the title of 'President of the Council' was indicative of the desire to return to normal political life. It noted that de Gaulle was very popular, especially among conservatives, that the 'Algiers Committee' were less popular and that he would have to be tactful not to disappoint the Resistance on the one hand, or moderate opinion on the other. The PCF leadership weakness was confirmed and Koenig's competent control of the situation was also noted, so there appeared to be no threat to public order from political sources. The only problems were the small groups of Resisters still wandering around the streets with guns, although sniping had long since finished. Thus the American military authorities were told that the arrival of de Gaulle and his nominees had met the situation, which was satisfactory at the end of August.

The State Department was receiving advice from several sources.

Winant, Ambassador in London, sent messages to Washington urging that they ensure the transfer of GPRF representatives to Paris without delay, because his contacts in London, and Massigli in particular, were afraid that the communists might cause confusion in the capital.[162] Bonbright (State Department, European Division) forwarded the reports of the OWI to Hull and these were even more jaundiced than those of Winant: 'The wisdom of American policy is surely confirmed by the unsettled political conditions in France.'[163] The OWI itself appeared to be confused. It said that the PCF 'controlled the opposition' which disturbed matters, but then said that the PCF did not seek power. It also thought that de Gaulle was having problems, 'negotiating with the *Secrétaires Généraux*', not realizing these men were in fact under de Gaulle's own control.

Confused or not, the overall impression of the reports was that Paris was calm, given the circumstances, and that there was a skeleton administration of the GPRF, who had just been recognized as the *de facto* government of France by the Allies. There was a strong communist presence in many areas of the city, but there had been no coup nor was there likely to be one. Indeed, the *communes* under communist control were among the better organized, and safest, in the city. The capital was short of food, but not starving, and there was no need for a greater Allied intervention than that represented by the civil affairs detachments. The major problems for the Allies seemed to be finding enough hotel rooms for all their personnel who needed to be based in Paris.

The Liberation of Paris was a vital turning point for all the parties involved. Those in the US State Deparment who had been leading the way in attempting to secure recognition for the GPRF had positive proof that de Gaulle was a popular and viable leader of the provisional government, and that there was no alternative administration which might have emerged in Paris. For the British, it was the justification of their pro-Gaullist line and, in particular, a satisfactory conclusion for the Foreign Office, who could now establish full diplomatic relations with the new regime. For both governments, it meant abandoning any lingering ideas about an AMGOT government for France. Any attempt at such an administration would lead to the civil war which they so feared might break out at Liberation, but which had not. For the Allied military, the change in plans had been most unwelcome, but with a sense of enormous relief, they could report success in the capture of a major strategic objective and the avoidance of a breakdown in civil order and public safety – their two nightmares.

De Gaulle and his group had entertained similar fears in the weeks before Liberation and, although control of the insurrection had slipped from their hands, its outcome had not been as dire as they imagined.

Indeed, in the midst of the fighting, GPRF representatives had established themselves, to be confirmed in their fragile posts by the public acclamation of de Gaulle. The representatives and de Gaulle's 'Cabinet' had stepped swiftly into the potential governmental vacuum, thus occupying the arena in which local autonomy might have flourished. As it turned out, the local Liberation committees failed to secure important posts before the uprising, and were unable to influence de Gaulle upon his arrival in Paris. They had to tackle massive problems of supply and found that their armed units were more concerned with chasing Germans, and subsequently collaborators, than they were with extending the political power of the domestic Resistance. The Liberation of territory up to this point, and the piecemeal establishment of local GPRF administrations, had served the functions of replacing Vichy and preventing the Allied military from taking sole charge of French affairs. It had certainly provided physical proof of the existence of a provisional government and given that government a certain level and area of political power. The outcome of the Liberation of Paris was symbolic and practical. The GPRF and de Gaulle had been allowed to represent themselves as the legitimate government of France, in the seat of national government, Paris. The extent to which they would be able to continue in this role would depend firstly on the attitude which the Resistance in various parts of France adopted, and secondly on the approach which the Allies took towards them.

## 6 The early days of the GPRF, September–December 1944

WITH THE Liberation of Paris, the provisional government was installed in the capital. This did not mean, however, that it was in control of the whole country. Parts of France were still under enemy occupation, and communications with areas that had been liberated were difficult in September 1944, and would remain so for several months. Out of 40,000 kilometres of railtrack only 18,000 were actually operational. The train link between Paris and Marseilles, for example, was not restored until 9 October, and telephone lines from Marseilles to other cities were not working properly until 29 September. At the first Cabinet meeting of the GPRF in Paris the Minister of the Interior admitted that: 'the government's authority was limited to Paris, the suburbs, and possibly the outer suburbs; no one knew very clearly what was happening in the departments, or what was the state of the departmental administration'.[1]

In fact the situation varied enormously from area to area, depending upon the way in which the locality had been liberated, and the strength and political complexion of the Resistance.

In Normandy, for example, Resistance had been weak and relatively insignificant. As the Allies noticed when they arrived in the region, the inhabitants seemed to have come out of the occupation reasonably prosperous. When Coulet appeared, to take over administration on behalf of the GPRF, he encountered considerable hostility, not as he had expected from determined members of the Resistance, but rather from local notables who were unrepentantly Pétainist. To begin with it was difficult to find ex-Resisters who could be appointed to responsible positions. When the committees of Liberation, formed secretly before June, emerged into the open, their members were found to be people who were largely unknown in the region and whose political views were at variance with those of the majority of the population. In the Department of La Manche, for example, there was a considerable gap between the Resistance post-Liberation, as represented by the *Comité Départemental de Libération*(CDL) at Cherbourg, and the peasant population of the department beyond the town. In this situation, the *Commissaire de la République* tended to act first as a stimulus, encouraging CDLs in the region to take office and operate, and then as a reminder to CDLs that they should take note of the views of the more conservative majority in the departments. The armed forces of the Resistance were asked by the *Commissaire* himself to take on local police-type duties.[2]

At the other end of the scale, the situation in a place like Toulouse was highly explosive. Armed Resistance groups had been active before the Liberation, and the communist FTP were an important part of the FFI in the region. The newly appointed *Commissaire de la République* claimed that rather than the city liberating itself, it was more a case of the Germans withdrawing from Toulouse and leaving the Resistance to get control as it wished. When the *Commissaire* arrived, he had received no briefing on what the situation was likely to be, largely because he was a late replacement for the man originally chosen and now thought to be dead. The number of those armed in the city was enormous, and grew even larger as the weeks went by. Relations between the GPRF nominee (a socialist sympathizer) and the Resistance were so uncertain to begin with that the *Commissaire* hesitated to leave the prefecture when he was warned that the Germans might be returning, in case this was a manoeuvre to get him out of the building so that FTP/FFI forces could take it over. With some 50,000 armed men in the Toulouse area, a spate of arrests and requisitioning took place. At one stage there were reportedly as many as 32 separate FFI secret services, each capturing and imprisoning their own suspected collaborators.[3]

Between the two extremes of Toulouse and Normandy, there was a whole range of different local situations. The parallel command structures which had been evident in French planning before the Liberation allowed space for competing centres of power to develop. The CNR with its military organization, COMAC, and its nominal control of the still ill-defined Liberation committees, stood in potential opposition to the GPRF and its locally appointed nominees. The problem, however, was not one of a national conflict: the Resistance/PCF or CNR against the government. Everything depended on the conditions and balance of power locally. As Madjarian suggests, the picture is less of 'one single and general power struggle', and more of 'a multiplicity of local conflicts'.[4]

Given the wide range of local situations and the problem with communications, the GPRF were clearly going to find it difficult to establish the control of central government throughout France. To begin with, at least, they would be dependent on the skills of the officials they had nominated, the *Commissaires de le République*, to take over the direction of the regions. These men had been given unprecedented administrative powers to enable them to fill the vacuum in authority at the Liberation. As Kramer points out, the attitude that CFLN nominees took to their job was by no means uniform. For example, Ingrand, the *Commissaire* at Clermont-Ferrand, disputed the necessity of fitting into a bureaucratic framework, designed for the *Commissaires* by Paris: 'The *Commissaires de la République* are not in my view civil servants who have to automatically agree'.[5] The GPRF, however, clearly envisaged that the *Commissaires* would behave entirely like government employees. As soon as communications with the regions were re-established, they were required to come to Paris for regular meetings, not only with their own minister, the Minister of the Interior, but also with General de Gaulle himself. Every fortnight the *Commissaires* wrote detailed situation reports, using a format carefully laid down by the ministry.[6]

In addition to this centralized framework within which the *Commissaires* were expected to work, the GPRF appointed roving *Commissaires* (*Commissaires en mission*) who were supposed to travel to particular regions, so that they could explain the importance of government policy to regional *Commissaires*, and act as a further reporting back channel in those cases where Paris became concerned that the *Commissaire* was not presenting a very faithful picture of his region. The classic example of the latter was Marseilles, where the roving *Commissaire* concluded that the local representative, Aubrac, had been sending back a series of tendentious reports to the ministry which bore no relation to the actual policies he had pursued locally, which included, to the annoyance of Paris, requisitions of industries without central government permission – 'disguised nationalizations' – unilateral imposition of a petrol tax, and an independent assessment of the banknote rate. To the supervising official concerned, all this indicated that the *Commissaire de la République* in Marseilles had stepped out of the role of a professional civil servant to assume an overtly political stance. Aubrac was duly dismissed in January 1945 and replaced by a more malleable career civil servant.[7]

The relationship which Paris wanted between *Commissaires* and central government was thus exactly the same as the traditional one of Paris/departmental prefect: the *Commissaires* should implement central government policy. Any attempt to stray outside that relationship – arranging to meet together without the permission of the Ministry of the Interior – was greeted with considerable suspicion. Even the exchange of reports between different *Commissaires* was thought to be unwise until the material had been examined and 'centralized' in Paris.[8] The job of the *Commissaires*, however it was clothed in language like, 'represent the government to the people . . . look after the permanent interests of the Nation',[9] was clearly to establish central government control in each region of France. In general, the difficulties the *Commissaires* faced in doing this were related to the presence of local armed troops (both FFI and *Milices Patriotiques*) and to the attitude and behaviour of the departmental Liberation committees. The importance of each of these factors depended very much on the particular local area concerned.

## *The* Forces Françaises de l'Intérieur *(FFI)*

AT A probably conservative estimate, the FFI represented in the autumn of 1944, a body of some 300,000 men, armed with rifles, sten guns, pistols, bren guns and bazookas.[10] They were a mixture of the different pre-Liberation forces, swelled at Liberation by a number of individuals, some inevitably with rather questionable motives, who wished to be involved in the act of Liberation.

The strength of the FFI varied considerably from region to region in France. In the Normandy area, for example, where the Allied troops were numerous, the FFI forces co-operated without apparent difficulties, and at the Liberation, generally melted back into civilian life. In Brittany the position was very different. Here, the FFI's initial role was of far greater military importance, since they contained in Brest, St Nazaire and other west coast ports, more than three German divisions. When the Allied army subsequently advanced, villages had been liberated at high speed, and the Allies disarmed local FFI brigades, only to find, a few hours later, that Germans retook the villages, with the disarmed FFI powerless to intervene.[11] This understandably resulted in the FFI refusing to be disarmed, and continuing to take an active part in the fight against the Germans. Relationships between the communist-dominated FTP and the rest of the FFI were sometimes acrimonious and further complications were created by the activities of the Breton Liberation movement which was reported to be attempting to set up a rival *maquis* group.[12] In neighbouring Departments the situation was often quite different. Thus, in the Marne, FFI forces were few in number, whilst in the Aube there were reportedly more than 3000 who, it was claimed in early September, had kitted themselves out with a stock of uniforms at Troyes belonging to the Armistice Army.[13]

In the south-west of France, on the Spanish border, two and often three different FFI groups competed for power. Reports about the supposed relationship of the Spanish troops with the French forces varied wildly. On the one hand, the prefect of the Pyrénées Orientales claimed that the communist *maquis* were preparing to enter Spain with their Spanish comrades, blessed by the French communist ex-international Brigadier, André Marty. On the other, the American consul in Barcelona reported that the FTP man in Perpignan had told him he wished to 'bring the Spaniards under control'.[14]

FFI attitudes and behaviour varied greatly, depending on the nature of local forces, and the type of external authority, if any, which they encountered. Thus, in Nancy the FFI had made contact with the Americans from the earliest moment and had worked with them in selected missions behind German lines. Local incidents between them and the newly established authorities had been smoothed over easily when the regional head of the Resistance had been made the commander of the 20th Region.[15] In general the continued presence of the American army in the region lessened the likelihood of civil unrest. In Poitiers, which remained in the war zone until the end of the war, the relationship between the *Commissaire* and General de Larminat, who commanded the local FFI troops, deteriorated steadily, worsened by the arrival of *maquis* groups from outside the region. A series of inexcusable incidents by rampaging bands, like the notorious *groupe soleil*, made the situation difficult for a long time.[16]

In some cases, particularly where an area had been liberated solely because of the efforts of the FFI, the forces took on a major, often highly political role from the outset. Thus, in the Limousin, the FTP imprisoned suspected collaborationist bosses in Limoges and then assumed control of the industries.[17] In Lyons, the FFI took over the Montluc fort, and, by the early days of September, had requisitioned a large number of buildings in the town, including at one stage the Spanish and Greek Consulates.[18]

In Lyons and Toulouse the *Commissaires* gave some official recognition to the fact that the FFI were an important feature of their regions. Farge in Lyons suggested that the FFI should be involved in social tasks, helping to solve the food distribution problems in the area: 'It's by giving them responsibility that we shall awaken their sense of discipline'.[19] In Toulouse, the *Commissaire* asked the Commander of the Lot FFI to re-establish control in the city himself, a wise move in view of the huge escalation in FFI recruitment since August 1944.[20]

If however the strength and political attitudes of FFI varied from region to region, there were some general interests which members tended to hold in common. As a SHAEF report explained:

> What their experience in Resistance has given them is a fervent desire for new men of action and new efficient institutions rather then definite constitutional and political ideas. They are impatient of military traditionalism and parliamentary procedure, and they have little respect for Third Republic parliamentarians and generals . . . .[21]

These desires centred on two particular issues: the need for a thorough purge of Vichy politicians and administrators; and the necessity of creating a 'new' French army, of which they would be the nucleus. Their experience fighting a guerilla war, their strong links with the local population and their political aspirations already marked them out from the 'normal' type of army.

To more traditional commentators, the FFI behaved in a way which was totally alien to army procedures. The *Commissaire de la République* of Limoges was appalled to find that they were publishing their own weekly newspapers: 'I am trying to control this press . . . and wonder whether its existence can be considered legal, since the Army was given no means of expressing its opinions under the Third Republic.'[22] The tendency of some FFI groups to check with their own hierarchy before executing an order, and their evident interest in matters which were considered non-military, like the purge of Vichy officials and officers, were both treated with suspicion.[23] Career army officers in particular found the FFI ethos difficult to accept. General Cochet, hearing that Resistance leaders favoured the creation of political committees in armed groups, reiterated the standard military line: 'We mustn't lose sight of the fact that the FFI are militarized and as such should be forbidden to take part in political activity, like other military groups'.[24] In this attitude he was strongly supported by de Gaulle, who regarded the 'irregular' aspect of the FFI as something to be deplored after the Liberation. When the General toured the various FFI barracks in the middle of September 1944, his preferences were evident. Units like those at Lyons which were commanded by a career officer and attempted to present themselves as regular formations drew unalloyed praise. With others he seemed more aware of the failures in training which 'proper' army officers could have ironed out, ruminating miserably on: 'What the forces of the Resistance could have been . . . had Vichy not prevented the regular officers from taking over their command'. Grades which the FFI had won in the Resistance were, as the Toulouse FFI bitterly noted, of considerably less interest to de Gaulle than the rank which men had held in the pre-war army.[25]

The conflict between members of the FFI, who expected to form the basis of a new 'popular' army, and the traditionalist GPRF plan which envisaged them integrating into the existing French army structure, had already erupted during the Liberation fighting. In the south in particular there had been arguments when career army officers from Algiers were brought in from the outside ('parachuted' in FFI parlance) to take command of operations over the heads of local FFI leaders.[26] The numbers of regular French army officers had incidentally increased dramatically at the Liberation as people who had retired to civilian life in France in 1942 donned their uniforms again – 'moth-balled' officers they were popularly called – and expected to assume their pre-war positions and ranks.

Pressure from the Allies to deal with the large number of armed personnel behind their lines had surfaced early on during the battle, with the Allied military trying on occasions to disarm the FFI themselves as soon as local fighting was over. The Commanding General of the 7th Army in the south of France was asking the French in mid-August 1944 to get the younger members of the FFI incorporated into regular territorial units.[27] At the end of August de Gaulle dissolved the FFI High Command and general staffs in Paris and all liberated departments. The idea was that FFI soldiers would now be incorporated into the national army on an individual basis, whilst their weaponry would be collected up under instructions issued by the newly appointed regional military commanders. An FFI department in the Ministry of Defence was established to begin the process.[28]

Opposition to what amounted to the swift dismantling of a separate FFI identity was immediate. On the same day that de Gaulle released his orders on the FFI, the CNR military organization, COMAC, commanded their FFI troops to continue the work of liberation until a new army structure, based on a chain of military committees, linked to the CDLs, had been created.[29] On the CNR, even a Gaullist member like Debû-Bridel argued against any move to destroy the cohesion of what seemed to be a popular army, on the model of 1793.[30] Duclos and the Central Committee of the PCF warned that the dissolution of the FFI would mean the end of hopes of reorganizing the army on popular bases.[31] Whilst the PCF was anxious that its often unruly FTP wing should now amalgamate with the rest of the FFI[32] their view was that the FTP should form an important part of a 'new' French army which would be, 'tightly linked to the French people'. They had no desire to integrate their men into the FFI only to see them swallowed up in the old-style regular army, with former Resisters commanded by those they regarded as the old officer class, which had already proved itself to be defeatist and culpable.

'On the ground', the evidence in September 1944 was that GPRF orders on the FFI were simply not being implemented in many areas. In the south in particular there was so much non-compliance that General Cochet's staff were forced to consider what measures they could take to make integration in the army more palatable. Suggestions included ensuring that the new regional command structure contained officers well-known for their Resistance records, and holding parades of the regular army with well-chosen, impressive troops.[33] In Toulouse, the President of the *Mouvement de Libération Nationale* (MLN) gave a radio broadcast in which he was bitterly critical of the army of 1939 (this just after de Gaulle's rather unfortunate meeting with the local FFI). Cochet's staff reported in mid-September 1944 that FTP units in the FFI had expressed the view that they would rather take to the *maquis* than accept 'officers imposed on them from a national army'.[34]

By the end of September the government's position was beginning to change. In decrees on 19 and 29 September COMAC was assigned a role in the making of decisions concerning the FFI. An FFI general staff would be created which would consider the appointment of ex-FFI officers to the new regional commands. It was still unclear whether officers would be retained with the FFI units they had commanded during the Liberation, but at least some concession had been made to the special identity of the FFI, although in practice this did not indicate the creation of a popular army.

The overall numbers of FFI volunteering to join the army increased spectacularly in the next few months – 40,000 in September, 60,000 in the middle of October, 137,000 in November.[35] The extent to which the integration of the FFI in the army was accepted still varied however from region to region. In Châlons-sur-Marne, the *Commissaire de la République* reported in early November 1944 that all those FFI who wished to be incorporated in the army had been accommodated and those who preferred to return to civilian life had now done so, 'there are no more isolated groups in the country or towns . . .'.[36] The *Commissaire* at Nancy indicated in mid-October that the FFI had generally submitted well in incorporation, but that elements of the FTP, some under the *Milices Patriotiques* label, were still marginal to the operation.[37] A police report for late September/early October mentioned an FTP unit in Fort de Bicêtre which refused to see itself as a unit of the regular army, claiming instead to be part of a 'popular army'.[38] In areas in the south in particular, FFI groups formed themselves into units which joined the army *en bloc*, forming virtual FFI regiments like, for example, the Schneider battalion. Such men were clearly voting with their feet – they wanted to take part in the fight against the Germans, but they were not prepared to be 'diluted' in the army of Africa.

The actual experience of incorporating was predictably difficult for both sides. From the regular Army's point of view, the FFI seemed to be richly overprovided with officers. Thus the Schneider column had 8.5 per cent officers and 20.8 per cent non-commissioned officers, when the regular army would have expected comparable figures of around 3 per cent and 13 per cent respectively.[39] In addition, for the career soldiers 'a certain number of FFI officers do not know the rules and customs of military administration, and do not have large unit command experience'.[40] As far as members of the FFI were concerned, the army could appear deliberately unwelcoming. FTP criticisms were especially severe on this score. Granville from the south reported that:

> In the general staffs, some officers showed little understanding, displaying a scarcely veiled contempt for their young colleagues. They have a tendency to forget that it is largely because of these young colleagues that they are where they are. For the soldiers there are daily difficulties of equipment, armament, food and pay.[41]

Commander Lamaison, asked how the Army of Africa had welcomed their new recruits, replied: 'Well . . . there'll be a lot written about that.

I have to say that, quite frankly, the reception they gave us was bad rather than good. There was a lot of unpleasantness about our men and about the ranks they held.'[42]

If by the end of 1944 considerable progress had been made in integrating the Resistance FFI with the former Army of Africa, the political question of what sort of army would emerge from the mixture had yet to be officially sorted out. For the FTP in the south-east, for example, the new democratic army would only be born if its former members remained a unified group: 'We'll only be strong in the general staffs if we stay together as a bloc . . . there are a whole group of officers who have no desire to understand our aspirations and wishes . . . they will have to break their teeth on the cement of our unity'.[43]

In the future, the concept of a popular army would remain on the political agenda only as long as the PCF, and to a lesser extent the socialists, were prepared to continue pressing for its establishment. But the indications at the end of 1944 were that the 'new' French Army was likely to be very little different in structure and hierarchy from the Army of before the war.

## *The* Milices Patriotiques *(MP)*

THE OTHER armed group which constituted a potential problem for the GPRF was the *Milices Patriotiques* (MP). The CNR had first discussed the idea of *Milices Patriotiques* in 1943, on the basis of a *Front National* (FN) proposal which had sought to mobilize Frenchmen in towns, villages and industries where weapons to join the FFI were not easily available. There had been initial suspicion about such a suggestion emanating from the FN, since some members of the CNR feared that the communists might want to use the militia as a secret army, in the event of the FTP merging with the rest of the FFI. The agreement which the CNR arrived at created the MP as a supplementary force to act in strikes and demonstrations during the occupation and then to assume civilian duties, like the arrest of suspected collaborators, at the Liberation. Whereas the exact status of the FFI had always been somewhat hazy, depending both on the GPRF (through the military hierarchy) and the CNR (through COMAC), the MP were clearly under the orders of the alternative Resistance institutions, the CDLs and the CNR. The FN, the trades unions and the PCF were the most enthusiastic and active supporters of the group.[44]

As with the FFI, the actual members of MP (called *Gardes Patriotiques* or *Civiques* after October 1944) varied a great deal from region to region. The most active of units by September/October 1944 were, not surprisingly, given its supporters, in urban, industrialized areas. Here, according to the CGT weekly, *La Vie Ouvrière*, they were involved in activities designed to start the purging of French society and afford some protection from fifth column attacks: seizures of goods, arrests of collaborators, defence of factories and protection of transport.[45] In the Rhône, the MP developed into armed organizations which saw themselves as keeping order and participating in police operations. The prefect tried to limit the numbers actually involved in police duties to a controllable 400, under the aegis of the regional director of police, but he was unsure in October 1944 about the extent to which the MP would accept these local restrictions on their role.[46] It was indeed evident that the functions and powers of the MP were being worked out 'on the ground' in the months following the Liberation of Paris, with different views and compromises being developed in different areas. In the Haute-Garonne/Ariège region (the 17th military region), for example, there was an argument in September 1944 between those who wished the MP to limit recruitment to a small elite group, chosen from the most respected Resistance elements, and those, like the majority of the political parties and trades unions, who favoured a far wider recruitment.[47]

Whilst the general uncertainty about the functions of the MP continued, and wide variations between actual practice were beginning to develop, the GPRF acted to take control of the situation, issuing a statement on 28 October 1944 which called for the dissolution of the MP on the grounds that the insurrectional period was now over and that their duties could be properly discharged by the government and police. This action effectively undermined the review process which the CNR was currently undertaking with the Minister of the Interior and the prefect of police.[48] The consultation process had been jettisoned in favour of government executive action. Frenay's recollection of the relevant Cabinet meeting was that the Minister of the Interior (the socialist, Tixier) had evidently cleared the matter in advance with General de Gaulle. All the non-communist ministers, with slight differences of emphasis, agreed with the dissolution. The two communist ministers, Billoux and Tillon, argued that the MP were still necessary to combat fifth column activity: 'We mustn't give the people the impression that we are afraid of them'. After listening to this, de Gaulle concluded the discussion with, in Frenay's words: ' "Republican order is based on the pre-eminence of the state. The state can only have one justice, one army, one police force, and this is why we agree with the proposals of the Minister of the Interior." In Cabinet, at least under de Gaulle, there was no voting. Silence . . . we passed on to the next item.'[49]

The GPRF had acted to dissolve the MP at a time when their major activity was policework against suspected collaborators, and, in some instances, seizure of their goods. In most regions, up to the dissolution order, there was no evidence that the MP had been more than a part-time civil order militia. Certainly they were not organized into a national formation which challenged the government for political power. On a local level, their existence, in certain areas in the south in particular, was one of the several factors which served to diffuse and disperse power, but their challenge, even in the regions in which they were strong, was generally directed towards speeding up the purge process, rather than attempting to seize power. For the GPRF the MP problem was one which the Cabinet of the Ministry of the Interior outlined in detail in the following months, in response to suggested CNR compromises: a 'duality of power', a second hierarchy which would try to set itself beside the government, owing its allegiance to the local Liberation committees, and having the armaments and weaponry to exercise executive power.[50] In such a context, the MP could be seen as dismembering the central authority of the state and dispersing it locally, at a time when the GPRF was already deeply concerned about its ability to establish its position throughout the whole nation.

The reaction to the government's banning order was stormy, particularly when detailed instructions were released on 31 October which made it clear that dissolution of the MPs was to be treated as a matter of individuals against the law: the only people now legally entitled to carry arms were the army and the police. All others must hand in their guns and weapons. The Paris Liberation Committee had already found itself divided over the issue, with some non-communist members suggesting that the government should carry on with its job of governing, and others, like Tollet, demanding that the CPL should support the CNR in its outright opposition to the banning order. There were incidentally strong objections on the Paris Liberation Committee to the way in which MP telephone lines had been cut off, and tension in the capital became so acute over the MP issue that the prefect of police felt it was necessary to put a special guard on the prison camp of Drancy, which now housed suspected collaborators, in case angry and frustrated militiamen attempted to storm it by force.[51]

The PCF led the public demonstrations of hostility against the banning order. The Political Bureau of the party spoke of the Prime Minister, 'once more . . . treating the French Resistance as a negligible quantity'. At Douai at the end of October 1944 Duclos addressed an estimated audience of some 30,000 people and castigated the dissolution of the MP as being like 'the reactionary, anti-Republican decrees of Daladier'.[52] Other demonstrations in the Vélodrome d'Hiver in Paris, and in Toulouse drew reportedly large audiences. The FTP/FN/ PCF press continued the campaign throughout the winter of 1944, using supposedly fifth column activity like the munitions train explosion at Vitry, or the attack on an FFI company near Pertuis, as indications that an organization like the MP was still very much needed.[53]

For the GPRF, there was to be a difference between issuing a banning order and ensuring that it was obeyed all over the country. The extent to which the decree was actually enforced again depended on the particular locality. Rural areas, for example in the Isère, where the MP had never been strong, generally showed a great degree of compliance. In other areas there was a massive failure to obey. In some places where the *Milices* apparently ceased carrying arms in public, the prefect was still convinced that their actual numbers were increasing rather than decreasing. Some local Liberation committees, like those in the Var for instance, actively continued to support the principle of an armed militia, even demanding that the prefect provide appropriate weaponry, in one case in December 1944, for as many as 10,000 men.[54]

In the Meurthe-et-Moselle at the end of December 1944, the compromise CNR version of the MP (the *Gardes Civiques Républicains*) were openly recruiting members, and the *Commissaire de la République* reported that they were starting talks with the FTP, designed to get their backing in a bid to persuade the departmental Liberation committee and the Nancy town council to provide the group with arms.[55] In Clermont-Ferrand, the MP demanded that they should be allowed to participate in the Armistice Day marchpast. In the Haute-Marne *Gardes Civiques* were still active in December 1944, policing PCF/FN rallies, and searching for suspected collaborators and blackmarketeers.[56]

In practice, despite the government's dissolution order, the MP continued to exist in many parts of France and to hold on to the weapons they had obtained just before or during the Liberation. It was a matter of 'fact . . . if not . . . law'. As the *Commissaire de la République* of Marseilles explained: 'You can hardly expect arms to be handed in spontaneously, and at the moment it's quite impossible to use coercion'.[57]

## The Departmental Liberation Committees (Comités Départementaux de Libération, *CDLs*)

THE OTHER major problem which the GPRF faced in re-establishing central government control was the behaviour and activity of the CDLs. Once again, this was largely conditioned by what had happened locally in the occupation and immediate Liberation period. In areas which had been directly occupied by the Germans, the CDLs often proved to be weak or virtually non-existent at Liberation. Thus Coulet reported that at Alençon the CDL had been decimated by the

Gestapo with the result that it would have to be totally reformed at Liberation. In Normandy indeed, the CDLs which did remain often appeared to be rather apathetic and when they were operational tended to reassure the newly appointed prefects by their general moderation and desire to co-operate.[58]

In the south, however, the composition of the CDLs was often hotly disputed before 1944, with conflicts becoming more acerbic as the moment of Liberation arrived. In the CDL of the Alpes-Maritimes, the original composition (one communist out of eight) in February 1944 was modified locally to include a higher communist representation (four out of ten) in June. An argument developed about the post of chairman of the CDL, originally a non-communist MUR candidate, and now disputed by the FN. After a stormy discussion on 6 June, the chairman refused to hold any further meetings before the landings, during which time he welcomed the prefect who had been nominated by Algiers, and presented non-communist representatives to him. By 15 August, the FN, CGT and PCF, taking advantage of the chairman's absence, set about forming a new enlarged CDL, including in it delegates of *Combat* (which had not accepted the chairman's authority), the prisoners' movement, and organizations associated with the FN like *Femmes de France*. This new CDL subsequently met each day after the Allied landings, considering the purge, the press, the composition of town councils, and the creation of an insurrection committee. After the fighting of 28 August, the CDL installed itself in the prefecture as the *de facto* power. The prefect, arriving soon after, took up residence in a different part of the same building. When the original chairman of the CDL arrived, the stage was set for a curious political situation; 'Which CDL do you represent – the real one or the false one ?'[59]

In some areas conditions just before the Liberation had enabled the CDL to assume a position of considerable local power. Thus in the Auvergne in early August, some regions had been virtually operating under Resistance control for weeks before the Liberation. In Mauriac, in the Cantal, each Vichy official had been given a Resistance 'double' who supervised his work and ensured that his contacts with the Germans by telephone were suitably innocuous. By the time the government-nominated prefect arrived two weeks after Liberation, the CDL had become accustomed to controlling the area and running affairs.[60] In the Allier, Montluçon was liberated a week before the arrival of the prefect. The CDL, between 26 August, when it was established in the *sous-préfecture*, and 8 September, published over 70 decrees, dealing with a wide range of social and economic matters. The chamber of commerce was suspended and its property temporarily transferred to an economic committee of the CDL. Management committees were set up in each firm employing more than 100 workers, with the CDL given the ultimate right to arbitrate in any difficult decision. In firms of 25 to 100 workers, a control committee was established which had to be consulted by the director of the firm in all matters to do with the running of the business, 'since the workers must be called on to participate in the management . . . of the firms'. Key administrative personnel from the previous regime were dismissed, and over 100 internment orders against individuals were issued. The *Commissaire de la République* made frequent visits to Montluçon after the arrival of the prefect in an attempt to mediate between him and the independent CDL, and by the end of October reported that he had declared the CDL's decrees null and void except in so far as they conformed to his own instructions.[61]

The approach of the CDLs to the exercise of power after the Liberation depended very much on the area. As Foulon suggests there were three main types of CDL in the post-Liberation period: those whose role had been restricted in the occupation, and whose members, largely moderates, were willing to obey the appointed prefect without difficulty; those who, irrespective of their role during the occupation, wanted to collaborate with the prefect and get their views heard and understood; and finally, those CDLs which had been very important before the Liberation, and which were unwilling to relinquish their previous powers.[62] Within a single region, the attitude of neighbouring CDLs could be quite different. Thus the *Commissaire de la République* at Châlons-sur-Marne noted in November that the CDL of the Aube was working well with the prefect; that of the Haute-Marne was 'more turbulent'; whilst the CDL of the Marne had not actually met for several weeks.[63] In some areas CDLs indeed seemed to lose their momentum as member organizations became involved in activities elsewhere or as prime CDL responsibilities, like the purge, were deemed to be completed. From the point of view of government officials, however, it was clear that considerable difficulties could be experienced getting CDLs to accept directives which stated that they were only consultative bodies: 'They fail to see why the plans made and discussed by them before the Liberation should not be executed by their own committees'.[64] The report of the CDL of the Garonne for September 1944 expressed some of this considerable frustration:

> With the *Commissaire de la République*, our relationship has not always been marked by the greatest cordiality . . . the CDL often has the impression that its decisions have been held back either by an exaggerated desire to keep everything legal, or through pusillanimity, or for some other reason . . . we have the feeling that the fight against the 'trusts' and the desire to have a full purge are not always pursued with the needed enthusiasm.[65]

In several instances the CDLs immediately asserted their independence by refusing to accept officials nominated by the GPRF. Thus, in the Alpes-Maritimes, the prefect who had favoured the originally constituted CDL found himself rejected by the second. Relations between the prefect and the new CDL, already tense, deteriorated further on 1 September 1944 when the prefect agreed that American troops should deal with public order problems, whilst the CDL demanded that the FFI should be called in. In the end, the *Commissaire de la République*, Aubrac, was forced to arbitrate in the issue. After an abortive attempt to get the CDL to give the prefect another chance, Aubrac agreed to replace him, clearly fearing that the situation might develop into a confrontation between American troops, supporting the prefect, and Resistance forces, supporting the CDL. The result was a notable victory for the CDL. Similar cases ocurred in the Savoie, whilst in the Jura and in Saône-et-Loire the CDL not only rejected the prefect, but designated their own chairmen as temporary replacements.[66]

Such CDLs were clearly well established locally and in a good position to take decisions and influence events. In the Alpes-Maritimes, for example, the CDL was active in a number of areas. In a particularly acute local problem, the food shortages, members of the CDL played a strong lobbying role, appealing to the Allied troops for short-term help, and having the director of the food department, who had anyway been one of their nominees, replaced by another of their members when progress seemed to be too slow. The CDL's food committee indeed maintained a constant stream of criticism about the way in which the whole problem was being tackled, and, with the agreement of the *Commissaire de la République*, sent delegations to Paris to present their grievances. The Minister of Food, Ramadier, in fact appeared before the CDL in December 1944 to hear a more detailed exposition of the issue. The CDL was also involved, both before and after the Liberation, in deciding what newspapers should be allowed to appear in the Alpes-Maritimes. Intervention in economic policy was confined to resolving immediate local problems, such as providing financial help to industries which had been badly damaged in the fighting, reorganizing the cinema industry, which had been controlled by the Italians since 1942, and trying to ensure that French and American troops vacated at least some of the region's hotels so that the important tourist industry could begin to develop once more. In more general terms, the CDL proposed the sequestration of 'trusts' in Nice and took some interest in the Nice/Côte d'Azur airport scheme.

Perhaps the most difficult job of the CDL was the organization of the purge of Vichy and collaborationist personnel. In the early days of the Liberation, the FFI had arrested an estimated 3000 people by the end of September 1944. Many summary executions had also taken place. Here the CDL exercised a controlling role early on, taking over responsibility from the FFI for assessing individual cases to see whether suspects should be dismissed from jobs, have property confiscated, or be sent for trial. The workload was very heavy. The CDL purge committee met around 119 times between September 1944 and February 1945, examining some 2550 cases.[67]

Despite the fact that some members of the Alpes-Maritimes CDL were regarded as 'red dictators', the evidence suggests that their main concerns were immediate local economic issues, and the prosecution, in some sort of good order, of the administrative and industrial purge. To this extent, even the more independent CDLs, who intended to operate with or without the agreement of the prefect, represented a challenge to central government appointees only in limited areas of competence. The threat was seldom political in the sense of attempts to take over the full reins of power, either by force or by the demonstration of mass support. As with the local armed groups, the CDLs were an additional factor, acting to disperse and diffuse power between several agencies. To the GPRF, however, the activity of some CDLs, albeit restricted to certain areas, represented an alternative power, alongside their nominees, and therefore, by definition, a challenge to their legitimacy.

It was not, however, simply a matter of possible dual responsibility between the CDL and the prefect or *Commissaire de la République*. There was, in fact, a multiplicity of committees, local and, in some cases, factory based, which had been formed before the Liberation, despite the evident hostility of the Algiers Committee, and which continued to be formed in the weeks following the Liberation. In the Ariège, the CDL had agreed to the creation of local Liberation committees between 30 July and 6 August, whilst in the Moselle in November, the prefect reported that three local committees had just been established, despite the fact that he had expressly discouraged them: 'When these committees submitted proposals to me, I told them that I could not give them any official recognition, especially as they were not mandated by the CNR or by a Departmental Committee'.[68] A letter from the Ministry of the Interior in the spring of 1945 gives some idea of the misgivings with which this proliferation of local committees was regarded officially:

> . . . no legal role has been given to the local committees which were set up and have continued to function after without precise powers . . . if the formation of these local committees becomes widespread, despite your intervention, you should consider them solely as organizations within the Resistance movement, and avoid giving official recognition to their intervention in the administration.[69]

With this widespread dispersal of power locally the GPRF found it was extremely difficult to put into practice the political plans agreed by the Consultative Assembly in Algiers before the Liberation. In particular, the section of the 21 April *ordonnance* which provided for the restoration of pre-war municipalities occasioned profound suspicion among many Resisters. To begin with, the text of the law was distributed so late in some parts of metropolitan France that alternative action had often been taken, with local Liberation committees forming their own provisional town councils. The *Commissaire de la République* of Nancy reported that the CDLs in his area would not accept the April *ordonnance*, 'fearing that . . . the Resistance movements would be suffocated by it'. The CDL of Meurthe-et-Moselle voted a unanimous motion calling for the committees of Liberation to be given a completely free hand in choosing the municipalities.[70] In the Basses-Alpes the local Liberation committee wanted the dismissal not only of collaborationist councillors but also of those who had been neutral or lukewarm towards the Resistance. In the Bouches-du-Rhône in late November 1944 the *Commissaire de la République* reported that none of the new town council chosen had been members of the pre-war body.[71] In Clermont-Ferrand, the *Commissaire de la République* claimed that the CDLs were proposing left-wing councils which were completely out of step with the true political complexion of the area, a reflection perhaps of the general over-representation of townspeople, as opposed to peasants, on the CDLs.[72]

The Minister of the Interior could do little more than note the fact that the April *ordonnance* was scarcely more than a theoretical document in many parts of France. A circular issued on 7 September indicated that the *ordonnance* could not be applied in every respect at this time, 'unless law and order were to be gravely compromised'.[73] The situation in local government was clearly one of considerable confusion. In one department, Bouches-du-Rhône, for example, the prefect reported that in some areas provisional councils had been set up which were being totally disregarded. In others, there were two rival councils. In certain places, the mayors and councillors from the pre-war elections were demanding to be reinstated in the new councils.[74] The rate at which town councils were re-established was, understandably given the conflicts involved, often slow. By the middle of December five were still unconstituted in the Alpes-Maritimes, 14 in the Var, four in the Basses-Alpes and six in the Bouches-du-Rhône where the prefect reported that he could not get the CDL to give him the remaining nominations.[75] The number of 'special delegations', as opposed to reconstituted municipal councils, varied considerably from region to region, being, as Foulon points out, much higher in the former southern zone where the CDLs were particularly strong: in January 1945 for example, there were 27 delegations out of 343 *communes* in the Marne, compared with 258 out of 325 *communes* in the Tarn.[76] Once town councils had been named, the network of Liberation committees did not automatically fade away. In the Bouches-du-Rhône, the CDL expressly demanded that local Liberation committees should continue to exist independently, alongside the reconstituted councils. In some areas, the CDLs insisted that Liberation committees represented the true will of the people until actual elections were held.[77]

The picture in many areas was thus one of chaos, with a variety of different bodies and institutions claiming authority for themselves. The position could change dramatically from one part of France to another. What was certain was that the confusion of the Liberation had led to a situation where considerable freedom of manoeuvre existed for local initiative. The GPRF was unable to re-establish its control quickly in large areas of the country, and on some particular issues (the *Milices Patriotiques*, and the establishment of town councils) its decrees were often deliberately flouted. Localist activity did not threaten a national revolution, or even a radical seizure of power at the regional level, but it did create a pattern where power was highly dispersed, and where the central control of the government in Paris was more notional than real in many areas. The big unknown was in the extent to which the Allies, facing the reality 'on the ground' as their troops progressed through France, would find the situation threatening and judge that its potential strategic and political consequences were unacceptable.

## Allied views of the situation

FACED WITH these variations, the Allied military adopted simple criteria of assessment. Was the position in this or that area 'under control'? Was there a potential threat of armed activity which might affect the Army, by diverting their attention from the battle with the enemy, or by jeopardizing lines of communication? In this light, Allied reports were generally reassuring. Although there was no question of the GPRF in Paris having established its control all over France, there was equally no evidence of a concerted national attempt by any group – like, for example, the PCF – to seize power. Power was evidently dispersed, with regional centres still operating in a virtually autonomous way, but the army observers spotted relatively few cases where this regional control seemed to be either politically or socially revolutionary. On the whole they described it as practical and effective administration, and remained indifferent as to whether the good order and stability was a product of FTP, communist or GPRF initiative.

In August and September 1944, despatches were full of admiration for the way in which local French administration was coping: 'Resistance much better disciplined in most areas than anticipated and rendering considerable assistance'.[78] The problems Civil Affairs faced were relatively minor and routine: looting by civilian and military personnel, out of hours buying of alcohol, merchant seamen and fishermen plying their trade without necessary documentation. When difficulties were caused by the Resistance, they seemed largely to be provoked by attempts to track down alleged traitors and pursue personal vengeance: 'rowdier elements of the Resistance movement who go as far as they can in their campaign against collaborators'.[79] In the north, the First Canadian Army reported that the FFI and *maquis* were maintaining excellent discipline, and in the south officers noted that the FFI were proving invaluable in such uncontroversial administrative tasks as traffic control. Overall, the impression was most favourable: 'The patient and realistic underground preparations of the French to assume civil administrative control upon their Liberation have produced increasingly impressive results.'[80] Even in areas like Marseilles where it was evident that those in control were not the officials of the GPRF, Civil Affairs commented that the attitude and effectiveness of the French were 'commendable'.[81]

There were, however, in August and September 1944, indications of future problems which the Allied military would have to watch. On occasions these proved to be false alarms. In Rouen for example the French authorities themselves asked the Allied forces to disarm the Resistance as soon as the town was liberated because, 'The Resistance movement contained a lot of rowdy elements who had not been genuine members . . . there might be trouble in the town if the Allied forces did not assist.'[82] In the event, the expected disorder did not materialize. Similarly, when civil affairs officers visited what they had been told was a hotbed of communist activity, Halluin, they found everything calm and apparently under control.[83] Other areas were clearly more genuinely troubled – in Douai and in Brittany there were reports of disorder, and of continuing tension between FFI and FTP troops. The First US Army claimed in early September that there was considerable public apprehension about the consequences of a withdrawal of American forces, which might leave the way open to *putsches* by 'FFI and comparable organizations'.[84] By November 1944 reports were coming in from the northern coastal areas and the Brest peninsula that the government seemed unable to control FFI and FTP factions. Observers registered greater communist activity in the north, and felt the conflict between the 'propertied' and the 'property-less' had become more obvious.[85]

The greatest concern was for the capital and for particular trouble spots in the south. SHAEF officers' first War Department summary of the political situation drew particular attention to Paris. Information from 'Com.Z' suggested that Paris was 'preparing for a large-scale communist revolution, and there is some indication that large stocks of small arms, automatic weapons and ammunition have gone underground.'[86]

Eighteen out of the 20 *arrondissements*, it was said, were headed by communist mayors who had surrounded themselves with quasi-private armies, which the French police were powerless to control without firm help from the national authorities. This apparently 'one-off' report was echoed in a slightly different form in a SHAEF counter intelligence summary, where the head of the *Service de la Surveillance du Territoire* told informants that although law and order was better in Paris than expected, there was still cause for concern in the number of weapons hidden (especially by the communists at Chateaudun), and in the continued existence of an irregular *deuxième bureau* (secret service) of the FFI.[87] A 'final report' from the headquarters of the public safety section of the first European Civil Affairs Regiment in late October 1944 described the situation as 'alarming', detailing accounts of wildcat arrests, and tortures by FFI groups:

> the regime is rapidly becoming a terrorist one, and the general opinion on all sides, is that a state of civil war may break out at any moment . . . There is no doubt that the Paris police are an excellent body of men . . . but it is doubtful if even they could control affairs . . . without the backing of the Allied Military to assist.

The version of this report submitted to the SAC in fact put the case even more bluntly:

> The French Military Authority has promised on several occasions to deal with the matter but conditions remain unchanged and the situation is becoming serious, and there has grown up an organised attempt to seize power by force of arms.[88]

A similar concern about the possibilities of an explosive situation in the south led the military command to demand that SHAEF should furnish them with specific information in October 1944: 'Further details on situation in south-west France urgently desired here, particularly steps which French are taking to solve problem, details on raids into Spain, precise areas and towns controlled by communists, names of their leaders. Information also desired on situation in Toulouse, Marseilles, Limoges and Tours where disorders have been reported.'[89]

SHAEF G2 had already become anxious about what was happening in the south-west of France where a large contingent of ex-Republican Spanish *maquis* soldiers – SHAEF estimates of the size varied dramatically, from 200 to 200,000, settling at around 20,000 – was marshalling dangerously close to the Spanish border. In general SHAEF noted that the influence of the communist FTP and of the PCF itself was strong in many southern towns. In Marseilles, the campaign for nationalizations had assumed a concrete form, and in the Nice/Cannes area the prefect was apparently finding it very difficult to control the FTP who were arresting a large number of people (put at 1,000 in early September) and had allegedly executed some 100 suspected collaborators by this time.[90]

In order to find out exactly how serious the political situation in these areas was, OSS agents Hughes, Rockefeller and Brinton were sent on tours of duty to the south, supplementing the findings of SOE agents like Freddie Ayer. Their reports were uniformly lukewarm on the validity of the 'red menace' theory. The evidence of a plot to seize power by the PCF was very thin. Neither their tactics locally nor the perceived national state of the party indicated that revolution was a near possibility. Major Hughes of OSS pointed out in September, for example, that the communists in the Alpes-Maritimes, who had caused SHAEF officers some anxiety, were not advocating class war or violent change, and that there could well be advantages:

> for public order in a situation where the extreme Left, which might have adopted a position of systematic opposition, has now been called on to assume the responsi-bilities of office, and hence must either silence or satisfy the discontent and criticism which every departmental administration must face.[91]

Whilst OSS officers noted signs of PCF activity, and signalled apparently 'extreme' decisions taken by certain CDLs, they were at pains to stress that PCF economic policies were either vague and moderate, or else distinctly non-revolutionary. The tactic of the PCF seemed to be evolving:

> Their first effort was to win mass membership for '*parti des fusillés*'. They have now shifted to an attempt to assume leadership of Resistance outside of the Communist Party by avoiding controversial issues and taking the initiative in pressing the Government for action on current popular grievances . . . almost exclusive concern with day-to-day issues.[92]

OSS agent David Rockefeller made the point that the communists appeared split in December between the main group directed from Paris, peaceful, co-operative and legalistic, and the other, mainly FTP faction, which was far more revolutionary. Information he had gleaned from government officials implied that the PCF would, if anything, wait for a post-war crisis to try and seize power, and that the party was divided between those who wanted French leadership of the PCF, those who sought guidance from Moscow, and those anarchistically inclined who took little note of central directives.[93]

SOE agents echoed this view of a party which was encountering considerable difficulties in establishing its monolithic pre-war identity: thus, when wondering how far local communists were centrally directed: 'On the whole the evidence points to the existence of a controlled police working under the same difficulties of communication as that of the Provisional Government.'[94] Similarly, they noted that the behaviour of the FTP depended largely upon the particular region in which it found itself, arbitrary when in oppositon, moderate when, as in Limoges and Toulouse, it was in control. To Ayer, and his colleagues, FTP conduct that they witnessed seemed so haphazard that it was difficult to regard it as centrally directed. If there was indeed a political tactic, they submitted, it was an especially poor one, since the trouble thus far stirred up was insufficient to bring down the government or produce a *coup*, but enough to alienate public opinion which might have been otherwise well disposed towards the PCF.[95]

OSS and SOE reports identified the trouble spots to which civil affairs officers had alluded but were generally optimistic in their prognosis. Thus Crane Brinton, putting to the test the 'wildest rumours' he had heard in Paris about the situation in the south in October, concluded that they were totally without foundation.[96] Rockefeller similarly reported in November that: 'At the present time the situation in Toulouse Region is calm and well-ordered although there is much Communist agitation. It is doubtful whether conditions were ever as critical as reports outside lead one to believe.'[97] In the same month he filed a report on the Lyons region, taking much the same moderate tone:

> It cannot be said that the authority of de Gaulle's Government is as yet complete everywhere in the Lyons region, but it is believed that the authority of the Regional Commissioner is growing constantly and there are no factors in the situation which, in the opinion of this officer, are capable of creating disturbances which might interfere with military operations or military supply.[98]

In the Lille area, OSS reported that there could well be trouble if the economic paralysis continued into the winter, but that even the middle class recognized that the gains the PCF had been making were the result of economic hardship rather than revolutionary sentiment.[99] SOE observers, commenting on the position in south-west France in October, agreed that the FTP in the area were undoubtedly storing arms, but since an armed *putsch* would not succeed and was highly unlikely, they thought it probable that the FTP were collecting weapons for use later in Spain. They stressed incidentally that other Resistance groups (ORA and Gaullist) were equally diligent in storing arms.[100] The conclusion on the situation in the south-west, which had exercised SHAEF minds throughout October and November, was noticeably positive: '. . . what is remarkable is not that there has been so much disorder in the south-west, but that it has been of such relatively slender consequence'.[101]

As the autumn and winter of 1944 advanced, the Allies were clearly concerned that central government had not established its control throughout the country. They were, however, generally sure that there was no immediate danger of a left-wing *putsch*. The problem was rather one of local disorder which manifested itself chiefly in illegal acts of vengeance on suspected collaborators, with armed groups often going so far as to break into prisons and lynch those whose trials they considered had been delayed for too long. The shortages of food and fuel were clearly exacerbating tensions and provoking, by December 1944, demonstrations and noisy demands for action. Allied observers on the ground were increasingly inclined to attribute trouble when it arose to these social and economic causes, accepting that local circumstances created specific local problems. Unrest in Brittany in December 1944 was felt to be the product of the enormous influx of refugees from other areas. The violent protests in Poitiers had been provoked by the appointment of a new 'outside' general to replace the colonel who had been in post since 'D' Day.[102]

The continued dispersal of power and the presence of a large number of weapons in the hands of people whose intentions were unpredictable were causes of concern. The potential for large-scale unrest still existed. Towards the end of December, Rockefeller identified four sources of possible future trouble in France: a lack of food and material; a conflict between the Army and the FFI; enemy agents and agitators, and finally, large stores of hidden arms under the control of the PCF, whose loyalty to the government could not be totally trusted.[103] The Allies would have to keep a watching brief and see how the situation developed.

## French–Allied relations

ALTHOUGH there was considerable confusion in many areas, it was evident that French indigenous authorities, albeit different ones in different places, had obtained control of civil affairs with remarkably little difficulty. By mid-September 1944 the US Office of War Information noted the fact that AMGOT had been definitively jettisoned: 'Under the policy laid down by SHAEF, military government has not been set up in liberated France, control of civil administration remaining with the local authorities.'[104] The job of Allied Civil Affairs now became one of 'assisting local authorities to maintain law and order and re-establish community services'. The change of tone since the AMGOT days of 1943 was visible in 7th US Army reports from southern France at the beginning of September:

> There is some confusion over the role of the American army in connection with the French government here, with some people wondering whether we eventually intend to establish an AMGOT. Plans to counteract any such impression by publicizing Army Civil Affairs policies are under way.[105]

By the end of September SHAEF G5 felt that the French were operating so well that it would be possible to withdraw the majority of civil affairs detachments, retaining them only at regional level.[106]

If, however, the Allied military were willing to respect the efficiency of French local administration, this did not necessarily imply that all of them regarded the Gaullist regime as the natural national government of France. The *Commissaire de la République* at Nancy was told by the first American General whom he saw: 'You are by no means obliged to follow General de Gaulle. If you think that another Government would be better, we're all ready to consider the matter'.[107] For this reason, French central government officials begged regional representatives to approach the question of dealing with Allied authorities with some care. Thus Laroque in the north warned the *Commissaire de la République* of Rennes that direct dealings with Allied soldiers at a local level might result in junior officials giving in to the Allies and ceding far too much, 'as a result of habits acquired during the German occupation'.[108] Cochet in the south was equally concerned at civil affairs officers visiting prefects without prior clearance or unaccompanied by a French administrative Liaison Officer, although it should be noted that the civilian French authority in the south, Aubrac, was himself complaining to Cochet at this time about the activities of French Liaison Officers, who were overstepping their purely military responsibilities.[109]

Reports of unacceptable Allied activity continued to reach French central authorities. In Caen for example it was claimed that the British had searched the PCF headquarters. Teams of British and American personnel were said to have conducted detailed inquiries on every aspect of French economic and industrial life. On occasions, the French and the Allies could be equally embarrassed by incidents. The presence of Allied officers who had led local Resistance groups during the pre-Liberation days, and then stayed on in the areas, operating like 'feudal lords', was something neither side greatly appreciated.[110]

On a local level, the wild enthusiasm which had generally greeted the arrival of Allied troops was inevitably replaced by a more wary coexistence as the problems of living together became evident. The First Canadian Army reports noted that there was a tendency on the part of the French population in September 1944 to feel that the war was now over as far as they were concerned.[111] Disillusionment set in when it was realized that Liberation meant neither the end of the war, nor the beginning of markedly improved economic conditions, and some of this disappointment was laid at the door of the Allies, to feed the complaints which were bound to arrive as a large foreign army wintered in a country: excessively generous treatment by the American army of German prisoners, requisitioning, an apparent tendency to behave in Lorraine as if already in German territory, and so on.[112] Some of the problems were cultural. Foulon, for example, describes the case of an American general congratulating the French on the good advertising skill shown in naming villages in the Rhône Valley after well-known wines![113] Others sprang from the tensions produced by having large numbers of armed troops, Allied and French, in the same areas.

As far as general behaviour was concerned, the *Commissaire de la République* in Nancy claimed, in November 1944, that relations with the Allied troops were good at the top, but considerably worse lower down. Compared with 1918, he felt the soldiers were more undisciplined, and cited cases of drunken behaviour, and damage of industrial premises occupied by troops.[114] This report was echoed by other sources, although a familiar refrain was that black troops were the ones largely responsible for incidents. The prefect of the Var indeed suggested that there could well be a link between mutinous behaviour by French Sengalese troops in Toulon and Hyères, and the influence of black American soldiers.[115] Clearly, as Rockefeller pointed out, there was some local resentment towards black American troops, and especially black military policemen.[116] Whatever the truth of the various incidents, French police reports suggested that, by the latter part of November 1944, the popularity of the Americans was waning in relation to that of the British, towards whom they claimed, the people had been initially rather reserved: 'The French feel a great deal closer to the British than they do to the Americans.'[117] If the Foreign Office treated the news of diminishing American popularity with some smugness, it should be said that public sympathy at the end of 1944 was probably related to the actual numbers of each nation's troops currently in France, hence perhaps the even greater warmth reportedly felt by the French for the USSR.[118]

On a governmental level, relations between the GPRF and the Allies were essentially ambivalent. The GPRF would acquire credibility as an independent government in the eyes of its Allies if it was shown to be able to produce the much-valued law and order in the country. To do this, however, it was at least partly dependent upon those same Allies for the wherewithal to keep order – weapons and armaments – and for the undoubted boost to its morale which diplomatic recognition would provide domestically. The result was that the GPRF trod a delicate path between requesting support from the Allied agencies, and declaring that all was under control without their assistance. On the one hand, GPRF officials told their Allied counterparts that peace was being obtained without outside foreign intervention. On the other, they insinuated that such a state of affairs might be only temporary, since the menace of communism and chaos could rear its head in the event of the GPRF failing to secure adequate backing and recognition in the diplomatic sphere.

At moments of possible internal tension French officials assured Allied representatives that there was no threat of general disorder. Thus, for example, Koenig informed the British Embassy military attaché that rumours of clashes between *Milices Patriotiques* and the police, after the government's dissolution announcement, had been greatly exaggerated.[119] Luizet, the prefect of the Paris police, had a long conversation in October 1944 with a British Embassy official about the latter's worries on the likelihood of a communist *coup* in the city. He agreed that the communist presence in the town halls of the capital was indeed formidable, but pointed out that: 'many of these mayors were good conscientious officials, were not Communists by conviction and relied for their support in the main on the less vocal Resistance elements, which were moderate in tendency.' The existing large armaments caches were a potential danger which the government could not immediately tackle, since any measures to eliminate mayors and seize arms would produce a reaction on the part of the PCF and might indeed result in greater general support for the party. He counselled going slow and waiting for the municipal elections rather than attempting at this stage to replace mayors:

> In the opinion of M. Luizet a Communist *putsch* was extremely improbable, as such action in war time would alienate much of the support which Communists at present draw from less extreme elements and could hardly meet with approval of the Soviet Government who could not be expected to favour civil war in France with Germany still unbeaten.[120]

Other GPRF representatives tended to give a slightly more nuanced picture of the situation, designed to elicit diplomatic support for the new French regime. Massigli, on his first visit to Eden as French ambassador, told him that:

> The Communists were co-operating for the present and the FFI would . . . gradually be assimilated. All the same, there was no escaping the fact that the only alternative to the present Administration, if it were unable to carry on, was one of the extreme left dominated by the Communists.[121]

Bidault, a few hours after assuming the post of Foreign Minister, told a visitor from the British Embassy that: 'unless we recognized the Provisional Government as such, chaos would ensue particularly from Communist quarters. Recognition would give stability and confidence to the Government.'[122]

In a sense, the GPRF was able to use the same sort of procedure, in reverse, to apply covert pressure on Frenchmen who felt inclined to challenge the new government's authority. The Minister of the Interior, writing to his *Commissaires de la République* about the need to control the maverick CDLs, suggested that they should draw attention to:

> the grave responsibility they will have in damaging the authority of the French Government . . . at the precise moment when it is in delicate and important negotiations with the Allies, designed to obtain respect for the independence of

France, and to enable the country to participate in the European Commission which will decide the terms of the armistice with Germany.[123]

Regional officials were certainly aware of the premium the Allied military were placing on the law and order question locally, and SOE observers noted that French civil administration tended to be fully supported by the FFI in those places where there was a large contingent of Allied troops, and where the population were therefore more aware of the lurking possibility of an AMGOT. Certainly after the British intervention in Belguim, French public opinion was said to be alerted to the dangers of allowing a situation to develop which would tempt similar action in France: 'The public has been very struck by the political situation in Belgium and hopes that the French Government will ensure that Republican legality is respected over the length and breadth of the country, without the intervention of foreign forces, even if they are Allied.'[124]

Despite the generally sanguine reports on the political situation in France in the autumn and winter of 1944, it was evident that the Allied military were still worried enough about particular pockets of unrest to consider possible contingency plans. G3 notes for a SHAEF Mission (France) conference on the subject of internal security in October 1944 indicated that:

> General de Gaulle has written to the Supreme Commander, through the Mission, stating the necessity for employing one French division in the hiatus area of Bordeaux, and one division in the Paris area.[125]

In its second draft report on the south-west hiatus area, G3 had alluded in detail to the worrying situation caused by the three problems of communist elements out of control in such areas as Toulouse and Limoges, the presence of large numbers of Spanish (communist) Republicans on the frontier, and the still apparently irreducible German redoubts on the coast. As the draft report pointed out:

> A comparatively stable political situation in France will be of the greatest importance to us when engaged in Germany either under *Overlord* or *Talisman*. We should not have to look over our shoulders, our lines of communication would be more secure, and less French troops would have to be permanently diverted to internal security. It is clear therefore that so far as it does not detract from the main offensive, the situation in South-West France should be cleared up before it deteriorates further.[126]

The draft recommendation for dealing with the situation was that the French should send garrison units to south-west France as soon as possible. In the longer term it might be possible to divert a French corps or French divisions to the region. The fear on the part of SHAEF that they might imminently have to deal with a 'conflagration in our rear', threatening lines of communication and, hence, the future conduct of the war, was a repeated theme: 'The threat is of sufficient magnitude to warrant energetic measures to remove it while there is yet time to do so, before mob law has an opportunity of establishing itself.'[127]

SHAEF's preferred method of dealing with the security situation in October and November was evidently via the French authorities, diverting French troops, trying to provide adequate armaments for the largely under-resourced French police, and ensuring that continued Allied arms' drops to *maquis* units, were, at the request of the French government, discontinued.[128] French government applications for weaponry and uniforms for their army were treated with sympathy even if demands were not always met. Koenig had emphasized to Eisenhower's staff the potential problems created by the huge number of armed and unarmed FFI operating in France in September 1944. To avert the difficulties it would be necessary to absorb as many as possible into the French Army, but there was a severe shortage of uniforms and equipment. A month later de Lattre reported that some 52,000 ex-FFI men had been absorbed into the Army, but were in desperate need of uniforms and clothing. 6th Army Group were fully prepared to support de Lattre's request, given the: 'political complications involved in allowing these 52,000 men to return to their homes where their presence may result in public disturbance in our rear areas'.[129] The hope was that the French government, if supported by Allied equipment, would be able to deal with the problem themselves, either by absorbing potential miscreants into the Army, or else by sending their own forces, released by SHAEF for this purpose, to particular trouble spots like south-west France in order to 'show the flag'.

The 21st Army Group prepared, however, during the early days of November 1944, to supply more direct 'help' to the French should the occasion arise. The historical survey for the 21st Army Group noted that: 'Civil Affairs at the level of this HQ and in France and Belgium in particular began to adopt a watching attitude towards the functions of National and Local government, than one of active participation.'[130] On 2 November 1944 the Group was considering ways in which the French authorities could be positively assisted in dealing with possible civil disturbances in the Line of Communications Zone, especially the Lille–Tourcoing area. In terms of the procedure to be used to set any such operation in motion, it was suggested that the same method applied in Belgium should be relied upon, 'so that there will be no delay in giving assistance to the civil authorities in an emergency'. A directive on internal security was accordingly issued, the object of the exercise: to intervene only, where possible, with the agreement of the

French civil authority. The draft instructions to officers employed in this task stressed that the action was to be concentrated on the defence of precise installations, damage to which might conceivably interfere with the Allied military war effort. A minimum of force should be used, and: 'When possible, you will endeavour, through a civil affairs officer if available, to persuade any mob to disperse without the use of force'.[131] The American and British political officers at SHAEF, it should be noted, were somewhat cynical about the likely usefulness of such a directive, regarding it as:

> doubtful whether the French Government will be either prepared or able to make forecasts about internal security problems, and even more doubtful whether they would be willing to communicate such forecasts to the SHAEF Mission, except in the case of grave emergency.

They counselled instead relying on the reports of the British and American Ambassadors in order to predict when a 'grave emergency' might arise.[132]

Neither diplomat was, however, inclined to suggest to his government that the time had come for Allied troops to intervene. The American Embassy on the one hand faithfully reported the strength and potential danger as they saw it of the PCF:

> The communists are in the minority, but . . . they are well organized; they are also aggressive and militant . . . If the Communists were to win the fight, the danger would arise that the entire continent of Europe might fall into the Russian orbit.[133]

Their despatches on the general situation of France were, however, almost entirely calming. Caffery, the Ambassador, informed the Secretary of State in early November that, 'The Government is extending its authority day by day and order and control are being established in more and more regions'.[134] A *'tour d'horizon'* enclosed by Chapin pointed out that the GPRF had indeed settled down, that the strength of the PCF had been exaggerated, and that generally, all was going well.[135] Chapin incidentally had already reported on an earlier PCF demonstration at the Père-Lachaise cemetery stressing that there seemed to be a 'new style' of communism in France: no clenched fists, no wild chanting and singing, emphasis on co-operation with the government and national recovery after the sacrifices of war.[136] John Boyd, from the American Consulate in Marseilles, described the allegedly troubled areas of southern France as 'calm and well-ordered', with the FFI and the FTP in the Montpellier area, 'now well disciplined'. There had been food riots in Perpignan, Béziers and Montpellier in November, but the 'French authorities consider the incidents of minor importance'.[137] Caffery, summing up the situation for the Secretary of State in December, claimed, 'As contrasted to the tense political situation obtaining in certain liberated countries such as Italy,

Greece and particularly Belgium . . . there has been a noticeable *détente* in the political atmosphere in Paris during the last two weeks'.[138]

The British Embassy was, if anything, even more inclined to underplay reports of disorder in the autumn of Liberation. Thus Duff Cooper, the Ambassador, claimed in mid-October that 'the existing lawlessness in the south is of a temporary character and much exaggerated'.[139] In his view, rumours of disorder were part of the 'revolution bogey' designed to discredit the new regime: 'Such excesses as may have been committed by young armed guerilla bands constitute little more than a natural phenomenon after an abnormal period of foreign occupation.'[140] In view of the prevailing analysis, it was not surprising that the Embassy was highly suspicious of suggestions that the Allies might be drawn to intervene directly in the affairs of France. Duff Cooper, reviewing *Combat's* treatment of events in Belgium, Italy and Poland, commented that an appeal by the French authorities to the Allies was firstly inconceivable, and secondly would fail.[141] In this context, the Ambassador was clearly concerned at the role and activities of SHAEF. News, for example, that CCOS had asked SHAEF G2 for political information indicated an 'extremely dangerous tendency . . . for CCOS to encourage SHAEF to undertake purely political activities. Heaven knows they need no encouragement.'[142] It was imperative for the SAC to have sure political guidance, and he mourned the absence of Harold Macmillan, or someone of comparable standing, who could help SHAEF, 'to deal with the political and administrative problems that are likely to arrive in the near future'.[143]

The Paris Embassy's despatches accorded well with the underlying Foreign Office view. Whilst reports of Russian or PCF activity in France were assiduously examined,[144] the general tenor of Foreign Office comments leaned towards calm and moderation. The purges and the rumours of nationalization measures were alike treated impassively. Harvey warned that the British government should not seek to intervene: 'one of the chief advantages of General de Gaulle would be that his regime would be sufficiently authoritarian in this transitional phase to carry out necessary executions.'[145] Even where Frenchmen representing British interests had been arrested in the course of the *épuration*, FO spokesmen felt intervention was wrong, and the Embassy indeed suggested that if any people who had administered British banks were suspected of collaboration, they should be removed directly. In general, French nationalization measures in this period – the requisitioning of Renault, and the beginning of state control of the northern coalmines – were not seen as threatening, although it was noted that British interests might well be affected by the nationalization of insurance companies, and some commentators signalled the possibility of repercussions on British public opinion of a successful programme of state control in France.[146] Harvey pointed out to the Ministry of Labour the importance of appointing a good labour attaché at the Paris Embassy: 'The French Labour and Trades Union situation will be very complicated and extraordinarily interesting to us in the months and years following the war . . .'.[147]

In the more immediate term, the Foreign Office continued their campaign for the recognition of the French administration. Telegrams and despatches which indicated concern at the public order situation in France were often, by tacit agreement, not shown to possibly hostile readers outside the Foreign Office, 'especially not to the War Office',[148] whilst positive reports, stressing the need to recognize, flowed in.

The Foreign Office position, not unexpectedly, was strong support for the GPRF. In a long memo in late June, Eden had argued that recognition of the GPRF would lessen the risk of 'civil war in France', drafted originally by Mack as, 'other groups raising their ugly heads'.[149] In the Foreign Office view, other Resistance groups and institutions, although possibly praiseworthy, should begin to disappear so that the 'legitimate' government could be strengthened. When the Foreign Office considered whether it was advisable to allow members of the CNR to visit London, they noted that the Resistance contained, 'nearly all the best elements in the new France', but doubted whether it was wise to give any kind of official recognition to bodies like the CNR which were seeking:

> to entrench themselves as rival governmental and administrative authorities to the Government and its ordinary administrative machine . . . While there is no doubt that the CNR and the Committees of Liberation, etc.,will continue to exist for some time to come, we think that the true interest of France is that they should gradually fade out and that the leading men of the Resistance should take their place in normal democratic institutions.[150]

The situation in which both the Foreign Office and the State Department urged recognition, and the two principals dragged their heels, was briefly repeated at this eleventh hour. The American Embassy in Paris had been filing a stream of despatches suggesting that recognition of the GPRF would be the most sensible course of action. Chapin pointed out that, from the American standpoint, recognition would dispose of the story that the American Government was encouraging neo-collaborationist elements. It would help France to improve the law and order situation. According to Chapin, the GPRF had given ample proofs by the middle of September of its democratic and republican credentials. De Gaulle was clearly accepted everywhere, his government was popular, was maintaining law and order, and had shown itself to be restrained in the treatment of collaborators. In addition, Chapin claimed, Eisenhower himself supported a policy of recognition.[151] Bonbright followed this up with a memo of his own to the President, indicating his view that the time was now ripe to recognize the French government. Matthews continued the assault, begging Hull to take a copy of his note to the President that very morning.[152]

As before, the President urged caution, and the Prime Minister procrastinated. Roosevelt told Hull on 22 September that: 'I still think . . . it is premature to recognize the French Government. We should remember that there are still several hundred thousand Germans in France'. Hull anxiously sought from the Paris Embassy evidence, presumably to help convince the President, that de Gaulle was broadening the base of his popular support.[153]

The Prime Minister meanwhile was still trying to moderate Foreign Office enthusiasm for recognition: 'Why cannot you leave it alone for a while and let things develop?' he wired waspishly to Eden.[154] The Foreign Office waited in some frustration: 'What are we waiting for ? . . . The President and Mr Hull are last-ditchers of the true blue brand.'[155]

Pressure was, however, building up outside the Foreign Office for recognition of the GPRF. On 28 September, Churchill announced to the House of Commons that recognition was being given to the Italian government. As far as France was concerned, the Allies were:

> most anxious to see emerge an entity which can truly be said to speak in the name of the people of France . . . As an interim stage, the Legislative Assembly would be transformed into an elected body, reinforced by the addition of new elements drawn from inside France . . . Such a step, once taken, . . . would greatly strengthen the position of France and would render possible . . . recognition of the Provisional Government of France . . .[156]

The reaction of MPs was lukewarm, and Eden was forced the next day in the House of Commons, answering a Harold Nicolson question, to provide a clarification of the Prime Minister's words, suggesting that Churchill had been referring to the setting up of a reorganized consultative body rather than the holding of elections which, as everyone knew, was likely to be a long process, dependent on the return of prisoners of war.[157] Further parliamentary questions on recognition from Bartlett, Shinwell and Cocks were tabled a few days later.[158] In a sense, the evolving Churchill/Eden condition was a compromise between the hard-line Roosevelt, 'no recognition without free elections' policy and the softer Foreign Office 'recognize as soon as possible' line. The State Department, it appeared, favoured a different sort of condition – recognition when an Interior Zone was declared in France.

It was evident that Churchill could no longer deny the concern which existed in British government circles, and within public opinion at the Allied failure to recognize the GPRF. On 14 October the Prime Minister telegraphed to the President his view that the situation had moved to such a point that some decision had to be made on recognizing the provisional government of France.[159] He suggested that either the enlarged assembly formula or the declaration of an Interior Zone would be suitable pegs on which to hang recognition. The President's reply indicated that he would be unwilling to recognize the GPRF until a 'real' Zone of the Interior had been set up, and that enlargement of the Assembly was also an important factor: 'hang recognition on the effective completion of both these acts.' Cadogan at least was encouraged by this telegram to hope that Roosevelt was on the point of changing his mind. The State Department, including Hull, was now solidly for recognition. The President's last ally, Leahy, had also apparently changed his mind.[160] The President was thus completely isolated and faced with an American public opinion which saw few reasons for the delay, a factor which doubtless weighed heavily with Roosevelt as the presidential elections drew near.

The message from the military on the ground was that the time was now ripe for power to pass officially to the GPRF in France, with the declaration of an Interior Zone. This had not been a decision rapidly arrived at. Once a Zone of the Interior was designated, the responsibility for assuring law and order in the area would pass from the military, SHAEF, to the GPRF. Neither the Allied military nor de Gaulle had been keen to have such a declaration immediately after the Liberation of Paris. In early September 1944 indeed de Gaulle had specifically informed the Supreme Commander that he did not want a Zone of the Interior agreed in the immediate future: 'It is apparent that de Gaulle wants [a] legal state of siege until he can reform his administration without undue interference from [the] Algiers Committee'.[161] The Foreign Office commented that de Gaulle presumably 'feared that the wilder elements of the FFI might get out of hand'.[162] In the event, however, de Gaulle asked for the creation of a Zone of the Interior at the beginning of October. According to Churchill's emissary, Morton, who had just completed a visit to France and Belgium, discussion of the Zone of the Interior had produced a 'stormy meeting' of the French Cabinet, where de Gaulle had found himself in a minority of one, and had been forced to bow to the wishes of his colleagues.[163] SHAEF meanwhile had some hesitation in declaring a Zone, in the light of news brought to them by Generals Defars and Patch of the current difficulties in the south between FFI troops and American transport units, which might potentially threaten the transport route from Marseilles.[164] The problem, as Peake explained, was that SHAEF feared they might have to 'reconvert' a Zone of the Interior if their lines of communications were threatened, which could enable critics to say the Allies were trying to establish the now mercifully forgotten AMGOT.

The solution was clearly to let the French themselves patrol the area by releasing French regiments from Allied military duty.[165] In effect, as SHAEF G3 pointed out in early October:

> The French have virtually exercised administrative control from the time of Liberation. The result has been that the liberated areas have approximated very closely to a Zone of the Interior.[166]

Finally, therefore, Eisenhower gave the CCOS formal notice of the creation of a Zone of the Interior on 20 October. In theory the agreement was to have been signed by de Gaulle in Paris on 23 October but, as it happened, the French Minister of Information released the news to the press who published it on 21 and 22 October.[167]

Pressure had clearly built up for recognition on all sides. According to Hull, Roosevelt, despite his earlier stipulation of two conditions, was now prepared to recognize the GPRF at the same time as a Zone of the Interior was announced.[168] Considering the long drawn-out history of Allied relations with the CFLN/GPRF, it was surprising that the final step should be taken, not by the British, who had thus far led the field, but by the Americans. The President had earlier suggested to the Prime Minister that any actions on recognition should be taken by the two of them together:

> I am anxious to handle this matter, for the present, directly between you and me and would prefer, for the moment, that the *modus operandi* not become a matter of discussion between the State Department and your Foreign Office.

The British representative at SHAEF, however, discovered that the American Ambassador in Paris had received instructions to tell de Gaulle informally that the American Government was ready to recognize the GPRF.[169] To the British it seemed that the USA was attempting to gain credit for being first in the field with recognition, to try and erase the memory of their delays. Cadogan expostulated, 'God help us! Is this simple inefficiency and crossing of wires or are the US trying to do us down?'[170] The State Department strenuously denied that they had tried to 'jump the gun', claiming that Caffery must have misunderstood his instructions. The President, on the other hand, apologized to Churchill that, 'my absence from Washington resulted in more precipitate action by State Department than was contemplated.'[171] In the end, the three powers all recognized the GPRF officially on 23 October. As Cadogan irreverently put it, 'At last! What a fuss about nothing! Due to that spiteful old great-aunt Leahy.'[172] De Gaulle's response to the whole episode was laconic: 'The French Government is satisfied to be called by its name.'[173]

Although Roosevelt hung on till the last minute in his desire to maintain an interim 'non-political' situation in France until the full democratic process had been re-established, it was evident that the Allies had needed an interim French administration to govern the country whilst they continued the fight against the Germans. The British and Americans had no group to put in the place of the GPRF and, by October 1944, it was clear to all parties that there *was* no real alternative to de Gaulle.

The official recognition by the Allies of the GPRF, long-awaited by the French, when it actually came was something of a damp squib. True to the pattern of Franco-Allied relations at this period, actions in the diplomatic sphere lagged behind events in France and the behaviour of Allied participants on the ground. Thus a putative French administration had been established before civil affairs negotiations were completed. Thus *de facto* recognition of the GPRF had been accorded when Allied military had already been treating the *Commissaires de la République* for some time as the 'real' administration of France. The *de jure* recognition of October 1944 came when the GPRF was clearly establishing itself throughout France. In the longer term, however, official recognition was more than a late postscript. The GPRF was undoubtedly the central administration of France, but it had not yet come to terms with the competing centres of power dispersed in the regions. There was no concerted attack on the position of the GPRF, but most observers agreed that a potential for conflict, albeit localized in certain regions, still existed. In this context, recognition would be an important indication for the rest of France that the central government in Paris was the one considered legitimate by the Allies. For Allied commentators, the situation in France might not be 'acute', but it was still 'delicate'.[174]

# 7 The establishment of GPRF authority, January–April 1945

DURING THE first quarter of 1945 de Gaulle's regime gradually asserted its control, and by the time the municipal elections were held at the end of April any possibility that the GPRF would be toppled, or its authority seriously threatened, had disappeared. There were two contributing factors. Firstly, the party which might have been able to turn the widespread dispersal of power into a coherent anti-government threat (the PCF) proved, after the return of its leader from exile, not merely unwilling to start a revolution, but actively concerned to support the claims and authority of the GPRF. Secondly, the Allies' own attitude towards the French government moved from often grudging acceptance to a clearer belief that the continuation of the Gaullist regime in France would best serve Allied interests. By April 1945 the British and the Americans regarded France as an independent, sovereign state, albeit with some difficulties. The diplomatic attention they paid to the GPRF in the wake of recognition gave it international confirmation as the legitimate and undisputed government of France. The attention was, however, well short of what the Gaullist regime and the people of France regarded as properly theirs.

## The Communist Party and the return of Thorez

THE Communist Party (PCF) leader, Thorez, explained in a *post hoc* analysis why the party had not taken advantage of the turbulent conditions at the end of 1944 to seize power. Firstly, he claimed, such behaviour would have provoked civil war, with the massive intervention of the Allies: 'With the Americans in France, the revolution would have been annihilated. France would have experienced the fate of Greece on an even larger scale . . .'. Secondly the great mass of the French people were not ready for revolution, and by no means all the sympathizers the PCF had won during the war could have been mobilized. Thirdly: 'you must take account of the international situation. To start a revolution would have meant ignoring this reality, it would have meant that we totally lacked the sense of our responsibilities.' Implicit in this last reason is the view that a revolution in France would have disrupted the Second Front in 1944 and put a strain on the

Allied alliance, to the detriment of the general war effort and the particular situation of the USSR.[1] Eight years after the Liberation, when the Central Committee of the party was accusing André Marty and Charles Tillon of planning, in defiance of the correct line, to seize power in September and October 1944, it was at pains to stress the first and the last points of Thorez's earlier analysis:

> What was our duty ? . . . To make war . . . In taking another course the PCF would have betrayed the working class and the nation . . . A reversal of alliances creating a coalition of capitalist powers against the Soviet Union was possible . . . the Party would have been quickly isolated if it had embarked on a course other than that of continuing the war against Hitler . . . A pretext would have been furnished to de Gaulle to call upon Anglo–American arms to crush the working class . . . the Communists are revolutionaries, not adventurers.[2]

Communist historians like Elleinstein have generally reflected this interpretation, pointing out that conditions in France were totally unpropitious for the seizure of power: de Gaulle was extremely popular and the communists, whilst experiencing a dramatic upturn in their fortunes, were still nowhere near the majority. In addition, those communists who had reached positions of influence and responsibility in September 1944 had done so largely as a function of national rather than class backing.[3] In ideological terms, the official communist thesis is thus that the Liberation period was not a revolution. On the other hand, it cannot be viewed as the re-establishment of the *status quo*. Rather it was to become characterized in PCF historiography as a situation entirely *sui generis*, difficult to define but, on balance, favourable to the party.[4] Non-communist observers and historians have often taken a more sceptical view of the validity of this interpretation of communist strategy and doctrine. Those former members of the party involved in the events themselves and often bitterly disappointed with the PCF, have criticized the doctrinal legitimacy of the communist position: thus Auguste Lecoeur suggested in 1963 that the concept of Liberation without proletarian revolution could only lead to the re-establishment of the bourgeoisie and the traditional parties, with the PCF actually contributing to the reinstatement of the bourgeois regime.[5] Marty accused the party of failing to exploit the favourable conditions which he claimed existed in 1944–5 to destroy the remnants of fascism in France.[6] Kriegel, reviewing the party's behaviour during the Fourth Republic, has argued for a more complex analysis of PCF strategy, positing the existence of three successive party strategies – the 'direct conquest of power' which was to fail, a strategy based on respect for the priority interests of the socialist camp, and the classic frontist approach, aimed at 'the conquest of power from within.'[7] Courtois on the other hand is more reserved about the existence of any clearly worked out and defined strategic line, speaking of, 'great uncertainty, fundamental indecision on the strategy to be adopted after the Liberation.'[8]

What is undoubtedly true is that the USSR did not regard France as a sphere of interest at the pre-Liberation and Liberation period. In July 1944 Harriman, the American Ambassador in Moscow, reported to the Secretary of State that: 'Molotov has told me several times since I have been back that it was the Soviet policy to leave the initiative in French policy to the British and ourselves.'[9] When the Soviet government did make representations to its Allies about the situation in France, these seemed generally to consist of complaints that the two had given a public impression of not adequately consulting the USSR. According to Ceretti, Thorez was told by Stalin, just before the French communist leader's return to Paris, that he should 'forge a national union around de Gaulle in order to complete the successful liquidation of Hitler.'[10] Certainly Stalin explained to Tito in 1948 that the Red Army 'did not and could not' have given the same assistance to the French (and indeed Italian) Communist Party as it had to the Yugoslav.[11] All this clearly indicated the preference in Moscow for the PCF to eschew any revolutionary path, and to co-operate with the de Gaulle government at least until the war was over.

What is more problematic is the extent to which this message had reached both the relevant leaders in Paris, and, more importantly, the rank and file in the country, before Thorez's return at the end of November 1944. As Agulhon points out, when the Central Committee met for the first time in Paris on 31 August, with Thorez still absent in Moscow, it is likely that the differences in emphasis between the Moscow, Paris and Algiers groups of leaders would have been discussed. The latter, men like Billoux, Grenier and Marty, were much less positive about the overall benefits of co-operation with de Gaulle. If Moscow, and to a certain extent Paris, were suspicious about the General, but unprepared to do anything which would lead to a break between the PCF and the GPRF, the Algiers group seemed in August 1944 more inclined to accept the likelihood of an eventual split.[12] Besides these differences of emphasis within the leadership, the PCF was faced with the same communication difficulties as the government itself as it attempted to impose some form of central control on its forces throughout France. Paradoxically the problem was exacerbated for the PCF by the very success that it had enjoyed in recruiting new members during the occupation and post-Liberation period. As Kriegel suggests, the new militants recruited were often entirely different from the sort of members the party had welcomed before the war. In class terms, they tended to be socially marginal, like much of the Resistance movement, without clear roots in the French working class. Ideologically, many of them had joined the PCF because it seemed in war to be the effective embodiment of the ideals for which Frenchmen were fighting, ideals it should be said which were implicitly patriotic. Their grasp of Marxist theory was inevitably not as secure as that of an average pre-war militant. The experience of Resistance was totally different from normal party experience in peacetime. For communist Resisters, 'the integration of military affairs into political matters was not necessarily seen in the same way as it was by the "purely political" members'.[13] Control of the rank and file and their subordination to a national policy was commensurately more difficult.

It was within this perplexing and uncertain context that the PCF developed its strategy until the return of Thorez in late November 1944. The party found itself in something of a dilemma. On the one hand it was keen to capitalize on the emotion generated by the Resistance, the *Milices Patriotiques* and the CDLs in order to persuade the government to consider introducing some form of popular democracy. On the other hand, its instinct was to look inward at its own party, attempting to rebuild its structures so that the party itself would be in a position to be the principal weapon for the future. Acceptance of the first course of action implied full-scale support for the alternative Resistance institutions, and with this, support for people who were entirely outside the control of the PCF. It also meant that those within the party who were too radical, and those new recruits who had not been shaped by party discipline, would be given considerable encouragement. The 'Resistance card' would inevitably tip the scales in favour of the Resistance leaders in the PCF to the detriment of the traditional 'party apparatus' leadership.

Until Thorez's return the communist leadership trod an uncertain path, never wholeheartedly following the pro-Resistance line, but equally never wholly rejecting it, by calling its more independent members in the FTP, *Milices Patriotiques* or CDLs to order. Courtois suggests that the strategy adopted at this time was a slowly evolving one, a product of developing circumstances rather than a set of conscious choices by the party. By mid-October 1944 it was clear that *l'Humanité*'s insistence during the previous weeks on the imminent victory of the Allies, and in particular of the USSR, who would advance faster than the Americans, was decidedly premature. Stalin's agreement to zones of influence in Europe, with his major interest being in the East, and the subsequent recognition of the GPRF by all three Allies, clearly closed off a number of possibilities for the PCF. From this time until the return of their leader, there was an ambivalence of tone both in the pronouncements of the party's cadres and in the apparent line which was being followed; a 'strategy of tension'.[14]

On the whole the PCF leadership treated de Gaulle implicitly, if not explicitly, at this time as a national leader rather than, as in more traditional communist rhetoric, the representative of the bourgeoisie. Even after the GPRF had announced the dissolution of the *Milices Patriotiques* in late October 1944, and Duclos had declared publicly that there was no 'providential man', the party forbore from direct attacks on the General, although the number of times he was actually mentioned by name in the communist press certainly diminished. All this did not, however, prevent the leadership from criticizing the whole government in the most acerbic terms. Thus Duclos, in a speech to Parisian militants at the end of October, denounced the ministers of Labour, Food and Industrial Production, as well as the Gaullist secret service (BCRA). More fundamentally, he pointed out that the legitimacy of the GPRF was based solely on the Resistance:

> The Resistance which was organised in clandestinity has, through its fight, created a new legality to oppose the false legality of Vichy. And today, it is the Resistance which constitutes the legal basis for the provisional government of the Republic. There are people who want to liquidate the Resistance. This would be most serious because it would leave the government without any legal basis.[15]

On 15 November 1944, Duclos set out the party's views on law and order: 'If the Provisional Government of the Republic returned purely and simply to the legality of 1939, by liquidating the Resistance, the basis of the new legality, it would no longer have any legal basis . . . In actual fact we are in a situation which somewhat recalls 1789. At that time there was, from one end of France to the other, a profound wish for change, because the old regime gave the appearance of being incoherent and impotent'.[16] Benoît Frachon echoed this call for change and an alternative style of democracy: there would be no economic renaissance in France 'unless in the political sphere there are profound changes . . . real democracy based on the ordinary people'.[17]

If the PCF co-operated as far as it could with the integration of the FFI into the regular Army – a measure to be supported as making the war more winnable in a shorter time – it was, as we have seen, far from co-operative in dismantling the other forms of Resistance alternative legitimacy, the *Milices Patriotiques* and the CDLs. Besides organizing demonstrations in support of the *Milices* after the government's dissolution initiative, Duclos announced publicly that the CNR were correct in demanding that the *Milices* should be placed under the authority of the town council or local committee of Liberation: 'The foundations of law and order must be democracy, authentic democracy, allowing the permanent control by the people of their representatives, making it impossible to have any form of personal or hidden power'.[18] Towards the CDLs, the official attitude of the party was slightly more nuanced. It was closely involved in early attempts to group committees of liberation together at the Valence congress in September 1944, and at the Avignon congress in early October. In both cases interestingly enough, communist participation tended towards moderation of CDL demands, and an emphasis on the need to establish a proper structure, via patriotic assemblies, and the summoning of an estates-general. In a sense, Duclos's championing of the latter allowed the PCF to declare itself for alternative Resistance institutions whilst not going as far as actually supporting the rights of the CDLs to exist in preference to municipal councils or delegations. The local estates-general would become, 'the organizers of national reconstruction', and at departmental and then national level would 'create the right conditions for the work of the future constituant assembly'.[19] Arguably the PCF had found it difficult to get the initiative in the area of the CDLs – Jean Chaintron, for example, then a member of the Central Committee, and prefect of the Haute-Vienne, claimed that the party had in fact lost control of the committees of Liberation, whilst Marty, in his later apologia, criticized the political bureau for its general passivity as regards policy being developed by the Avignon congress.[20]

The position of the PCF then before the return of Thorez was a rather curious one. Its attacks on the legitimacy of the GPRF, if not on the still sacrosanct figure of de Gaulle, and its defence of an alternative legitimacy, that of Resistance institutions – wholeheartedly in the case of the *Milices Patriotiques* – placed it in the opposition camp, seeking alliances within the Resistance movement which it was very far from being in a position to dominate. Thus the party tried to encourage the merger of the two major movements of the Resistance, the *Front National*, which it controlled, and the *Mouvement de Libération Nationale* which it did not, and thus also, it called for joint Resistance lists for the forthcoming municipal elections. At the same time, the PCF continued to have two of its members represented in the government whose legitimacy it was, at least verbally, contesting. The problem with the PCF in the September–December 1944 period is not whether it intended to seize power in the immediate term (it clearly did not) but what objectives it was pursuing in the rather uncertain tactics of tension without open conflict.

There is no doubt that the return of Thorez clarified the overall strategy. Thorez had been condemned as a deserter from the army in 1939 and had spent much of the subsequent time in Moscow. There is evidence that the USSR, doubtless concerned to have a man in whom they had total confidence leading the PCF, started to put out feelers about the return of Thorez soon after the German invasion of the USSR. At the end of 1943 the initiative was taken up again, via the CFLN representative in Moscow, Garreau, who met Thorez and sent back a favourable report of the interview to de Gaulle, stressing that Thorez had emphasized his desire to collaborate with de Gaulle as soon as he returned to Algiers. The reply, which Garreau read to Thorez in January 1944, described Thorez as a 'deserter' who could, therefore, not be permitted to return to Algiers. Thorez was provoked by this to point out to Garreau, in an official letter at the beginning of March 1944, that the CFLN were displaying towards him precisely the same attitude which the Allies had taken towards the General: 'the CFLN feels that my arrival might produce a reaction in public opinion. The same pretext was used last year to delay General de Gaulle's arrival in Algiers'.[21] As Courtois indicates, the parallel PCF campaign to be allowed to choose their own appointments to the CFLN, both candidates being people who had occupied official positions of responsibility in the party before 1940, was not unrelated to the campaign to bring Thorez back – an acceptance by de Gaulle of the PCF nominees would have been tantamount to the rehabilitation of the party after criticisms of its early behaviour, leaving the door open, as the next logical step, for the return of the man who had been leader of the party in this controversial period.[22]

With the party's 44th anniversary in May 1944, *l'Humanité* launched a massive campaign, demanding the return of Thorez – around 10 articles in three months attesting the importance attached to the issue. At the same time the party sought to secure supporting resolutions from the CGT, the CNR and various committees of Liberation. The campaign was stepped up even further with the Liberation of Paris. It was not, however, until the prospect of a visit by de Gaulle to the USSR arose that permission was given *de facto* with the promulgation of an amnesty to be accorded in certain cases to those condemned before 17 June 1940, under the clauses of the military code which had operated in Thorez's case. Thorez's personal amnesty was published on 6 November. De Gaulle flew out to meet Stalin at more or less the same time as Thorez was arriving back at Orly. Fauvet claims that de Gaulle said in confidence that he was going to Moscow 'to obtain from the PCF the year of peace I needed to get the situation under control'.[23]

In fact the visit had major importance in the context of de Gaulle's diplomatic offensive. In his memoirs, the General makes no mention of discussions on the PCF, other than Stalin's cynical advice not to put Thorez in prison, at least for the time being.[24] Harriman, meeting de Gaulle during his Russian visit, reported that the French leader said that:

The Communist Party in his country took its orders from Moscow; that he thought it would abandon its revolutionary aims but that under the guise of urging radical social programs would continue to create trouble. He was satisfied that the Soviet Government would use the French party as a means of furthering its own policy rather than in an effort to bring about a Communist France.[25]

Thorez's first speech on his return to France on 30 November 1944 already demonstrated a softening of the ambivalent but conflictual stance which the party had latterly been pursuing. Notable for its tendency to deal in generalities and patriotic appeals, the speech called on its listeners to continue the war, work hard, and ensure that traitors were punished. On the latter point, however, it was interesting that Thorez made a distinction between those definite collaborators, whose goods should be seized forthwith, and ordinary bosses who were currently complaining that they were not able to get on with work and produce what was required. On the other hand, alluding to the recent bomb incident in the Vaucluse, Thorez accused the government of being reluctant to put confidence in the people's ability to stamp out the fifth column, 'the people . . . are very willing to undertake the police duties in the country'. To this coded, but nonetheless clear, reference to the maintenance of the *Milices Patriotiques*, was added a similar note of support for the CDLs: 'organizations which have come out of the heroic struggle, like the committees of liberation'.[26]

Nearly two months later at the Central Committee meeting in Ivry between 21 and 23 January 1945, the non-conflict tone had developed into a definite party line. Thorez now firmly underlined the legitimacy of the GPRF – 'one state, one army, one police' – and the consequent illegitimacy of competing Resistance institutions. Thus, on the *Milices Patriotiques*:

> These armed groups had their *raison d'être* before and during the insurrection against the Hitlerian occupier and his Vichy accomplices. But now the situation is different. Public security must be provided by the regular forces of the police, formed for this purpose. The *gardes civiques* and all the irregular armed groups in general, must continue no longer. . . .

Similarly, on the CDLs, the communist leader paid tribute to their former work, but stated firmly that:

> the local and departmental Committees of Liberation must not act as substitutes for the municipal and departmental administration, any more than the CNR must act instead of the government. The task of the Committees of Liberation is not to administer, but to provide help to those who administer. Their job above all is to mobilise, train and organise the masses so that there is the maximum war effort and support for the provisional government in its application of the Resistance programme.[27]

The line was resolutely governmentalist:

> We Communists are not at present making any demands of a Socialist or Communist character. We say this at the risk of seeming weak and tepid to those who are always talking about revolution . . . We want to respond to the appeal of the CGT and participate with enthusiasm in the battle of production.[28]

The extent to which the period in between Thorez's two speeches had been marked by disagreements within the leadership about the change of policy is difficult to gauge. Lecoeur claimed that the tactic was never discussed in the Central Committee either before or after its adoption, and Fauvet's understanding is that Marty and Tillon privately protested about the Ivry speech.[29] Later, in 1952, the Central Committee admitted that: 'Some excellent comrades may have believed, on the basis of an inexact understanding of the forces of that moment, that the working class should have seized power at the Liberation'.[30] Certainly there is a suggestion that relations in general between those who had stayed in France throughout the war, and the newly returned exiles from Moscow were sometimes strained.[31]

In the dilemma which the PCF had faced in September 1944, Thorez had taken a clear and unmistakable line, coming down in favour of rebuilding the party and against support for the Resistance institutions. To begin with he had re-established his own authority in the party, and secondly, he had set aside any confusion within the PCF by deciding that the best chance of gaining power lay in reconstructing the normal political systems in France which would enable the PCF to win power through the ballot box. In this analysis, the way to attract votes was to enhance the Resistance image of the party as Jacobin patriots, the ancestors of the '*sans-culottes*' of 1789. Anything which impeded the re-emergence of the normal political systems necessary for the PCF to win power, or which tarnished the image of a fiercely patriotic party, would have to be speedily jettisoned. Hence Thorez's unequivocal abandonment of the alternative Resistance institutions which many of his own members had hitherto supported.

For many communist militants throughout the country, Thorez's speech came as a considerable shock. Two days after the Ivry speech he found it necessary to declare publicly that there was no right or left wing in the PCF, and that the membership had never been as united as it currently was around its Central Committee.[32] He and the other communist leaders then embarked on a tour in the provinces, including Toulouse and Marseilles, presumably designed to reassure the membership and ensure that the policy was fully understood. In June 1945 at the party's 10th national Congress, Fajon's speech implied that the argument was not yet over:

> Marxism–Leninism teaches us . . . that we must discern what can be achieved in a given period. For example, the chit-chat about the establishment of socialism in France, at the present time, has absolutely no meaning or else is the product of provocateurs, ordered to divide the democratic forces.[33]

Non-communist observers meanwhile were explicit in their reports that militants had found the change difficult to understand. Thus the prefect of the Vaucluse reported surprise among local members, but noted that they were disciplined, and that the PCF would not hesitate to purge itself of disobedient elements, and the prefect of the Ain observed much the same initial disorientation at orders which 'do not correspond to what they had been doing up to now'.[34] In some areas, early astonishment developed into threats of insubordination. The prefect of the Puy-de-Dôme claimed in late February–early March 1945 that a party circular addressed to local cells had stipulatd that any member found in possession of a weapon whose use he could not adequately justify would be excluded immediately from the PCF. In the Bouches-du-Rhône, information suggested that the local communist *député*, Cristofal, had told party members in early February: 'We should be obliged to consider those who refuse to give up their weapons as real saboteurs of the Party.'[35]

The *Contrôles Techniques* (censorship of post) reported that communist militants in the *Milices Patriotiques* who refused to recognize the necessity of dissolution had been 'sharply recalled to order'.[36] Some prefects, like those of the Allier and Deux-Sèvres, detected definite signs of unrest among PCF members and sympathizers: 'It would be most premature to talk of actual party divisions but it is however true that in some cases the word has been pronounced.'[37]

Whilst the PCF leadership may have had difficulties in ensuring that the line developed in Thorez's Ivry speech was palatable to all its members, the evidence is overwhelming that the militants largely obeyed. The fact that after all the uncertainty, Thorez's change of line was so completely implemented is some indication of the extent to which the party had managed to rebuild its internal structures and successfully begin the task of regaining control of its membership. Democratic centralism had returned, and it was to be sufficiently strong for Thorez to wield power much as he had done in the heydays of the early 1930s.

Crucially, the instructions given to local communists and the enthusiasm with which they were disseminated caused a major change in the still uncertain relations between the GPRF and the alternative Resistance institutions, the *Milices Patriotiques* and the CDLs. The effect of Thorez's speech was a general relaxation of the overt political tensions which had existed in many areas at the end of 1944. The new *Commissaire de la République* at Marseilles, appointed after the pro-communist official had been dismissed, was amazed to find that the local communist press made very little of his arrival: 'Doubtless the recent speech of M. Thorez . . . had helped me to benefit from a calmer climate.'[38]

In general, astonished prefects did their best to ensure that PCF instructions received the widest possible publicity, in some places, as in the Alpes-Maritimes, for example, putting the radio at the disposal of the local party representative so that he could stress the importance of Thorez's injunctions.[39]

In some areas the position regarding the *Milices Patriotiques* appeared to change virtually overnight. Thus the prefect of the Var reported that, whereas the month before he had been involved in an acrimonious argument with the CDL about the formation of a *Garde Civique Républicaine*, by mid-February, the communist leadership was advocating respect for law and order, and the need for one single police force, controlled by central government. The local Communist *député*, Bartolini, had indeed proposed to the prefect that he should hold a series of lectures, 'to encourage his friends to give in their weapons'.[40] In La Nièvre, the PCF representative on the CDL demanded that the committee should order the dissolution of the armed groups as soon as possible, and the handing in of guns and rifles. In the Haute-Marne, a section of *Milices Patriotiques* which had been formed under the former leader of the *Front National* at St Dizier dispersed almost immediately after Thorez's speech. In other areas, attempts which had been going on to organize new groups of armed men seemed to founder as the *Front National*/PCF members reportedly lost interest. It was clearly difficult for such bodies to maintain their enthusiasm and *raison d'être* if their previously most committed members left. As the *Gardes Civiques* of the Allier noted, in the resolution by which they voted to accept their own dissolution: 'A sense of discipline is depriving us in a large measure of our members from the Communist Party and its sympathisers.'[41] Of course such votes did not necessarily mean that weapons held by individuals would be handed in, and several prefects remained sceptical about the extent to which this part of the dissolution order was being obeyed. However, the point remained that the authority of the PCF had largely achieved what central government could not, the virtual disbandonment of potentially hostile armed groups. As the police expressed it, Thorez's speech had produced 'a very pleasant surprise'.[42]

The attitude of the PCF towards that other pillar of Resistance legitimacy, the CDLs, had always been slightly more cautious than their outright defence of the *Milices Patriotiques*. The general change in the party's policy was, however, observable in the more moderate and co-operative tone adopted by many local committees. Thus the *Commissaire de la République* of Châlons-sur-Marne reported in mid-February 1945 that there had been, 'a complete reversal . . . in the policy of the Departmental Liberation Committee since M. Thorez's speech at Ivry', whilst the communist influence on the CDL of the Vaucluse was said to be instrumental in pushing that body towards greater collaboration with the prefect.[43] The loss of the *Milices Patriotiques* and the change in PCF tactics were clearly two of several factors which operated to weaken the influence of the CDLs in the early months of 1945. In a sense the process was one of attrition, with the gradual nomination of rival interim town councils, and the prospect of imminent municipal elections. The very fact that the first elections in Liberated France were to be local elections is a measure of the seriousness with which the government regarded the situation in the provinces, and the importance which they attached to legitimate institutions regaining control. The effect would clearly be to squeeze the Liberation committees out of existence. As *Combat* noted in January 1945: the committees of Liberation: 'are called on to act as understudies for the traditional municipal and regional bodies. This "overhanging" position is not designed to simplify our political life . . . Led as it has been to create a real State, but one without real power, the Resistance has been hovering for four months between respectful inaction and anarchic activity . . . '.[44]

Increasingly, reports from the provinces indicated that members of CDLs were finding themselves caught uncomfortably in the kind of powerless position to which the paper alluded. Thus, some members appeared to be turning their attention to finding a seat in the forthcoming local elections, whilst others sought to divert public animosity about food shortages and adverse economic conditions by making a virtue of necessity and pointing out that the CDL was only a consultative body which could not be blamed.[45] The picture emerging from regional and departmental despatches of the period is that the power of the CDLs was gradually falling away in early 1945, either because the committees voluntarily accepted a limitation in their role – a more exclusive preoccupation with social affairs was a fairly common pattern – or because the interest of the public, and of members themselves was fast diminishing. In the Bouches-du-Rhône the departmental Liberation committee could only attract an audience of 50 to a public meeting it had organized at the beginning of March 1945, and in the Allier, where the CDL had been particularly active, the prefect reported that his contacts with the members had ceased altogether. At a lower tier, the local Liberation committees were often close to extinction – by the end of April, the prefect of the Vaucluse claimed that in his department they were all dead, with the exception of that of Carpentras which consisted of one active member who continued on his own to write agenda which nobody else bothered to read.[46] Whilst there were exceptions – the Regional Liberation Committee in Marseilles was holding an extremely lively protest meeting in early April[47] – the general impression is one of markedly decreasing activity.

The alternative Resistance institutions which were posing some threat to the GPRF at the end of 1944 had virtually withered away by April 1945. With the PCF adopting a resolutely governmentalist line, the de Gaulle regime faced no real domestic challenge to the wide-spread establishment of its authority.

## *Allied attitudes*

THE LONGER the GPRF remained in power, apparently accepted by the French people, the more difficult it became for the Allies to contemplate its removal, even if they had had some suitable substitute to put in its place. Allied reports in 1945 implicitly acknowledged that the Gaullist regime was the national government of France. Whereas observers in 1944 had been mainly interested in the extent to which some form of order could be said to exist throughout France, des-patches in the first part of 1945 concentrated on how long the GPRF might be able to maintain the present situation of 'unstable equili-brium'.[48] More and more, Allied military and diplomatic personnel regarded the continued existence of the GPRF as essential. The Foreign Office, for example, was convinced that the strong France Great Britain desired for foreign policy reasons would best emerge from the existing Gaullist regime:

> de Gaulle is the only man today around whom a strong France can be recreated; I fear that General de Gaulle stands between us and a pretty chaotic France.
> There are good grounds for thinking that . . . de Gaulle's government, with all his shortcomings, is the only alternative to civil strife and the emergence of a single party government which it would be difficult for us to work with.[49]

The crucial factor, as Duff Cooper pointed out, in determining whether problems in France would produce a situation like that in Belgium, where the Allies might intervene directly, was the attitude and behaviour of the PCF.[50]

Thorez's return from Moscow had led the British Ambassador to conclude that the communist 'danger' had been largely dissipated:

> For some time after the Liberation it was believed that the Communists might be working against the Government. Whatever the truth of that may be, they certainly never ventured out into open opposition. Now, no doubt following their directive from Moscow, they are committed to cooperation with the Administration, if M. Thorez's declaration is to be taken at its face value. Thus France appears for the time being to have escaped the most serious of all potential dangers, namely, open conflict between the united Resistance movement and the Government.[51]

The OSS broadly supported this view, pointing out, for example, that Villon, at the *Front National* congress, had employed strikingly similar terms to those recently used by Thorez in calling for national unity, and had soft-pedalled all criticisms of the government, even on contentious issues like food-shortages and the purge, where the *Front National* had formerly been vociferous.[52] It also appeared as if the CGT and the unions were unlikely to take issue with the government.[53] The

OSS noted that the communists were still actively criticizing GPRF ministers in the Consultative Assembly, but felt that, 'The sharpness of criticism in the Assembly is due in some measure to its ineffectualness'.[54] There was still a cleavage in the country between the government and the Resistance:

> The Government sees its duty simply as the restoration of the French state by traditionally acceptable legal means. The Resistance thesis is that the Government should be concerned above all with the full accomplishment of the aims of the national insurrection as primarily embodied in the CNR program.

The failure to recognize this cleavage publicly, however, put the communist and socialist parties, in the eyes of OSS, in a difficult position since neither wished to withdraw from the government unless they could form an official opposition, and neither was likely, separately or together, to get the mass of the people to understand their reasons for leaving.[55] In late winter/early spring of 1945, therefore, the OSS seemed ready to endorse the view that there was probably less danger from the communists than from provocative anti-communists.[56]

The question for Allied observers was chiefly: how long would the communists continue with their present attitude ? As SHAEF Mission (France) put it in March:

> The Communist Party maintains towards the French Provisional and the Allied Governments, the moderate and conciliatory attitude which it has adopted since the return of Thorez from Moscow. This is in contrast with its extremist and outspoken attitude of earlier days and the criticisms voiced at present by more conservative parties. The Communists retain their opinions, but, for the time being at any rate, they are not prepared to take action which might adversely affect the united war effort of France.[57]

Significantly, the Joint Intelligence Committee of SHAEF sought information from the British Embassy at the end of March 1945 on [the]:

> Future of the present French Government – its inherent weakness – possibility of Thorez and Communist Party no longer supporting Government after cessation of hostilities.[58]

With the end of hostilities in Europe, SHAEF did note that the attitude of left-wing parties began to change. There was a marked stiffening of anti-government articles in the communist and socialist press:

> While it is the opinion of informed Allied observers that, for the time being, the Left parties will successfully restrain organized labour from a course of direct economic action on a large scale, it is to be expected that the maximum of pressure will be exerted on the Government by political means in the Consultative Assembly, in the Press and in a rising crescendo of public demonstrations.[59]

Order itself was being maintained, but the general prognosis of SHAEF as regards the future of the present French government was still not sanguine in mid-June: 'It is apparent that France politically at the present moment is basically unstable.'[60]

The main danger as SHAEF saw it in 1945, lay in the desperate food deficiencies: 'Stocks of food in the large centers of population are still dangerously low, and symptoms of unrest in consequence have begun to appear in Paris and Lille.'[61] In the north, which had always been more favoured in food provision during the occupation, there were real shortages now. Captain Norton-Griffiths from G2 reported that there could well be internal disturbances in the south-west as well if the 1945 winter was bad.[62] The Parliamentary Secretary at the Ministry of Food commented, on his visit to Paris in January 1945 that: 'London would be in uproar long before it had reached the condition of scarcity which Paris has . . . endured quietly'. He counselled the British government to send help as soon as possible, 'if civil disorder, quite apart from serious physical deterioration, is to be avoided'.[63]

Other more specific public order problems in particular areas of France complicated the general unease which SHAEF felt was being caused by physical hardships. Groups of foreigners who had fought in the Resistance and Liberation, or were refugees from German atrocities, now formed large, often armed, enclaves which could present potential difficulties to the forces of law and order in those regions. Thus Lt. Col. Sawyer of G5 reported that he had found armed Russians in the Lille area who were raiding the surrounding countryside. The 21st Army Group was ordered to disarm them, but 'on urgent representations', had been told to hold their hands. In the same region, he had encountered 200,000 Poles who were divided between the Lublin Poles and the London Poles, the former apparently intimidating and even killing some of the latter.[64] The perennial problem of Spanish refugees along the Franco–Spanish border was still smouldering on in early April 1945, with SHAEF showing concern that the Spanish government might decide their presence was a security threat and thus take pre-emptive action which could result in irregular fighting along the length of the border.[65] At least by May the problem of the Spanish *maquis* camped in the Departments close to Spain appeared to be resolved by the French authorities, who had given them civilian status and regular identity cards as foreign workers. The Spaniards were persuaded to relinquish their weapons, and the GPRF had placed those whose homes were still in Spain, and who intended to return there, in labour battalions with a semi-military status, engaged in cutting wood and making charcoal. Those whose homes were now in France or who had signified no desire to return to Spain were, on the other hand, left to their own devices, in the expectation that they would subsequently be absorbed into the immigrant labour market.[66]

SHAEF continued in this period to plan for possible Allied military intervention in France, in order to safeguard the war effort, but the plans were now predicated on the need to involve, and where necessary support, the Gaullist regime. Towards the end of January 1945 a directive on internal security had been issued. This posited a situation where:

> economic and political factors may induce a feeling of unrest in France which may, in turn, result in internal disorder and strife. Such disorders may require military force to restore order . . . The sole concern of the military authorities is to ensure that the Allied war effort is not impeded by internal disorders in France. We have no desire to interfere in French internal affairs, but it is our duty adequately to secure our installations and lines of communication.

The directive enjoined SHAEF Mission (France) to co-ordinate information on the internal security situation from the Army groups, the embassies, and the French government, and to communicate pertinent material to the GPRF. Two headings were suggested for Allied intervention: cases where the French government requested assistance, and instances where, as in 'riots, strikes, picketing', direct military action was advisable to 'protect life and property and safeguard the war effort'. The communiqué stressed that, wherever possible, the first case should be operative, with the French government taking the initiative. 'Since the political repercussions of Allied intervention tend to be so violent', there should be, 'irrefutable evidence of the desire of the French Provisional Government for Allied military intervention', and such evidence should be preferably written; if verbal, it must come from someone of 'cabinet rank if possible'.[67] Brigadier-General Nevins, head of Operations Section of SHAEF, defended the wisdom of issuing such a directive in early 1945:

> I do not think that we are proposing to issue this directive because we are 'windy'. France has been quiet since its Liberation and there is nothing to indicate at the moment that it will not remain quiet. The French, however, have a great name for internal strife and it cannot be doubted that the economic situation and political development in the country provide a potential of trouble. I believe it would be better to get this directive out while all is quiet and let our doctrine of controlled interference filter down to the lower levels . . .[68]

SHAEF Mission (France) was thus placed in a key position with regard to internal security in France, and accordingly began to plan the means by which it would get access to the precious information required in order to make an informed judgment of the type implied by the directive.[69] Experience in Poitiers had suggested to SHAEF observers that French intelligence was often unreliable, and they would have preferred to rely on their own men who could be expected to report more 'impartially'.[70] SHAEF Mission (G2) survey of existing British and American intelligence provision connected to SHAEF indicated however that in areas like the south-west where there were no Allied troops, the few remaining Allied officers were already being withdrawn. It would thus be extremely difficult to get a picture of what was happening in this area, without the co-operation of the French authorities: 'preliminary and quite informal contact with the French authorities makes it clear that the question is one of extreme delicacy for the French Government.'[71] By the end of February, however, G2 noted that the Director-General of the *Sûreté Nationale* had arranged for the director of the Secret Service in his Department to be in immediate contact with G2 Mission: 'in order to transmit any information of importance which comes into his possession on the internal security situation'.[72] Towards the end of March 1945, a plan for the co-ordination of internal security in France had been prepared by SHAEF Mission (France) ready to be sent to the appropriate French officials. The details provided for the exchange of information between SHAEF and the GPRF, with the actual mechanics by which this would be achieved being left to later discussions between SHAEF and the Ministry of War. The plan suggested that support for the French authorities would develop in three stages: firstly, disorders would be dealt with by the French police: 'The presence of Allied military police, who would be given definite orders not to take an active part, is considered as being of assistance at this stage.' Secondly, if the GPRF were unable to control the situation using police, it was assumed the next step would be for them to call on the services of the French military: 'In order to reduce the likelihood of intervention by Allied military forces, the French provisional government takes into account the security situation when arranging the disposition of French troops throughout France. It was proposed that Army Groups and Communications Zone should, if they think fit, suggest the redisposition of local French forces 'so that these may be most suitably located for supporting the maintenance of public order.' Finally, direct action by Allied military personnel would only take place in the exceptional circumstances outlined in the original directive. Where the French authorities requested aid, it was presumed that the request would come from central government, but provision was made for local French authorities in extremis to apply directly, in writing, for Allied help. A chart of the channels by which the French would seek military assistance was enclosed, so that the process would be clear at each stage.[73]

In April however, with parties intent on the election campaign, SHAEF Mission reported that their French informants regarded the position as much calmer:

The Ministry of the Interior consider . . . on the basis of information received from all sections of France, that the political situation is well in hand and is not likely to necessitate AEF intervention.[74]

The message appeared to have registered with SHAEF headquarters because G3 ordered the French Mission not to publish the plans for internal security, but to hold them instead in readiness: 'circumstances and conditions . . . [have] changed to such an extent that it is now considered highly improbable that security difficulties . . . will ever occur. It is also felt that the French may, at this time, take offence at an inference of their inability to cope with internal disturbances'.[75] The American Political Advisor, Robert Murphy, wrote a long paper in mid-June pointing out that substantial changes in the directive and plan were necessitated by the changing political circumstances:

> With the termination of hostilities in the European Theater, the urgency of possible military action on our part to safeguard the security of our installations in France is reduced, whereas the political implications of such intervention become correspondingly greater.

He recommended that strong safeguards should be attached to the plan to ensure that local American commanders were brought more fully under Communications Zone Headquarters control for crucial policy decisions like intervention in support of the civilian power. Any requests from the GPRF for military aid should only be acceded to 'under most cogent circumstances of necessity' with 'irrefutable evidence of the military necessity for such intervention'.[76]

## Diplomatic relations

WHEN THE Allies had accepted that the Gaullist regime was the legitimate government of a sovereign state, they began to accord it some of the diplomatic attention for which de Gaulle had craved during the dark days before the landings. In the field of international relations, the GPRF had very specific objectives, and ones moreover which were generally supported by all post-Liberation political tendencies. As Caffery, the American Ambassador, noted:

> De Gaulle's activities in the international field until recently tended to enhance his prestige in France, and his government took advantage of that prestige to arrange a great many things in the domestic field to their own liking.[77]

Certainly opinion polls at the beginning of January, February and April 1945 showed respondents to be solidly behind the foreign policy that the GPRF was pursuing.

De Gaulle's personal influence on the formulation and prosecution of French foreign policy was massive. Catroux, for example, describes how he received his instructions for the job of Ambassador in the USSR not from the Foreign Minister, but from the General himself, and that this was clearly the norm.[78] For de Gaulle it was of pre-eminent importance for France to gain admittance to the debates of the 'Big three', where issues which he considered vital to France's future interests were being discussed.[79] Here France would serve as an all-important bridge between East and West, since, according to Bidault, the Foreign Secretary, France understood Russian conceptions of the world, but could equally boast a spiritual and geographical proximity to the Anglo-Saxon countries. Speakers in the Consultative Assembly tended to echo this neutralist, independent theme. Five speakers in a foreign affairs debate in 1944, for example, claimed France was the bridge or link between the Allies: 'France is in a way the wedding ring of the great marriage, as she was the forward guard of the coalition.'[80]

At the nub of French foreign policy was, of course, the German question. De Gaulle insisted that France should be represented in all Allied discussions on the future of Germany. Otherwise, as he stressed in the Consultative Assembly before his departure for Moscow in December 1944, France would not be bound by arrangements which had been arrived at by others in its absence. French security in the future could not be entrusted exclusively to a new world peace organization. There would have to be alliances in eastern Europe, and possibly some form of regional understanding in western Europe, but France would need in addition reliable guarantees about the future control of Germany – in effect the total occupation and disarmament of the country. In practice, the details of whether this meant annexation of territory or international control, and what form the latter should take, varied somewhat from political group to political group. What was clear, however, as Deporte points out, is that the general policy of the GPRF – independent great power status, firm control of Germany – met widespread support across the political spectrum, and accorded well with the exigencies of domestic politics, enabling a government, formed of elements ranging from the PCF to the right, to maintain its unity on foreign policy with little difficulty at all.[81]

The British, whilst not fully endorsing French pretensions to great power status, went some way towards giving the idea approval, for reasons of their own. During the earlier argument between Britain and the USA about which country should control which zone in occupied Germany, France's possible role had been an ever-present undercurrent in discussions. Both countries had assumed that they would 'lead' the minor western European states adjacent to their own occupation zone. Thus the southern occupier would 'lead' France, whilst the northern would 'lead' Norway and the Netherlands, with Belgium probably falling under northern leadership as well. When, however, the disagreement was finally settled at the September Quebec conference, with the British given the northern zone, the Foreign Office did not abandon their declared intention to build up French power. A restored France was needed for future western European security, as well as to share the responsibilities and incumbent expenses of occupying Germany. Harvey indicated in early 1944 that:

> We want France, for good British reasons, to play a large part in occupying and controlling Germany after the war, and it would be only natural therefore that she should take her place in the control machinery of Berlin.[82]

Later, as the French authorities began to argue their own need for an occupation zone, the Foreign Office remained sympathetic, but clearly felt that the priority was the establishment of the north-west British zone, particularly as they presumed France would be too weak to administer Germany immediately after the war. Instead, they inclined towards joint British–French control of part of the British zone as a first step towards giving the French what they sought.[83]

When Churchill and Eden visited Paris in November 1944, the ambivalence of this position was evident. The British were cautious about French demands for help in re-equipping the army and frankly 'evasive' when French thinking on Germany was spelled out to them. De Gaulle explained that the French would require their own occupation zone: 'not only as a symbol of French participation in the occupation but also because France must effectively cover French territory in the East'. Bidault stressed that there had to be international military, economic and political control of Germany, and western control of the economy of the Rhineland.[84] Churchill, whilst expressing sympathy with this: 'knowing well that there will be a time not many years distant when the American armies will go home and when the British will have great difficulty in maintaining large forces overseas', pointed out that 'all this must be settled at an inter-Allied table'.[85] When de Gaulle attempted to persuade the Prime Minister that the two countries, weakened by comparison with the superpowers, would have an interest in co-ordinating their policies in many areas, Churchill said that it was better to guide the stronger powers rather than work against them:

> The Americans have vast resources. They do not always use them wisely. I am trying to enlighten them . . . As for France . . . don't be impatient ! . . . You'll come, in the natural course of time, to have a chair during discussions. Nothing will prevent us then from working together. Until then, let me get on with it ![86]

Despite this, however, both Churchill and Eden were at pains to underline the theoretical recognition of great power status given to France in her Dumbarton Oaks role, and in her participation in the European Advisory Commission (EAC).

In a sense, Churchill's problem was that of maintaining his own privileged position among the Allies, whilst clearly realizing that Britain would be dependent on the help of a restored France, if she were to have any hope of meeting her European security commitments. In his reports on the meeting to Roosevelt, Churchill was a good deal more eloquent in pleading the case of France than he had been with de Gaulle:

> Here is another reason why we should have a triple meeting if U.J. [Uncle Joe Stalin] will not come, or a quadruple meeting if he will. In the latter case the French would be in on some subjects and out on others. One must always realize that before five years are out there must be made a French army to take on the main task of holding down Germany.[87]

Roosevelt's non-committal reply, coupled with his statement that he would have to bring American troops home as soon as possible, worried the Prime Minister a great deal:

> If after Germany's collapse you 'must bring the American troops home as rapidly as transportation problems will permit' and if the French are to have no equipped post-war army or time to make one . . . how will it be possible to hold down western Germany beyond the present Russian occupied line ? We certainly could not undertake the task without your aid and that of the French. All would therefore rapidly disintegrate as it did last time.[88]

On the American side, the State Department was generally sympathetic to the British case. In the preparation for the British–American talks at Malta, Dunn forwarded to Stettinius the British Embassy's position that France, Belgium and Holland should be rearmed so that they could take part in the occupation of Germany, making those countries 'militarily strong within the British idea of a "defensive" confederation'.[89] In a later memo on French participaton in tripartite plans for the control of Germany, Stettinius suggested to the President that the British view on France was broadly correct:

> It is in the interests of the United States to assist France to regain her former position in world affairs in order that she may increase her contribution in the war effort and play an appropriate part in the maintenance of peace.

Since the USA might well withdraw a sizeable proportion of its troops quite early in the occupation, Stettinius argued that French forces could then act as replacements, and that if this were the case, it would be sensible to involve the French in planning for the occupation from the outset. Presumably anticipating Roosevelt's likely response, he admitted that such treatment could be regarded as being out of proportion with the present power of France:

> In the long run this Government will undoubtedly gain more by making concessions to French prestige and by treating France on the basis of her potential power and influence, than we will by treating her on the basis of her actual strength at this time.[90]

When the French submitted their demand to participate in the forth-coming Yalta conference, Matthews warned Stettinius that it was quite likely that the British and Russians would tell the French that they had no problems accepting their presence, thus leaving the USA isolated to bear the onus of the refusal.[91]

Once more, however, the stumbling block appeared to be Roosevelt. The President was adamant that de Gaulle could not be invited to the meeting of the 'Big three' at Yalta: 'I still adhere to my position that any attempt to include de Gaulle in the meeting of the three of us would merely introduce a complicating and undesirable factor'. In addition, any parallel agreements with France, of the type proposed by the Prime Minister, to include France, the USSR and Britain, were, Roosevelt implied, inadvisable, since they might be interpreted publi-cly as some sort of rival to a future world peace organization.[92] The President was aware of the likely embarrassment in Franco–American relations that such an attitude would provoke and the presidential special adviser, Hopkins, was despatched to de Gaulle to soften the blow of France's enforced absence from Yalta. According to Caffery, the General was in an 'icy mood', characterizing the American government's approach, not entirely unjustly, as follows:

> the USA has done an enormous number of very helpful things for us . . . but you always seem to do it under pressure and grudgingly.[93]

By the beginning of February 1945, however, the British and Ameri-cans had managed to agree a joint approach on France to be presented to the Russians at Yalta. The President was now disposed to give the French an occupation zone in Germany, and it was settled that the USSR would be asked to approve a proposal that Britain and the USA should work out an appropriate zone with the French, and that the French government should be included in the control machinery.

The attitude of the Soviet government to the future status of France was doubtless less obvious to the GPRF than was that of Roosevelt. Certainly there is considerable evidence that Stalin had a generally low opinion of French participation in the war and hence regarded their claims to be treated on a par with the three Allies as totally unrealistic. In November though the Russians had pressed for the addition of France as a permanent member of the EAC, thereby perhaps giving de Gaulle hope that the USSR might be prevailed upon to urge the whole French case more forcibly.[94] Deporte suggests that, whilst the motives of the GPRF in seeking a Franco–Russian pact were clear in the light of de Gaulle's general diplomatic offensive, Stalin's motives in enter-taining the idea of an agreement were a good deal more obscure. He knew of course that a pact would enhance the status of the PCF, and thus perhaps was willing to 'strengthen the international position of the Gaullist government in order to consolidate the position of the French Communist Party within that Government and within France . . .'.[95] In the event, negotiations between the two sides in early December 1944 were difficult, and from the GPRF's point of view, rather unsatisfactory. To begin with Stalin refused de Gaulle's suggestion that they should present a joint policy on Germany to the other Allies: 'it was impossible to decide this question without the knowledge and agreement of our chief Allies'.[96] After this, two major obstacles to the signature of a treaty emerged. Firstly, Churchill, in reply to a note from Stalin seeking advice on the matter of a Franco–Soviet pact, had advanced the view that a tripartite treaty between Britain, France and the USSR might well be a preferable idea. The British Ambassador in Moscow reported that the Russians appeared to be using the Prime Minister's suggestion to rub salt in the wound of French pride and independence, and de Gaulle reacted angrily to the manner in which the proposal had been made, claiming later to Duff Cooper that the British action had enabled the Russians to sell the pact to the French at a higher price.[97]

The second problem, predictably enough, concerned the vexed and uncertain Polish question. De Gaulle had indicated to Stalin that he would raise no objection to German territory up to the Oder-Neisse line being given to Poland. However, on the matter of recognition of the Lublin Committee, on which the Russians pressed him hard, the General was unyielding.[98] The disagreement stayed between the two delegations for the duration of the talks, threatening any possible treaty up to the very last moment. A member of the French delegation reported to the British Ambassador that it was extremely important:

from the domestic point of view in France for General de Gaulle to conclude a pact with the Russians before leaving Moscow . . . he [de Charbonnière] was very bitter about the Russians, who he said, had tried to exploit the French wish for a pact by driving them hard to commit themselves publicly on the Polish question.[99]

Finally, however, without such a public declaration, a pact between the two countries was agreed which contained the significant clause that the USSR would discuss the post-war settlement with France, and that they would both monitor the behaviour of Germany to prevent it representing a danger in the future. In a sense, such a treaty indicated that France was, in theory at least, likely to be treated on the same level as the other Allies, an interpretation given some credence when the Soviet ambassador to France, referred to the fact that: 'all the powers which have been the most active in this war – that is, Great Britain, the United States, Russia and France – understand that they must act in common to reach the goal'.[100]

At the Yalta Conference (4–11 February 1945), however, from which the French were excluded, Stalin made it clear that, whatever hopes the French might have entertained about the Franco–Soviet pact, his own opinion of the country was as low as ever. He explained to Roosevelt, in a talk without Churchill, that he had found de Gaulle to be unrealistic: 'in the sense that France had not done very much fighting in this war and De Gaulle demanded full rights with the Americans, British and Russians'. Roosevelt, after recounting the tale of de Gaulle comparing himself with Joan of Arc and Clemenceau, proceeded to break ranks with the British position:

> The President said he would now tell the Marshal something indiscreet, since he would not wish to say it in front of Prime Minister Churchill, namely that the British for two years have had the idea of artificially building up France into a strong power which would have 200,000 troops on the eastern border of France to hold the line for the period required to assemble a strong British army. He said the British were a peculiar people and wished to have their cake and eat it too.

When asked directly by Stalin whether he considered it to be a good idea to give the French an occupation zone in Germany, Roosevelt's response was far from the firm advocacy which the Malta Agreement between the British and Americans had implied:

> The President said he thought it was not a bad idea, but he added that it was only out of kindness. Both Marshal Stalin and Mr Molotov spoke up vigorously and said that would be the only reason to give France a zone.[101]

This initial exchange set the tone for much of the later discussion between the Allies on France. When, at the second plenary session, Churchill argued the case for a French zone in Germany to be allocated out of the existing American–British zones, Stalin objected that he could not take this to mean that France would also have a place in the Allied control machinery. The Prime Minister pointed out once more that the French would have to be called on to assume long-term control in Germany, since the Americans would be withdrawing their troops within a short time, confirmed by the President as under two years. Roosevelt, again at variance with the earlier agreed position, indicated that, whilst he believed France should be given a zone, he was not personally in favour of allowing her into the control of Germany. From this point until the last plenary session, Churchill and Eden continued to present the case for France's admittance to the control commission:

> It would be inconvenient to add France to the present group of major Allies, but . . . British public opinion would not understand why France was being excluded from a problem which was of such direct concern to her . . . the destiny of great nations was not decided by the temporary state of their technical apparatus.[102]

Eden pressed the point that France would never accept an occupation zone if she were denied a place in the control machinery, whilst the Prime Minister claimed that French participation need not necessarily entitle the country to attend conferences such as Yalta in the future.[103]

Whilst Churchill and the Foreign Secretary were, in Hopkins's words, fighting 'like tigers for France', he and his colleagues attempted, behind the scenes, to modify the President's attitude to French membership of the control commission.[104] Before the seventh meeting on 10 February, the President had changed his mind, and sent word privately to Stalin, via Harriman, that he was now in favour of the British position. Thus, at the end of the Yalta Conference, Roosevelt and Stalin agreed that France would be given both a zone, and a place on the control commission, although their acceptance was at best grudging: 'it would be easier to deal with the French if they were on the Commission than if they were not'.[105]

Whilst Yalta accorded some rights to France in the matter of Germany's future, the published protocol underlined the fact that she was still not accepted as a full partner of the 'Big three'. Like China, France was granted the rank of major power in formal organizations, but when non-organizational meetings (like periodic foreign ministers' discussions) were to be held, it was once more excluded. Equal rank extended to the execution of decisions but not to the process by which the decisions were actually made. Bidault reported to Duff Cooper that he had had the greatest difficulty in calming de Gaulle down when the latter received the notes from the Crimean conference, and the General's state of mind was doubtless not improved by what he regarded as Roosevelt's insulting invitation to come and see him in Algiers.[106] Massigli felt that the section of the communiqué on foreign ministers' meetings had been deliberately worded to exclude GPRF representatives.[107] The Foreign Office meanwhile suggested the 'need for some discreet publicity about our role at Yalta',[108] so that the French would realize that opposition to their case had come from the USA and the USSR despite what the respective publicity machines of those countries might be indicating.

The French press of the period was increasingly critical of American behaviour in the diplomatic sphere. To begin with there was considerable anger at the way that France had been excluded from full participation in important Allied conferences. Since the recognition of the GPRF in October, continuous demands had been made in French newspapers for the country to be included in discussions with the major Allies. The tendency to restrict participation to a purely consultative role was roundly condemned, and the failure to invite France to the conference at Yalta provoked a spate of bitterly angry articles.[109] Further mistrust was occasioned by the American theory of trusteeship, discussed at Yalta, which might imply that the Americans would seek to control former French possessions in the Pacific recaptured from the enemy.[110] Allied delay in giving the French details about the boundaries of the French zone of occupation in Germany was yet another source of public grievance, and sections of the French press alluded to the fact that Allied policy in general towards liberated countries was proving far from adequate. *L'Aurore* published an article by the American correspondent, Walter Lippmann, stressing the need to involve France in future international arrangements in order to avoid the 'errors' already committed in Belgium, Greece and Italy,[111] and *Le Monde* carried an outright condemnation of the conservative attitude which the American government was said to have taken towards the Resistance movement in Belgium and Greece.[112] Oliver Harvey, from the Foreign Office, describing a visit he had paid to Paris in March 1945, claimed to detect great dislike, 'even hatred' of the Americans, and perplexity on the part of pro-British French officials that His Majesty's Government[113] was not 'as confiding with France as our mutual interests demanded'.[113] As SHAEF Mission (France) admitted, reviewing the situation during June 1945:

> Although Franco–Allied relations may be described as satisfactory, from the volume and tone of reports received during this period, it must be concluded that there has been some increase in popular misgivings about the Allies, and, to a lesser extent, in actual unfriendliness. This is largely attributable to the current state of international affairs. The nationalistic foreign policy of De Gaulle is very popular, and the repeated checks it has met at the hands of the Allies cannot but result in an unfavourable public impression, especially when taken with the normal discomfort a nation undergoes while large bodies of foreign troops are within its territory, and with widespread, if uninformed, popular opinions of what the Allies are, or are not, doing to alleviate France's economic suffering.[114]

The increasing unpopularity of the Americans was not unrelated to the fact that, with the advance of the 21st Army Group into Belgium and Holland, remaining British commitments in France had passed to the American forces. Understandably the malaise could be more acute in those areas where a large number of troops were concentrated. Thus the *Commissaire de la République* of Châlons-sur-Marne, where there were large military barracks, addressed a number of despatches to the Ministry of the Interior pointing to the difficulties of local relations with the troops. Whilst on the surface conduct was courteous, he claimed that when the Americans needed something they were not over scrupulous about how it was obtained, an approach the French had already endured for the previous four years of occupation:

> The American mentality is so very different from the French that only the gratitude we feel towards the Americans for the Liberation can lessen what is in effect a complete change in public opinion. In this region, saturated with troops, the actions of the American army . . . and those of the American Government are very unfavourably regarded.[115]

Incidents were particularly frequent where French personnel were working for American employers (as in the docks at Le Havre, the mines in the Nancy region, or the construction site at Gray, in the Haute-Saône, where the Americans were faced with a strike after the sacking of the local secretary of the building union, against the explicit advice of the prefect). In other areas, however, where the Allied presence was much less obtrusive, there were still reports of anti-American feeling and of a general decline in American prestige and popularity.[116]

The economic situation, in particular the food shortage, played its part in the mounting criticism of the Americans. SHAEF Mission (France) reported in March 1945 that:

> The shortage of food continues to be critical, especially in urban areas, and an average family, with insufficient resources to buy on the black market, finds it difficult to exist. The general civilian supply situation is unquestionably inferior to that which existed during the German occupation.[117]

In March, the scale of rations issued in the city of Paris per person per month was: 210g of meat, 180g pork, 80g cheese, 500g sugar, 10,850g bread, 6,000g potatoes and 5,500g vegetables. The total value of the diet was estimated at 1,515 calories, whereas the goal originally established by SHAEF to provide against disease was 2,000 calories, although it was suggested that an additional 300 calories per day were probably being consumed by French families, from outside sources like the black market, social services and factory canteens.[118] In April, however, SHAEF reported that no meat had actually been issued in Paris for three consecutive weeks, and the butter ration had not been distributed for three months.[119] An opinion poll, asking French people whether the food situation in early spring 1945 was better or worse than the position before the Liberation, found 59 per cent of respondents claiming that it was worse, and 79 per cent worse than it had been in October 1944.[120] In these circumstances it was unsurprising that food demonstrations were reported in many areas of France – the police recorded 51 in the mid-February to mid-March period, with 10,000 people involved in Lyons, 2,000 in Angoulême, Vannes, Clermont, Bron and Bayonne, and 4,000 in Agen.[121]

Inevitably the Allied agencies felt they had been caught as 'piggy-in-the-middle', a convenient, and not altogether innocent, scapegoat. The Joint Intelligence Committee of SHAEF noted in February 1945 that the French government might well be tempted to deflect some of the opprobium resulting from its economic problems to the Allies, who could be blamed for supply and transport deficiencies; 'If little or nothing can be done to meet these demands, we may expect considerable resentment and friction . . . '.[122] The public relations division of SHAEF had indeed begun to consider ways of presenting the Allied aid programme in a more positive light, 'in view of the world-wide controversy and comment'.[123] A confidential paper pointed out that the problem was, in practice, a matter of French criticisms of the American government:

> There is a growing breach between France and the United States . . . One of the main troubles is that De Gaulle is under pressure for action of all kinds and he does not hesitate to shift shortcomings to Allied shoulders. What he says gets French press space. What we do does not.[124]

When SHAEF produced a communiqué claiming that their record on aid to the military programme and civilian economy was in fact extremely good, the French press neither reported nor commented on it, although Paris radio broadcast an *Agence France Presse* statement suggesting that the SHAEF list of supplies had been presented in an ambiguous way, whilst the French embassy in Washington pointed out that more had been withdrawn from France than had actually been imported.[125]

It is a measure of the American government's concern that the American political officer at SHAEF, supported by the Ambassador, indicated in March 1945 that a co-ordinating committee on public relations among American services and agencies was urgently needed. Caffery himself had sent a note on the present destitution in France to an American journal, and this at least received some publicity in the French media, with extracts on the food shortages being reproduced by several papers.[126] *Le Populaire* commented bitterly that such articles had not yet been followed up by practical measures from the USA, although the arrival of shipments of condensed milk, fats, rice and medical supplies was promised all the time.[127] Meanwhile, press protests on the slowness of deliveries, and the general lack of shipping facilities continued. The impression the French press generally gave its readers was that military and naval needs always took precedence for the Americans over the carriage of food, clothing and supplies.

The USA, whilst being badgered to give the French a seat at Yalta, an occupation zone, and a place on the control commission, was hardly put in the most receptive mood by such reports of growing anti-Americanism. American agencies like the State Department, which favoured giving concessions to France in foreign policy matters, were put in a particularly difficult position by the news that large sections of the French press were blaming the USA for worsening domestic economic conditions.

# 8 Economic reconstruction and the Allies

AS FAR AS its economic future was concerned, it was clear that Liberated France was dependent for its very survival on help given by the Allies. This desperate need placed the Allies, and in particular the Americans, in an apparently strong position from which to demand a *quid pro quo* from the provisional government, namely liberalization of the French economy. Given the country's extreme economic weakness, it was remarkable that the French managed to be as unco-operative as they were in this area. By the technique of verbal agreement followed by lengthy procrastination, the French government delayed giving the USA what it demanded. In a sense the Allies were hoist with their own petard. Having allowed the GPRF to take power and having underpinned its authority it was difficult in practice to do a great deal about French independence. It was not, however, until tensions between East and West sharpened that the USA began to consider abandoning its attempt to exact a return for financial and economic help proffered.

France before the war exhibited many symptoms of economic malaise even before the colossal problems provoked by the Occupation and subseqent Liberation. Whilst it was true that the 1929 depression had hit France later than other industrialized countries, its effects had taken longer to reverse. The very factors which had protected the French economy in the early 1930s — its comparatively large agricultural sector, and more particularly its relative independence within the international economy – served as barriers to recovery when the multilateral system of the Gold Exchange Standard broke down and other countries began to set up their own trading systems for domestic recovery. France was left virtually isolated and unable to reverse the impact of the Depression. The pattern of pre-war French finances had been to run a constant and often very large trade deficit; indeed there were only two occasions in the 40 years before the war when French exports had been able to pay for the nation's imports.[1]

The effect of the German Occupation was to deplete France's finances and diminish its industrial potential still further. In the period of 1940–4, it was estimated that France transferred to Germany a cash sum equivalent to 169 per cent of the whole of its income in taxation.[2] The Germans confiscated some two-thirds of French production for their own uses and French stockpiles were ruthlessly pruned. Between 1938 and 1943, the Allies estimated that total industrial production in France had decreased by around 40 per cent and reckoned that Liberated France and its Empire would be able to supply only approximately 2 million of the 7 million tons of raw materials required. Despite these estimates, and the recognition that the initial economic situation of the country would be worsened by the inevitable demands that the Allied war machine would make on it, the Allies had not envisaged the sheer scale of the additional devastation visited on the French by the Normandy Landings: some 83,000 civilians killed, including around 4000 children.[3] In the middle of September 1944 the Prime Minister had demanded actual details on the health and food supply situation in the Low Countries, France and Germany, starting from the assumption that, 'they will be found very much better off than we have been led to believe'.[4] The Stopford Mission, reporting on the position in October, was much less optimistic in its conclusions on France. The nutritional standard of the population was better than expected, but there was very little margin of safety, and the appalling transport situation was likely to aggravate both food supply and economic problems: 'The primary need of the French is for the means of transport and raw materials, though a certain quantity of fats and temporarily at least, milk for children and meat, should be imported as soon as possible.'

Later in September, a joint British–American team, the Weir–Green Mission, produced a more detailed analysis of the current industrial potential of France. Whilst the Foreign Office commented that some of its remarks were patronizing to the French and that there were instances where the team had appeared rather too anxious to see French industry revert speedily to the use of natural raw materials which the Allies themselves could supply,[5] the report provided an excellent picture of the economic situation of Liberated France. The devastation, wrought firstly by the Occupation, and then by the Liberation, was graphically portrayed. In terms of railway rolling stock for example, the pre-war situation had been around 300,000 wagons (not including passenger stock), and 6,000 locomotives. By June 1944 the vicissitudes of the Occupation had reduced that number to 250,000 and 5,000, respectively. By the post-Liberation period serviceable wagons and locomotives had fallen to 31,000 and 1233. Since the Germans had left the country, virtually all supplies of raw materials had stopped and no alternatives had been found. French industries were, therefore, at a standstill and could not restart operations until raw materials had been brought in and transported to individual factories, and supplies of fuel and power made available. Social unrest and large-scale unemployment, 'which might well be prejudicial to the successful development of operations and to the stability of the French administration', seemed inevitable. The Weir–Green Mission suggested that French demands for raw materials to alleviate this situation were currently unrealistically high, and that the best course of action would be for the Allies to aim to re-establish industrial employment in the short term at the level, an admittedly low one, that had pertained during the German Occupation.[6]

Two further reports in early 1945, one by President Roosevelt's friend, Judge Samuel Rosenman, and one from the British Embassy in Paris, updated these findings on the economy.[7] Both emphasized that the food problem was still acute. Before the war the country had been 80 per cent self-sufficient in foodstuffs. The Occupation had radically altered the balance of agriculture, since the Germans had extracted large quantities of food, whilst production had generally declined in the wake of lower supplies of labour and fertilizers, and reduced feed imports. The transport situation was hindering post-Liberation attempts to distribute what the farmers were now producing, and the government was finding it difficult to persuade peasant producers to adhere to agreed systems of collection and distribution.

Both reports pinpointed the coal shortage as one of the major difficulties in the reconstruction of the French economy. In early December 1944 the Minister for Industrial Production claimed that deliveries of coal had fallen to 2,000 tons per day, whereas 5,000 tons per day were needed to supply Paris alone with gas and electricity. Before the war the French economy had used something in the order of 75 million tons each year, 30 million tons of which had been imported. By February 1945 coal production in the Nord–Pas de Calais fields was at around 70 per cent of pre-war production, but even this, given the still acute transport situation, could not guarantee domestic heating in Paris. The import of coal from the Allies meanwhile was signally failing to fill the gap in home production. In December indeed the French protested that the Allies might at least import to France as much coal – 400,000 tons each month – as they were currently consuming in the country. Rosenman's conclusion on the French economic situation in January 1945 was bleak. Short-term Allied help to restore the French manufacturing base by supplying raw materials had proved to be a drop in the ocean, since most had gone to the rearmament programme. What was needed to reconstruct the economy was a sustained long-term effort so extensive that Rosenman was unable to cost it. The normally optimistic Jean Monnet underlined the magnitude of the task facing the GPRF: 'In spite of what has been done, the economic life of France is steadily approaching extinction'.[8]

In these conditions it was evident that France would firstly need aid to begin to reconstruct its economy, and secondly would be forced to abandon its former isolated position and become much more dependent on international trade. When the French government signed the Bretton Woods agreement at the end of 1945, it accepted that France would participate in a multilateral trading system, although there was the proviso that such participation could only follow economic reconstruction and modernization, the latter clearly dependent on Allied, and more particularly American, help.

The American attitude to the economic future of France was conditioned by two factors – one specific to France and a product of its political relations with the Gaullists; and the other springing from its general preconceptions about the desirability of reconstructing a multilateral system of world trade in which barriers to trade would be lowered and made non-discriminatory in their application. Economic relations between the American government and the Free French had been marked by the uncertainty which had characterized their political relations. Thus in 1941 when the Free French had sought some form of Lend Lease to support the Resistance colonies, and suggested that the Americans might like, as it were in return, to establish military installations in Equatorial Africa, they had been met by a chilly response. The State Department initially refused to receive the Gaullist emissary, Pleven, and Welles pointed out that Lend Lease could apply only to legally constituted governments. Hopkins expressed the prevailing mood: direct aid to the Free French, 'is a very touchy subject and must be explored only through the State Department. It gets into the matter of foreign policy and the decisions must finally rest there.'[9] Aid could only be provided by a system of retransfer from the British government. After the American entry into the war, the subject of direct aid to the French was again discussed, and the President specifically rejected the idea of negotiations with the Free French for a formal Lend Lease agreement. As the war progressed and French North African territory was liberated, however, Roosevelt accepted that the rather *ad hoc* retransfer system should be replaced by an agreement on reciprocal aid to French North and West Africa. Such an agreement distinguished clearly between Lend Lease nations and the CFLN since the French authorities were expected to pay cash for civilian goods rather than obtaining the material on credit. The American government defended this position on the grounds that France had adequate funds to pay for the goods. France's participation in the war effort had been brief, and it had not, therefore, incurred the huge financial debt which plagued the British. In addition, the areas concerned in the agreement, North and West Africa, had, the Americans argued, been out of the war altogether. The ambivalence of the French situation was precisely illustrated by the American contention that France's economic problems could not be considered as acute as those of Britain, since the French held, under

Morgenthau's estimate, over 2.5 billion dollars in gold and American dollars in the USA. Since however the CFLN had not been recognized as the government of France, it was difficult to see how they could draw on these reserves, and it was not indeed until the Allied recognition of France in October 1944 that French government funds in the USA were unfrozen.[10]

American uncertainty in the political sphere over recognition of the CFLN was matched by a similar delay over negotiating a formal Lend Lease agreement which would cover the needs and problems of Liberated France. Six months after the Normandy landings, France was the only major recipient of Allied aid with whom the American government had not yet concluded a master Lend Lease agreement. In a sense the legacy of suspicion about the French, fed on occasions by the way in which the GPRF presented its case for economic assistance, continued in some American circles, long after the demise of the one-time leader of the anti-Gaullist camp, President Roosevelt. Truman, for example, told Sir John Balfour of his unfavourable impressions of the French people and their government in August 1945. After his visit to Europe, the President had been struck by the contrast between the Belgian and French people – the latter, 'appeared to be listless and waiting for outside relief to put them on their feet'. He doubted whether de Gaulle was really the man to pull the nation together: 'the General took himself and his ideas of French prestige altogether too seriously and "to use a saying that we have way back in Missouri", he was something of a pinhead'.[11]

If American economic relations with France were anomalous as far as the existence of a Lend Lease agreement was concerned, their general attitude towards the future pattern of trade with France was very much in line with that displayed to other Allied and liberated countries. From the beginning the French were aware of strong American pressure to liberalize trade. In the September 1943 agreement on aid to French North and West Africa, the American negotiators had insisted on a supplemental document stipulating that 'nothing in the agreement shall be interpreted as precluding the early resumption of private trade when conditions permit'.[12] In the USA the Lend Lease agency itself was coming under mounting pressure from the private sector to facilitate the restoration of American international commercial trade as soon as possible, and a special economic mission to investigate the prospects for this had been set up in July 1944, under the aegis of the Foreign Economic Administration (FEA) and the State Department. At the end of August 1944, the mission exchanged views with GPRF officials, still in Algiers, on the likelihood of an early resumption of private trade with the French empire and metropolitan France. The chairman, Culbertson, received a highly unfavourable impression, concluding that, whilst there were some differences of opinion between French Cabinet members, the majority appeared to advocate 'government control and monopoly of trade and industry'. Culbertson's recommendation was that the American government should pursue a 'firm, realistic, non-benevolent policy toward the French in Paris in order to achieve the economic policy which gave rise to the Mission'.[13]

With the Liberation, the French response to these pressures tended to take the form of procrastination, followed by verbal agreement, followed by further procrastination. Early in September 1944, the French provisional government suggested that private trade would be unlikely to resume until the French people had elected a new government, a process which could take anything from six months to a year. Whilst there was by no means unanimity among American agencies in late 1944 about the wisdom of exerting further pressure on France in its present weakened state, the Embassy pointed out to the French Foreign Ministry in December 1944 that American policy was to foster private trade through commercial channels, and that the forth-coming ending of the agreement on aid to French Africa would provide an ideal opportunity to begin to normalize commercial trade in this area. The GPRF was asked to send commercial agents to the USA in order to promote the desired contact between American and French firms. The French replied by conditionally accepting and promising to issue export licences. They pointed out, however, that they would not be able to move to private purchase in all cases, since a great deal of material was presently being imported for state organizations, and these orders would have to be placed via government channels. In a later talk with Culbertson's mission, the French reiterated that they would have to continue to procure bulk items in this way, but suggested that private trade could begin immediately in such areas as lorries, cars and farm equipment.[14] In March 1945 the GPRF agreed to the restoration of private trade with West Africa, a move which stimulated over 1,000 American firms to write letters of inquiry to the American Consulate at Dakar.

In practice the actual effects of French trade liberalization tended to be notional. In early 1945 the French had signalled their intention to establish tariffs and controls on imports because of their severe economic difficulties, whilst restating their acceptance of the free trade spirit of undertakings already taken. They suggested that one way forward might be the convening of expert talks on the subject, a suggestion that the Americans had broadened out to an interminister-ial conference designed to reduce all trade barriers.[15] In April Stettinius was ordering Caffery to remind the French of the importance which the American government attached to such a measure to deal with restrictive practices and trade barriers.[16] As far as private trade with metropolitan France was concerned, the GPRF continued delaying tactics. The chairman of the French Supply Council claimed in March 1945 that he had received no instructions at all in this matter and that the subject of private trade was barely discussed in Paris.[17] The earlier accord on private trade with the French empire did not produce an agreed list of commodities until the end of April, and it was not until September 1945 that the GPRF accepted the resumption of private trade with metropolitan France, whilst insisting again that the French Mission would have to continue buying most French imports for the time being: 'the French Provisional Government feels that the execution of its extensive reconstruction program requires supervision by governmental authority and an impetus which only these authorities can give'.[18] The French government continued to exercise firm control over imports, asking American exporters to justify the contribution their goods would make to the national reconstruction programme, and severely limiting the commodities for which export licences would be granted.

The British government for its part was, of course, facing many of the same pressures from the USA as was the GPRF, whilst acknowledging their different relationship with the Americans. The British attitude towards the economic reconstruction of France was, therefore, slightly ambivalent. The Foreign Office and the War Office both saw advantages in the establishment of a future western bloc, based on an alliance with France, and to this extent supported the idea of a financial agreement with the GPRF, which, if not to the immediate economic interest of the British, would provide a basis for long-term co-operation. The Treasury could see the advantage of an early foothold in the French market as a means of increasing exports to Europe to plug the gap which would be left by the collapse of Germany. In addition, speedily re-established trading links with France might well pre-empt what British observers took to be signs of growing protectionist tendencies in several GPRF ministries.[19] On the other hand, French proposals, and there were several, to form joint manufacturing complexes with the British were firmly rejected on the grounds that it would be nothing more than a market-sharing operation which would go against the multilateral trading interests of both Britain and the USA. The Board of Trade showed some reluctance, in the present state of the British economy, to take anything more than the minimum of French imports. There was a tendency among British spokesmen, particularly in the Treasury, to assume that the right course of action was for the modernization of the French economy to be postponed until the British economy had recovered. Churchill had already spoken out forcibly against the suggestion that the French should be accorded

Lend Lease and after this had been granted and then suspended, Keynes had sought to persuade the French not to negotiate a new loan from the American government until Congress had ratified the British loan. The Foreign Office, it should be said, warned that such behaviour might revive unfortunate memories for the French of the aftermath of the First World War.[20]

Immediately after the Liberation, France's desperate need for imports made the GPRF turn naturally towards the British government. Before, however, a financial agreement could be made between the two countries, they had to deal with the problem presented by private French assets held in Britain, which the French government were keen to assess, and, where possible, requisition. The difficulty was clearly the procedure by which confidential information about the assets of foreign nationals residing in Britain would be disclosed to outside sources. When Pleven came over to London in the beginning of February 1945, the Chancellor of the Exchequer agreed in principle that he would assist the French government by providing the required details. Interestingly enough a parliamentary question was tabled, asking Anderson whether he was satisfied that such disclosure would not prejudice the tradition of secrecy for which the British banking community was respected world-wide. The Chancellor defended the agreement on the grounds that it was a 'wholly abnormal interruption of the relationship between banker and client, for which the banks cannot be held responsible'.[21]

After this, the main difficulty in the path of a Franco–British financial agreement was, predictably enough, the means by which the French would pay for the imports they required. Estimated payments for supplies for the first quarter of 1945 alone would be £16 million, but according to Pleven, the GPRF had only £11 million in the foreign exchange account, and much of this would be rapidly exhausted by diplomatic expenses and debts.[22] The Chancellor was keen to ensure that the terms of the agreement stipulated that the French would make some payments to the British in gold, 'since we shall end the war with inadequate gold reserves and very large external liabilities, while France will end the war with her considerable reserves of gold and foreign exchange almost unimpaired and no substantial liabilities'.[23] It became apparent, however, that Pleven, whatever his personal view might have been, would have found it impossible to persuade his colleagues to part with any gold whilst the French economy was in such a bad state, and whilst the French would have little chance of importing more than a fraction of their actual requirements.[24] In the end, therefore, a compromise was agreed whereby, if France bought more from Britain in the current year than Britain bought from France, part of the difference would be settled in gold. Secondly, an arrangement would be made by which dollars paid by the French before the capitulation to settle munitions contracts in the USA, which had been subsequently taken over by the British, would be used by the French ($158 million in gold or dollars) to purchase goods and materials from Britain.[25] The final agreement signed in April 1945 opened a credit of £100 million to the French and an equivalent one in francs to the British, 20,000 million francs.

To the British it was apparent that the exchange rate for the franc was set too high, making it difficult for potential buyers in Britain to purchase French goods and thus use up some of the credit surplus. In June 1945 the British Embassy sounded out Pleven about a possible change in the rate of exchange. The Minister explained that he was unwilling to do this until prices and wages had begun to settle. At present he had no idea where exactly the value of the franc should be placed, and he was concerned to avoid a 'shot in the dark' devaluation which might necessitate a second devaluation later. The GPRF was naturally feeling considerably frustrated about its economic relations with the Allies, and Pleven accused the British and Americans of 'treating France as though she would be of no account in the World for the next fifty years . . . of wishing to act as a screen between Europe and raw materials from the outside world'.[26] By August, however, Pleven suggested that, since the Japanese war had ended and the French might now be given more access to coal, it could be a good idea to adjust the rate of the franc before the end of August. If not, devaluation would have to be postponed till after the elections.[27] In the event, the GPRF decided to do nothing about the value of the franc until after that date. Duff Cooper reported that the American ratification of the Bretton Woods Agreement had made the Minister of Finance feel that any devaluation should have the moral support of the same agreement, if adverse psychological effects on the French were to be avoided.[28]

Some of the inadequacies which the French detected in early Allied programmes for France related to the fact that immediate help for the French economy had taken the form of an import programme administered by the Army under Stimson's 'prevention of disease and unrest' formula. To begin with, the amount of damage which French harbours had suffered made it very difficult to supply the volume of goods originally designated. In 1944, for example, SHAEF imported only 21 per cent of the minimum food programme in the north, and 75 per cent in the south. Secondly, the Army could hardly give priority to rehabilitating the economy when it was urgently involved in fighting the war. The French pressed actively for a national import programme which would replace the Army's first aid, but the War Department delayed agreeing to this, fearing that their claims on already scarce shipping would be badly affected if they gave up the job of importing food and supplies to the French economy. The military were nervous anyway that the lessening of control in such a critical economic area might engender repercussions on operational effectiveness.[29] Pressure was nevertheless growing for the Allies to allow civilian agencies to take over and produce a wider ranging programme for the French economy – as Rosenman pointed out to the President in April 1945, 'To limit the standard of assistance to the military level of provision any longer than is necessary, is to restrict treatment to first aid long after the patient is in need of a major operation'.[30]

The major infusion of blood which the French economy sought would be provided, the GPRF hoped, by an agreement with the Americans on Lend Lease. Monnet had drawn up two import programmes in the summer of 1944, one as an emergency supplement to the military's programme, and the other, covering the period November 1944 to June 1945, specifying not only those materials needed to enable France to participate in the war effort, but also those required to begin the process of reconstructing the French economy. By presenting the needs of the French economy in global terms like this Monnet aimed to include imports like coal for factories, which only fostered the Allied war effort indirectly: 'the recovery plan is the kingpin of the agreements for Lend Lease and reciprocal aid. It is essential that President Roosevelt approves the main outline of the plan specifying the goods we need to set the economy back on its feet at the same time as we sign the Lend Lease agreement.'[31] The State Department, underlining France's obvious difficulties, and emphasizing the connection between France's economic situation and likely political stability, supported a liberal interpretation of Lend Lease credit to cover the post-war period. The American Treasury was strongly against such a move, arguing that there was no sanction from Congress for an interpretation of Lend Lease which would clearly facilitate the reconstruction of post-war France. At the second Quebec Conference, with Churchill equally opposed to the French beginning economic recovery through Lend Lease, Morgenthau, the American Secretary of the Treasury, carried the day and Roosevelt ordered the indefinite postponement of the agreement.[32] With the recognition of France, however, the State Department came under increasing pressure to finalize a Lend Lease agreement. Stettinius noted: 'we've got a full Ambassador now and the French are needling the hell out of our fellows and we've got to say something to them'.[33] At an American Cabinet meeting in January 1945, Morgenthau, though still against the proposals the French had presented, did agree that it was necessary to get some kind of accord. He was adamant, however, that since the British had been obliged to discuss their holdings of gold and foreign exchange before Lend Lease had been granted to them, the same process must also apply to the French. The result of all this was to reduce the amount of Lend Lease offered, and a final agreement, incorporating changes, was given to the French in early February 1945. The document firstly analysed the civilian programme drawn up in 1944 in considerable detail, omitting from it all services and supplies which were needed solely for reconstruction. The rest of the requests were placed on two lists, one for short-life goods and services covered by Lend Lease up to the end of the war, and the other detailing long-life equipment for the war effort, but also beyond. These goods would have to be paid in their entirety on the basis of a 20 per cent down payment and 80 per cent on credit over 30 years from July 1946. The demands for transport, a particularly critical area for the French, had been quite severely cut, so that France would still largely be dependent on Allied transport for the supply of goods promised. Some members of the French Economic Committee were far from satisfied – 'we are getting nothing for nothing' – but the agreement was signed on 24 February.[34]

The reception of the French Lend Lease deal by Republican and conservative Democrat Congressmen was extremely hostile. Unlike other Lend Lease agreements, the French document specifically provided for the supply of civilian materials which would have a post-war utility. The pressure from Congress, including the passage of an amendment to the Lend Lease Act prohibiting its application to the post-war period, undoubtedly influenced the Presidency's behaviour in this area, and President Truman terminated all Lend Lease at the end of the Pacific War. By the time the USA had called a halt to Lend Lease in August 1945, only a small proportion of the import programme had actually been shipped to France. It was then essential for the GPRF to arrange some form of emergency financing to maintain the supply of materials to the economy. In September the State Department discussed with Monnet the possibility of opening overall financial and commercial policy talks, similar to those currently being held with the British.[35] In the meantime, Congress approved a loan to the French from the Export–Import Bank to cover the remainder of the goods ordered but not yet delivered. The Assistant Secretary of State, Will Clayton, exerted pressure to make the loan conditional on the French undertaking commercial commitments additional to the Article VII commitments of the Lend Lease agreement, which had specified a readiness to reduce barriers and tariffs and liberalize trade as the American government wanted.[36] Clayton was particularly interested in the French opening access to the USA to all air routes, lifting restrictions on American films, and eliminating tax measures which the American government thought to be unfair. The French, obviously hard-pressed by this, agreed to an exchange of letters by which they repeated their willingness to comply with Article VII. They pointed out, however, that the first priority had to be to reconstruct the economy: 'The French Government therefore proposes that, before entering into negotiations relative to customs barriers and commerical policy, our two Governments undertake together an inquiry into the total needs of France, and the resources which are at present available, or may be rendered available, to place France in a position to participate in the orderly development of international trade'.[37] Caffery reported that highly placed French commentators considered that the French Cabinet had made a conscious decision, signified by the letters, to move in the long term towards multilateral trade, with all that this implied for the domestic economy. The Ambassador felt that the French strategy was to get the USA to recognize France as a major economic power, entitled to the same treatment as Britain – 'Their argument runs that France's decisions rather than the UK's will predominately control the foreign trade policies of Western Europe'. Secondly, the French appeared to be aiming to substitute generalities as the *quid pro quo* for the loan, rather than the specific actions and commitments which the USA required. Caffery believed that careful negotiation could secure some of the concessions the USA desired in return for a loan. With the November government reshuffle which brought the communist Billoux into the Ministry of the National Economy, the Ambassador was even more convinced that financial discussions with the French should not take place without simultaneous examination of commercial policy and specific trade problems: 'it is clear that the program of the *Délégation [sic] des Gauches* has so many closed economy aspects that it will be extremely difficult to reconcile it either with our broad commercial policy objectives or with the specific concessions which we need from the French Government'.[38] Eventually, however, a loan contract was signed in December 1945 at the rate of 2⅜ per cent to be repaid over 30 years.

The argument about the speed with which the French would move towards liberalizing trade continued into 1946. The French government had explained, in signing the Bretton Woods Agreement at the end of 1945, that the country could only participate in a mutilateral system once the domestic economy had been reconstructed and modernized. They hoped that imports to effect this recovery would be financed largely by American credits on the scale of the recently negotiated British loan. The government informed the Embassy that they would need a lump sum for this purpose, rather than piecemeal credits. Caffery's staff advised that there should be prior assessment of the French attitude to changes in fiscal and monetary policies, to nationalization, taxation and exchange controls.[39] In the middle of January

1946, three days after General de Gaulle had resigned from power, the new Prime Minister, Léon Blum, informed the Ambassador that he would like to go to the USA himself, in order to stress how desperate France's need was for coal, wheat and other raw materials and to reassure the President that the country had not 'gone red'.[40]

Faced with the current political situation in France, Caffery's reports indicated a new ordering of priorities as far as French economic demands were concerned:

> As you are aware, I have always favoured a realistic and comprehensive settlement of unfinished business with the French in return for any dollar credits. At this time, however, I desire to emphasize my belief that it is in our national interest to grant France a substantial dollar credit even though to a banker's eye France might not be considered an A-1 risk. It is in our interest that public discouragement should not reach the point where extremists appear to offer the only chance of improvement. Under these circumstances, I believe that the loan France will request of us should be weighed in terms of its political importance.[41]

# 9 Conclusions: the reconstruction of the state

BY APRIL 1945 a sovereign France was being created. From the chaos and dishonour of 1940, and the often humiliating dependency on the Allies in the subsequent years, an independent French regime emerged with clear political objectives of its own, and a surprising tendency to withhold co-operation with the Allies if French interests might be compromised.

This book has explored how far the Allies conditioned this outcome. The evidence suggests that the influence was predominantly indirect and often unwitting. The silence before 'D' Day on Allied intentions, for example, fuelled French fears of an Allied-imposed solution. This, in turn, encouraged the Gaullists to demonstrate that they had the democratic credentials which might have persuaded the Americans to recognize them as the future government of France. Hence the enlargement of the CFLN, the creation of the CNR and the Consultative Assembly, and the official integration of the parties into the Resistance bodies. The less the Allies told the French about their political plans, the more the French were stimulated to work out their own plans for the Liberation in considerable detail. The CLFN in fact used fears of an AMGOT to promote unity among the Resistance and to obtain assent to the interim Liberation measures which were planned.

During the actual Liberation, Allied influence varied enormously from area to area. When the dust of the fighting settled, it was clear that the Allies had observed, and in some cases assiduously aided, the assumption of power by the French themselves. Who the 'French' were depended on which part of the country one was in. The Allied military proved willing to accept all sorts of political arrangements provided – and it was an important proviso – that they maintained a reasonable level of law and order locally, and thus caused no trouble behind Allied lines. The Liberation of Paris showed starkly how far the Allies had been reduced to the role of observer in the transfer of power.

In the absence of an agreed Allied policy, and hence of overt interference in French affairs, the main barrier to the CFLN/GPRF assuming power was the likely behaviour of the PCF. We have attempted to examine the intentions and actions of the PCF as they developed before, during and after the Liberation. The evidence, admittedly imperfect, supports the view that the party had no intention of staging a coup and of seizing power at the Liberation. Instead the communists wished to place themselves in as advantageous a position as possible from which to fight and win an election, coming to power through the ballot-box as a Jacobin party. Before the return of Thorez, however, there was still some uncertainty in communist tactics, and the last months of 1944 were marked by the PCF defending, at least publicly, the existence of the alternative Resistance institutions which de Gaulle was keen to discourage.

Just as there is no evidence of a 'communist plot' to seize power, so there is no evidence of a more general Resistance/left-wing plot to subvert the GPRF. In many areas of France the provisional government found it difficult to re-establish control, but the situation was one of competing centres of power rather than of an organized attempt on the national scale to wrest power from de Gaulle. In general, the alternative Resistance institutions showed themselves to be interested mainly in chasing collaborators, and in low-level police work, and only occasionally in economic and social reform, and this in a strictly limited local context.

The final establishment of GPRF power throughout France was a product of two factors, both dependent on the Allies. Firstly, Thorez returned from Moscow, doubtless with instructions from Stalin about the need to respect Allied spheres of influence, and bend all efforts to winning the war. The tactics of the PCF were clarified almost immediately, and the alternative Resistance institutions largely withered away. Secondly, the Allies underpinned GPRF authority both by the diplomatic recognition and attention they accorded it, and by their continued failure to produce any alternative of their own. The longer the French government stayed in power, the more unlikely it became that the Allies would interfere or even seek to use the security measures they had drafted in the event of an emergency. The British in particular, but later the Americans too, were convinced that it was in their interests to support a regime which was already in power and seemed both democratic and likely to keep some control of the Left. The British government was keen to advance at least some of the French claims to 'great power' status, hoping that a strong French government would share the costs of European defence once the Americans had gone.

The fall of France in 1940 had brought down with it the whole structure of the Third Republic. As we have seen, the metropolitan Resistance in particular regarded these events as signalling a watershed in French life. The post-war world would have to represent a new beginning, a 'renovated' France. Different groups gave different nuances to the 'revolution' required, but most agreed on the basic premise that what came after the Liberation would have to remedy the clear political and constitutional defects which were felt to have contributed to the *débâcle* of defeat. There would have to be a new and uncompromised personnel to carry out the necessary changes. The CNR programme called for a society in which social and economic relationships would have been profoundly altered in comparison with the pre-war world.

## The balance of political forces

TO BEGIN WITH the Resistance movements seemed likely to hold their own against the political parties. The latter, although integrated into the CNR and the GPRF by de Gaulle, were still – with the exception of the PCF – trying to rebuild their organizations after the blow dealt them by the defeat. The two major umbrella groups of the Resistance, the *Mouvement de Libération Nationale* (MLN) – non-communist – and the *Front National* (FN) – dominated by the PCF – did not simply disappear at the Liberation. Both launched vigorous recruitment drives, and by December 1944, *Le Monde* could describe them as 'real political formations'.[1] In many areas the Resistance movements seemed to be at least as active and successful as the re-emerging political parties. In the November–December 1944 period, for instance, both movements were recorded as holding more political meetings than the Socialist Party: 117 for the MLN, 152 for the *Front National*, and only 78 for the SFIO. In the Clermont region the MLN was reported as being the major mass movement, whilst its membership in the Puy-de-Dôme area was put at 100,000 and still growing in October 1944. In Marseilles in early November, the most active organizations were again reported to be the MLN and FN rather than the political parties.[2] The problem with this startling success lay in the nature of these movements themselves. Before the Liberation both had been heterogeneous in membership, in the case of the FN deliberately so since, although the movement was largely controlled by the PCF, it had opened its doors to as wide a spectrum of political views as possible, numbering, for example, François Mauriac, Father Philippe and Monsignor Chevrot among its prominent members. For the MLN heterogeneity was built into its structure, since it had been formed by merging several existing Resistance groups (*Combat, Libération, Franc-Tireur, France au Combat, Résistance, Lorraine*) which were each individually highly varied in membership. The additional members who had joined in the months immediately following the Liberation, often attracted by the message of change, reform and renewal which the movements preached, clearly increased the potential problems. If some form of effective political expression was to be given to the aspirations of the membership, the movements would presumably need to define and agree a programme, or at the least a set of immediate goals.

Some of the difficulties involved in this process were illustrated by the congresses of the two movements in early 1945. At the MLN Congress (23–28 January) an argument on church–school subsidy, a traditional pre-war bone of contention between the political parties, threatened to break out. To avoid what might clearly have been a damaging dispute, the Congress decided to accept the status quo on the issue and refer the matter to a special committee for more detailed discussion. At the end of the Congress, whilst some delegates bemoaned the fact that there had been so little serious consideration of the need to turn the movement into a proper political formation, others were pleased that such an opportunity, which they felt to be contrary to the spirit of the Resistance, had been lost.[3] By contrast, the *Front National* Congress (30 January–3 February) seemed to be extremely disciplined, with a tendency for speakers to add information to the previous speech rather than engage in a full-scale debate. Discussion of programmes appeared even less in evidence, with the tone of contributions resolutely practical – a delegate from the Nord suggesting, for example, that destitute Parisian children should be temporarily fostered in homes in his area.[4]

Both the MLN and the FN congresses had been dominated by the question of whether the two movements should merge. At the MLN Congress the debate had been fierce and prolonged, underlining the fundamental differences of opinion which existed as to which direction the movement should take. To begin with, three motions were put before the membership. One, backed by Pierre Hervé, called for a federation of Resistance movements, or a *travailliste rassemblement*, open initially to the PCF, the SFIO and the CGT, as well as the two existing major Resistance movements. A second option, proposed by Alban, was close to the Hervé resolution, but had a less *travailliste* tone, suggesting simply that all Resistance movements should unite in a front of national Liberation. A motion opposing these two, and defended by André Malraux, eschewed any idea of organic mergers, calling instead for a vaguer sort of Resistance unit, and demanding specifically that the MLN should support General de Gaulle and develop its own programme, including a package of socialist economic measures and the nationalization of credit facilities. After discussion, Alban's motion was removed and the membership was asked to choose between the resolutions of Hervé and Malraux. Whilst it was true that Hervé's motion did not call for a merger between the MLN and the FN, it clearly advocated a federation of movements as a first step towards achieving some kind of organizational unity. Malraux's resolution equally clearly intended each movement to retain its own character and structure, and the writer urged the congress to develop the MLN into a separate political formation, as disciplined and single-minded as a party like the PCF:

> . . . if we want to maintain the resources of energy that we have mobilised, then we have to use techniques similar to those of the Communist Party . . . we must observe within our Movement a sense of discipline which is as great as that Party's.[5]

The vote rejected the Hervé merger motion by 250 votes to 119. As *Combat* commented, the argument over merger or non-merger had as its subtext the still running dispute between the Socialist Party, a major 'shareholder' in the MLN, and the PCF, a dominant partner in the FN. Yet, according to the Resistance paper, MLN delegates who had voted against the merger motion were less worried about the potential domination of the PCF, and more concerned to avoid what they felt to be the basically conservative approach adopted by the FN in welcoming members of former right-wing parties into membership, and in toning down anything in its programme which might scare voters away.[6]

Such a judgment of the FN's moderate stance was amply confirmed by the movement's Congress where, for example, the President, Pierre Villon, protested that nationalization measures should only be taken with the total assent of the nation: 'And don't let anyone get onto us with all this radical nonsense . . . we are serious people. We're fighting the war and trying to get national unity.'[7] Clearly the FN were disappointed at the MLN Congress decision to refuse a merger, but Villon suggested that they should accept for the moment unity of action, in the absence of any form of organic unity.[8]

The argument about mergers continued. In the MLN departmental Congress at Lyons in May 1945, the Rhône branch of the movement voted to merge with the FN and were promptly suspended by the national executive committee. By June the minority (merger) wing of the MLN nationally had split with the majority in the movement, joined the FN and formed a new joint movement, the *Mouvement Unifié de la Renaissance Française*. The majority MLN tendency had, meanwhile, fused with two smaller independent Resistance movements, *Libération-Nord* and *Organisation Civile et Militaire* (OCM), to form the *Union Démocratique et Sociale de la Résistance* (UDSR).

Against this background of mergers, doctrine and programmes, the Resistance movements faced the build-up to the municipal elections in April 1945. As the *Commissaire de la République* of Dijon reported in late February: 'The Resistance movements are disorientated . . . and don't know exactly how to approach the electoral problem'. At Marseilles at the same time it appeared as if the political parties were moving into the foreground compared to the Resistance groups.[9] A measure of this was the number of political meetings held in the pre-election period, where the SFIO, trailing behind the PCF, had overtaken the MLN and FN in three consecutive monthly reports, although the Resistance movements were still far ahead of the embryonic *Mouvement Républicain Populaire* (MRP), and the barely revived Radical and Radical-socialist Party.[10] As the major parties of the Left discussed at national and local level the tactics that they should pursue in the forthcoming municipal elections, the Resistance movements found themselves either acting as the battlefield for the covert conflict, or else regarded as an irritating irrelevancy. The PCF and SFIO were both suspicious of movements which they could not totally control, and which might well become election rivals for them, making inroads in their traditional electoral clienteles.[11] The experience, organization and single-mindedness of established political parties were more than a match for the enthusiastic but amorphous resistance groups. By March and early April 1945 reports suggested that the MLN and FN had either been subsumed into the parties, or had become satellites, 'branches' of the parties. With the decisions on electoral lists announced it was evident that the major political parties had reasserted control: 'The Resistance seems rather to have melted away at the first breath of the election lists . . . the former parties and their leaders have re-emerged from the shadows.'[12]

The Resistance movements, which could have proved a national challenge to the GPRF in a way in which the dispersed units of alternative local adminstration had not, took considerable time to see what their common interests were, and decide on the best way of organizing nationally. In the act of uniting, they could find neither a basis for unity, nor a separate electoral role for their groups. They were thus swiftly overtaken by the eminently normal Republican practice of a local election, and turned their attention to the task of winning (or helping a particular political party to win) within the existing structure. Any thought that the Resistance movements might overturn the political system was thereby lost.

That it took at least some of the political parties time to 're-emerge from the shadows' is an indication of the problems several of them faced at the Liberation. The PCF was in many ways the best placed to profit from the situation. With an undeniably courageous Resistance record and considerable public sympathy for the USSR, it embarked on a vigorous campaign to capitalize on the favourable climate of opinion and expand the number of its members and sympathizers. In the autumn and winter of 1944 it was undoubtedly the most active party in terms of meetings held (10 of which attracted over 1000–2000, and nine more than 2000), with the next highest political group on the list recorded as having only 117 meetings.[13] The impression in several regions was that the party was giving first priority to recruitment, 'it's trying to extend its surface, rather than concentrate its forces', and certainly the PCF made use of the now flourishing press, printing blank application forms in many of the provincial papers.[14] It made special efforts with sections of the population among whom its appeal had formerly been slight. Thus, in an attempt to penetrate the peasant masses, it fused PCF peasant Resistance groups (*Comités de Défense et d'Action Paysanne*) with the socialist-founded *Confédération Générale d'Agriculture*, and instructed its members in rural *communes* to act moderately and even to stand up against the 'sectarianism' of certain Liberation committees whose activities were clearly dismaying local peasant farmers.[15] Very often the broadening of appeal required the party to downplay its traditional themes of class conflict in favour of a vaguer and more general 'unity' message. Thus, for example, the Political Bureau of the Region of the Vienne explained to a comrade in February 1945 that his draft article on the early history of the church would not be published because it would inevitably have had to refer to class conflict and the revolutionary nature of the communist ideology: 'Now it is awkward to evoke these two points at a time when our position can be summed up in the following directive: "Union of the French Nation." '[16]

In the more traditional bastions of trades unions and workers' organizations, the party worked to increase its influence to the detriment of the SFIO. The communists profited here from the effect that the celebrated collaboration of '*confédéré*' leaders like René Belin had created in workers' circles after the war. On a local level, communist trade unionists were initially better organized than their opponents and often succeeded in identifying themselves with the Resistance and their rivals with the collaboration. The composition of the *Bureau Confédéral* changed in March 1945 to the advantage of the PCF who, in the absence of the imprisoned general-secretary, took control of the central organization of the union.

In terms of recruitment to the party, the effect of this dynamic activity was enormous. In September 1937, the membership of the PCF was put at around 300,000. In January 1945 it was still estimated as under 400,000, but by the beginning of June 1946 it would reach 800,000. There were, of course, potential difficulties in this success. If the leadership remained virtually identical to the pre-war one in this period, the base had changed in quality as well as quantity. Numbers in Paris had stagnated or actually declined, whereas in the rural regions they had dramatically increased – ten-fold in Brittany, for example, where there had been hardly any PCF presence before the war. The proportion of cells based on factories and the shopfloor had sharply decreased (31.1 per cent of all the cells in 1937, compared with 20.1 per cent in 1945), an indication of the relative reduction in the percentage of working-class members in the PCF after the war. Such an influx of members drawn from backgrounds atypical in normal PCF recruitment posed the problem of training, control and internal discipline. Thorez's return, as well as clarifying the party's strategy, signalled a re-emphasis of the tradition of democratic centralism, a stress on the need to discipline, to avoid 'the family-type atmosphere which rapidly stifles the spirit of the Party'.[17] Reports suggested that the PCF was reorganizing itself and beginning to impose a very firm structure of internal party discipline in the early part of 1945. In time it would shed some of the militants whose Resistance record might have been impeccable, but whose social background was deemed inappropriate.[18]

By comparison, the Socialist Party experienced more difficulties in restarting political activity. Since socialists had tended to resist as individuals rather than establish a specifically socialist Resistance group, and since the party had, like others of the Third Republic, its share of *Pétainistes* and *attentistes*, it emerged from the war years with a less gilded reputation than that of the PCF, and initially devoid of the charismatic drawing power of the latter. Gradually the party set about restoring its organization in the regions. The Central Executive met for the first time on 30 August and arranged a special delegate conference in September. At their first national congress in November 1944 the party excluded all those socialist *députés* who had voted in favour of granting full powers to the Marshal in July 1940. By this time 96 out of the pre-war 101 federations had been reconstituted, and membership was estimated as being around 120,000, about the equivalent of 1939 figures.[19] If the SFIO was rebuilding itself, however, its political activity in the provinces was markedly less than that of its left-wing rival. In the period when the PCF was holding over 300 meetings, socialists were recorded as having only 75, two of which drew 1,000–2,000 and one over 2,000.[20] Through 1945 its activity steadily increased and overtook that of the Resistance movements, but still trailed far behind the PCF, as indeed did its membership figures, some 250,000 in the middle of 1945.[21]

To an extent, many of the members who had entered the party by the Liberation (and about half of the membership was estimated as new) were politically inexperienced and thus not a match for the more politically sophisticated local PCF organizers. In addition, it was clear that there was some lack of sympathy between the aspirations of these newer militants and the longer standing members of the party.

The intentions of the Resistance leadership, dominated, until Léon Blum's return, by Daniel Mayer, were viewed with suspicion by more traditionalist militants. Thus, at the November congress, Mayer expressed his views on the 'new' revolution called for by the Resistance, and alluded to the possibility of future agreements with communists and Christian democrats, whilst at the same time anti-clerical delegates from Normandy and Brittany spoke passionately against the executive's attempts to tone down a typically pre-war anti-clerical motion. As far as the organization of the party was concerned, a similar argument ensued about the merits of the pre-war decentralized model and a centralized system, favoured by the leadership, that would enable the *comité directeur* to control the federations via federal secretaries and, hence, go some way towards suppressing pre-war factionalism.[22] At a local level the same sort of disputes between old and new guard were repeated: in the Saône-et-Loire for example, the older militants reacted badly to the purge measures taken at the national Congress against their former colleagues, whilst 'the religious question creates a real abyss between the two elements'.[23]

The fundamental division within the party about the salience of the old anti-clerical issue militated against any meaningful attempt to create an '*entente*' between the SFIO and Christian democrats, although the party made a half-hearted step in that direction in November 1944, inviting Christian socialists to join them on an individual basis. In that month, however, the Christian democrats themselves took the initiative by officially forming their own political party, the *Mouvement Républicain Populaire* (MRP). The ground which they sought to occupy had been pioneered before the war by Christian groups like the *Parti Démocrate Populaire* and *Jeune République*, but these had been largely unsuccessful, polling in total only some 3 per cent of the vote in the 1936 elections. The experience of the Resistance paved the way, however, for a spectacular renaissance of Christian democracy. Firstly, it proved that Catholics could co-operate well with other Republicans. Secondly, it had provided a core of leaders who had learnt their skills in Resistance organizations and councils. Among future MRP leaders, Bidault had been president of the CNR, Max André Vice-President of the CPL, François de Menthon and Pierre-Henri Teitgen, members of the CNR.[24] Much of the early part of the MRP's existence was taken up with deciding the internal structures of the party, and evolving a set of agreed policies, but an increasing number of public meetings were held in the build-up to the municipal elections, attesting to the growing activity of the movement.[25]

If the cause of Christian democracy was given considerable impetus by wartime experiences, that of the Radicals/Radical socialists, and of more conservative formations, was markedly retarded. In both cases their responsibility for and participation in the Vichy and Paris regimes had been extensive, and the resurgent parties of the left, as well as the Resistance movements, were careful to continue stressing the complicity of their rivals. Slowly, however, the Radical parties emerged from the shadows and started to reform. In November 1944 a group of former Radical *députés* held a conference, and in December the Radicals and Radical socialists met in a 'small congress' at which it was agreed to recommend a rather limited (by comparison with the SFIO) purging of senior members: 34 former parliamentary representatives were excluded, and another two temporarily suspended. Radical Party public activity in the first months of 1945 was extremely limited, but in the period immediately preceding the first round of the municipal elections, the party held more meetings than the embryonic MRP, although its total of 65 (with only two over 2,000) contrasts poorly with the two major parties of the left and the Resistance formations – PCF : 750, SFIO : 430, FN : 318, MLN : 113.[26]

By comparison, the political activity of conservative politicians was even more severely restricted. By April 1945, just before the municipal elections, two federations had appeared, regrouping members of the right in the resistance, with the addition of some pre-war conservatives: the *Fédération Républicaine*, led by Louis Marin, and the *Alliance Démocratique*, led by Joseph Laniel. The initiative in the months following the Liberation had, however, clearly moved to the left of French political life.

In purely electoral terms the PCF, despite its strength, was unlikely to secure a dominant position, without the support of other groups and movements. Hence the party's attempts in late 1944 and early 1945 to encourage Resistance institutions to underwrite common lists for the elections, and hence too their efforts to arrive at a merger of the leading Resistance movements, the MLN and FN. Above all, the PCF had to obtain the good will and support of its major contender on the left, the SFIO. The socialists, whilst traditionally wary in their dealings with the PCF, were receptive to the idea of discussions on unity after the Liberation. Indeed Mayer had urged the communists as early as September 1944 to begin talks as soon as possible. There were, however, limits which the SFIO were clearly inclined to put on the concept of left-wing unity. At the party's November 1944 Congress, for example, there was a vote in support of Jules Moch's motion to discuss organic unity with the PCF at the same time as the members decided to present their own separate list in the first round of the forthcoming municipal elections. As Kramer points out, the *comité directeur* were by no means unanimous on the view to take towards unity discussions with the communists. Some people, like Andrée Marty-Capgras, were strongly in favour, whilst the majority of the committee remained generally attracted to the idea of unity, provided it could be achieved with the agreement of the whole party and on terms which seemed fair to the SFIO.[27] The *comité d'entente* of socialists and communists, designed to discuss the issue, met for the first time on 19 December 1944. The PCF, strongly advocating an organizational unity between the two parties, suggested at this meeting that local and regional *comités d'entente* should be formed to advance the matter at grass-roots level. The socialist members of the group, clearly fearing a PCF manoeuvre by which the more dynamic communist cadres would outwit their socialist colleagues, rejected the proposal at the meeting, and warned their federations to beware of such a tactic locally.[28] Talks continued, however.

By early spring 1945 it was apparent that the SFIO was becoming increasingly sceptical about actual organizational unity with the PCF, arguing instead for a looser form of alliance, into which the MRP, for example, might ultimately be drawn. The very dynamism of the PCF, added to the growing fear that exclusive dealings with the PCF might alienate potential middle-class voters for the socialists, contributed to the cooling of SFIO ardour. Faced with the evident reluctance of the socialists, and the failure of FN plans to merge with the MLN, the communists turned their attention, at the end of March 1945, to ensuring that the SFIO was effectively isolated from the MRP and, hence, forced into some kind of cohabitation with them. The tactic used was to resuscitate the old right/left cleavage in French politics, based on the now smouldering issue of church–state relations and education. Thus, largely through PCF support, the Consultative Assembly voted for the immediate suppression of government monies to church schools, posing the Socialist Party with the stark prospect of an anti-clerical alliance (PCF, SFIO and Radicals) against the MRP. By the end of the first round of voting in April, however, the Socialist Party was still maintaining its policy of *'ouverture'* to both the PCF and the Christian democrats, driving the communist press to angry denunciations of both the SFIO and the Christian democrats, who were portrayed as a Trojan horse of the moribund right: MRP – *Machine pour ramasser les Pétainistes* (Machine for picking up Pétainists), *Mensonge, Réaction, Perfidie* (lies, reaction and perfidy).[29] The party's *Bureau Politique* went so far as to demand that the MRP be excluded from common lists for the second round of the elections.[30]

In practice, despite SFIO clear instructions to federations that there should be no participation in common lists in the first round, and PCF contrary orders to their militants, the tactics adopted by local organizers on the ground tended to be far more flexible. Areas where socialists had large working-class support – Nord, Pas-de-Calais, Haute Vienne, Bouches-du-Rhône – were understandably averse to organic unity with the communists, whereas in Departments where their electoral base was different from that of the PCF, or where the local SFIO thought it might outflank the PCF, socialists were more sympathetic to the idea of common lists. In the Rhône, the Aisne (Laon), Ariège (Foix) and the Doubs (Besançon), for example, local socialist federations had joint lists with the PCF on the first round. In the Nièvre (Nevers) and the Seine-et-Oise (Rueil-Malmaison) SFIO candidates on the other hand shared a list with the MRP.[31]

Outside the political parties, public interest in the municipal election campaign often seemed slow to develop. Many of the potential electors (an estimated 3 million) were of course still absent in prisoner of war camps and many in France had apparently failed to register themselves as electors. In some cases, like that of French women – voting for the first time ever – this was because they were new to the whole process; in others, because of general apathy, or because they were still attached to the discredited Vichy regime. In some areas, the abstention rate in the elections was high – 38 per cent in Nancy, 25–30 per cent in Meurthe-et-Moselle, 30–35 per cent in the Charente-Maritime – although officials reported that voters in some regions voted more numerously in the second round as they appeared to become more used to the procedures.[32]

Apart from the voting system itself which caused some difficulties, it was evident that the pattern of alliances concluded by parties, different in different areas of France, made for a rather blurred picture nationally for the electors. This was confirmed by *Le Monde* which reported that the electorate appeared to be finding problems in making sense of the artificial lists:

Something which was totally unknown in the annals of the Third Republic, newspapers have received letters from their readers asking them which names 'they should be voting for in order to vote correctly'.[33]

Voting did however take place, and the results indicated both the distance which had been travelled since the days of the Liberation and the post-war electoral strength of the political parties. Although the elections as a whole represented a clear triumph for the ideas and programme of the CNR, with all the groups who polled well strongly underwriting CNR aspirations, they also confirmed the virtual disappearance of the Resistance movements as political entities. *Combat* noted that, where the Resistance had stood in the elections separately from the political parties, it received only minor local successes. Certainly candidates had made much of their Resistance records, but largely from the shelter of an established political party and its joint or separate list: 'the Resistance spirit was ratified by these elections, the Resistance movements were buried by them'.[34]

Table 1. Municipal elections 29 April and 13 May 1945

*Situation in 1935*

|  | *Communes* |
|---|---|
| Communist | 317 |
| SFIO | 1,376 |
| *Socialistes indépendants et Républicains socialistes* | 944 |
| *Radicaux–Socialistes* | 9,162 |
| *Démocrates populaires* | 280 |
| *Radicaux indépendants* | 3,120 |
| *Républicains de gauche* | 8,473 |
| *Fédération République et URD* | 9,489 |
| *Conservateurs* | 1,603 |
| Unknown* | 1,074 |
|  | 35,838 |

*Not including *communes* in Bas-Rhin, Haut Rhin, Moselle, Territory of Belfort, and 348 'coastal pockets'.

*Results in 1945*

| Communist | 1,462 |
|---|---|
| *Socialistes–Communistes* | 247 |
| SFIO | 4,133 |
| *Socialistes indépendants et Républicains socialistes* | 1,501 |
| *Radicaux–Socialistes* | 6,501 |
| Left (no dominant party) | 913 |
| *Mouvement Républicain Populaire* | 609 |
| *Radicaux indépendants* | 1,797 |
| *Républicains de gauche et Alliance démocratique* | 5,499 |
| *Féderation Républicaine et URD* | 5,809 |
| Right (no dominant party) | 2,007 |
| *Conservateurs* | 552 |
| Unknown* | 4,736 |
| Did not vote | 72 |
|  | 35,838 |

*Because of number of councillors elected under the name of a Resistance organization, and without political labels.

*Source*: adapted from *L'Année Politique, 1944–45* (Paris, 1946), table, 491.

The most striking feature of the results was the clear success for the parties of the left, and in particular for the PCF. In the previous municipal elections in 1935, the communists had majority control in 317 councils. In 1945, they shot to 1,462. The SFIO also made considerable gains, passing from 1,376 councils in 1935 to 4,133. Jointly, the Socialists and Communists in 1935 had control of 279 of the larger *communes* (over 4,000 inhabitants). In the 1945 elections the figure rose to 458. The MRP was effectively isolated by the electoral alliances of existing parties, and ended up with control of some 477 *communes*, a success more interesting for the potential which it suggested for future legislative elections than for the present municipals.[35]

The loser on the other hand was evidently the traditional right, and even the centre-left. In 1935 the moderate parties had won power in 22 685 councils out of a total of 35,838. In 1945, the figure slumped to 15 655, and in the larger *communes* from 484 to 110. Furthermore, in many of the councils controlled by the right a minority of left-wing representatives found themselves elected for the first time. The Radical–Socialists were equally punished by the results, their control slipping from some 2,700 councils. Whilst conservative politicians like Louis Marin suggested that the conditions in which parties had operated – very limited poster campaigning and no published election tracts – impeded the progress of the recently formed moderate alliances,[36] it was evident that what had really happened was a marked shift on the part of the electorate towards the parties of the Left. In the circumstances, however, the Right could have been said to have done reasonably well. In the smaller *communes* at least they had often held on, bolstered by inbuilt traditions and country fiefs, and by the anti-communism of that vast majority of voters who had taken no active part in the Resistance.

The municipal elections clearly demonstrated that the parties had recaptured the central ground of the political debate, and that those on the left were in the ascendancy. The PCF and the SFIO were in commanding positions and the MRP had shown that it would be a force to reckon with in the future. It was these three groups, with the Radical Socialists as a subsidiary contributor, which would dominate the next few years of party politics in liberated France. Intent on splitting the socialists from any form of alliance with the MRP, the PCF found the SFIO increasingly determined to steer a middle course away from direct union with itself. As Mayer expressed it: 'must not our role be to serve, on the left of the MRP, as a pole of attraction in opposition to the other attraction appearing on their opposite side ?' With the return of Léon Blum in early May, the position of the Socialist Party as the future linchpin of the tripartite relationship was confirmed.[37] The electors had signalled their desire for some kind of political change, and certainly the parties which had scored well in the municipal elections favoured a new constitution which would finish with the 1875 model which many people felt had contributed to the discreditable defeat of 1940. In practice, however, the 'new' French state of 1945 was a good deal less radical than the CNR charter had promised it would be.

## The épuration

ONE OF THE most consistent demands of the Resisters had been that the men and women of 1940 who had compromised with Vichy and the Germans should be purged from French public life. This was not only, or even primarily, a desire for revenge to assuage the blood of comrades shed during the war. Rather the *épuration* was a kind of guarantee that the post-war world would not resemble what had gone before: there would be a total renewal in French public life, administration, economic management and cultural activities. As the CNR programme forcefully expressed it in its preamble on measures to be applied at the Liberation: '. . . ensure the punishment of traitors and the dismissal from the administration and working life in general of all those who compromised with the enemy . . . confiscate the goods of traitors and black-marketeers'.[38]

The priority which Resistance opinion attached to this renewal was speedily emphasized to the CFLN. As Novick points out, one of the first acts of the newly constituted Consultative Assembly in Algiers was to pass a unanimous resolution calling on the committee to act in this area more swiftly and resolutely, and this was followed up two months later by another unanimous motion on the subject, this time openly critical of CFLN delays.[39] The catalyst to this concern had undoubtedly been the public hesitations of the CFLN when faced with the presence in Algiers of politicians like Pucheu, Peyrouton, Boisson and Flandin, considered in Resistance circles as traitors. The last three, accused of less serious offences, benefited from some measure of Allied support. In the case of Pucheu, however, his status, and hence his symbolism to the Resistance as an indication of de Gaulle's likely views of the *épuration*, forced the CFLN into a trial and an execution, which the General upheld: *la raison d'état* required a swift example.[40] The case was a clear pointer – a Minister of Vichy had been executed solely on the basis of his ministerial acts, despite the fact that he had attempted in his trial to question the competence of the tribunal considering his case, in particular the judge who had, Pucheu claimed, sworn an oath of loyalty to the very regime Pucheu stood condemned for supporting.

De Gaulle's public alignment to the Resistance position on the purge did not signify that there was total agreement on the methods to be used, and the extent to which the policy should be fully prosecuted on the return to France. Some sections of the Resistance, generally strongly committed to the legal norms, nevertheless felt that summary justice at the Liberation for certain notorious and well-known collaborators was acceptable and indeed desirable; a necessary police operation which would enable the people to let off steam, a sort of catharsis before the rebuilding of the country could begin. De Gaulle was deeply hostile to any such 'wildcat' settling of scores. Justice was the prerogative of the state and could only be administered under the aegis of the restored French government. Quite apart from moral considerations, it was clear that the Allies regarded the speed with which the GPRF got control of the illegal punishment of suspected collaborators as an important indicator of their ability to maintain law and order and, hence, act as a legitimate government. In early October 1944, in a speech at Evreux, de Gaulle pointed out to his audience that it was necessary for the purge to be conducted with compassion in order to reassure the Allies, and win the war speedily so that the vital reconstruction work could begin.[41]

Once some control had been established, the central problems of the 'épuration' still remained. To begin with, there was considerable reluctance to tackle the fundamental, but clearly highly sensitive, question of the legitimacy of the Vichy regime. The Pucheu trial had indicated some of the pitfalls inherent in political trials, based on *prima facie* culpability of anyone associated with a particular political system. The likely repercussions of this in view both of the GPRF's own, not unstained, pedigree of legitimacy, and the fact that the majority evidently had accepted, or at least lived peaceably under, the previous regime, made such a path an especially dangerous one to follow. As Madjarian suggests,[42] the only way out of this dilemma was to avoid it, by putting individuals on trial rather than the actual regime. This course of action had certain definite consequences. If individuals were to be tried and evidence secured which would convict them in court, then visibility of collaboration became one of the easiest criteria to adopt. When the *Commissares de le République* had begun their local purges, the GPRF had indeed instructed them to bear this principle firmly in mind: 'the criterion [should be] public scandal . . . the impossibility of maintaining an individual in office in the face of hostile criticism from the population . . . Obedience to legal measures, weakness of character, lack of courage – these are all regrettable, but should not by themselves be the cause of suspension'.[43] Similarly, the early showcase trials tended to involve journalists whose collaboration had left clear and tangible evidence, seen by all the public, rather than economic collaborators, where the actions were less visible, and the evidence considerably more difficult to establish.

In the pre-Liberation days considerable attention had been given to the vital purging of the administration, and detailed plans had been drawn up. De Gaulle and the *Comité General d'Études* (CGE) certainly took the view that the *épuration* should be swift and not too radical within the civil service. Purge commissions were rapidly set up in all government departments, comprising ministerial employees and members of the resistance nominated by the CNR or other respected Resistance body. These commissions considered all complaints against personnel (except in the case of anonymous denunciations) and made appropriate recommendations to the Minister concerned. The evidence that historians have assembled suggests that the purge did not strike all ministries equally. It was most severe, again presumably on the visibility criterion, in the Ministry of Information where, for example, something like three-quarters of employees in the central Paris office were sanctioned in some way. Political ministries like Justice, the Interior, and the *Conseil d'État* had relatively more staff penalized than the so-called technical ministries like Public Health and Finance. The Ministry of Finance and the Ministry of Foreign Affairs were both purged only very lightly. In an area where it has been difficult to establish figures, Novick suggests that out of 1 million central government civil servants, around 11,300 received punishment, about 5,000 of these actually being dismissed.[44] The passive resistance of many, the *esprit de corps* of some ministries, and the general desire of the GPRF to complete the operation speedily so that the wheels of government could again begin to turn, militated against removing a greater number from office.

In the case of trials of alleged collaborators, public disillusionment was extreme. The task which faced the judiciary was enormous. By early October 1944 a total of around 10,000 people in Paris alone had been imprisoned and were awaiting trial. Over the whole of France the numbers were estimated to be around 80,000 at the height of the process. Understandably, a 'judicial log-jam of unprecedented dimensions' developed,[45] with public frustration mounting monthly as the delays in bringing people to trial continued. Trials were still being conducted in the summer of 1949. In addition there was much evidence that the severity of the courts varied from Department to Department, so that general perceptions of the verdicts as slow, lenient and disproportionate grew. Opinion polls in the winter of 1944–5 showed increasing frustration with the conduct of the *épuration*, which became a convenient stick with which all political and Resistance groups could beat the GPRF. As the purge had been the symbol of renewal in pre-Liberation programmes, so its perceived failure became the proof for many that a major opportunity to change the face of France had been lost. The Foreign Office, keen to keep as far as possible out of the whole purge process in France – on occasions difficult to do when former Vichy officials implicated His Majesty's Government[46] – noted in January 1945 that, 'The general impression is that the purge is now on the downgrade and that surprisingly few collaborators in high quarters have been brought to justice.'[47] What started off as a renewal had evidently become an adjustment of the more unacceptable and visible aspects of a largely restored system. In the end, the more visible and obvious collaborators, such as those in the Ministry of Information and of the Interior, were removed, but many thousands collaborating less conspicuously in other ministries were left. Political, intellectual and entertainment personalities were hounded, but lesser lights were left undisturbed. The regime had changed, but many of the personnel within the system remained the same.

## Social and economic reforms

THIS continuity of personnel was undoubtedly one factor in discouraging large-scale social and economic reform. Another was the ambivalent nature of French institutions in the immediate post-Liberation period which provided for little parliamentary influence on the government, and even less government accountability. What existed in institutional terms was an unelected government, operating in parallel with, but not responsible to, an unelected Consultative Assembly. As Wright suggests:

> For fourteen months after Charles de Gaulle's triumphal return to Paris, the Government of France was essentially a dictatorship by consent. There were no formal limitations on de Gaulle's authority except those which he himself voluntarily accepted. The cabinet was handpicked by de Gaulle and was responsible to him alone; he in turn was accountable only to the people. But this responsibility was totally without sanctions, and presumably the people could only exercise their powers by an uprising or a threat thereof.[48]

As far as the Cabinet was concerned, the General's choice of 9 September 1944 (modified only slightly before May 1945 after the death of one Minister and the later resignation of Pierre Mendès–France) included representatives of most political tendencies: communists, socialists, popular democrats, radical socialists and several members of Resistance movements.

Already, at this early stage of political Gaullism, it was evident not only that de Gaulle saw it as his personal responsibility to pick and dismiss members of the government, but also that he considered that his Ministers, once in post, should drop party political loyalties and, where possible, active party membership. Thus, he discouraged Ministers from speaking in their governmental capacity at congresses and conferences of their particular groups. In a revealing interview with the SFIO's temporary leader, Daniel Mayer, the General specifically rejected the idea that the Socialist Party had delegated its members to enter the government: 'You have delegated no one. I am the one who has asked certain men to join the Government. They are not delegated by you, but chosen by me.' De Gaulle's attitude to political parties and their deleterious influence on the country's affairs was already well established: 'You tried in 1936 to form a Government with the parties. It's impossible. You should realise just what happened because of that.'[49]

Towards the Consultative Assembly his behaviour, though outwardly courteous, was dismissive. When Pineau was due to appear before it, the General enquired: 'Don't you have anything better to do?'[50] His decision to house the Consultative Assembly in the Luxembourg Palace – the former home of the Senate – rather than in the Palais Bourbon (traditional home of the National Assembly) was indicative of his attitude towards it: the Consultative Assembly should be given a role which remained purely and simply consultative, without any power to supervise or control the executive. Largely because of the speed with which the Liberation took place, plans for converting the Consultative Assembly into a provisional one by electing representatives from each Department were never put into effect. Before the Assembly had inaugurated its first Paris session in November, the socialists had already made an unsuccessful attempt to enlarge the functions of the House, to include some form of supervisory function. The *ordonnance* of 12 October 1944, however, regulating the position of the transferred Consultative Assembly, made it clear that, whilst its membership was to be increased in relation to the Algiers Assembly, its powers were to stay exactly the same. As time went on, the frustration of many of its members became clear, as representatives attempted to play a parliamentary role, criticizing Ministers and voting reductions in the Budget, only to discover that much of its work was completely ignored. For example, in early March 1945 the Finance Committee of the Assembly recommended the immediate abolition of the previous Vichy subsidy to church schools. The Education Committee suggested that it should be continued until the end of the present term in July. The Assembly, however, voted to approve the Finance Committee's tougher resolution by 128 to 49. In response, the provisional government ignored the vote and stated that it intended to continue the subsidy until July.[51] A delegation of Consultative Assembly members went to see the Prime Minister to demand that the executive should henceforth take no decisions which were contrary to the position adopted by the Assembly, that is to say that the Consultative Assembly should begin to operate as a true Parliament. De Gaulle's reply was characteristic: 'Only the people are sovereign. Until they are in a position to express their will, I have taken it upon myself to lead them'.[52]

One of the largest bones of contention between the GPRF and members of the Consultative Assembly was the perceived reluctance of the government to undertake major structural reforms. Socialists, in particular, mounted an early campaign to remind the new administration of its responsibilities in this area. *Le Populaire* ran a series of articles on the subject in September 1944, calling on the GPRF to nationalize the banks, insurance and heavy industry as quickly as possible, undertake a census of fortunes and begin the process of taxing profits made during the occupation. When the party had still received no satisfaction, they took up the matter directly with de Gaulle. The General's case had the same tone as his dismissal of the argument for a stronger Consultative Assembly – nothing could be done until the people had been given a chance to choose:

> There have not been elections. The Nation has not pronounced and you would want me to transform the economic structure of the country. Don't count on it. I won't do anything fascistically . . . I promised to prevent the trusts from imposing their law, but I could not say that I would tranform the structure of the country without the country's having pronounced.[53]

By the beginning of February 1945 large sections of the press were involved in a vigorous debate on the advisability of structural reforms. *Le Monde* quoted the official government line that until peace and the conditions for a return to democratic politics were restored, the government had no mandate for the changes demanded. *Combat* replied that de Gaulle had had a golden opportunity in September 1944 to undertake sweeping reforms without any open opposition.[54] The CNR joined the mounting pressure for the government to institute real changes, calling for the application of its Resistance charter and for the GPRF to take proper account of what the Consultative Assembly was saying.[55]

To a large extent, the Socialist Party, backed by the Resistance movement, had made the running in this campaign and reports from the provinces confirmed that it was indeed SFIO members locally who were proving the most hostile to government policies compared with the resolutely governmentalist PCF: 'It has the tendency to move to the extreme left, leap-frogging over the Communists'.[56] As the campaign grew in momentum, however, and the PCF saw the possible danger of being outflanked and of losing support at the grass roots, a slight adjustment in the public presentation of policy was discernible, with Thorez, for example, proclaiming that the PCF wanted the principal means of production, monopolized by the trusts, returned to the nation. On 2 March 1945, *L'Humanité* and *Le Populaire* published a joint manifesto, demanding a nationalization programme.[57]

The effect of all this pressure was to force the government into at least discussing the issue of structural reform in the Consultative Assembly, where de Gaulle made an important speech on domestic policy on 2 March. Here he reaffirmed the need to nationalize coal, electricity, oil, the principal means of transport and the banks, but was extremely vague about exactly how this programme would be implemented, suggesting that it was up to a future representative assembly to take the major steps in this area. Speeches in the Assembly, particularly from left-wing members, demonstrated dissatisfaction with the government's failure to act decisively on structural reforms, and the press reaction was generally equally impatient, with *L'Humanité* giving pride of place to the very hostile speech which Duclos had given:

> This Assembly, if it is not elected, is none the less representative of the various political parties with their millions of electors . . . The problem we have at the moment is that of the . . . collaboration between the Government and the people.[58]

If the malaise that existed between the GPRF and the principal political parties had become acute, it is nonetheless true that they continued their participation in the government. The PCF, despite the cosmetic changes made in its public presentation of policies, and the continued tendency to criticize specific Ministers in the press or the Consultative Assembly, was clearly resolved to stay in government at least until the war was over and they had built up the most advantageous position from which to seek power legitimately. If either of the principal parties left the government it might find itself isolated in opposition, with its rival using a governmental position to discredit it. If both parties left simultaneously, which was unlikely, the socialists would find themselves alone and possibly overpowered by the resurgent PCF. The situation thus continued, with the political parties highly critical of the GPRF, but still maintaining their members as part of the government team. The overall impression was of lively and vigorous political debate both within the Consultative Assembly and in the rapidly burgeoning press,[59] but of a debate which had virtually no impact on the government or the political process. It was as if the political parties and the GPRF existed in mutually exclusive watertight compartments.

What is interesting about this curious institutional interregnum is the clear existence of quite widespread discontent in the country which was not being channelled or mobilized by the political parties. In the field of industrial relations, the PCF, which might have been expected to exploit grievances in an area to which it had easy access, acted as a moderate and calming influence, exhorting the work-force to greater efforts in work and production. Thorez's exhortations had clearly been noted by the CGT. In the Nancy region for example, the *Commissaire* reported that the trades union delegates appeared to have received orders to modify their attitudes to the bosses, and were now seeing their role as that of liaison between workers and management, reprimanding workers who stepped out of line and presenting their demands to the bosses in a very co-operative way, 'in short moderating influences, whose sole objective is to increase production'.[60] In the Jura, the local CGT secretary intervened in two disputes to get the men back to work. 'He is as much convinced as I am', reported the prefect, 'of the need to ensure that government instructions prohibiting wage increases are respected.'[61] This approach by trade union organizers, however, did not succeed in damping down all signs of industrial unrest. In the mid-January to mid-February 1945 period, a total of 17 strikes were reported, with around 24 in the next cycle, mid-February to mid-March, and 25 mid-March to mid-April. Many of these were token strikes lasting a day or under, but some, like that of the miners in the Isère, or the SNCF in Plaine St-Denis, lasted five and three days. The major causes of these strikes were listed as wages or food (34/66), with the next highest being the purge (7/66).[62]

Industrial unrest thus simmered, largely outside the control of the political parties and trade union organizations. Politicians in the Consultative Assembly expressed considerable hostility to the GPRF, but appeared to have little influence on the government, despite their own participation in the Cabinet.

The relative conservatism of the GPRF was nowhere better illustrated than in its approach to economic reconstruction and reform. Post-war planning in Resistance circles had been dominated by a total rejection of the principles of economic liberalism associated, not always accurately, with the economy of the Nazis. The CNR March 1944 programme, for example, had called for a 'rational organization of the economy, subordinating individual interests to the general interest', a national plan to establish a framework for production and the nationalization of the principal means of production, sources of energy, raw materials, insurance companies and banks.[63]

The Vichy regime had fundamentally changed economic relationships with the state, bequeathing to the GPRF a battery of planning organizations and rationing and price control measures virtually unprecedented in the pre-war management of the French economy. The inclination, therefore, was to take over the levers of Vichy planning and use them for different ends. Such views seemed particularly appropriate to the situation of widespread economic and social dislocation which greeted the GPRF on its return to France. There were, however, strong differences of emphasis between the school of thought which wanted state intervention to promote social change, and those who regarded a directed economy as a necessary, but temporary, expedient to make industry more efficient. Modernizing elements among industrialists, for example, called for state intervention in the economy, but they tended to make the point that the *'dirigisme'* which was now essential should be combined with liberalism as regards the actual running of individual businesses. Much emphasis was laid in such groups on the British model of nationalization which had given independence to the management of nationalized companies, and allowed the employees little more than a consultative role.

Within the GPRF the form that state intervention in the economy should take, and the exact parameters within which it should operate, were matters of considerable dispute, with views ranging from limited and pragmatic *'dirigisme'* through to rigorous control, accompanied by immediate structural reforms. In November 1943, Mendès-France had taken over the *Commissariat* of Finance in Algiers. He had initially tried to set up an overarching Ministry of the Economy which would take over the co-ordination of production, monetary policy, the Treasury, and Budget responsibilities at Liberation. He immediately encountered opposition from some of his colleagues, particularly Diethelm at the *Commissariat* of Production and Food. In view of this, Mendès-France abandoned the maximalist approach and concentrated instead on ensuring that his strongly interventionist policies received a fair hearing before the return to France. In February 1944 he submitted a paper on the economy which set out the radical *'dirigiste'* case. In the management of food supply, he argued that it would be impossible at the Liberation to re-establish economic liberalism. An overall plan should be prepared by some kind of central authority, prefigured by Vichy's *Délégation Générale à l'Equipment National*. To ensure that the poor were not adversely affected, restrictions and restraints would be necessary. As far as monetary policy was concerned, Mendès-France recommended freezing bank accounts and establishing the exchange of banknotes as had been done in Tunisia and Corsica. In this way, he claimed, it should be possible to absorb the massive amount of notes in circulation, cancel the reserves built up by those involved in the Occupation, and get control of profits made by certain industrialists during the war. This policy, coupled with a tough set of fiscal measures, would have the effect of restoring the long-term balance of the French economy as well as exacting swift punishment upon those who had made money out of the war. The *Commissaire* was aware that such an approach, which clearly entailed austerity measures, was unlikely to commend itself to a people who had just suffered the privations of the Occupation, and he suggested that Algiers should begin a deliberate campaign on the radio to prepare the French for the reality of the situation, explaining to them that austerity and sacrifice would be necessary at Liberation, and that a temporary wages and prices freeze would be one of the first actions of the provisional government.[64]

By March 1944 it was evident that Mendès-France's views had met considerable opposition within the CFLN and he tendered his resignation to de Gaulle. When the General appeared to move closer to the Mendès position, Mendès-France withdrew his resignation. He reported that he had managed to secure the all important agreement of the *Commissariat* of Agriculture, but there was a great deal of opposition elsewhere in the Cabinet: 'there are scores of the most ardent defenders of agriculture, including the General, who are terrified at the idea of provoking protests or complaints'.[65] A more limited and pragmatic course of action was advocated by one of de Gaulle's closest confidants, René Pleven, *Commissaire* for the Colonies. Instead of austerity and an attempt to reduce the money supply, Pleven leant towards building up public confidence and optimism, as a background for the launching of a government loan. The hope was that the problem of note circulation would right itself when normal production returned. In the meantime classic *ad hoc* measures, like the taxation of illicit profits, would be sufficient to control the development of the economy.

The financial situation which was to greet the provisional government on its arrival in France was serious. The payment of the occupation indemnity in the war (400 million – 600 million francs per day) had combined with the evident scarcity of goods to produce high levels of inflation. A massive number of banknotes was in circulation[66] – at the beginning of October the estimate was 632 billion francs. The position was further complicated by the black market which had thrived during the war and would continue to profit in the post-Liberation period, and by the wage policy which Vichy had operated during the Occupation under which wages in industries working for the Germans had been raised, whereas in other sectors they had fallen far behind. It was difficult for the government in this situation to avoid accepting a general wage rise when it returned to France, but even so, earnings were generally still lagging behind the cost of living.

On the GPRF's return to France, it was evident that the Pleven philosophy of economic management was, at least temporarily, in the ascendancy. Mendès-France was not given the financial portfolio in the first government formed, on the grounds, he claimed, that his presence at the Ministry, with his well-known views on money supply, would prejudice the launching of a government loan.[67] The Liberation loan was a success: when it was closed in the middle of December 1944, a total of 164,000 million francs had been raised, although some commentators noted that it could have been even more popular if the deficiencies in the transport system had not made it impossible to deliver bond certificates in time to certain areas. The note circulation had been reduced to 572,000 million francs by the end of December. Even so, the volume of money in notes and bank deposits was reckoned to be over four times the pre-war figure. Alongside the loan strategy, the government attempted at the outset to peg prices at pre-Liberation rates, especially in agricultural goods, although there were loud protests about this in peasant circles, in particular the small winegrowers in the south.

All this, of course, went nowhere near as far as Mendès-France wanted. He, meanwhile, had taken over the Ministry of the National Economy, believing that he was getting a major ministry post from which to begin reshaping the French economy. It soon became apparent that this was far from the case. The Minister realized rapidly that any attempt to assume a co-ordinating role in economic planning foundered firstly on the fact that the Ministry as established was really little more than a fragment of the Ministry of Finance, which the General evidently considered to be the 'serious' part of the operation, and secondly, on the obstructions which it encountered from other ministries, many of which seemed to retain the attitudes which had shaped their departments in the 1930s – in the Inspectorate of Finance, for example, 97 per cent of the inspectors-general had also served under the Vichy regime, as had 75 per cent of the more junior inspectors.[68] De Gaulle himself made it clear that the new ministry should be careful not to encroach on the powers of the Quai d'Orsay. It might, for example, help in the preparations for international economic negotiations, but the actual conduct of talks with foreign powers should be the responsibility of the Ministry of Foreign Affairs. A decree in the middle of November 1944 did seek to concentrate more economic control in the hands of the Ministry of the National Economy, but the ministries with which Mendès-France largely had to deal – Finance, Agriculture and Industry – managed to evade any real check of their activities in this area, and thus maintained their virtual independence from his planning process.

A further sign that Mendès-France's views were unlikely to prevail was given in November 1944 after the death of the then Finance Minster, Aimé Lepercq, in a road accident. Clearly the appointment of his successor would be a vital touchstone for the economic policy of

France. According to Mendès-France, de Gaulle, obsessed at this time with foreign affairs, and more immediately with his forthcoming visit to the front with Churchill, told him to fill in temporarily as Finance Minister. On the General's return, however, Pleven rather than Mendès-France was chosen to be the new Minister. Mendès-France speculated after the event to his biographer that the influence of Churchill, who regarded him as rather like Stafford Cripps, may have played some part in the eventual choice, but Pleven claimed that Lepercq himself had earlier suggested to de Gaulle that his natural successor would be Pleven.[69] Pleven's nomination to the key ministry tipped the balance in policy-making even more clearly towards the classic *ad hoc* methods which Mendès-France deplored. Despite this, the Minister for National Production presented his economic plan to the Cabinet in January 1945. Basically Mendès called for an overall five-year plan which would include the structural reforms which some Resistance groups and political parties had consistently advocated. He strongly held the view that nationalizations were necessary as a means of improving the effectiveness of the economy, and could not be delayed at will (until for example the government had received a specific mandate in this area) without embarking in the short term on an entirely different course of action which would inevitably rule out later nationalizations. The measures which the government had so far taken – increase of salaries, loan and commissions of confiscation – were at total variance with the policies he had prepared in Algiers, and were manifestly inadequate to deal with the situation. A change in monetary policy was an essential prerequisite to the kind of planned economy Mendès-France proposed, and he repeated once more his demands for a wages/prices freeze, the exchange of banknotes and the freezing of bank accounts.

The Cabinet response to Mendès-France's proposals was decidedly chilly. The majority of socialists - Lacoste, Minister of Production, Tanguy-Prigent at Agriculture – opposed him, and as time went on, only Laurent, Minister for Postal Services, and Tixier at the Interior, gave him some support. The MRP Ministers were divided, and Pleven, as Minister of Finance, suggested that the idea of a five-year plan would be especially distasteful to the British and Americans, 'who would regard it as a socialization measure and as one which would place restrictions on international trade'.[70] The communist members were equally critical of Mendès-France's proposed nationalization measures. An earlier indication of their attitude had been provided with the discussions over the status of banks in Alsace-Lorraine. These had been forcibly bought by the Germans during the war. Pleven had advised that the banks should be simply handed back to their original owners at the Liberation. Mendès-France objected that the owners had received payment for the banks from the occupiers, and that since the government was intending to nationalize the banks anyway, it would be better to sequester them temporarily and get them run by the state in the meantime. The communists backed Pleven in this argument, explaining that they wished to avoid transforming 'a principle, the nationalization of banks, into a local problem'.[71] On the other hand, the party criticized Mendès-France's general nationalization plans as being too partial, and, since the Minister wished to treat nationalized industries as being as competitive as the private sector, having the intention of bankrupting public industry.

As far as financial policy was concerned, the PCF fully supported the Pleven line. In the Consultative Assembly debate on economic policy in March 1945, Duclos was adamant that the way to remedy the money supply situation was to increase production, and, hence, the volume of goods available on the market. A strategy of exchanging banknotes would indicate that the country was in the grip of an 'inferiority complex'. The more cynical suggested that the PCF's opposition to Mendès-France was actually based on a reluctance to part with the considerable amounts of currency their members were said to have acquired in the early days of Liberation. The PCF was equally opposed to that other plank of Mendès orthodoxy, the freezing of accounts, in this case taking the part of the small savers, peasants, tradesmen and artisans who, they claimed, would be badly hit by the measure.[72] The major support for Mendès-France outside the government came from the socialists in the Consultative Assembly, and from sections of the press who were, as we have seen, impatient at the GPRF's failure to enact substantial structural reforms.

By January 1945, Mendès-France had offered to resign for the second time, and a compromise between him and Pleven had been patched up, largely through de Gaulle's good offices, with the Minister of Finance at least accepting that some form of exchange of notes was necessary. The government was still holding largely to the Pleven course, and in April, Mendès-France decided he could take no more and resigned. This effectively spelt the temporary end of discussions on the need for a planned economy. General de Gaulle appointed Cusin to Mendès-France's post, although at the request of the new appointee, the job was made that of a delegate rather than a Minister, which meant that Pleven, as Minister of Finance, had really subsumed the planning ministry under his control. As Lynch demonstrates, examination of a national plan did not re-emerge until the autumn of 1945, and then mainly as a reaction to the failure of Potsdam to give priority to French reconstruction over that of Germany and to allow for French utilization of the resources of German industry. After Potsdam, 'delicate questions such as the future role of the Ministry of National

Economy, the treatment of wartime illicit profits, the nationalization of key industries, were all neatly shelved in order to devote more attention to questions of "national" interest such as the future of Germany'. Planning and state intervention in the economy could thus be depoliticized, metamorphosed for a domestic audience into a matter of uncontentious foreign policy. Equally, French attitudes to Germany, which had often appeared to the Allies as unacceptably *'revanchist'*, could be presented as dictated by the evident needs of France's planned economic reconstruction. In this political climate Jean Monnet would be able to convince de Gaulle, at the end of 1945, of the need to create a planning and modernization programme for the French economy, in which trade unionists, industrialists and civil servants would participate, under the *Commissariat Général du Plan* in 1946.[73]

Pleven was later to argue in 1980 that it was too simplistic to present the conflict over the development of the French economy in 1944–5 in terms of austerity versus *laissez-faire*. It was rather a question of how much intervention in the economy was politically acceptable at that stage: 'my point of view tended towards not wanting to crush the French people by forcing too heavy a collar on them. The French had the right to breathe a bit.' Quoting his own experiences of the Breton peasants, Pleven suggested that any attempt to impose *'dirigiste'* policies would have resulted in their reacting badly, and possibly hanging on to the produce which was so desperately needed in the towns. De Gaulle apparently repeated much of the same defence to Mendès-France during the Fifth Republic: 'If I'd said you were right I should have been completely sunk; we wouldn't have had any more food, the markets would have been emptied straight away, the butchers would have shut up shop.' Bloch-Lainé makes the point that France, unlike Belgium where interventionist policies of this sort had been tried, still had several competing centres of power. It could well have been difficult to take a Jacobin approach to the economy when the control and power of Paris was being disputed in the early months of the Liberation.[74]

Curiously enough, parallel with economic policies which were increasingly liberal in tone, there was a wave of state intervention in particular sectors of the economy. As Madjarian points out, the post-Liberation nationalization programme operated in two phases: the first, more Jacobin and anti-capitalist, with the requisitions carried out by CDLs, the take-over of the mines in the Nord/Pas de Calais in December 1944, and the confiscation without compensation of companies which had collaborated during the occupation (for example, *Renault, Gnôme et Rhône*) transferred to the state in January and April 1945. From the spring of 1945 to spring 1946, there was a second batch of nationalization measures, parliamentary, modernist and technocratic, inaugurated by the joint Socialist Party/Communist Party manifesto in March 1945. The impetus was provided by the Constituent Assembly, where nationalization bills were generally passed in virtual unanimity. The language of the debates, however, tended to have changed from 'war on the trusts', to modernization and productivity.[75] *Air France, Air Bleu,* and *Air France-Transatlantique* were taken over by the state in June 1945, and the *Banque de France* and other major banking companies were nationalized in November 1945. In April 1946, insurance companies were taken over and the *Electricité de France* and *Gaz de France* set up. In May 1946 remaining French mines were nationalized.

These measures were much less radical than they appeared on paper. As in Britain, much of the nationalization had taken place in the backward sector of heavy industry which had failed before the war to provide the kind of profits which might attract private investment. In the case of the airlines, the state had already been a shareholder before 1940, and the Bank of France had come under the direct control of the government in 1936. As far as the banks were concerned, however, there was much less unanimity, and the measure agreed, buying the shares of the Bank of France and four credit banks (*Crédit Lyonnais, Société Générale, Comptoir National d'Escompte* and *Banque Nationale pour le Commerce et l'Industrie*), was less radical than many had expected, and left the actual running of the banks very much as they had been before. Similarly, the nationalization of insurance companies left something like 50 per cent of the insurance business in the hands of private companies, and made very little difference to the way in which the new state insurance companies did their business. In all cases, nationalization could be justified by the necessity to provide raw materials and investment which would reconstruct the French economy, to the ultimate benefit of all industrialists and entrepreneurs.

Even a measure like the institution of *comités d'entreprise* (industrial committees) approved in principle in late September 1944, was not actually promulgated until the middle of the following February, and turned out to be a rather anodyne form of worker participation, designed to be a good deal less threatening than the 'management' or 'production' committees which had grown up in the early months of the Liberation, generally in areas over which central government had not yet established its full control. By comparison with these, the GPRF's model was deliberately limited and non-executive: 'These Committees are not decision-making bodies. It has seemed indispensable to leave the manager with the responsibility for the business he is managing.'[76] No wonder perhaps that the British Embassy, asked to comment on the current economic situation of France in February 1945,

alluded to: 'what seems to some a rather timid series of measures . . .
the Government have followed a cautious policy and evidently do not
intend to make widespread and drastic changes in the general
economy or in the structure of industry without careful thought or
without a mandate from the country.'[77]

In the field of economics, the limited nature of the change which had
occurred with the establishment of a new administration became
apparent. The political movements which might have been expected to
demand a radical renewal of the economic structure, like the PCF,
turned out to favour fairly orthodox economic measures and the
proponents of particular initiatives, like the SFIO with nationalizations, seemed content with what could be done in the difficult
post-Liberation period. There were some radical measures and an
impetus for change generated by the Resistance groups and grass roots
movements, but the policy of the provisional government was in
general terms a triumph for conservative economics.

For many Resisters, the regime which emerged in France proved to
be a deep disappointment – an opportunity to change the face of
France was lost. Certainly the actions of the GPRF suggest an essential
continuity with the past rather than the radical change the Resistance
had called for. In this area the influence of the Allies was indirect,
although they were sometimes used by the government as an alibi for
particular political choices. The large-scale American military presence
in France undoubtedly discouraged those who might have espoused
the cause of revolution, and played its part, alongside Stalin's instructions, in calming the PCF. The constitution of French domestic politics,
and the policy goals of the provisional government were, however,
even more critical in leading the country towards a relatively conservative solution of its problems. The institutional context in which the
GPRF existed, the disappearance of the Resistance as a major political
force, and the re-emergence of the parties all contributed to making the
new system surprisingly impervious to change. The nature of the
difficulties to be tackled – the purge, or economic reform – was often so
problematic and potentially divisive, that the government tended to
eschew radical solutions in an attempt to maintain its credibility in the
eyes of that majority of Frenchmen who had not participated in the
Resistance.

Instead of new political groups imbued with the ideology of the
Resistance, the old political parties (with the crucial addition of one
new formation) speedily regained the central stage of political debate.
The parties of the centre and right which had dominated the Third
Republic were certainly punished by the electorate for their hesitations
and compromises in the war, and it was the parties of the left which
emerged as the clear political victors of the Liberation. However, any

hope of a 'Resistance' unity between them outlasting the war was soon disappointed. The divisions between the three major parties were as bitter and acrimonious as any which had existed in the Third Republic.

After the trauma of 1940 and the complete disintegration of the Third Republic structures, the France which emerged from the Liberation was recognizably the same country as that which had plunged head-long to defeat. In a sense this continuity was a powerful tribute to the careful planning, and painstaking assertion of central authority, before and during the Liberation process. To many French men and women, however, the aftermath of the Liberation seemed to be a betrayal of the bright hopes of the Resistance: 'The mountain has given birth to a mouse.'[78]

# Abbreviations used in the notes

NOTE: Places of publication are given only for works published outside the United Kingdom. Commonly recognized abbreviations such as *J.* for *Journal*, *Rev.* for *Review*, have been used; other abbreviations are listed below.

| | |
|---|---|
| AN | Archives Nationales, Paris |
| Archives Ivry | Association du Musée de la Résistance (which has changed both name and location from Ivry to Champigny-sur-Marne) |
| FRUS | Foreign Relations of the US |
| IHTP | Institut d'Histoire du Temps Présent |
| NA | United States National Archives, Washington |
| PRO | Public Record Office, London |

Where the documents contained in the collection entitled Foreign Relations of the United States were seen in the US National Archives, they have been given their archival reference number (the one that appears in FRUS), but where they were not seen in the National Archives, they have been given an FRUS volume and page number.

# Notes

## 1    The disintegration of the Republic

1.  Of the many books on the fall of France, R. Jackson, *The Fall of France 1940* (1975), is a concise account; J. Williams, *The Ides of May: The Defeat of France May–June 1940* (1968), is a longer narrative; A. Horne, *To Lose a Battle: France 1940* (1959), is dramatic; and L. F. Ellis, *The War in France and Flanders 1939–1940* (1953), is the official British history. B. Bond in *France and Belgium 1939–1940* (1975), demonstrates the link between defeat in Belgium and that in France.
2.  On the French side General Maxime Weygand gives his account in *Recalled to Service* (trans.), (1952), and General Gamelin in *Servir* (Paris, 1946–7). Paul Reynaud explains his actions in *In The Thick of the Fight* (trans.), (1955), and in his *Mémoires* (Paris, 1960). M. Bloch, *The Strange Defeat* (trans.), (1949), is still a good insight into the psychology of the times.
3.  The struggle between 'defeatists' and 'defenders' can be seen in the works of Pétainists such as P. Baudouin, *Neuf Mois au Gouvernement* (Paris, 1948); and *The Private Diaries of Paul Baudouin* (trans.), (1948); Y. Bouthillier, *Le Drame de Vichy*, vol. 1 (Paris, 1950). Those who were 'undecided' are represented by C. Chautemps, *Cahiers Secrets de l'Armistice* (Paris, 1963); and those who opposed by J. Paul-Boncour, *Entre Deux Guerres: Souvenirs sur la IIIe République*, vol. 3 (Paris, 1946). The group who wanted to transfer the government to North Africa are chronicled in C. Rimbaud, *L'Affaire du Massilia* (Paris, 1984).
4.  P. Heracles (ed.), *La Loi Nazie en France 1940–1944* (Paris, 1974); and E. Jackel, *La France dans l'Europe d'Hitler* (Paris, 1968). P. Ory, *La France Allemande* (Paris, 1977).
5.  Pétain's speeches can be found in a number of places including *Paroles aux Français: Messages et Ecrits 1939–1941*, introduction G. L. Jarry (Lyon, 1941); and more recently in J. Isorni (ed.), *Philippe Pétain: Actes et Ecrits* (Paris, 1974). Jules Jeanneney's *Journal Politique* (Paris, 1972) gives an interesting and selectively detailed account of this period; and E. Herriot, a less precise picture, in his *Episodes: 1940–1944* (Paris, 1950).
6.  An account of 10 July at Vichy from the *Journal Officiel* is reproduced in E. Berl, *La Fin de la IIIe République* (Paris, 1968). For the establishment of Vichy, and its nature see H. Michel, *Vichy: Année 40* (Paris, 1966); R. D. Paxton, *Vichy France: Old Guard and New Order 1940–1944* (New York, 1972) which is still the best account; R. Aron, *The Vichy Regime* (trans.), (1958); G. Warner, *Pierre Laval and the Eclipse of France*, (1968); and H. Michel, *Pétain et le Régime de Vichy* (Paris, 1978).
7.  For views sympathetic to the PCF see J. Duclos and V. Joannes (eds), *Le Parti Communiste Français dans la Résistance* (Paris, 1967); G. Willard, *De Munich à Vichy: La Drôle de Guerre* (Paris, 1969); G. Willard, *La Gestapo Contre le Parti Communiste* (Paris, 1984); F. Crémieux and J. Estager, *Sur le Parti 1939–1940* (Paris, 1983); and R. Bourderon *et al.*, *Le PCF Etapes et Problemes 1920–1972* (Paris, 1981). A more balanced picture is provided by R. Kedward, 'Behind the

Polemics; French Communists and the Resistance', in Hawes and White (eds), *Resistance in Europe 1939–1945* (1975); S. Courtois, *Le PCF dans la Guerre* (Paris, 1980); and J. Simmonds, 'The French Communist Party and the Beginnings of Resistance: September 1939–June 1941', *European Studies Review* 11, 1981. Critical of the PCF are: A. Rossi, *Les Communistes Français Pendant la Drôle de Guerre 1939–1940* (Paris, 1972); A. Rossi, *La Guerre des Papillons* (Paris, 1954); A. Rossi, *Les Cahiers du Bolchevisme Pendant la Campagne 1939–1940* (Paris, 1951); R. Gaucher, *Histoire Secrète du PCF* (Paris, 1974); R. de Jonchay, *Les Communistes et la Résistance* (Paris, 1970); and A. Lecoeur, *Le PCF et la Résistance: Août 1939–Juin 1941* (Paris, 1968).

## 2  Preparations for the Liberation: the Allies

1. Accounts of Allied relations with de Gaulle: L. Woodward, *British Foreign Policy in the Second World War*, vols 1, 2, 3 (1970–1); F. Kersaudy, *Churchill and De Gaulle* (1981); E. Barker, *Churchill and Eden at War*, (1978); A. Funk, *The Politics of Torch: the Allied Landings and the Algiers Putsch* (Kansas, 1974); D. White, *Seeds of Discord and De Gaulle, Free France and the Allies* (New York, 1964).

2. On 12 June Churchill telegrammed Roosevelt asking for his support for Reynaud and noting, 'a young General de Gaulle who believes much can be done.' See J. P. Lash, *Churchill and Roosevelt 1939–1941* (New York, 1976). See also Kersaudy, *op.cit.*, M. Gilbert, *Winston S. Churchill*, vol.6 1939–41 (1983), and W. S. Churchill, *The Second World War*, vol. 2 (1948).

3. For a highly partial view of the Muselier affair, see E. Muselier, *De Gaulle contre le Gaullisme* (Paris, 1946). For the Saint Pierre and Miquelon incident and its ramifications see D. G. Anglin, *The St Pierre and Miquelon Affair of 1941* (Toronto, 1966).

4. R. T. Thomas in *Britain and Vichy* (1979), deals concisely with these remaining contacts and the British attitude to Vichy, and for a partial view of the Rougier Mission from Vichy to London see L. Rougier, *Les Accords Secrets Pétain-Churchill: Histoire d'une Mission Secrète* (Montreal, 1945).

5. See Cordell Hull's *Memoirs*, vol. 2 (New York, 1948); W. Kimball, *Churchill and Roosevelt* (1980), 45 and 47; and D. L. Porter, *The 76th Congress and World War II 1939–1940* (Columbia, 1979).

6. Roosevelt to Pétain, 25 Oct. 1940: see Hull to Matthews, NA, 740.0019 European Wars 1939/530a, see also R. Murphy, *Diplomat Among Warriors* (1964), 56.

7. Murphy, *ibid.*, 67–98 and Secretary of State to Leahy, 15 Jan. 1941, NA, 851.48/127. See a summary in J-C. Beam, 'The intelligence background of operation Torch', *Parameters 13* (1983), on intelligence resources provided by presence of American agents under Murphy–Weygand agreements, 26 Feb. 1941.

8. W. D. Leahy, *I Was There* (1950); Leahy to Secretary of State, 11 Jan. 1941, NA, 851.48/123 and Leahy to Roosevelt, 25 Jan. 1941, NA, 740.0011 EW 1939/7908 1/2.

9. Welles memo of conversation with Halifax, 31 March 1941, NA, 741.00112 European War 1939/2548; Secretary of State to Leahy, 30 April 1941, NA, 740.0011 European War 1939/10536a. For an apologia/exposition of US policy towards Vichy see W. Langer, *Our Vichy Gamble* (New York, 1947). The Vichy point of view on relations with Britain and the USA is expressed in P. Queuille, *Histoire Diplomatique de Vichy* (Paris, 1976) and A. D. Hytier, *Two Years of French Foreign Policy: Vichy 1940–1942* (trans.), (Westport, 1974).

10. Hull to Roosevelt, 2 Feb. 1942 (on Saint Pierre and Miquelon) NA, 851. A

01/2–242. The US State Department had given Vichy Admiral Robert authority over the islands: see memo of European Division of State Department 28 Nov. 1941, quoted in Langer, *op.cit.*, 196. Also Roosevelt to Pétain, 13 Dec. 1941 via Leahy; see Leahy to State Department NA, 851.33/211, and Donovan to Roosevelt, 24 Dec. 1941 in Secretary of State to Leahy, 25 Dec. 1941, NA, 851 A 01/15.

11. Welles to Leahy, 16 April 1942, NA, 124.51/234a and 124.51/236a.

12. For the difference in British/American attitudes to the Free French at this stage, see: British statement on the Free French, 14 May 1942, US Embassy (London) to State Department NA, 851/)01.452 1/2 and Roosevelt statement, 17 Nov. 1942, see annex I of memo by Welles, 18 Nov. 1942, NA, 851.R.01/12 3/4.

13. Matthews to Secretary of State on meeting with Eden, 8 Jan. 1943, NA, 851.R20/ 49.

14. 23 Sept. 1943, PRO, FO 371, 36036. Macmillan to FO, 21 Oct. 1943, PRO, FO 371, 36036.

15. See, for example, FO to Washington Embassy, 10 May 1943, PRO, FO 371, 35994. 'Mr Hull is really hypersensitive', Washington Embassy Report, 29 Jan. 1943, PRO, FO 371, 35993; Memo of conversation with Sir Ronald Campbell by Secretary of State, 1 Jan. 1943, NA, 851.01/965 Secretary of State to Matthews, 1 Jan. 1943, NA, 740.00115 European War 1939/5545 and Matthews to Secretary of State on meeting with Eden, 8 Jan. 1943, NA, 851.R20/49.

16. See Winant to Secretary of State, 6 April 1943, NA, 851.01/2016; Murphy to Secretary of State, 3 April 1943, NA, 851.01/2008; Secretary of State to Murphy, 13 April 1943, NA, 851.01/2008; Winant to Secretary of State, 15 April 1943, NA, 851.01/2054; Murphy to Secretary of State, 24 April 1943, NA, 851.01/537; Murphy to Secretary of State, 6 May 1943, NA, 851.01/2105; President to Secretary of State, memo, 8 May 1943, Roosevelt Papers (FDRL). See also Kersaudy, *op.cit.*, 272–3, and telegram to Prime Minister from Deputy Prime Minister and Foreign Secretary, Alcove 370371 and 372, Secretary's Standard File, 23 May 1943, PRO, CAB 65 (38) WM 75 (43) l; Prime Minister to Deputy Prime Minister and Foreign Secretary, Pencil 227, 24 May 1943, PRO, FO 371, 36047.

17. Murphy to Secretary of State, 7 June 1943, and 8 June 1943 on conversations with de Gaulle, NA, 851.01/2234 and NA, 851.00/2223; Matthews to Leahy, 8 June 1943, NA. Matthews/Hickerson file, M–1244, roll 13 (known hereafter as M–H file); Hull, *op.cit.*, 1221; C. Pogue, *George C. Marshall: Organiser of the Victory* (New York, 1973, 236).

18. For the American reaction to this development, see Murphy to Secretary of State and President, 16 June 1943, NA, 851.01/2283. Roosevelt to Churchill, 17 June 1943, Roosevelt Papers (FDRL), *ibid.*, copy of telegram sent to Eisenhower and to Churchill, and W. D. Leahy, *op.cit.*, 221.

19. A. Cadogan, *Diaries 1938–45*, ed. L. Dilks (1971), 21 Aug. 1943; Kersaudy, *op.cit.*, 296.

20. Roosevelt to Churchill, 1 Jan. 1943, FRUS (1943), vol. 2 (Washington, 1964), 23.

21. Comment on Strang's memo, 15 March 1943, PRO, FO 371, 36036. Secretary's Standard File, 13 April 1943, PRO, CAB 65 (38), WM. 53 (43) 2.

22. 18 Jan. 1944, PRO, FO 371, 41931.

23. Comment on Morton's paper, 26 Feb. 1944, PRO, FO 371 41876.

24. English and American texts, Kersaudy, *op.cit.*, 296–7.

25. War Office note, 12 June 1942, PRO, CAB 78, 3/Misc. 29(42) 23 June 1942.

26. 8 March 1943, PRO, CAB 66, 34/WP(43) 78.

27. For a full discussion of this struggle see H. Coles and A. Weinberg, *Civil Affairs: Soldiers Become Governors* (Washington, 1964).

28. F. Donnison, *Civil Affairs and Military Government, North-West Europe 1944–1946* (1961), 19.
29. Coles and Weinberg, *op.cit.*, 116.
30. For a good summary of the sequence of events, see FO notes for discussion with WO, 28 Sept. 1943, PRO, FO 371, 35237.
31. 22 Sept. 1943, PRO, FO 371, 35237; Sargent to Bovenschen, 9 Oct. 1943, PRO, FO 371, 35237; 20 Sept. 1943, PRO, CAB 88 63; 23–24 Sept. 1943, PRO, CAB 122 409. Text of American draft in Washington to FO, 24 Sept. 1943, PRO, FO 371, 35237; 7 Oct. 1943, PRO, FO 371, 35239; 29 Oct. 1943 PRO, FO 371, 35238; FO comments, 4 Oct. 1943 and Washington to FO, 3 Oct. 1943, PRO, FO 371, 35239.
32. Comments of FO on Strang's meeting with WO, 7 Oct. 1943, and on telegram outlining American proposals, 7 Oct. 1943, PRO, FO 371, 35238.
33. 28 Oct. 1943, PRO, FO 371, 35238; 11 Oct. 1943, PRO, PREM 3, 177/6, response FS to PM, 9 Oct. 1943, PRO, FO 371, 35239 Cadogan to PM, draft minute, 4 Oct. 1943, PRO, FO 371, 35239. Morton forwards Macmillan's letter to PM, 9 Oct. 1943, PRO, PREM 3 177/6. Strang's comments on using letter in meeting with Bovenschen ('It shook them up considerably'), PRO, FO 371 35238 and 35239.
34. Ward to Carver, 23 Nov. 1943, PRO, FO 371, 35238.
35. FO comment on difficulties on using EAC, 12 Nov. 1943, PRO, FO 371 35239. Useful table setting out English, American and French drafts at this stage, 7 Oct. 1943, in PRO, FO 371, 35239.
36. See, for example, Stalin's suspicion of Anglo–American discussions in D. W. Ellwood, *The Politics of Liberation: Italy, 1943–1945* (1985), 27.
37. FO Comment, 30 April 1944, PRO, FO 371, 40363.
38. 11 Nov. 1943, PRO, CAB 66/43 WP (43); Cabinet discussion on Eden's attempts to persuade McCloy, and HMG policy after, 23 Nov. 1943, PRO, CAB 87/83, ACA (43).
39. Kersaudy, *op.cit.*, 303, 305.
40. British views of American immobility in FO to FS, 4 Dec. 1943, PRO. PREM 3, 177/6; note on State Department, December 1943, PRO, FO 371, 35238.
41. Reports of Eisenhower's last meeting with de Gaulle before he left Algiers in A. D. Chandler, *The Papers of Dwight D. Eisenhower*, vol. 3 (1970), 592 and 1668; and H. Butcher, *My Three Years with Eisenhower* (New York, 1947), 473. War Department reprimand HQ COSSAC to CA Division and replies, 26 Nov. 1943, NA, CAD 014 Fr (3 8–43) (1) (?).
42. Wilson to State Department, 10 Nov. 1943, NA. 851.01/3174 1/2 and 12 Nov. 1943, NA, 851.0/3174 1/2.
43. See also Chandler, *op.cit.*, 1592–1668.
44. Bonbright to Secretary of State, 9 Sept. 1943, NA, 851.01 2941.
45. OSS R and A Report (Bruce), 17 Sept. 1943, NA, 321, AF, 61595.
46. *Ibid.*
47. OSS Washington. Report on France no. R. 2137, 15 Nov. 1943, NA, OSS 53666 and 6 Dec. 1943, report no. 252438–48, NA, OSS 49786; Gumbel (OWI) to Platt (OSS), 18 Oct. 1943, NA, RG.266. Entry 99 Box 32; OSS R and A report no. 15831, Dec. 1943, NA, OSS 355.4. AH 611115.
48. JCS Memo for information, CCAC files 12 Oct. 1943, NA, 851. 014 Fr (9 Dec. 1945) (1).
49. Hull, *Memoirs, op.cit.*, 245; 27 Nov. 1943, Matthews/Hickerson file, NA, M 1244 roll 13; FDR to Churchill FDR Personal Letters, *op.cit.*, 31 Dec. 1943.
50. Chandler, *op.cit.*, 1667 and note 1668 and Secretary of State to Winant, 14 Jan. 1944, FRUS 1944, vol. 3, (Washington, 1965), 641–2. See also S. E. Ambrose, *Eisenhower*, (1984), 279–80.

51. See, for example Stimson and Bundy, *On Active Service in Peace and War* (New York, 1947), 546–77 and Hull to Roosevelt, 14 Jan. 1944, NA, 851.01/3369B.

52. 22 Jan. 1944, PRO, WO 219, 45.

53. Halifax to Eden, 22 Jan. 1944, 17 Feb. 1944, PRO, CAB 122, 409; Washington to FO, 10 Feb. 1944, PRO, FO 371, 40361.

54. 12 Feb. 1944, PRO, CAB 122, 409; FO comment on 20 Jan. 1944, PRO, FO 371, 40361; also 12 Feb. 1944, PRO, FO 371, 40361.

55. Halifax to FO, 24 Feb. 1944, PRO, CAB 122, 409; 28 Feb. 1944, PRO, FO 371, 40362.

56. 29 Feb. 1944, PRO. PREM 3, 177/3.

57. FDR to Hull, 25 Feb. 1944, NA, M/H file, M 1244 Roll 13; Stimson and Bundy, *op.cit.*, 548; President's directive to Eisenhower, 15 March 1944, Na M/H file, M1244 Roll 13; Roosevelt's meeting with Edwin C. Wilson (US rep to the CFLN), 24 March 1944, NA, 851′00/3185 1/2; President to SAC via Hull, 11 March 1944, NA, CAD 014 Fr (3–8–43).

58. Halifax to FO, 3 March 1944, PRO, FO 371, 40362 and report in FO to Algiers, 10 March 1944, 40362; see also 2 March 1944, PRO, CAB 122, 410.

59. OSS Historical file 1 Jan. 1944 RG 226. Entry 99 Box 1; SOE A no. 331 6 Jan. 1944, AN, 72 AJ, 37; see also Donovan Report for many other examples. AN, 72 AJ, 85.

60. Political Résumé for 1943, 5 Feb. 1944 NA, OSS 56831; Report no. 29804-2 (OSS Washington. Origin New York), 2 Feb. 1944, NA, OSS 56441; Weekly Airgram no. 16 OSS (OID) Algiers, 24 Feb. 1944, NA, OSS 60272; summary of Views on Currents in the Resistance (no. 7B 97) 3 March 1944, NA, OSS 60656.

61. See also OSS R and A Report no. 1697, 25 May 1944, NA, 323, 2AF, 6200S and 21st Army Group report, PRO, WO 171, 165. For a whole series of MID (Military Intelligence Division of the U.S. Department) reports, mainly originating in Madrid, see NA, OSS 63882, 64722, 73143, 69442, 81927.

62. FO commentary to Duff Cooper describing their attitude as standing aside and letting the President and his advisers fight it out, 10 March 1944, PRO, FO 371, 40362; PM to FS, 30 Jan. 1944, PRO, FO 371, 41876; PM to FS, 13 March 1944, PRO FO 371, 40362; PM to Washington, 4 March 1944, PRO FO 371, 40362.

63. For a flavour of procrastination, see record of telephone call from Law, 15 April 1944, PRO FO 371, 40363; PM to Cadogan, 9 April 1944, PRO, FO 371, 40363; 20 April 1944, PRO, FO 371, 40364.

64. Memo to Secretary of State from Matthews on talks with Harvey and Mack of FO 12 April 1944, NA, 851. 01/4–1244; T. M. Campbell and M. Herring, *The Diaries of Edward R. Stettinius Jr. 1943–1946* (New York, 1975), 18, 19 April 1944.

65. Hull, *op.cit.*, 1210–12, and NA, CAD 014 Fr (3–8–43).

66. Hilldring to Secretary of State for War, 19 April 1944, NA, CAD, 014 Fr (3–8–43) (1)(3); notes on a proposal for de Gaulle to visit Washington, Hull to Roosevelt, 20/6, 21 April 1944, NA, 851.00/49.

67. Further complications arose because of the downgrading of Giraud, and the Indo-China problem. For the Prime Minister's insistence that he would not let the issue separate him from the President see W. S. Churchill, *The Second World War*, vol. 5 (1968), Appendix C. For a history of the USA's dropping of Giraud from around October 1943 see Murphy to Hull, 8 Aug. 1943 NA, 851.01/3053: 'In my opinion, politically, he has played his cards badly, frequently stubbornly; against our advice. Our policies . . . should not be tied to the person of General Giraud;' Chapin to Hull, 9 Feb. 1944, NA, 851.01/1–2845; Murphy to Hull, 6 April 1944, NA, 851.01/3639; Chandler, *op.cit.*, 1834, 26 April 1944, Eisenhower to Marshall; Leahy, *op.cit.*, 277, 8 April 1944, an account of a holiday with Roosevelt at Hob Caw.

For a flavour of Roosevelt's attitude to Indo-China see FDR to Cordell Hull 24 Jan. 1944: 'I saw Halifax last week and told him quite firmly that it was perfectly true that I had for over a year, expressed the opinion that Indo-China should not go back to the French, but that it should be administered by an international trusteeship,' in E. Roosevelt and J. P. Lash, *FDR: the Personal Letters 1928–1945* (New York, 1970); Roosevelt briefing to Edwin C. Wilson, 23 March 1944, NA, 851.00/3183 1/2. He suggested that Australia and New Zealand should control New Caledonia, that Indo-China should not be returned to France. But Chiang Kai-Shek, to whom he offered the colony, refused his 'gift'. T. M. Campbell and G. C. Herring, *The Diaries of Edward R. Stettinius Jr, op.cit.*, 17 March 1944, Roosevelt complained, as he did frequently, about French stewardship of Indo-China.

68. Washington to FO, 10 May 1944, PRO, FO 371, 41879.
69. Reported in 28 Jan. 1944, PRO, CAB 122, 409.
70. See, for example, 18 March 1944, PRO, WD 219, 3729.
71. Grasset to McSherry, 26 April 1944, PRO, WO 219, 3845.
72. Comment 13 April 1944 on PRO, FO 371, 40363.
73. 5 April 1944, PRO, WO 219, 45.
74. Memo of conversation by Matthews, 25 April 1944, NA, M/H file M-1244 Roll 17 and Campbell and Herring, *op.cit.*
75. 11 April 1944, PRO, WO 219, 45, gives an idea of how desperate the situation was becoming. On SAC's move 13 April 1944, PRO, FO 371, 41878, and 20 April 1944, PRO, FO 371, 40363. Biddle/Koenig opening moves, 18 April 1944, PRO, WO 219 45.
76. SAC's request, 20 April 1944, PRO, WO 219 45; 20 April 1944, PRO, FO 371, 40363; Leahy to Marshall, April 1944, NA, CAD 014 Fr (3-8-43), Roosevelt to Churchill, 12 May 1944, FRUS 1944, vol. 3, *op.cit.*, 683 and Roosevelt to Churchill, 27 May 1944; F.L. lowenheim *et al.*, *Roosevelt and Churchill* (New York, 1975).
77. 25 April 1944, PRO, FO 371, 40364.
78. Hilldring to Chief of Staff, 11 May 1944, NA, CAD 014, Fr (3-8-43).
79. Eden comments, 17 May 1944, PRO FO 371, 40364; FO on the necessity of adopting a low profile, 1 May 1944, PRO, FO 371, 40364, and 5 May 1944, PRO, FO 371, 41879; FO note on Koenig/SHAEF talks, 4 May 1944, PRO, FO 371 40364.
80. Eisenhower to AGWAR, CCS, 11 May 1944, in Chandler, *op.cit.*, 1896; compare Roosevelt at Cabinet meeting of 20 May 1944 declaring that he would not change his position unless someone could give him a certificate saying that de Gaulle was a representative of the French people. Winant to Secretary of State, 24 and 25 May 1944, NA 851.01/383c/77 and Stettinius to Matthews, 24 May 1944, NA, 851.01/3859.

# 3   Preparations for the Liberation: the French

1. For a good summary of the steps leading to the creation of the *Conseil National de la Résistance*, see D. Cordier, *'Jean Moulin et le Conseil de la Résistance,'* in *Institut d'Histoire du Temps Présent* conference, June 1983.
2. See *Rapport Passy*, May/June 1943, AN, 72 AJ, 438, *Rapport Rex*, 7 May 1943, AN, 72 AJ, 410.
3. Text in H. Michel et B. Mirkine-Guétzevitch, *Les Idées Politiques et Sociales de la Résistance* (Paris, 1954), 110.
4. 3 April 1943, AN, F1a 3735.

5. Quoted in H. Noguères, *Histoire de la Résistance en France*, vol. 4 (Paris, 1976), 164.
6. Rapport Rex, 7 May 1943, AN, 72 AJ, 410.
7. C. de Gaulle, *Mémoires de Guerre* (Livre de Poche), vol. 2 (Paris, 1956), 122.
8. H. Frenay in *Combat*, Algiers, 2 Oct. 1943.
9. J. Sweets, *The Politics of Resistance in France, 1940–1944* (Illinois, 1976), 124.
10. See, for example, Passy/Manuel/Rachet conversation, 5 March 1944, AN, 72AJ, 410; d'Astier/de Gaulle interview, 7 March 1944, and Passy/Bloch/Pelabon/Rachet conversation, 29 Feb. 1944, AN, 72 AJ, 410 . . .'*entre d'Astier et moi, c'est la guerre au couteau.*' Also Fouche Report no. 4, undated, AN, 72 AJ,410.
11. R. de Jonchay, *Le Parti Communiste et la Résistance, op.cit.*; A. Rossi, *La Guerre des Papillons* (Paris, 1954); A. Kriegel, *Communismes au Miroir Français*, (Paris, 1974); and A. J. Rieber, *Stalin and the French Communist Party* (New York, 1962).
12. The Central Committee of the PCF to the President of the CNR, 3 Jan. 1944, AN, 72 AJ 3.
13. In S. Hawes and R. White (eds), *Resistance in Europe: 1939–1945* (1976), 101.
14. Laroque to Col. Dumas, 19 Oct. 1943, AN, F1a, 3836, and Record of conversation 21 Oct. 1943, PRO, FO 371, 36036.
15. M. Agulhon in the Liberation Colloquium, *Comité d'Histoire de la 2ème Guerre Mondiale, La Libération de la France* (Paris, 1974), 67–90.
16. Garreau to de Gaulle, 23 Jan. 1944, AN, F1a 3816 and Bloch to d'Astier, 29 Jan. 1944, AN, F1a, 3816.
17. See, for example, R. Hervé interview with J. C. Simmonds, 12 Feb. 1969, and R. Pannequin interview with J. C. Simmonds, 1 Feb. 1969.
18. Speaight, 31 Nov. 1943, PRO, FO 317, 36037.
19. Interview, 24 Sept. 1943, between Victor (PS) and member of the Central Committee of the PCF, AN, F1a 3751.
20. *La Vie du Parti*, February 1944, 4.
21. H. Michel, *Les Courants de Pensée de la Résistance* (Paris, 1962).
22. See BBC monitor of Soviet European Service, 18 May 1944, PRO, FO 371, 41879.
23. H. Michel in *Revue d'Histoire de la Deuxième Guerre Mondiale* (1952), no. 8, 81.
24. Michel and Mirkine-Guétzevitch, *op.cit.*, 60.
25. Diagrammatic comparison of plans in PRO, FO 371, 41877 and *Journal Officiel, Compte rendu Analytique des débats de l'Assemblée Consultative Provisoire*, 21/22 Jan. 1944, and 18/22/30 March, 1944.
26. 28 Sept. 1943, AN, F1a 3734.
27. For copy in English, see PRO, WO 219, 45.
28. AN, 72 AJ, 449.
29. See supplement to review of the foreign press, series F, no. 32, 1 May 1944, PRO, FO 371, 41878.
30. See AN, 72 AJ, I or Noguères, *op.cit.*, vol. 4, annexe no. 5, 672.
31. For an excellent study of the *Commissaires*, see C-L. Foulon, *Le Pouvoir en Province à la Libération* (Paris, 1975). D. de Bellescize, *Les Neuf Sages de la Résistance (le comité général d'études dans la clandestinité)*, (Paris, 1979) is good on the 'think-tank' which preceded the *Commission des Désignations*. See also Debré's own estimate of the *Commissaires* in 'Un grand mouvement préfectoral', *Les Cahiers Politiques* (1948).
32. Vincent (Fouche) 26 March 1944, AN, F1a 3234.
33. Foulon, *op.cit.*, 78 and C-L. Foulon, *Les Commissaires de la République 1943–1946*, *thèse pour le doctorat de recherches* (1973).
34. Papers of Serreules, quoted in Sweets, *op. cit.*; and Fouche report no. 2, 10 Oct. 1943, AN, 72 AJ, 410.
35. Fouche report no. 3, 11 Nov. 1943, AN, 72 AJ, 410.

36. F-L. Closon, *Le Temps des Passions* (Paris, 1974), 140; and Fouche report no. 3, 11 Nov. 1943, AN, 72 AJ, 410.
37. Fouche report no. 2, 10 Oct. 1943, AN, 72 AJ, 410.
38. From Briand to London, 23 Nov. 1943, AN, 72 AJ, 236 and to Secnord, 12 Dec. 1943, AN, 72 AJ, 235.
39. D'Astier to de Gaulle, 21 Jan. 1944, AN, 72 AJ, 409, and also in AN, F1a, 3840; 15 Feb. 1944, AN, 72 AJ, 409; d'Astier to Salard, 11 Feb. 1944, AN, F1a, 3816; Bloch to d'Astier, 7 Feb. 1944 and note from Sauvier, 8 March 1944, AN, 72 AJ, 234.
40. See, for example, Secnord, Léandre, 4 April 1944, AN, 72 AJ, 36; Sudsec, Cléante, 10 Jan. 1944, AN, 72 AJ, 236.
41. 31 Dec. 1943, AN, 72 AJ, 234.
42. *Bulletin d'Information du Front National*, 6, 15 Feb. 1944, quoted in J. Sweets, *op.cit.*, 133.
43. Bulletin no. 6 of *Front National*, 15 Feb. 1944, AN, F1a, 3763.
44. 23 Nov. 1943, AN, 72 AJ, 236; see copy of the monitoring report on this Provisional Consultative Assembly speech, 10 Jan. 1944, PRO, FO 371, 41923; Massigli, note 8 Jan. 1944, AN, 72 AJ, 221.
45. Telegram, Polygone to BCRAL, 1 Jan. 1944, AN, 72 AJ, 237.
46. Military Role of the French Resistance, 6 March 1944, AN, 72 AJ, 471.
47. General d'Astier to *Comité d'Action en France*, 10 Feb. 1944, AN, F1a, 3727.
48. Koenig to COMAC in AN, 72 AJ, 512, no. D440/FF1; Rivier to all FFI in region 5, 25 July 1944, AN, 72 AJ, 586; undated note from Arc, AN, 72 AJ, 512.
49. E. d'Astier de la Vigerie, *Seven Times Seven Days* (1958), 157.
50. Passy quoted in Sweets, *op.cit.*, 87.
51. See, for example, AN, F1a, 3750, 37 and 3752.
52. Note from Sauvier, 8 March 1944, AN, F1a, 3234; Polygone to BCRAL, 28 Feb. 1944, AN, 72 AJ, 237. See also A. de Dainville, *L'ORA, la Résistance de l'Armée/Guerre 1939–1945* (Paris, 1974). Polygone to BCRAL, 26 Jan. 1944, 10 Feb. 1944, 21 Feb. 1944, AN, 72 AJ, 237.
53. Resolutions voted by the *Comité Directeur* of *Front National* in meeting of 29 May 1944, AN, F1a, 3753; *Assemblée Consultative Provisoire*, 8 Jan. 1944, 2 March 1944.
54. See, for example, Soustelle/Grenier polemic, *Les Lettres Francaises*, 23 Oct. 1947.
55. Telegram from Secnord, 25 April 1944, AN, 72 AJ, 236; Necker Report, 31 Oct. 1943, AN, 72 AJ, 409.
56. See 30 Aug. 1943, AN, F1a, 3818.
57. Letter, Massigli to British resident minister at Algiers, 7 Sept. 1943, PRO, WO 219, 45.
58. 27 Dec. 1943, AN, 72 AJ, 447.
59. Undated note, AN, 72 AJ, 438.
60. 23 Oct. 1943, AN, F1a 3836. Report by Laroque, 14 Sept. 1943.
61. Report no. 15, 15 Jan. 1944, AN, F1a, 3831.
62. Report by 2nd Lt. Saville 18 Jan. 1944 – 19 Feb. 1944, AN, F1a, 3831.
63. See 23 Oct. 1943 and 4 Nov. 1943, AN, F1a, 3836.
64. Lion (*Secrétariat du Comité de la Défense Nationale*), 10 April 1944, AN, F1a, 3836.

# 4 The Allies, the French, and the beginnings of Liberation

1. F. Philips (British Supply Council in North America) to W. Bell, 6 Feb. 1943, NA, CAD. 123 (2-6-43) sec. 7 and Under Secretary of State to Treasury, 23 Sept, 1943, NA, CAD. 123 (2-6-43) (2-6-43).

Meeting in McCloy's office 23 Sept. 1943 NA, CAD. 123 (2-6-43) SHAEF to War Department, 23 Sept. 1943 NA, CAD. 123 (2-6-43) sec. 1 CM—IN–4980 and Hilldring to McCloy, 12 Dec. 1943 NA, CAD. 123 (2-6-43) sec. 1 CM—out 1927.

2. CCAC to SHAEF 29 Jan. 1944 NA, CCAC. 123 (10-30-43) sec. 1 CM—OUT 12364 and M. Blum, *The Morgenthau Diaries* (New York, 1965), 167–8.

3. SHAEF Draft Directive, 2 May 1944 PRO, FO 371, 40365, U4624; Eisenhower to AGWAR, 4 May 1944, PRO, WO 219, 12 51235; Hilldring to Chiefs of Staff, 11 May 1944, NA, CAD. 014 Fr (3-8-43) (1) (3); Hilldring memo, 14 May 1944, PRO, WO 219, 45.092.

4. Foreign Office French Department, 30 May 1944, PRO, FO 371, 40365, 23636.

5. The CFLN draft memo on the administration of France, sent to Washington on 4 Sept. 1943, included a statement on Liaison Officers. See Donnison, *op.cit.*, 66.

6. EACS, SHAEF War Diary, 7 June 1944, PRO, WO 178, 82 and War Diary. June. Analysis Sheet. 7 June 1944, PRO, WO 219, 3879.

7. HQ 21st Army Group, SHAEF G. (Ops), 11 May 1944, PRO, WO 171, 104.

8. SHAEF G3 Conference, 29 May 1944, PRO, WO 219, 45. 092 Fr; SHAEF G3 Conference, 29 May 1944, PRO, FO 371, 41879.

9. 5 May 1944, PRO, FO 371, 41980; 3 May 1944, PRO, FO 371, 23162, 4 May 1944, PRO, WO 219, 12, additional message, Prime Minister to Foreign Secretary, M 524/4, 7 May 1944, PRO, FO 371, 41980.

10. PRO, FO 371, 41980; 8 May 1944, PRO, WO 219, 45; PRO CAB 122 410, 3/6 48; Eisenhower to AFHQ, PRO, WO 219, 45 092 and 11 May 1944, Ike to CCOS, PRO, WO 219, 45 092.

11. SHAEF to Cadogan, 11 May 1944 PRO, WO 219, 45 092; Prime Minister to Roosevelt, 11 May 1944, PRO, FO 371, 41980; FO to Washington Embassy, 12 May 1944, PRO, FO 371, 41992.

12. President to Eisenhower, PRO, WO 219, 45 092; Foreign Secretary to Prime Minister, 16 May 1944 and Prime Minister to Foreign Secretary, 17 May 1944, PRO, FO 371, 41980; Prime Minister to Foreign Secretary, 17 May 1944, PRO, FO 371, 41980.

13. 19 May 1944, PRO, FO 371, 41992; COS meeting, 18 May 1944, PRO FO 371, 41992.

14. Winston Churchill to Foreign Secretary, 14 May 1944, PRO, FO 371, 41992; 18 May 1944, PRO, FO 371, 41992, and 21 May 1944, PRO, FO 371, 41992.

15. A.D. Duff Cooper, *Old Men Forget* (1953), 326–7, 21 May 1944, PRO, FO 371, 41992, 23 May 1944, PRO FO 371, 41992.

16. 23 May 1944, PRO FO 371, 41980; Duff Cooper to FO, 26 May 1944, PRO, PRO, FO 371, 51992; and PRO FO 371, 41879.

17. 20 June 1944, N, 851.01/6. 2044.

18. Winston Churchill to Foreign Secretary, 4 June 1944, PRO, PREM 3, 182/3.

19. 7 June 1944, PRO, CAB 65/46, 19146; Roosevelt to Churchill, 12 June 1944, FDRL; 8 June 1944, PRO. CAB 122, 410 3/6 64C and NA, 851.01/3921.

20. 10 June 1944, PRO, CAB 122, 410 3/6 66.

21. Duff Cooper, *op.cit.*, 319–20; and PRO, FO 371, 41879. 11 June 1944, PRO, CAB 122, 410 3/6 7.B.

22. Cabinet meeting, 6.30 p.m. 5 June 1944, PRO, CAB 65/46 019146.

23. Winston Churchill to FDR, 5 June 1944, PRO, PREM 3, 181, 10; PRO, CAB 65/46, 019146 and Cadogan Diaries, 634; Duff Cooper, *op.cit.*, 330–1 and A. Gillois, *Histoire Secrète des Français à Londres* (Paris, 1975), 24.

24. B. Lockhart, *Comes the Reckoning* (1948), 635.

25. Duff Cooper, *op.cit.*, 332.

26. Duff Cooper, conversation with de Gaulle, 6 June 1944, PRO, FO 371, 41993.

27. Eden to Prime Minister, 6 June 1944, PRO, FO 371, 14993.
28. Cadogan Diaries, *op.cit.*, 5 June 1944.
29. 7 June 1944, PRO. CAB 65/46, 019146.
30. Matthews's draft statement for the Stettinius Final Report, 12 June 1944, NA, M-1248 MA 13, and Washington to Foreign Office 18 June 1944, PRO, FO 371, 41937.
31. Washington to Foreign Office, 18 June 1944, PRO, FO 371, 41957, and I. Berlin, *Washington Despatches*, ed. H. G. Nicholas, (1981).
32. Stimson diaries for June 12–14 1944 from Stimson and Bundy, *On Active Service in Peace and War* (New York, 1947), 547–50.
33. T.M. Campbell and G.C. Herring (eds), *The Diaries of Edward R. Stettinius Jr* (New York, 1975), 14 June 1944.
34. FO to Algiers, 6 June 1944, PRO, FO 371, 42000; Eden to Holman, 5 June 1944, PRO, FO 371, 41993; Eden to Duff Cooper etc., 6 June 1944, PRO, FO 371, 42000; Duff Cooper–de Gaulle, conversation for records, 6 June 1944, PRO, FO 371, 41993.
35. Cadogan Diaries 10 and 11 June 1944; 12 June 1944, PRO, FO 371, 41879; PRO, FO 371, 41880; 14 June 1944, PRO, FO 371, 441879 and inclosure; PRO, FO 371, 40366.
36. SHAEF CA Instructions, PRO, WO 219, 3729; 2nd British Army CA Instructions, PRO, WO 219, 3729; 30th Corps CA Operation Instructions, PRO, WO 171, 365.
37. CAREP (Civil Affairs Report) 21st Army Group, 12 June 1944, PRO, FO 371, 42017.
38. A. Renaud, *Saint-Mère Eglise* (Paris, 1984), 124; see Eisenhower Proclamation draft 7, PRO, FO 371, 40364 and final proclamation PRO, WO 219, 12 561; CA 1st Corps HQ War Diary, 7 June 1944 PRO, WO 171, 283; 21st Army Group SHAEF, G2. Ops, 12 May 1944 PRO, WO 171, 151.
39. CA 30 Corps, Staff Intelligence Summary no. 1, 15 May 1944, PRO WO 171, 365.
40. CA Detachment 202 Report, 7 June 1944, PRO, WO 171, 3566.
41. Eisenhower Report, 9 June 1944, PRO, WO 219 3728.
42. CA Detachment 203 Report 8 June 1944, PRO, WO 171, 3567; J. J. Maginnis, *Military Government Journal* (Boston, 1975), 10–11; Report of recce by Lt.Col. D. R. Ellias, 9–12 June 1944, NA, CAD 014 Fr (3-8-43) (1) (3). Ellias was sent by DCCAO of 21st Army Group to make a reconnaissance 48 hours after the landings. See also report by E. J. Bolton in 1st US. Army area noted in PRO, WO 219, 3729; see also Prime Minister to Foreign Secretary on Montgomery's report, 12 June 1944, PRO, PREM 3, 339/723.
43. HQ 12th Army Group daily CA report, NA, SHAEF G5 file 204.32, 5654/152; SHAEF G5 CAREP 11 June 1944, PRO, FO 371, 42017; 1st US Army CASUM 19 and 20 June 1944, PRO, FO 317, 42017.
44. 9–12 June 1944, NA, CAD 014 Fr (3-8-43) (1) (3); see also Holmes to Hilldring, 13 June 1944, NA CAD 014 Fr (3-8-43); Lt. Koren to Mr Hill, (OSS R and A), 17 June 1944, NA, OSS 83335; see also SHAEF Political Warfare Division. Intelligence Section HQ, PWD, FUSA, 8 July 1944, NA, OSS 83285.
45. Béthouart reported to Duff Cooper (PRO, WO 106 4278) that he was 'universally acclaimed', Koenig told Biddle (PRO, WO 171 82) that he got a great reception and de Courcel seconded this: Lewis, SCAO 2nd Army, reported (PRO, WO 171, 1232) that his reception was not impressive and Holmes (NA, CAD 014 Fr. (3-8-43) (1)) summarized the reports that he had received as indicating that de Gaulle was 'well received', but had hoped for more enthisiasm. See also 21st Army Group Historical Survey PRO, WO 219,

3727; Montgomery to Prime Minister, 14 June 1944, PRO, PREM 3, 339/7.8; Pink report on de Gaulle's visit, 14 June 1944, PRO, FO 371, 41994; Admiralty to Prime Minister, 23 June 1944, PRO, PREM 3, 339/7.3; de Gaulle, *War Memoirs, Unity* (trans.) (1959), 233; Coulet to *Délégué Militaire Général*, 18 June 1944, AN, F1a 4005.

46. Coulet to *Délégué Militaire Général*, 18 June 1944, *ibid.*, F. Coulet, *le Vertu des Temps Difficiles* (Paris, 1967), 225–38; see Coulet's first proclamation announcing the provisional government of the French Republic, quoted in M. Viost, *Hostile Allies: FDR and Charles de Gaulle* (1965), 204.

47. A. Béthouart, *Cinq Années d'Espérance* (Paris, 1966), 251.

48. Summary of negotiations on legal aid and judicial matters between French authorities and CA 2nd Army (nd), PR, WO 171, 252.

49. 2nd Army CA Weekly Report, 19 June 1944, PRO, WO 171 252; Coulet to Délégué Militaire Général, 18 June 1944, *op.cit.*, also 2nd British Army, French Civil Administration Report, PRO, WO 219, 3780.

50. June War Diary Analysis, 12 June 1944, PRO, WO 219, 3879, 5644/117; 13 June 1944, PRO, PREM 3, 177/2 71; 15 June 1944, AN, AJ 72, 449 and 12 June 1944, PRO, FO 371, 42017.

51. 12 June 1944, PRO, FO 371, 42000; 12 June 1944, PRO, WO 219 3879. 5644/17; Cadogan Diaries, *op.cit.*, 13 June 1944; PREM 3 177/2. 68 and NA, CAD. 014. Fr (3-8-43) (1) (3) CM–OUT, 50351.

52. EACS War Diary, 7 June 1944, PRO, WO 178, 82.

53. Biddle for record, SH/6/EAC, 14 June 1944, PRO, WO 178, 82.

54. Biddle/Koenig conversations, 16 June 1944, PRO, WO 219, 3879; SHAEF War Diary, SH/6/EAC, 25 June 1944, PRO, WO 171, 82; SHAEF AGP, HS/SHAEF/3/1, 26 June 1944, PRO, WO 171, 20.

55. SHAEF CA Report no. 4, 24 June 1944, PRO, FO 371, 42017; Eisenhower to AGWAR, 4 July 1944, PRO, WO 219, 130 and SHAEF G5 CA Summary no. 6, 20 July 1944, PRO, FO 371, 42018.

56. PRO, FO 371, 42005; Coulet to Koenig, 18 June 1944, AN, 72 AJ, F1a, 4005; 20 June 1944, Coulet to Koenig, AN, 72 AJ, F1a 4005 and 27 June 1944, AN, 72 AJ, F1a 4005.

57. Coulet Report, 27 June 1944, AN, 72 AJ, F1a 4005 no. 79.

58. 21st Army Group CA/Military Government Branch Historical Summary PRO, WO 219, 3727.

59. PRO, WO 219, 3527; PRO, WO 219, 3845.

60. PRO, WO 219, 12,; Coulet to Koenig, AN, F1a, 4005; 2nd Army CA Report, 9 July 1944, PRO, WO 171, 252; Foreign Secretary to Prime Minister, 3 July 1944, PRO, PREM 3, 177/8, 654. Eisenhower did say that de Gaulle should be told that continuing currency difficulties could not be tolerated, but he did not threaten Coulet. 4 July 1944, PRO, WO 219, 130.

61. Report of Meeting of SCAO (Lewis) with Coulet 20 June 1944, PRO WO 171 252; 'de Gaulle's bolted'—PRO, FO 371 41944; see also 21st Army Group CA Historical Survey—Stainforth Report PRO, WO 219, 3727; for an example of Coulet's edicts see 6 July 1944, PRO WO 171, 252.

62. Maginnis, *op.cit.*, 26–27.

63. Report of Lt. Col. Nolan (SHAEF) and Lt. Col. Heywood (HQ 21st Army Group) in Normandy, 22–25 June 1944, NA, CAD 014 Fr. (3-8-43).

64. Perry, CA 1st US Army to DCCAO Main 21st Army Group, NA, CAD, 014 Fr (3-8-43).

65. Maginnis, *op.cit.*, 3.

66. Marcus to Hilldring, 3 July 1944, NA, CAD 014 Fr (3-8-43).

67. 944.AD.3709, NA, OSS 2375.

68. Minutes of Conference of representatives of Regional Commissioners and 1st Corps HQ CA, 30 June 1944, PRO, WO 171, 283; see also Report of de Pury to DCCAO 21st Army Group, 12 July 1944, PRO, WO 171 165.
69. CA Det. 208 Report, June–July 1944, PRO, WO 171, 3571.
70. Lewis 2nd Army Group SCAO Report no. 3, 23 July 1944, PRO, WO 171, 252.
71. SHAEF PWD, HQ, PWD FUSA Intelligence Section, 8 July 1944, NA, OSS 83285.
72. 1 July 1944, PRO, FO 371 41862.
73. G5 SHAEF, 7 July 1944, PRO, WO 219, 12 51.552.
74. 2 July 1944, PRO, FO 371, 92017.
75. SHAEF G5, CA no. 5 14 July 1944, PRO, FO 371, 42017.
76. 1st US Army CASUM to 20 July 1944, PRO, FO 371, 42017.
77. SHAEF French Country Unit, 22 July 1944, NA, OSS 85124.
78. 21 July 1944, PRO, WO 106, 4273.
79. Recce on Cherbourg, 29 July 1944, PRO, WO 171, 164.
80. SHAEF G5, 28 July 1944, PRO, FO 371, 42017; SHAEF G5 Ops, 28 July 1944, PRO, FO 371, 42018.
81. HS/SHAEF G5, 1 Aug. 1944, PRO, WO 171, 54; 4 Aug. 1944, PRO, WO 171, 54.
82. SHAEF G5 Guidance for PWD, 6 Aug. 1944, PRO, WO 171, 54.
83. SHAEF G5, Summary of field reports no. 9, 11 Aug. 1944, PRO, WO 220, 19.
84. Maj. Scully for Col. Ryan, 13 Aug. 1944, NA, SHAEF G5 file, 17.16; SHAEF French Country Unit, 14 Aug. 1944, NA, SHAEF G5 file 17.04 and 21st Army Group CA, 15 Aug. 1944, PRO, WO 171, 65.
85. Grasset to 21st Army Group, 3 Aug. 1944, PRO, WO 219, 3845.
86. Eisenhower to AGWAR, 4 Aug. 1944, PRO, WO 219 130–85.
87. SHAEF G5, 4 July 1944, PRO, WO 171, 54 and PRO, FO 371, 42017, 8 July 1944, PRO, WO 219, 12.51.579.
88. 2nd Army CA, Lewis (SCAO), 9 July 1944, PRO, WO 171, 252.
89. SHAEF G5 CA Summary no. 5, 14 July 1944, PRO, FO 371, 42017, and PRO, FO 371, 42005; 17 July 1944, PRO, FO 371, 42006.
90. FUSA 2nd fortnightly report, 7 July 1944, PRO, WO 219, 3527; 22 July 1944, PRO, WO 219, 12, 51.492; SHAEF G5 Ops, 4 Aug. 1944, PRO, WO 171, 54; SHAEF (Exec.) 11th Meeting of Branch Chiefs, PRO, WO 171, 54.
91. Capt. Langelon (PWO), 1 July 1944, PRO, WO 219, 3845.
92. 1 July 1944, PRO, WO 219, 3845.
93. SHAEF G5 CA Summary, 4 Aug. 1944, PRO, WO 171, 54.
94. The Resistance in larger cities like Cherbourg and Rouen had been expected to be more 'political' because of the stronger pre-war left-wing presence in these places. See Civil Affairs Handbook for France, *op.cit.*
95. 27 Jan. 1944, PRO, PREM 3, 181/10; 28 Jan. 1944, PRO, PREM 3, 185/1; see also E. d'Astier de la Vigerie, *Les Dieux et les Hommes* (Paris, 1965), 33–41; US opposition to the 'Planners Committee', FRUS, 1944, vol. 3, 654 and NA OPD France (3) 169; PRO, WO 219, 212; SHAEF G5, PRO, WO 171, 19 HS/SHAEF/2/10 PRO, WO 219, 45 and SHAEF G1 OPs, 'Resistance by the General Public in France' 29 April 1944, 1 May 1944, PRO, WO 219, 212 and PRO, FO 371, 42000.
96. OSS R and A, Civil Affairs Information Guide for the War Department, 25 May 1944, NA, OSS 1697; NA, 323, 2AF. 6200S; NA, OSS 2172.
97. Donovan to Marshal, NA, RG 226, Entry 99, Box 13; SHAEF G3 Ops to Chiefs of Staff, PRO, WO 219, 609.
98. Military Intelligence Division of WDGS (Military Attaché in Madrid), 14 April 1944, NA, OSS 73143; 17 and 20 April 1944, NA, OSS 69442; May, NA, OSS 81972; 7 June 1944, NA, OSS 79.74; 3 July 1944, NA, OSS 83599, OSS 83579, OSS 82550.

99. 'The Communist Party in France and in North Africa', 27 June 1944, NA, OSS 84092.
100. OSS Algiers, 'The Communists and the Invasion', 29 June 1944, NA, OSS 84092.
101. NA, RG 226, Entry 99, box 13.
102. Donovan Report, AN, 72 AJ, 513, and 72 AJ, 83.
103. *Ibid.,* and AN, 72 AJ, 84.
104. PRO, WO 219, 213 52–640.
105. Roosevelt to Churchill, 12 June 1944 in Roosevelt Papers (FDRL) and PRO, PREM 3, 177/2, 53.
106. McCloy to Stimson in Roosevelt to Eisenhower telegram, 19 June 1944, NA, CAD 014 Fr (3-8-43); President to Prime Minister, 19 June 1944, PRO, FO 371, 41994 and Matthews/Hickerson file (hereafter known as M/H file) NA, M 1244 Roll 13.
107. Eden to Prime Minister, 15 June 1944, PRO, FO 371, 41974, and Prime Minister to Roosevelt, 21 June 1944, NA, 851.01/6. 2344.
108. Stimson and Bundy, *op.cit.*, 550; Halifax conversation with Stimson and McCloy, PRO, FO 371, 41974; Matthews for Stettinius Mission final report, 12 June 1944, NA, M/H file, M 1244 roll 13 and JSM to War Cabinet, 12 June 1944, PRO, CAB 122, 410; Stimson diaries, 12 June 1944, in Stimson and Bundy, *op.cit.*, 547–51.
109. W. D. Hassett, *Off the Record with FDR* (1960), Press Conference, 23 June 1944.
110. Stimson and Bundy, *op.cit.*, 546.
111. FO to Washington, 24 June 1944, copy of President to Prime Minister, 23 June 1944, PRO, FO 371, 41975.
112. 7 June 1944, PRO, CAB 65/46, XC/A/019146; Churchill to Roosevelt, 7 June 1944, in Lowenheim *op.cit.*, 523; FO to Washington, 8 June 1944, PRO, FO 371, FO 371, 41994; Lindley called de Gaulle's behaviour 'close to being a stab in the back'. 18 June 1944, PRO, FO 371 41957.
113. 8 June 1944, PRO, PREM 3, 339/7.28 and PRO, PREM 3, 177/8, 649 Prime Minister to Foreign Secretary, 12 June 1944, PRO, PREM 3, 339/7.23.
114. See House of Commons question time in F. Kersaudy, *Churchill and de Gaulle, op.cit.*, 353–4.
115. SHAEF G5 Historical files, NA, 300, 21st Army Group (Brit.) CA Sec and PRO, CAB 66, (51) WP 44–337, also 22 June 1944, PRO, PREM 3 17718.
116. Cadogan, 11 June 1944, PRO, FO 371, 41993.
117. 12 June 1944, PRO CAB 65/42 WM (75) (44) 3; Cadogan, 13 June 1944 PRO, FO 371, 41993, and PRO, FO 371, 42000.
118. Peake to FO, 15 June 1944, PRO, FO 371, 41862.
119. Analysis Sheet, June War Diary, 12 June 1944, PRO, WO 219, 3879 Biddle/Koenig talks 16 June 1944, PRO, WO 219, 3579; SHAEF EACS War Diary, 21 June 1944, PRO, WO 171, 82.
120. 22 June 1944, PRO, WO 219, 12, and WO 219, 3845; 28 June 1944, PRO WO 219, 3845.
121. McCloy to Dunn on Holmes notes, 27 June 1944, NA, 851, 004 and Holmes to Grasset, 29 June 1944, PRO, WO 219, 3845.
122. 24 June 1944, PRO, CAB 122, 410.86 and PRO, FO 371, 41975.
123. 19 June 1944, PRO, FO 371, 40366, and PRO 371, 40365. For the British view: 20 June 1944, PRO, FO 371, 42000; PRO, FO 371, 40368.
124. PRO, FO 371, 40366.
125. Mack to Cabinet, PRO, FO 371, 40318.
126. SHAEF (Holmes for Eisenhower) to WAR (McCloy), 18 June 1944, NA, CAD 014 Fr (3-8-43).

127. Holmes to McCloy, 23 June 1944, NA, CAD 014, Fr (3-8-43) (1) (4); and PRO, FO 371, 41862.
128. Copy of President to Prime Minister, 23 June 1944, PRO, FO 371, 41975.
129. Copy of Prime Minister to President, 24 June 1944, PRO, FO 371, 418809; PRO, FO 371, 41880; 27 June 1944, Halifax to FO, PRO, FO 371, 41880; Eden note, PRO, FO 371, 40367.
130. 3 July 1944, PRO, CAB 65/43, WM 85 (44)3.
131. PRO, FO 371, 40367.
132. Eden had been pressing Churchill to announce British *de facto* recognition on 14 July, PRO, FO 371, 40368.
133. Washington to FO, 6 July 1944, PRO, FO 371, 41457; Washington to FO, 9 July 1944, PRO, FO 371, 41958; I. Berlin, *Washington Despatches*, 9 and 15 July 1944 (1981).
134. Washington to FO, 9 July 1944, FO 371, 41958; S. I. Rosenman, *The Public Papers and Addresses of Franklin D. Roosevelt, Toast at the State Luncheon for General Charles de Gaulle*, 7 July 1944. As late as 1 July Roosevelt was still threatening, W. D. Hassell, *Off the Record, op.cit.*, 257; Hull, *op.cit.*, 1432–4; Campbell and Herring, *op.cit.*, 246.
135. 9 July 1944, PRO, FO 371, 41958; 11 July 1944, PRO, FO 371, 41958.
136. Berlin, *op.cit.*, 9 July 1944, 287–8; Leahy, *I Was There* (1950).
137. McCloy to Eisenhower and Stimson, 10 July 1944, NA, CAD 014 Fr (3-8-43) (1) (3),
138. Washington (Sir Ian Campbell) to FO, 11 July 1944, account of the President's statement PRO, WO 106, 9278.
139. CAD to General Bedell Smith, 12 July 1944, PRO, WO 219, 31–539; de Gaulle's Washington press conference, 12 July 1944, PRO, FO 371, 41758; SHAEF French Country Unit, 22 July 1944, OSS 85124.
140. Foreign Secretary to PM correspondence, 11, 13 and 18 July 1944, PRO, FO 371, 41958; PRO, FO 371, 42006.
141. PRO, WO 219, 57–539; Campbell (Washington) to Eden, 26 July 1944, PRO, FO 371, 41958; Berlin, *op.cit.*, 15 July 1955, 295.
142. 10 July 1944, PRO, FO 371, 40368; 12 July 1944, PRO 371, 41856; 12 July 1944 (US draft) PRO, FO 371, 41856.
143. Prime Minister to President, 13 July 1944, PRO, FO 371, 41881, Roosevelt to Prime Minister, 14 July 1944, PRO, FO 371, 41881.
144. 12 July 1944, PRO, WO 219, 12 51–539, 17 July 1944, PRO, FO 371 42001.
145. Lord General Maitland H. Wilson, *Eight Years Overseas* (1950); A. Funk, 'Considérations stratégiques sur l'invasion du sud de la France', in *La Guerre en Méditerranée (colloque)* CNRS (Paris, 1969).
146. Wilson, *op.cit.*, 194. In January, Eisenhower had told Marshall he wanted ANVIL so as to capitalize on Allied 'French investment', see A. D. Chandler *Papers of Dwight D. Eisenhower*, vol. 3, 17 Jan. 1944.
147. Wilson, *op.cit.*, 215–16.
148. AFHQ to Commanding General 7th Army, 8 Jan. 1944, NA, CAD 014 Fr (3-8-43) (1) (5); see also SHAEF to SACMED, 14 May 1944, NA, CAD 014 Fr (3-8-43) (1) (5).
149. *Ibid.*
150. SHAEF G5 6th Army Group History, NA, CAD 014 Fr (3-8-43) (1) (5).
151. British Embassy (Washington) to Bonbright (US State Department), 23 June 1944, NA, 851.01/6-2044.
152. Coles and Weinberg, *op.cit.*, 700.
153. Donnison, *op.cit.*, 93.
154. Duff Cooper to FO, 25 July 1944, PRO, FO 371, 41906.

155. G5 AFHQ to War Department and British War Office, 6 Aug. 1944, NA, CAD 014 Fr (3-8-43) (1) (5).
156. *Ibid.*, point 9.
157. G5 6th Army Group Historical Report, SHAEF G5 504, 6th Army Group Field Reports, NA, CAD 014 Fr (3-8-43) (1) (5).
158. A. C. Brown, *The Secret War Report of the OSS* (New York, 1976), 196.
159. See reports of JED teams LEE and COLLODION-LOCH in the Donovan Report, AN, 72 AJ, 89.
160. JED team ANTAGONIST in the Donovan Report, *ibid.*
161. JED team LEE in the Donovan Report, *ibid.*
162. JED team MILS (OSS and French BCRA) in Donovan Report, *ibid.*
163. *Ibid.*
164. History of CA Operations for southern France Pt2, NA, SHAEF G5 17.17.
165. CAO 30th Division weekly report, SHAEF G5 Historical Reports and 18 Aug. 1944, HQ 7th Army CA report no. 1, PRO, WO 171, 252.
166. AFHQ G5 CA report for southern France, 18–23 Aug. 1944, PRO, WO 220/09, also CAHQ 7th Army report to G5 AFHQ, 18 Aug. 1944, Coles and Weinberg, *op.cit.*, 757.
167. Report of first impressions of France by Lt. Cmdr. G. G. Schroeder, Military Attaché's Report (JICANA) to Military Intelligence Division WDGS, 19 Aug. 1944, NA, OSS, 91582.
168. *Ibid.*
169. AFHQ G5 French Section, CA Report for southern France, 18–23 Aug. 1944 PRO, WO 220, 69.
170. *Ibid.*
171. CAHQ 7th Army Report to SACMED, 22 Aug. 1944, NA, SHAEF G5 17.17.
172. AFHQ G5 French Section CA Report on Southern France, 18–23 Aug. 1944, *op.cit.*
173. *Ibid.*, see also JED team MILES in the Donovan Report AN, 72 AJ, 84.
174. CAHQ Report to CG 7th Army, 21 Aug. 1944, NA, SHAEF G5 17.17.
175. CG US Army (London) ETO to War Department. Report on France, 25 Aug. 1944, NA, CAD 014 Fr (3-8-43) (1) (5); JED team ANTAGONIST report, 13 Aug. 1944, and JED team LEE report in Donovan Report, AN, 72 AJ 84.
176. JED team SALESMAN. Report of Capt. E. L. Fraser, 7 June 1944 to 22 Sept. 1944 in the Donovan Report, *ibid.*
177. JED team SALESMAN. Report of 2nd Lieut. J-C Guiet in Donovan Report, *ibid.*
178. History of CA Operations for Southern France, Part 3, NA, SHAEF, G5 17.17.
179. AFHQ SAC Despatch (General Sir H. Maitland Wilson) Invasion of Southern France, PRO, WO 32, 11422.
180. AFHQ G5, CA Report on Southern France, 23–30 Aug. 1944, PRO, WO 220, 69; and Memo from Parkman to CG 7th Army, 25 Aug. 1944, NA, SHAEF G5 17.17.
181. *Ibid.*
182. AFHQ G5, CA Report on Southern France, 23–30 Aug. 1944, *op.cit.*
183. *Ibid.*
184. Donnison, *op.cit.*, 93 and History of Civil Affairs Operations for Southern France Part IX, NA, SHAEF G5 17.17.
185. Donnison, *ibid.*

# 5   The Liberation of Paris

1. Maclean (Washington) to Mack (FO), 12 July 1944, PRO, FO 371, 41881 and US Draft, 12 July 1944 PRO, FO 371, 40368.

2.  PM to President, 13 July 1944, PRO, 371, 41881.
3.  FO to Moscow, 10 July 1944, PRO, FO 371 42035 Ward for FO, 18 July 1944 PRO, FO 371, 41880.
4.  CCAC (London), 10 Aug. 1944, PRO, CAB 88, 63 Stettinius to US Embassy (London), 11 Aug. 1944 PRO, WO 219, 12; FO Comment on Agreement on Currency Procedure, 4 Aug. 1944, PRO, FO 371, 41973; Washington Embassy to FO, 5 Aug. 1944 PRO, FO 371, 41974; Washington Embassy to FO, 14 Aug. 1944, PRO, FO 371, 41974; FO to Washington Embassy, 14 Aug. 1944, PRO, FO 371, 41974.
5.  See Chapter 4.
6.  Coles and Weinberger, *op.cit.*, 749–50.
7.  D. D. Eisenhower, *Crusade in Europe* (1948), 296; P. C. Pogue, *Supreme Command* (Washington, 1954), 240; W. S. Churchill, *The Second World War*, vol. 4 (1948), 31.
8.  G. Patton, *War As I Knew It* (Boston, 1947); see also Eisenhower to Montgomery, 20 Aug. 1944, 21 A Gp Situation and Directive M-519 in NA, SHAEF SGS, 381.
9.  War Department Special Staff Historical Division, vol. 7, 1238, AN, 72 AJ, 514.
10.  France: Zone Handbook No. 16. Paris, Part I, 31 Jan. 1944, PRO, WO 220, 175.
11.  FO comment on CNR document, 9 July 1944 and 10 July 1944, PRO, FO 371, 41880.
12.  Peake to Mack, 9 Aug. 1944, PRO, FO 371, 41906; Chiefs of Staff Committee, 24 Aug. 1944, PRO, WO 106, 4322 A.
13.  G5 (Supply) 2045, 2 Aug. 1944 Brig. L. F. Field for SHAEF, PRO, WO 171, 54; see also F.S.V. Donnison, *Civil Affairs and Military Government. Northwest Europe 1944–46* (1961), 40–7.
14.  Scowden Report on trip to France, 10 Aug. 1944, PRO, WO 171, 54; SHAEF to CG 12th A Gp for G5, 16 Aug. 1944, PRO, WO 219, 14; also in SHAEF G5 History, PRO, WO 202, 2.
15.  G5 Sec. Narrative Report for August 1944, NA, SHAEF G5, 17.16.
16.  SHAEF G5 Weekly Summary no. 16, 18 Aug. 1944, PRO, FO 371, 42019; see also FUSA G5 Monthly Report, Col. Dittmar, August 1944, NA, SHAEF G5 Com Z Historical Documents.
17.  Grasset (AC of S.G5) to Chief of Staff SHAEF G5, 5 Aug. 1944 PRO, WO 171 54.
18.  Col. Howley. Det A1A1 interview 27 Feb. 1945, NA, SHAEF G5, 17.23.
19.  CPL, *Procès verbal de la 26ème séance* (nd), Archives Ivry, Fonds Tollet, also CPL *Procès verbal de la 27 ème séance* (nd), *ibid.*
20.  CPL, *Procès verbal de la 26 ème séance* (nd), Archives Ivry, Fonds Tollet.
21.  CPL, *Procès verbal de las 31 ème séance* (nd), Archives Ivry, Fonds Tollet; Secnord de Belladone to BCRA, 18 July 1944, AN, 72 AJ, 235, 1575.
22.  CPL, *Procès verbal de la 32 ème séance* (nd), Archives Ivry, Fonds Tollet.
23.  Secnord de Belladone to BCRA, 4 July 1944, AN, 72 AJ, 235, 1498; Secnord de Belladone to BCRA, 18 July 1944, AN, 72 AJ, 235, 1575; Secnord de Belladone to BCRA, 2 Aug. 1944, AN, 72 AJ, 235, 1676.
24.  CNR *Commission des Comités de Libération*, 'Statut des Comités Départmentaux de la Libération', 23 mars 1944, Archives Ivry, Fonds Tollet and 'Instruction du CNR', 11 avril 1944, cited in G. Madjarian, *Conflits, Pouvoirs et Société à la Libération* (Paris, 1968), 117.
25.  CNR, 'Programme d'Action de la Résistance', 15 March 1944, Archives Ivry, Fonds Tollet.
26.  CNR, 'Statut des Comités Départementaux de la Libération', *op.cit.*
27.  CPL, 'Appel au Peuple de Paris', 1 Sept. 1943, Archives Ivry, Fonds Tollet; also

cited in Madjarian, *op.cit.*, 117; also in H. Denis, *Le Comité Parisien de la Libération* (Paris, 1963).

28.   CNR, *'Statut des Comités Départementaux de las Libération'*, *op.cit.*

29.   CPL, *Procès verbal de la 34 ème séance*, Archives Ivry, Fonds Tollet.

30.   *Ibid.*

31.   C. de Gaulle, *Discours et Messages*, vol. 4 (Paris, 1980), 182.

32.   Le Crapouillot, *La Libération sans Bobards* (Paris, 1974), 47 and R. de Jonchay, *Les Communistes et la Résistance* (Paris, 1976).

33.   *Rapport Laffont* 20 July 1944 quoted in C-L. Foulon, *'Le Général de Gaulle et la Libération de la France'*, in H. Michel (ed.), *op.cit.*, 44.

34.   M.R.D. Foot, *SOE in France* (1966), 418; and L. Collins and D. Lapierre, *Is Paris Burning?* (1965).

35.   See M. Kriegel-Valrimont, *La Libération: Les Archives du COMAC* (Paris, 1946), 27; and F. Crémieux, *La Vérité sur la Libération de Paris* (Paris, 1971), 14–16.

36.   A. Tollet, *La Classe Ouvrière dans la Résistance* (Paris, 1969); and in Crémieux, *ibid.*; also M. Agulhon, *'Les Communistes et la Libération de la France'*, in Michel, *'La Libération de la France'*, *op.cit.*

37.   Tract of the CGT, *'Métallos parisiens aux Armes'*, Archives Ivry, Fonds Tollet.

38.   *'Unions des Syndicats a Toutes les IB'*, *Union des Syndicats de Paris*, 26 July 1944, Archives Ivry, Fonds Tollet.

39.   PCF *Comité Central*, *'Aux Régions et Inter-Régions'*, June 1944 Archives Ivry, Fonds Tollet.

40.   *'Les Communistes et les Comités Locaux de la Libération,'* *Les Régions Parisiennes du PCF*, June 1944, Archives Ivry, Fonds Tollet. See also the patriotic appeals of the CPL to local Liberation committees, Archives Ivry, AR 2, 89, CDL/CPL.

41.   *'Directives pour la Préparation et la Conduite de l'Insurrection Nationale'*, *Comité Central PCF*, May 1944, Archives Ivry, Fonds Tollet.

42.   *'Aux Directions Régionales'*, PCF, 6 Aug. 1944, Archives Ivry, Fonds Tollet.

43.   De Jonchay, *op.cit.*; A. Rossi, *La Guerre des Papillons: Quatre Ans de Politique Communiste 1940–1944* (Paris, 1954); see also R. Aron, *Histoire de la Libération de France* (Paris, 1959) 632; A. J. Rieber, *Stalin and the French Communist Party* (New York, 1962); S. Courtois, *Le PCF dans la Guerre* (Paris, 1980); A. Kriegel, *Les Communistes au Miroir Français* (Paris, 1974), and at *Colloque Historique Italo-Français de Naples* (1977), also with M. Perrot, *Le Socialisme Français et le Pouvoir* (Paris, 1966).

44.   C. Tillon, *Les FTP* (Paris, 1962) and *On Chantait Rouge* (Paris, 1977).

45.   P. Hervé, *Dieu et César Sont-ils Communistes?* (Paris, 1956), 22; J. Elleinstein in G. Willard, V. Joannes, F. Hincker and J. Elleinstein, *De la Guerre à la Libération: France de 1939 à 1945* (Paris, 1972). See also *Cahiers du Communisme*, Special Number June 1979, *Etudes et Recherche 30* supplement to *Cahiers d'Histoire de L'Institut Maurice Thorez* (Spring, 1980) and articles by J-P. Scott and G. Willard in *Cahiers de LIMT*.

46.   *'En Avant Peuple de Paris'*, in *Cahiers du Communisme*, 1er trimestre 1944 and as a tract in Archives Ivry, Fonds Tollet.

47.   *Procès verbal du 34ème séance du CPL*, Archives Ivry, Fonds Tollet.

48.   Kriegel-Valrimont, *op.cit.*, 171.

49.   FFI EMN A2043 2ème Bureau, Archives Ivry, Fonds Breton and War Department, Special Staff History Division: Liberation of Paris, vol. 7, 4/9–17, 1235, AN 72 AJ, 514.

50.   In J. Soustelle, *Envers et Contre Tout*, vol. 2 (Paris, 1956), 420 and also in H. Noguères *et.al.*, *Histoire de la Résistance en France*, vol. 5 (Paris, 1976) and R. Hostache, *de Gaulle 1944*, (Paris, 1978), 114–16.

51.   Soustelle, *ibid.*, 422.

52. Secnord de Belladone to BCRA, 3 Aug. 1944, AN, AJ 72, 235.
53. Crémieux, *op.cit.*, 12–13.
54. Secnord de Belladone to BCRA, 11 Aug. 1944, AN, 72 AJ, 235.
55. Crémieux, *op.cit.*, 14.
56. Courtois, *op.cit.*, Chapter 16; A. Tollet, *La Classe Ouvrière dans la Résistance, op.cit.*; R. Massiet, *La Préparation de l'Insurrection et la Bataille de Paris* (Paris, 1945).
57. Text 2 in *'Documents sur la Grève Insurrectionelle dans la Région Parisienne'* in *Cahiers d'Histoire de l'Institut Maurice Thorez 8–9* (1974) and Courtois, *op.cit.*, 54.
58. Text 3 in *'Documents sur la Grève Insurrectionnelle dans la Région Parisienne'*, *op.cit.*
59. See Noguères *et al.*, *op.cit.*, vol. 5, 259–60.
60. See J-P. Very (Maurice Sentuc) in *'Documents sur la Grève Insurrectionnelle dans la Région Parisienne'*, *op.cit.*, 58; and M. Choury, *Les Cheminots dans la Bataille du Rail* (Paris, 1970).
61. Tillon, *On Chantait Rouge*, 388–9.
62. *'Union des Syndicats à Toutes les I.B.'*, 26 July 1944, Archives Ivry, Fonds Tollet.
63. *'Documents sur la Grève Insurrectionelle dans la Région Parisienne'*, *op.cit.*, 58.
64. See Crémieux, *op.cit.*, 31–4.
65. See Courtois, *op.cit.*, 454.
66. *Cahiers d'Histoire de l'Institut Maurice Thorez 8–9* (1974), Annex 8 237; also Noguères, *op.cit.*, vol. 5, 459–60.
67. IHTP, 72 AJ, 61 AI, FFI Region P2, 16 Aug. 1944 and IHTP, 72 AJ, 61 AI, FFI Region P1, 16 Aug. 1944 and Tillon, *On Chantait Rouge*, 392.
68. AN, 72 AJ, 235 1781, Secnord de Belladone to BCRA, 15 Aug. 1944 and AN, 72 AJ 235 1780, Secnord de Belladone to BCRA, 15 Aug. 1944.
69. Kriegel-Valrimont, *op.cit.*, 185.
70. R. Hostache, *Le Conseil National de la Résistance* (Paris, 1958), 129; Secnord de Belladone to BCRA, 17 Aug. 1944, AN, 72 AJ, 235 1789–92.
71. A. Ouzoulias, *Les Bataillons de la Jeunesse* (Paris, 1969), 424; Tillon, *On Chantait Rouge*, 393.
72. IHTP, 72 AJ 61 A no. 4 (I), 18 Aug. 1944.
73. IHTP, 72 AJ, 61 AI, FFI Region I, 19 Aug. 1944, *'Ordre Général'* and A. Dansette, *Histoire de la Libération de Paris* (Paris, 1946), Annex 16, 371.
74. Dansette, *ibid.*, Annex 17, 372–3.
75. Noguères, *op.cit.* vol. 5, 438–71; *Cahiers d'Histoire de l'Institut Maurice Thorez 8–9* (1974), 245–6; Crémieux, *op.cit.*, 20; Hamon claims that the Bureau of the CPL did not decide to order the insurrection on 18 August.
76. AN, 72 AJ 235 1789–92, Secnord de Belladone to BCRA, 17 Aug. 1944.
77. Noguères, *op.cit.*, vol. 5, 470–1; Dansette, *op.cit.*, Annex 18, 373 and IHTP, 72 AJ, J61, Archives Blocq-Mascart, CNR *'Appel'*, 17 Aug. 1944.
78. AN, 72 AJ, 235 1796–1801, Secnord de Belladone to BCRA, 18 Aug. 1944.
79. Tillon, *On Chantait Rouge*, 390–3.
80. IHTP, 72 AJ, 61 A, no. 4,I, 18 Aug. 1944 (c) *'Appel du CNR'*.
81. IHTP, 72 AJ, 61 A, no. 4, I, 18 Aug. 1944 (b), Boucher (Bayet) to *Comité de Libération de la Police*. For a slightly different version see Noguères, *op.cit.*, vol. 5, 473 and Dansette, *op.cit.*, 133.
82. See Dansette, *op.cit.*, Annex 20, 374–5.
83. Crémieux, *op.cit.*, 44–6, A. Parodi in *Le Figaro*, 19 Aug. 1964, also Noguères, *op.cit.*, vol. 5, 472–3.
84. IHTP, 72 AJ, 61 A no. 4, I, (c) and Dansette, *op,cit.*, Annex 19, 373–4.
85. IHTP, 72 AJ, 61 AI, FFI Région P1 *'Ordre Général*, 19 Aug. 1944.
86. Tillon, *On Chantait Rouge*, 396–7.
87. Dansette, *op.cit.*, Annex 22, 475.

88.  R. Hostache, *De Gaulle, 1944, op.cit.*, 153–4 and AN, 72 AJ, 235 502 no. 50, Secnord de Belladone, 12 Aug. 1944.

89.  Foot, *op.cit.*, footnote, 418.

90.  R. Massiet, *La Préparation de l'Insurrection et la Bataille de Paris* (1947), 138–9.

91.  A. Parodi, in *Le Figaro*, 18 Aug. 1964.

92.  See L. Hamon in Crémieux, *op.cit.*, 68–72, and Noguères, *op.cit.*, vol. 5, 484.

93.  Dansette, *op.cit.*

94.  Dansette, *op.cit.*, Annex 25, 377–80; Noguères, *op.cit.*, vol. 5, 489–95 and J. Debû-Bridel, *De Gaulle et le CNR* (Paris, 1978), 156–8.

95.  Dansette, *op.cit.*, Annex 26, 380–3 and Noguéres, *op.cit.*, vol. 5, 495.

96.  Dansette, *op.cit.*, Annex 27, 383.

97.  IHTP, 72 AJ 61, CI 18, FFI Région Ile-de-France, 20 Aug 1944 (07.40).

98.  IHTP, 72 AJ 61, CI 18, FFI Région Ile-de-France, 20 Aug. 1944.

99.  Dansette, *op.cit.*, Annexes 28, 29 and 30, 383–4 and also , IHTP, 72 AJ, 61 CF 21, '*Carnet de Notes du Capt. Walter*' to the effect that the loudspeaker vans announced the truce but that written instructions were for '*guérilla à l'outrance*', which naturally had more authority.

100.  Noguères, *op.cit.*, vol. 5, 498–500.

101.  Tillon, *On Chantait Rouge*, 397.

102.  Dansette, *op.cit.*, Annex 34 (2), 392.

103.  Dansette, *op.cit.*, Annex 33, 386.

104.  Dansette, *op.cit.*, Annexes 32, 385–6, and 35, 393; Crémieux, *op.cit.*, 89–91.

105.  Dansette, *op.cit.*, Annex 34, 387–90, '*Procès verbal de la seance plenière tenue par le Conseil National de la Résistance*', 21 Aug. 1944.

106.  Dansette, *op.cit.*, Annex 31, 393; IHTP, 72 AJ, 62, *Affiches*, and IHTP, 72 AJ, 61 AI, F.F.I., 22 Aug. 1944.

107.  Tillon, *On Chantait Rouge*, 398.

108.  IHTP, 72 AJ, 61 AII, H. Frenay Papers, and IHTP, 72 AJ, 61 c, Y. Morandot papers.

109.  IHTP, 72 AJ, 61 AI, FFI P1 178/3, 23 Aug. 1944, '*Ordre Particulier*'.

110.  Noguères, *op.cit.*, vol. 5, 536–7.

111.  See facsimile of the original (indetermined) in Archives Ivry, Fonds Tollet and IHTP, 72 AJ, 61 AI 1 No. 31, Message no. 4, 24 Aug. 1944.

112.  PRO, FO 954, 9B 44/232.

113.  Churchill, *Memoirs*, vol. 6, 31.

114.  Foreign Secretary to Prime Minister, 22 Aug. 1944, PRO, WO 106, 4322A and Eden to Duff Cooper, 22 Aug. 1944, PRO, FO 371, 41863.

115.  War Department, Special Staff History Division, 'Liberation of Paris', AN, 72 AJ, J14 FR vol. 7.

116.  C. de Gaulle, *War Memoirs: Unity, op.cit.*, 301; de Gaulle to Eisenhower, 21 Aug. 1944, NA, SHAEF SGS, 092 (France). See also Diaries of Oliver Hardy, *op.cit.*, 302.

117.  Eisenhower to Bedell Smith, NA, SHAEF SGS, 092 (France), vol. 2, also in A. D. Chandler, *Papers of Dwight D. Eisenhower, op.cit.*, 2089.

118.  *Mission de Lt. Gallois* (Cocteau), IHTP, 72 AJ, 61 A No. 17 I.

119.  D. D. Eisenhower, *Crusade in Europe*, 323; P. C. Pogue, *Supreme Command*, p. 241 suggests that Eisenhower had changed his mind before the arrival of Gallois; also IHTP, 72 AJ, 61 A No. 17 I.

120.  C. de Gaulle, *War Memoirs: Unity, op.cit.*, 704, Letter to Luizet, 23 Aug. 1944.

121.  De Gaulle, *War Memoirs: Unity, op.cit.*, 307.

122.  De Gaulle, *War Memoirs: Unity, op.cit.*, 306.

123.  Dansette, *op.cit.*, Annex XLIII, 399; War Report Oxford 1946, Robert Reid, BBC, 202–4.

124. Gerow to Leclerc, in Dansette, *op.cit.* Annex 38.
125. C. de Gaulle, *War Memoirs: Unity*, *op.cit.*, 308, quoted in J. Debû-Bridel, *De Gaulle et le CNR* (Paris, 1978), 191.
126. *Ibid.*
127. J. Debû-Bridel, *ibid.*, 192, 198–9; IHTP, 72 AJ, 62, 27 Aug. 1944, *Affiches.*
128. Le Général de Gaulle, No. 7 CAB-Mil/PA, 27 Aug. 1944, Archives Ivry, Fonds Tollet.
129. Archives Ivry, Fonds Tollet, COMAC, 31 Aug. 1944.
130. Villon to de Gaulle, 31 Aug. 1944, Archives Ivry, Fonds Tollet.
131. De Gaulle to Villon, 1 September 1944, Archives Ivry, Fonds Tollet.
132. *Commissariat de l'Intérieur* file *'Service Central de Commissaires de la République'* AN, F1a, 4020.
133. *Ibid.*
134. *Ibid.*
135. *Procès verbal du Comité Parisien de la Libération*, 28 Aug. 1944 (Supplement to the *Bulletin Municipal Officiel de la Ville de Paris*), Archives Ivry, Fonds Tollet.
136. *Procès verbal du Comité Parisien de la Libération*, 4 Sept. 1944, *ibid.*
137. *Procès verbal du Comité Parisien de la Libération*, 25 Sept. 1944, *ibid.*
138. P. C. Pogue, *Supreme Command, op.cit.*, 242–9; D. L. Chandler, *The Papers of Dwight D. Eisenhower, op.cit.*, 2189–2200; PRO, WO 219, 3528, 18–1199; NA, CAD 014 Fr (3-8-43); PRO, WO 219 14 59-1-1088 Col. Vissering's Report, 30 Aug. 1944; D. D. Eisenhower, *Crusade in Europe* (1948), 326, 327.
139. Eisenhower to AGWAR, 6 Sept. 1944, PRO, WO 219, 3528 18-1199 and NA, CAD 014 Fr (3-8-43), 6 Sept. 1944.
140. Gammell to Bedell Smith, 29 Aug. 1944, PRO, WO 106, 4279; Bedell Smith to G5 SHAEF, 28 Aug. 1944, NA, SHAEF G5, File 30 (Comm. Z, G5 Historical Documents) and PRO, FO 371, 42071, 29 Aug. 1944. Comment by Speaight.
141. PWE, Political Intelligence Directive, 10 Aug. 1944, AN, F1a, 3725/16 and PWD, 44/12/14, Directive for the BBC French Services, AN, F1a, 3725/16.
142. *Les Voix de la Liberté: Ici Londres*, vol. 5 (Paris, 1978) 161.
143. *Les Voix de la Liberté, ibid.*, vol. 5, 175–6.
144. *Les Voix de la Liberté, ibid.*, vol. 5, 170–88.
145. Telegram no. 85, 22 Aug. 1944, PRO, FO 371, 41863.
146. PWE French directive meeting, 17 Aug. 1944, AN, F1a 3725/16.
147. SHAEF G5/RR/1202/7, 20 Aug. 1944, PRO, WO 171, 54.
148. AGWAR (Hilldring) to SHAEF (Eisenhower for Holmes), 20 Aug. 1944, PRO, WO 106, 4279.
149. War Department Special Staff, History Division, *The Liberation of Paris*, vol. 7, 1255, AN, 72 AJ, 514.
150. FO to Algiers, 25 Aug. 1944, PRO, FO 371 42018. Duff Cooper also congratulated CFLN leaders in Algiers on 23 August, PRO, FO 371, 42018.
151. PWE/OWI/44/1/11 Special Guidance on the Liberation of Paris, 24 Aug. 1944, AN, F1a, 3726/16.
152. PWE/CD/44/1733 general directive, 24 Aug. 1944, AN, F1a 3725/16.
153. See Coles and Weinberger, *op.cit.* 742–6.
154. Coles and Weinberger, *op.cit.*, 743, Col. Ryan, G5 12th A Gp to C of S 12th A Gp, 27 Aug. 1944.
155. PRO, FO 371, 42019, and PRO, FO 371, 41863.
156. CA Report on Paris, 27 Aug. 1944, PRO, WO 219, 14.59.1081.
157. Holman to FO from Paris, 5 Sept. 1944, PRO, WO 106, 4279. See also PRO, FO 371, 42008.
158. Holmes to Grasset, 31 Aug. 1944, NA, SHAEF G5, File 20, Communications Zone History File.

159. SHAEF G5 (Ops) 104, 31 Aug. 1944, NA, SHAEF G5, File 20, Communications Zone Historical Documents 'Appendix A' and PRO WO 219, 3846.
160. Telephone Conference, Scowden and Hilldring, 31 Aug. 1944, NA CAD 014 Fr (3-8-43) (1) (5).
161. SHAEF G5 Ops/800/6, 2 Sept. 1944, PRO, WO 171, 55 and PRO, WO 220, 69.
162. Winant to Secretary of State, 26 Aug. 1944, NA, 851.01/8 2644.
163. OWI Report from Paris, 5 Sept. 1944, NA, 851.01/9–844.

# 6 The early days of the GPRF, September–December 1944

1. H. Michel (ed.), *Colloque sur la Libération, op.cit.*, P. H. Teitgen, p. 101.
2. On Normandy, see M. Baudot, *Libération de la Normandie* (Paris, 1974); and S. Kramer, 'The provisional republic, the collapse of the French resistance front and the origins of post-war politics' (PhD thesis, Princeton University, 1971), 84–8; F. Coulet, *Vertu des temps difficiles* (Paris, 1967).
3. For Toulouse, see P. Bertaux, *Libération de Toulouse et de sa Région* (Paris, 1973); Kramer, *op.cit.*, 93–104.
4. Madjarian, *op.cit.*, 101.
5. Kramer, *op.cit.*; CR Clermont-Ferrand, 1–15 Nov. 1944, AN, F1a, 4021.
6. For an excellent study of the *Commissaires de la République*, see Foulon, *op.cit.*
7. *Ibid.*, 239. The Aubrac affair is in Minister of Interior to Aubrac, 11 Nov. 1944, AN F1a 3291; Aubrac's reply, 14 Nov. 1944, AN, F1a 14 Nov. 1944; Minister of Interior to Tissier, 16 Nov. 1944, AN, F1a 4023; Report by Tissier on 22 Jan. 1945 to 3 Feb. 1945, AN, F1a 3291.
8. Note on CR (S. Zone) exchange of views, pencilled comment, 24 Sept. 1944, AN, F1a 4022.
9. See chapter 3, note 27.
10. Estimates for example in SHAEF Mission (France), 'Report on the FFI', 25 Nov. 1944, PRO, WO 219 214; SHAEF Mission (France) G2, 'Concealment of Arms in the Provinces of France', 8 Nov. 1944, PRO, WO 219, 214.
11. SHAEF PWD Intelligence Section, Special Report (France), no. 10, 9 Oct. 1944, PRO, WO 219 112.
12. Bulletin extracted from report of CR Rennes, 1 Nov. 1944, AN, F1a 4028.
13. Note on Châlons region, 1 Sept. 1944, AN, F1a 4020.
14. *Journal de marche*, DMOS 'R', No. 17, 25 Aug. 1944, AN, 72 AJ 444; Report of American Consul General in Barcelona on conditions in the Midi, OSS 98417, 29 Sept. 1944, PRO, WO 106 4409A. General Cochet negotiated a 20 kilometre 'no-go' area at beginning of September 1944.
15. CR Nancy, 15 Oct. 1944, AN, F1a 4024.
16. See Kramer, *op.cit.*
17. Account by G. Gingouin, *4 Ans de Lutte Sur le Sol Limousin* (Paris, 1974).
18. F. Rude, *Libération de Lyon et de sa Région* (Paris, 1974).
19. *Service Central des Commissariats de la République*, 13 Sept. 1944, AN, F1a 4022.
20. See Bertaux, *op.cit.*, 49, 50. Bertaux gives figures of FFI membership as: 1000 pre-landings, 3000–4000 a week later, 6000–7000 a fortnight after, the 'September FFI'.
21. SHAEF Mission (France), 'FFI/FTP Political aspects, Tab. 11', 27 Nov. 1944, PRO, WO 219, 214.
22. Quoted in Madjarian, *op.cit.*, 105.
23. Report by Col. Zeller, dated 20 Sept. 1944, AN, 72 AJ, 449; *compte rendu de la*

*mission de reconnaissance*, Cpt. C. Claude, 8 Sept. 1944, AN, 72 AJ, 62. See also, Bulletin no. 30, CR Limoges, 15–31 Dec. 1944, AN, F1a 4028.

24. Cochet to Pres. of *Comité d'Action en France*, no. 40 (undated), AN, 72 AJ, 446.
25. Noguères, *op.cit.*, vol. 4, 775, 776, 777.
26. Commander J. Rollet to Cochet, 1 Sept. 1944, AN, 72 AJ, 449.
27. *Rapport du Cptn de Borde* (undated), AN, 72 AJ, 443; HQ. 7th Army, *Civil Affairs Report no. 3*, 20 Aug. 1944, PRO, FO 371 42018.
28. For information on this, see Michel (ed.), *Colloque sur la Libération, op.cit.*, P. Le Goyet. See also, IHTP, 72 AJ 62, 27 Aug. 1944, *Affiches*; Gen. de Gaulle, No.7 CAB-Mil/PA, 27 Aug. 1944, Archives Ivry, Fonds Tollet.
29. Madjarian, *op.cit.*, 108.
30. 'There can be no question of destroying its cohesion', *ibid.*, 109.
31. *Ibid.* See also, Archives Ivry, Fonds Tollet, COMAC (*Commandment de l'Etat Major National des FF1*, 31 Aug. 1944. See as well, Villon to de Gaulle, 31 Aug. 1944, Archives Ivry, Fonds Tollet, and de Gaulle to Villon, 1 Sept. 1944, Archives Ivry, Fonds Tollet.
32. See note of the military committee of FTPF, 20 Sept. 1944, quoted in Michel (ed.), *Colloque sur la Libération, op.cit.*, P. Le Goyet; for reactions on the ground from FTP commanders, see, for example, *Combattre (organe des FFI de Provence)*, no. 3, 8 Oct. 1944. For difficulties in integration see, Report of Prefect of L'Aube, 24 Sept. 1944, AN, F1a 4020; for a critical view, C. Tillon, *On Chantait Rouge* (Paris, 1977).
33. Proposition of Col. Cappart, 12 Sept. 1944, AN, 72 AJ, 443; *compte rendue of Cptn D'Astier*, 5 Sept. 1944, An, 72 Aj. 449. See also Grandval's attitude in, G. Grandval and A. Colin, *La Libération de l'Est de la France* (Paris, 1974), 193.
34. Cappart to DMOS, situation report on Toulouse, 20 Sept. 1944, AN, 72 AJ 443.
35. Figures in Madjarian, *op.cit.*, 111.
36. *Service Central des Commissariats de la République*, 9 Nov. 1944, AN, F1a 4020.
37. 15–31 Oct. 1944, AN, F1a 4024.
38. *Gendarmerie Nationale* report, *Synthèses*, 15 Sept. 1944–15 Oct. 1944, AN, 72 AJ, 384.
39. See H. Michel (ed.), *Colloque sur la Libération, op.cit.*, R. Michalon, 616.
40. *Ibid.*
41. *Combattre*, no. 10, 26 Nov. 1944.
42. *Combattre*, no. 11, 3 Dec. 1944.
43. *Combattre*, no. 10, 26 Nov. 1944.
44. See J. Debû-Bridel, *De Gaulle et le CNR* (Paris, 1978), 135; for recruiters' view see *La Vie du Parti* (August 1944).
45. *La Vie Ouvrière*, 2 Nov. 1944.
46. Prefect of Rhône, 1 Oct. 1944, AN, F1c III 1225.
47. Col. G. Bonneau to *Commissaire Militaire de la 17e Région*, 19 Sept. 1944, AN, 72 AJ, 443.
48. *Humanité*, 29 Oct. 1944; *France-Libre*, 4 Oct. 1944.
49. H. Frenay, *'La Nuit Finira'* (Paris, 1973), 474; see also, F. Billoux, *Quand Nous Étions Ministres'* (Paris, 1972), 61; C. Tillon, *'Les FTP–La guérilla en France'* (Paris, 1967) 417, footnote.
50. Note to Minister of Interior from Valabrègue, 29 Nov. 1944, AN, F1a 3347.
51. Séance du CPL, 31 Oct. 1944, AN, 72 AJ 62, *Gendarmerie Nationale* report, *Synthèses*, 15 Oct.–15 Nov. 1944, AN, 72 AJ, 384; for the CNR and de Gaulle, see de Gaulle, *Mémoires, op.cit.*, vol. 3, 49.
52. *Humanité* 31 Oct. 1944.
53. Madjarian, *op.cit.*, 159; A. Siegfried, *'L'Année Politique, 1944–5'* (Paris, 1946), 47; *Combattre*, no. 13, 17 Dec. 1944.

54. Prefect of Isère, 4 Dec. 1944, AN, Flc III 1219; *Service des Commissariats de la République Seine-et-Oise*, no. 11, 15–30 Nov. 1944, AN, F1a 4028; CR Marseille, 2nd *quinzaine* Dec. 1944, AN, F1a 4023.
55. CR Nancy, 15–30 Nov. 1944, AN, F1a 4024.
56. Report of prefect, 10 Dec. 1944–31 Jan. 1945, AN, Flc III 1222.
57. CR Marseille, 2nd *quinzaine* October 1944, AN, Fla 4023; prefect of La Nièvre, 2nd *quinzaine* Dec. 1944, AN, Flc III 1223.
58. Coulet to *Commissaire à l'Intérieur*, no. 416, 17 Aug. 1944, AN, Fla 4008, and no. 1328, 14 Aug. 1944, AN, Fla 4008; see also, Baudot, *op.cit.*, 233.
59. J. L. Panicacci, '*Le Comité Départemental de Libération des Alpes-Maritimes* (1944–47), RHDGM, no. 127, vol. 32, July 1982.
60. H. Ingrand, '*Libération de l'Auvergne*' (Paris, 1974), 142.
61. *Bulletin Officiel du CDL de l'Allier*, no. 1 Aug.–Sept. 1944, AN, Flc III 1205; Ingrand, *op.cit.*, 161; CR Clermont-Ferrand, 15–31 Oct. 1944, AN, Fla 4021.
62. In Michel (ed.), *Colloque sur la Libération*, *op.cit.*; Foulon, *op.cit.*,509.
63. CR Châlons-sur-Marne, 9 Nov. 1944, AN, Fla 4020.
64. CR, Châlons-sur-Marne, 10 Sept. 1944, AN, Fla 4020.
65. Bertaux, *op.cit.*, 159.
66. Panicacci, *op.cit.*; SHAEF G5 (Ops.), 5 Oct. 1944, PRO, WO 171 56; Alban to d'Astier de la Vigerie, 11 Sept. 1944, AN, Flc III 1219.
67. Panicacci, *op.cit.*
68. Bertaux, *op.cit.*, 61; Prefect Moselle, 1–15 Nov. 1944, AN, Flc 1222. For work of CLLs see, for example, *Gendarmerie Nationale* report, *Synthèses*, 15 Sept.–15 Oct. 1944.
69. In F. L'Huillier, '*Libération de l'Alsace*' (Paris, 1975), 170.
70. CR Nancy, 15–31 Oct. 1944, AN, Fla 4024.
71. CR Marseille, 2nd *quinzaine* Nov. 1944, AN, Fla 4023.
72. CR Clermont-Ferrand, 6 Oct. 1944, AN, Fla 4021; Madjarian, *op.cit.*, 123.
73. Madjarian, *op.cit.*, 128.
74. Prefect Bouches-du-Rhône, Sept, 1944, AN, Flc III 1210.
75. CR Marseille, 1–15 Dec. 1944, AN, Fla 4023.
76. C. Foulon, *Le Pouvoir en Province*, *op.cit.*, 222.
77. CR Marseille, 2nd *quinzaine* Nov. 1944, AN, Fla 4023.
78. Summary of civil affairs up to 31 Aug. 1944, VOG 119, PRO, FO 371 42018; CA weekly summary no. 11, 26 Aug. 1944, PRO, FO 371 42019.
79. CA summary of field reports, no. 9 up to 11 Aug. 1944, PRO, FO 371 42018.
80. CA summary no. 3, 14 Sept. 1944, PRO, WO 220; see also fortnightly report no. 4, 21 Army group L of C (CA) HQ, 2–16 Sept. 1944, PRO, WO 171 722; CA Report S. France, 23–30 Sept. 1944, PRO, WO 220 69.
81. Field reports through 26 Aug. and results Inspection Asst. COS G5, Cadrep no. 2, PRO, FO 371 42019.
82. Minutes of meeting 28 Sept. 1944, PRO, WO 219 3906; also SHAEF G5 to AGWAR, VOG 129, Sept. 1944, PRO, WO 220.
83. Major Fry, CA det. 329, 12/12 Sept. 1944, PRO, WO 171 3622.
84. HQ central gp. of armies rear to SHAEF, 410551, 4 Sept. 1944, PRO, WO 219 13; see also, CA fortnightly report, No. 4 (1st Canadian Army), up to 16 Sept. 1944, PRO, FO 371 42020.
85. SHAEF G5 weekly CA summary, no. 19, up to 21 Oct. 1944, PRO, FO 371 42020; SHAEF G5 weekly CA summary, no. 18, up to 13 Oct. 1944, PRO, FO 371 42020; SHAEF G5 (Ops) 850/6 CA weekly summary No. 18, 14 Oct. 1944, PRO, WO 174 56; SHAEF G5 850/6, weekly summary no. 2, 11 Nov. 1944, PRO, WO 220 69.
86. 'Political situation in France', 19 Oct. 1944, PRO, WO 219 3846, quoted in

information from 6th Army Group, 7 Oct. 1944, PRO, WO 219 3735; compare SHAEF G5 (Ops) 850/6 CA weekly summary no. 17, 5 Oct. 1944, PRO, WO 171 56.

87. SHAEF counter intelligence summary no. 2, week ending 27 Oct. 1944, PRO, WO 219 601.

88. Maj. Palfrey, HQ Paris CA dets., 1st European CA Regiment, 27 Oct. 1944, PRO, WO 219 3528 report to SAC, appendix A of this report.

89. AGWAR to SHAEF, 24 Oct. 1944, PRO, WO 219 601; response, SHAEF to AGWAR, 26 Oct. 1944, PRO WO 219 601.

90. See, for example, SHAEF analysis sheet, 20 Oct. 1944, PRO, WO 219 3753; on situation and numbers on Spanish border, see: Military adviser to SHAEF, 14 Oct. 1944, PRO, WO 106 4409A; telegrams Cappart, no. 271, AN, 72 AJ 444; note from prefect at Perpignan on situation of frontiers, 9 Sept. 1944, AN, 72 AJ 449; SHAEF to AGWAR, 5 Nov. 1944, WO 219 601; supplementary report Cpt Pietsch, 3 Oct. 1944, AN, 72 AJ 84; CA report S. France, 16 Sept. 1944–23 Sept. 1944, PRO, FO 371 42020; summary of field reports through 3 Sept. 1944, CADREP no. 3, PRO, FO 371 42019; CA report S. France 31 Aug. 1944–6 Sept. 1944, PRO, FO 371 42018; see report by Maj. Hughes, OSS, attached to CA HQ 7th Army, 17 Sept. 1944, PRO, WO 219 3753.

91. Allied Force HQ G5 APO 512, report by Maj. Hughes, 'Political Conditions in the Alpes-Maritimes', 17 Sept. 1944, PRO, Wo 219 3753.

92. 'Report on Conditions in S. France', JIC ANA (Naples) to AFH OSS 96519, up to 16 Sept. 1944, PWE/OSS Daily Int. Reports no. 96, 12 Sept. 1944, Military Int. Div., no. 21639, OSS 94041, 5 Sept. 1944, PWE/OSS Daily Int. reports, no. 94, 10 Sept. 1944, OSS ETOUSA R and A branch Paris, OSS 94990, 26 Sept. 1944; 7 Dec. 1944, OSS (ETO) US Army, R and A Paris, 14 Dec. 1944, OSS APO 887, 7 Dec. 1944.

93. JIC ANA (Naples), OSS 108946, 19 Dec. 1944; JIC ANA, 'Political Tendencies in Lyon Region', OSS 102512, 7 Nov. 1944.

94. Memo on liberation of S. France from Lt Commander Brooks-Richards (SOE), Maj, Ayer (SOE), Cpt Storrs (SOE), 7 Oct. 1944, PRO, FO 371, 41907.

95. Report no. 2 on 'Political Situation in SW France', 22 Oct. 1944, PRO, FO 371 41907.

96. C. Brinton, 'Letters from Liberated France', in *French Historical Studies* 2 (Spring, 1961).

97. JIC ANA (Naples) Toulouse, Political tendencies, OSS 105488, 29 Nov. 1944.

98. JIC ANA, 'Political Tendencies in Lyon Region', OSS 102512, 17 Nov. 1944.

99. ETOUA, R and A Paris, 'Report on the Lille Region', OSS 103350, 13 Nov. 1944.

100. Memo on liberation of S. France, *op.cit.*, footnote 94.

101. Report no. 2 on SW France, *op.cit.*, footnote 95.

102. SHAEF to AGWAR, VOG 234, 18 Dec. 1944, PRO, FO 371 42021; CA weekly summary no. 26, 9 Dec. 1944, PRO, WO 121 57; SHAEF Mission (France), no. 7, 15 Dec. 1944, PRO, WO 202 753.

103. JIC ANA (Naples) SN 16595, OSS 108946, 19 Dec. 1944.

104. US Office of War Information, Work of CA dets. in France, 15 Sept. 1944, PRO, FO 371 42020; see also, 7th US Army HQ, CA summary, 2 Sept. 1944, PRO, WO 220 69.

105. CA semi-weekly summary, S. France, no. 2, 2 Sept. 1944, PRO, FO 371 42018.

106. 21st Army Group CA report for Sept. 1944, dated 19 Oct. 1944.

107. Quoted in C. Foulon, *Le Pouvoir en Province, op.cit.*, 205.

108. Note P. Laroque to DM Zone nord, 13 Aug. 1944, AN, Fla 4008.

109. In supplement to report S. France, Lt. Col. Mitchell, 31 Aug. 1944–6 Sept. 1944, PRO. WO 220 69, Letter Aubrac to Cochet, 28 Aug. 1944, AN, 72 AJ 449.

110. CR Toulouse, report on Allied relations, 15 Nov. 1944, AN, Fla 3304; also 3 Sept. 1944, An, 72 AJ 449. On Allied Officers remaining in France, see MRD Foot, 'SOE in France' (1966), 420, 421; Ayers memo, footnote 94; Bertaux, *op.cit.*, 82.

111. First Canadian Army CA fortnightly report, no. 3, 21 Sept. 1944, PRO, FO 371 42018.

112. See, for example, *Gendarmerie Nationale* report, *Synthèses*, 15 Nov. 1944–15 Dec. 1944, AN, 72 AJ 384; weekly CA summary, no. 90, 28 Sept. 1944, PRO, FO 371, 42020.

113. C. Foulon, *Le Pouvoir en Province, op.cit.*, 202, footnote 7.

114. CR Nancy, 1–15 Nov. 1944, AN, Fla 4024; see also, Bulletin no. 2, *Service des Commissariats de la République*, 15–28 Oct. 1944, AN, Fla 4028.

115. Minister of Interior to Minister of War, 13 Nov. 1944, AN, Fla 3246; see also reports in AN, Fla 4028 and Fla 3291.

116. Report on Franco–American relations in S. France, T force, 6th Army group AFHQ, 15 Dec. 1944, CAD 014 Fr. 8-3-43; for an interesting fictionalized account of this problem see L. Guilloux, *Salido Suivi de OK Joe!* (Paris, 1976).

117. *Gendarmerie Nationale* report, *Synthèses*, 15 Dec. 1944–15 Jan. 1945, AN, 72 AJ, 384; but see also, opinion polls quoted by J. P. Rioux, '*La France de la 4e République*' (Paris, 1980), 19, footnote 1; early Dec. 1944, 71 per cent satisfied with behaviour of American troops.

118. *Gendarmerie Nationale* report, *Synthèses*, 15 Dec. 1944–15 Jan. 1945, AN, 72 AJ 384.

119. Duff Cooper to FO, no. 245 Saving, 1 Nov. 1944, PRO, FO 371 41926.

120. Holman despatch, no. 233 Saving, 28 Oct. 1944, PRO, FO 371 42083.

121. FS to Duff Cooper, 27 Sept. 1944, PRO, FO 954 9B; Speaight's conversation with Col. Kowaleswki, 29 Oct. 1944, PRO, FO 371 42083; less optimistic despatches from San Sebastián office, Viscount Templewood, 8 Sept, 1944, PRO, WO 106 4409A.

122. Holman to Harvey, 11 Sept. 1944, PRO, FO 371 42081.

123. Letter from Minister of the Interior, 1 Oct. 1944, quoted in Bertaux, *op.cit.*, 162.

124. CR Rennes, 16 Nov. 1944, AN, Fla 3304; CR Nancy, 15–30 Nov. 1944, AN, Fla 4024.

125. SHAEF Mission (France), Notes for conference, 16 Oct. 1944, PRO, WO 219 2748.

126. Second draft of study, 'Hiatus Area of SW France' (PS SHAEF 44/54), 19 Oct. 1944, PRO, WO 219 2748.

127. SHAEF Mission (France), Progress Report no. 2, 15–30 Sept, 1944, Appendix 2, G2 and Devers to SHAEF (ZONE NATOUSA), Oct. 1944, PRO, WO 219 112; Minutes of ACOS Conference with Branch chiefs, 20 Oct. 1944, PRO, WO 171 56.

128. See, for example, views on how to deal with SW France, SHAEF G2 Analysis sheet, 20 Oct. 1944, 30 Nov. 1944, PRO WO 219 3753; views expressed by Col. Pedron at conference at Supreme HQ, 17 Oct. 1944, PRO, WO 219 3753 ('Show the flag'); French division should be enough, without Allied aircraft, SHAEF G3, 19 Oct. 1944, PRO, WO 219 3753.

129. Ref. PWD 14014, 6 Sept. 1944, PRO, WO 219 3528; 6th Army group to SHAEF, 7 Oct. 1944, PRO, WO 219 611; requests to arm French police, supported by PM, Ismay to PM, 14 Nov. 1944, PRO, PREM 3 180/3 and telegram, 26 Nov. 1944, PRO, FO 371 42084, Z189/4.

130. 21st Army Group Historical Survey for Nov. 1944, Part ImPRO, WO 219 3732 1187/178.

131. 21st Army Group Ops A, 2 Nov. 1944, PRO, WO 219 1598A 7–640.

132. SHAEF/17516/Ops. C. Reber and Peake, 29 Dec. 1944, PRO, WO 219 2265. A novel request for direct American intervention was made by Prince Louis of Monaco and his PM who were said to be so afraid of the locals that they asked if Monaco could become a protectorate of the USA, see Coles and Weinberg, *op.cit.*, 764, and SHAEF G5 Ops. 850/6 Appendix A to GA weekly summary, 5 Oct. 1944, PRO, WO 171 56.

133. Caffery to Secretary of State, no. 45, 27 Oct. 1944, NA, 851.01/11–944.

134. Caffery to Secretary of State, 9 Nov. 1944, NA, 851.01/11–944.

135. Chapin memo, 'General Political Situation in France', 9 Nov. 1944, NA, 850.01/11–944.

136. 12 Oct. 1944, NA, 851/00B/10–1244.

137. Fullerton to State dept., Boyd's report on Toulouse, 8 Dec. 1944, NA, 851.00/12–844; memo from Boyd on Montpellier, 29 Nov. 1944, NA, 851.00/12–844; Caffery to Secretary of State, report of Boyd, 27 Nov. 1944, NA, 851.00/11–2744.

138. Caffery to Secretary of State, Telegram 784, 3 Dec. 1944, NA, 851.00/12–344.

139. Duff Cooper's comment, enclosing Reilly/Muggeridge conversation with Mauriac, 8 Oct. 1944, PRO, FO 371 42083.

140. Situation report no. 1, Saving 175, 14 Oct. 1944, FO 371 42083; see also, Situation report no. 3, Saving 291, 11 Nov. 1944, PRO, FO 371 42084.

141. Telegram no. 330, 2 Dec. 1944, PRO, FO 371 41926.

142. Duff Cooper to Harvey, 17 Oct. 1944, PRO, FO 371 41864.

143. Duff Cooper to FS, Saving 34, 17 Sept. 1944, PRO, FO 954 9B.

144. E.g. Passy's claim that the USSR was subsidizing French right-wing papers, treated with scepticism, and collaboration between French and British Communist Parties, copied by Hollis to Philby: see, Speaight to Holman, 11 Oct. 1944, PRO, FO 371 41864, Holman to Speaight, 21 Nov. 1944, PRO, FO 371 41864; Box no. 500 enclosure, 17 Dec. 1944, PRO, FO 371 42131.

145. Harvey comment, 8 Sept. 1944, PRO, FO 371 42012.

146. Simpson comment, 1 Nov. 1944, PRO, FO 371 42012; Holman to Harvey, 12 Sept. 1944, PRO, FO 371 42081.

147. Harvey to Leggett, 7 August 1944, PRO, FO 371 42061.

148. See note on report of Mr Child's visit to south of France, 19 Sept. 1944, PRO, FO 371 42020. FS forwarded to PM on other hand report from Paris that US chargé d'affaires was recommending recognition, 'It pays to be first in the field', Telegram FS to PM, Cordite 150, 12 Sept. 1944, PRO, FO 371 42024.

149. Eden to PM, 'Note on advantages and disadvantages of recognition', 26 June 1944, PRO, FO 371 42024.

150. Holman to Harvey, 24 Dec. 1944, PRO, FO 371 49146.

151. Chapin to Secretary of State, 15 Sept. 1944, FRUS, vol. 3, 1944, 664.01.c. 14.76; 851.01/9.1544; further confirmation of Eisenhower's views, Duff Cooper to FO, 19 Sept. 1944, PRO, FO 371 41958.

152. Bonbright to President, 17 Sept. 1944, NA, 851.01/9–1744; Matthews to Hull, 21 Sept. 1944, NA, 851.01/9–2144; Matthews to Hopkins, 25 Sept. 1944, NA, 851.01/9.2544.

153. FDR to Hull, 22 Sept. 1944, NA, 851.01/9–2244; Hull to American Embassy, Paris, 29 Sept. 1944, NA, 851.01/9–1544.

154. PM to FS, Gunfire 93, 12 Sept. 1944, PRO, FO 371 42024.

155. Harvey's comment, 18 Sept. 1944, on PM to FS, Gunfire 198, 16 Sept. 1944, PRO, FO 371 42024; Simpson's comment on Hull's reply at 1 Sept. press conference, PRO, FO 371 41958.

156. In FO to Paris, Saving 140, 28 Sept. 1944, PRO, FO 371 42024.

157. In FO to Paris, Saving 169, 2 Oct. 1944, PRO, FO 371 42024.

158. See 4 Oct. 1944, PRO, FO 371 42024, and 11 Oct. 1944, PRO, FO 371 42025.

159.  See Speaight memo updating the situation, 4 Oct. 1944, PRO, FO 371 42025; note Bidault surprise at HMG's condition, Paris to FO, 6 Oct. 1944, PRO, FO 371 41883.
160.  President to PM, 20 Oct. 1944, PRO, FO 371 42025; for Leahy, see Washington to FO, no. 5486, 8 Oct. 1944, PRO, FO 371 42024.
161.  SHAEF FWD to AGWAR, FWD 13533, 2 Sept. 1944, PRO, WO 219 3846.
162.  Speaight's comment, 1 Oct. 1944, PRO, FO 371 42024.
163.  See WP (44) 551 on Morton's visit, 25 Sept. 1944, PRO, FO 371 41864; also, PM/44/651, 6 Oct. 1944, PRO, FO 371 42090.
164.  Telegram Peake to FO, no. 115, PRO, FO 371 42090.
165.  SHAEF/1/Pol., 27 Sept. 1944, PRO, WO/371 42090.
166.  SHAEF G3, 3 Oct. 1944, PRO, WO 219 3753.
167.  AGWAR to SHAEF, 28 Nov. 1944, PRO, WO 219 3753; also, Duff Cooper to FO, no. 265, 21 Oct. 1944, PRO, WO 106 4279.
168.  President to PM, no. 631, 20 Oct. 1944, PRO, PREM 3 177/7 633.
169.  Hull to Paris Embassy, 19 Oct. 1944, NA 851.01/10–1544; Cadogan to FS, no. 1405, 21 Oct. 1944, PRO, FO 371 42025; Cadogan to PM, Drasic 189, 21 Oct. 1944, PRO, WO 106 4279.
170.  Cadogan diaries, *op.cit.*, 23 Oct. 1944. For the American version, see J. Hurstfield, *America and the French Nation, 1939–1945* (N. Carolina, 1986), 221.
171.  Washington to FO, no. 5718, 21 Oct. 1944, PRO, FO 371 42025; President to PM, no. 633, 23 Oct. 1944, PRO, FO 371 42026.
172.  Cadogan diaries, *op.cit.*, 23 Oct. 1944.
173.  De Gaulle, *'Mémoires de Guerre'*, *op.cit.*, vol. 3, 54.
174.  Donovan to Secretary of State, 6 Oct. 1944, NA, 851 01/10–644.

# 7    The establishment of GPRF authority, January–April 1945

1.  Quoted in E. Mortimer in *Communist Power in Europe 1944–49*, ed. M. McCauley (1979), 151.
2.  *Humanité*, 4 Oct. 1952.
3.  In G. Willard, V. Joannes, F. Hincker and J. Elleinstein, *De la guerre à la Libération, la France de 1939 à 1945* (Paris, 1972), 101–2.
4.  M. Agulhon in H. Michel (ed.) *Colloque sur la Libération, op.cit.*, 87–8.
5.  See A. Lecoeur, *L'Autocritique Attendue* (Paris, 1955).
6.  In A. Rieber, *Stalin and the French Communist Party 1941–47* (Columbia, 1962).
7.  A. Kriegel, *Communismes au Miroir Français* (Paris, 1974) 162.
8.  *Le PCF dans la guerre* (Paris, 1980), 466.
9.  FRUS, 1944, vol. 5, 723.
10.  G. Ceretti, *A l'Ombre des deux T, 40 ans avec P. Togliatti et M. Thorez* (Paris, 1973) 385.
11.  Quotes in Mortimer, *op.cit.*, 151.
12.  Agulhon, *op.cit.*, 70–7.
13.  A. Kriegel, *Les Communistes Français* (Paris, 1970), 76, 75, 73.
14.  Courtois, *op.cit.*, 466.
15.  *Ibid.*, 462.
16.  *Ibid.*, 463.
17.  *Ibid.*, 464.
18.  *Ibid.*
19.  *Ibid.*, 463.
20.  Quoted in Madjarian, *op.cit.*, 136.

21. Quoted in J. Fauvet, *'Histoire du PCF'*, vol. 2 (Paris, 1965) 139.
22. Courtois, *op.cit.*, 406.
23. Fauvet, *op.cit.*, 148.
24. De Gaulle, *op.cit.*, 77.
25. In Feis, *op.cit.*, 475.
26. P. Robrieux, *'M. Thorez vie secrète et vie publique'* (Paris, 1975), 285.
27. *Année Politique, 1944–45, op.cit.*, 92.
28. Fauvet, *op.cit.*, 151.
29. *Ibid.*, 166, 147.
30. *Humanité*, 4 Oct. 1952.
31. See Fauvet, *op.cit.*, 167.
32. Madjarian, *op.cit.*, 199.
33. Quoted in G. Elgey, *'Histoire de la 4e République, la République des Illusions, 1945–51'* (Paris, 1965), 22.
34. Prefect Vaucluse, 1 Sept. 1944–1 Feb. 1945, AN, Flc III 1230; Prefect Ain, 15 Jan. 1945–15 Feb. 1945, AN, Flc III 1205.
35. Prefect Puy-de-Dôme, 16 Feb. 1945–15 March 1945, AN, Flc III 1223; Bouches-du-Rhône, 15 Jan. 1945–15 Feb. 1945, AN, Flc III 1210.
36. See *Contrôles Techniques*, no. 4, *2e quinzaine* Feb. 1945, AN, F7 14936; no. 5, 20 March 1945, AN, F7 14936.
37. Prefect L'Allier, 15 Jan. 1945–15 Feb. 1945, AN, Flc III 1205; prefect Deux-Sèvres, 15 Feb. 1945–15 March 1945, AN, Flc III 1229.
38. Letter CR Marseille to Minister of Interior, 1 Feb. 1945, AN, Fla 3291.
39. Madjarian, *op.cit.*, 202.
40. Prefect Var, 16 Feb. 1945, AN, Flc III 1230.
41. Prefect la Nièvre, 25 Feb. 1945, AN, Flc III 1230; prefect Haute-Marne, 31 Jan. 1945–28 Feb. 1945, AN, Flc III 1222; prefect Saône et Loire, 1–10 March 1945, AN, Flc III 1225; prefect L'Allier, 15 Jan. 1945–15 Feb. 1945, AN, Flc III 1205.
42. See, for example, prefect Rhône, 15 Jan. 1945–15 Feb. 1945, AN, Flc III 1225; CR, *2e quinzaine* Feb. 1945, AN, Fla 1225; prefect Gard, 15 March 1945, AN, Fla 4028; *Gendarmerie Nationale* Synthèses 15 Jan. 1945–15 Feb. 1945, AN, 72 AJ 384.
43. *Service central des CR*, 15 Feb. 1945, AN, Fla 4020; also CR Châlons-sur-Marne, 1 Feb. 1945, AN, Fla 4020; prefect Vaucluse, 1 Feb. 1945–15 March 1945, AN, Flc III 1230.
44. *Combat*, 16 Jan. 1945.
45. Prefect Charente-Maritime, 10 Feb. 1945–10 March 1945, AN, Flc III 1213; prefect Ain, 15 Feb. 1945–15 March 1945, AN, Flc III 1205.
46. *Service central des CR*, 1–15 Feb. 1945, AN, Fla 4022; *service central des CR*, Toulouse, 15 Jan. 1945–16 Feb. 1945, AN, Fla 4028; prefect Bouches-du-Rhône, 15 Feb. 1945–16 March 1945, AN, Flc III 1210; prefect L'Allier, 15 March 1945–15 April 1945, AN, Flc III 1205; prefect Vaucluse, 15 April 1945–15 May 1945, AN, Flc III 1230.
47. *CR Marseille*, 1st *quinzaine* April 1945, AN, Fla 4023.
48. See SHAEF (France) enclosure to Minister of Interior of report by Lt. Col. Sawyer (20 Feb. 1945) visit to Lille, AN, Fla 3373.
49. Kirk to Secretary of State, quoting Macmillan, FRUS, *op.cit.*, 675; Harvey to Cadogan, 15 Jan. 1945, PRO, FO 371 49154; Fleece 354, 9 Feb. 1945 PRO, PREM 3 185/2.
50. Duff Cooper no. 152, forwarding Kay's despatch, 9 Feb. 1945, PRO, FO 371 49096. For Belgium, see G. Warner, *The Politics of Liberation: Belgium*, forthcoming.
51. Duff Cooper to Eden, no. 150, 9 Feb. 1945, PRO, FO 371 49146.
52. OSS Paris Intelligence weekly, no. 20, 1 Feb. 1945, PRO, WO 219 3754.

53. OSS Paris Intelligence weekly, no. 22, 15 Feb. 1945, PRO, WO 219 3754.
54. OSS Paris Intelligence weekly, no. 23, 22 Feb. 1945, PRO, WO 219 3754.
55. OSS Paris Intelligence weekly, no. 25, 8 March 1945, PRO, WO 219 3754.
56. OSS Supplement to Paris Intelligence weekly, no. 20, 1 Feb. 1945, 'Report on Catholic Progressives', PRO, WO 219 3754.
57. SHAEF Mission (France), Report no. 1 on Internal security in France, 10 March 1945, PRO, WO 219 2265.
58. F. Brown (SHAEF) to Reilly, 30 March 1945, PRO, FO 371 49073.
59. SHAEF Mission (France), Internal security in France, report no. 7, 2 June 1945, PRO, WO 219 1599 and WO 219 2265.
60. SHAEF Mission (France), report no. 8, 16 June 1945, PRO, WO 219 1599. See also, Wintour to Baumer, 1 June 1945: 'The considered opinion of the SHAEF Mission (France) is that the French administration may break down in the autumn and winter.' PRO, WO 219 2265.
61. SHAEF Progress report no. 12, 16–28 Feb. 1945, PRO, FO 371 49096.
62. Internal Security France no. 1, 10 March 1945, PRO, WO 219 2265; report Cpt. Norton-Griffiths, 25 Nov. 1944–10 Jan. 1945, PRO, WO 219 2265.
63. W. Mabane report on visit to Paris, Jan. 1945, PRO FO 371 49130.
64. SHAEF enclosure to Minister of Interior of report of Lt. Col. Sawyer's visit to Lille, 20 Feb. 1945, AN, Fla 3373.
65. SHAEF Mission (France), Internal security in France, report no. 4, 6 April 1945, PRO, WO 219 1599.
66. SHAEF Mission (France), Internal security in France, report no. 6, PRO, WO 219 1599.
67. SHAEF/17516/Ops (C), Directive on Internal security, 23 Jan. 1945, PRO, WO 219 210.
68. SHAEF/17516/Ops (C), to DAC of S-G-3 from Nevins, 20 Jan. 1945, PRO, WO 219 2265.
69. SHAEF Mission to France, no. 10, 16–31 Jan. 1945, Appendix B-G2 and Appendix C-G3, 1 Feb. 1945, PRO, WO 202 755.
70. SHAEF/17516/Ops (C)-G3 to COS, 20 Jan. 1945, PRO, WO 219 210, and WO 219 2265.
71. SHAEF Mission to France, Progress report no. 11, 1–15 Feb. 1945 and Appendix B(ii)G2, PRO, WO 202 756, also PRO, FO 371 49096.
72. SHAEF Mission (France), Progress report no. 12, 16–28 Feb. 1945, and Appendix B(ii)G2, PRO, WO 202 757.
73. 'Plan for the co-ordination of internal security in France', March 1945, PRO, WO 219 2265.
74. SHAEF Mission (France), Internal security in France, report no. 4, April 1945, PRO, WO 219 2265.
75. G3 to AEF Mission France, 22 April 1945, PRO, WO 219 1599; also, Chiefs Ops A subsection to G3 Whitely, 16 April 1945, PRO, WO 219 2265.
76. US Political office to G3 SHAEF, Internal security in France, 16 June 1945, PRO, WO 219 2265.
77. Caffery to Secretary of State, *FRUS, Conferences at Malta and Yalta*, 1945, 675; *Combat*, 30 Jan. 1945.
78. Gen. Catroux, *J'ai vu Tomber le Rideau de Fer* (Paris, 1952), 23.
79. C. de Gaulle, *Mémoires de Guerre, op.cit.*, vol. 3, 58.
80. A. W. Deporte, *De Gaulle's Foreign Policy, 1944–46* (Cambridge, Mass., 1968), 72, 70.
81. *Ibid.*, 73.
82. Harvey, 12 Jan. 1944, quoted in V. Rothwell, *Britain and the Cold War, 1941–47* (1982), 66.

83. *Ibid.*
84. DO Telegram, D. no. 1700, 18 Nov. 1944, PRO, FO 371 42117.
85. FO to Wash. No. 9833, copy of PM to President, 15 Nov. 1944, PRO, FO 371 42117.
86. C. de Gaulle, *Mémoires, op.cit.*, vol. 3, 64–5.
87. FO to Wash. No. 9833, copy of PM to President, 15 Nov. 1944, PRO, FO 371 42117.
88. PM to President, 19 Nov. 1944, *FRUS, Conferences at Malta and Yalta*, 287.
89. Dunn to Stettinius, 10 Nov. 1944, *FRUS, Malta/Yalta*, 293.
90. *Ibid.*, Stettinius to President, 4 Jan. 1945, 293.
91. *Ibid.*, Matthews to Stettinius, 19 Jan. 1945, 297.
92. *Ibid.*, Roosevelt to PM, 6 Dec. 1944, 291.
93. Caffery to Secretary of State, 28 Jan. 1945, *FRUS, 1945, vol. 6*, 665.
94. See 6 Nov. 1944, PRO, CAB 65 (44) WM 146 (44) 5.
95. Deporte, *op.cit.*, 76.
96. Stalin to PM, 3 Dec. 1944, in Churchill, vol. 6, 224.
97. C. de Gaulle, *Mémoires, op.cit.*, vol. 3, 82; Duff Cooper to Eden, 10 Jan. 1945, PRO, PREM 3 173/1 6.
98. Besides de Gaulle, *op.cit.*, see H. Feis, *Churchill, Roosevelt, Stalin* (Princeton, 1957), 475.
99. Moscow to FO, 10 Dec. 1944, PRO, PREM 3 173/1 20.
100. Quote in Deporte, *op.cit.*, 79.
101. FRUS, *Malta/Yalta, op.cit.*, 572.
102. *Ibid.*, 616.
103. *Ibid.*, 616, and 4th Plenary, 7 Feb. 1945.
104. R. Sherwood, *Roosevelt and Hopkins* (New York, 1950), 858.
105. FRUS, *Malta/Yalta*, 897.
106. Deporte, *op.cit.*, 94.
107. Memo, Sargent, 14 Feb. 1945, PRO, FO 371 49154.
108. Harvey, 18 Feb. 1945, PRO, FO 371 49154; Harvey to Western Dept., 18 Feb. 1945, PRO, FO 371 49125; Hoyer Millar to Harvey, 23 Feb. 1945, PRO, FO 371 49066.
109. See, for example, *Le Populaire*, 25–26 Feb. 1945, and *L'Aube*, 16 March 1945.
110. *Libération*, 8 March 1945; *L'Aube*, 16 March 1945.
111. *L'Aurore*, 18 Dec. 1944.
112. *Le Monde* (Y. Cézy), 10 March 1945.
113. Harvey to FS, 30 March 1945, PRO, FO 371 49073.
114. SHAEF Mission (France), Internal security in France, report no. 8, 16 June 1945, PRO, WO 219 1599.
115. Report CR, 1 Feb. 1945, AN, Fla 4020; CR, 1 March 1945, AN, Fla 3373 and Fla 4020. See also, CR, 15 Feb. 1945, AN, Fla 4020.
116. On Le Havre, note 6 Feb. 1945, AN, Fla 3373; on Nancy, CR, 15–31 March 1945, AN, Fla 4024; on Haute Savoie, prefect's report, Feb. 1945, AN, Flc III 1225. For example, CR Marseille, 2e quinzaine, March 1945, AN, Fla 3373; Prefect Cantal, 16 Feb. 1945–15 March 1945, AN, Flc III 1211; on South-east France, military attaché's report, 13–24 April 1945, PRO, FO 371 49097; South-west France, air attaché and second secretary, from 27 March 1945, PRO, FO 371 49097.
117. SHAEF Mission (France), Internal security in France, report no. 3, 31 March 1945, PRO, WO 219 1599.
118. SHAEF Mission (France), Internal secuirty in France, report no. 5, 5 May 1945, PRO, WO 219 1599.
119. SHAEF Mission (France), Internal security in France, report no. 4, 6 April 1945, PRO, WO 219 1599.

120. Quoted in SHAEF Mission (France), Internal security in France, report no. 3, 31 March 1945, PRO, WO 219 1599.
121. *Gendarmerie nationale* report, *Synthèses*, no. 18, 15 Feb. 1945–15 March 1945, Annexe 2, AN, 72AJ 384.
122. JIC SHAEF (45) Final, 12 Feb. 1945, PRO, WO 219 3754.
123. 'Publicizing of Allied Aid to France', SHAEF PR Division, 3 Feb. 1945, PRO, WO 219 169.
124. Confidential report, R. Hannegan, (FEA) Tabf, footnote 17, PRO, WO 219 169.
125. See SHAEF Public Relation Division, 'Allied Aid to France', 2 March 1945, PRO, WO 219 169; AFP statement, 3 April 1945; *Washington Times Herald*, 4 April 1945.
126. S. Reber to COS, 18 March 1945, PRO, WO 219 169; *Le Populaire*, 25–6 March 1945; *Le Monde*, 12 April 1945.
127. *Le Populaire*, 5 April 1945.

# 8   Economic reconstruction and the Allies

1. J. J. Dougherty, *The Politics of Wartime Aid: American Economic Assistance to France and French North Africa, 1940–46* (Westport, 1978) and F. M. B. Lynch, 'The Political and Economic Reconstruction of France, 1944–1947, in the International Context' (PhD thesis, UMIST, 1981).
2. A. S. Milward, *The New Order and the French Economy* (1970), 272.
3. Dougherty, *op.cit.*, 163.
4. PM to FS, Gunfire 284, 19 Sept., PRO, FO 371, 40964; Stopford (War Office) Report, 14–17 Oct. 1944, PRO, FO 371, 40964.
5. Comment by Coulson, 6 Nov. 1944, on the Weir–Green Mission, PRO, FO 371, 40964.
6. *Weir–Green Mission Report*, October 1944, PRO, FO 371, 40964.
7. For Rosenman's Report see Dougherty, *op.cit.*, 165; and British Embassy Report (Gridley Report), 7 Feb. 1945, PRO, FO 371, 49130.
8. Quoted in Dougherty, *op.cit.*, 167.
9. *Ibid.*, 56; Stettinius to Acheson, 851.R24/7, 13 Nov. 1942, FRUS 1943, 3, Washington 1962, 436.
10. See, for example, memo by Hull and discussion, 30 Aug. 1943, 851.01/2830, FRUS 1943, 2, Washington 1964, 188.
11. Balfour to FO, no. 5638, 16 Aug. 1945, PRO, FO 371, 49088.
12. Dougherty, *op.cit.*, 110.
13. *Ibid.*, 150; Culbertson to Secretary of State, 851R.50/9–44, 11 Sept. 1944, FRUS 1944, III, Washington 1965, 763; American Embassy to Ministry of Foreign Affairs, 851.50/4–745, 12 Dec. 1944, FRUS 1944, III, *ibid*.
14. Ministry of Foreign Affairs to American Embassy, 851.50/7–245, 27 Dec. 1944, FRUS, 1944, III, *ibid.*, 766.
15. Bidault to Caffery, 611.5131/1–1145, 9 Jan. 1945, FRUS 1945, IV, Washington 1968, 758; Stimson to Caffery, 611.5131/1–1145, 21 Feb. 1945, FRUS 1945, IV, *ibid*.
16. Secretary of State to Caffery, 10 April 1945, FRUS 1945, IV, *ibid.*, 761–2.
17. Dougherty, *op.cit.*, 155.
18. *Ibid.*, 158.
19. See Lynch, *op.cit.*, 346.
20. For example, Treasury Files, memo by Assistant to the Secretary of the Treasury on 20 Sept. 1944 meeting, Malta/Yalta, FRUS 1944, III, *op.cit.*, 139; Lynch, *op.cit.*, 348.

21. Wing-Commander James PQ, 20 Feb. 1945 and Anderson's response, PRO, FO 371, 49080; see also PRO, FO 371, 49081.
22. Lynch, *op.cit.*, 341.
23. Memo by Chancellor of the Exchequer, WP (45) 169, 16 March 1945, PRO, FO 371, 49081.
24. See letter, Ellis-Rees to Harvey, 8 Feb. 1945, PRO, FO 371, 49080.
25. Memo by Chancellor of the Exchequer, WP (45) 169, 16 March 1945, PRO, FO 371, 49081.
26. Penton to Ellis-Rees, 11 June 1945, PRO, FO 371, 49082.
27. Duff Cooper to FO, no. 8 Remac, 12 Aug. 1945, PRO, FO 371, 49082.
28. Duff Cooper to FO for Chancellor of the Exchequer, no. 1127, 21 Aug. 1945, PRO, FO 371, 49082.
29. Dougherty, *op.cit.*, 172.
30. *Ibid.*
31. Lynch, *op.cit.*, 291.
32. See, for example, Treasury files memo by the Assistant to the Secretary of the Treasury on meeting, 20 Sept. 1944, in FRUS, *op.cit.*, 139.
33. Quoted in Dougherty, *op.cit.*, 179.
34. Lynch, *op.cit.*, 295.
35. *Ibid.*, 296.
36. *Ibid.*, 301.
37. Lacoste to the Secretary of State, 8 Nov. 1945, FRUS 1945, *op.cit.*, vol. 4, 770.
38. Caffery to Secretary of State, 14 Nov. 1945, 611. 5131/11–2545, *ibid*, 771 and Caffery to Secretary of State, 25 Nov. 1945, 611.5131/11–2545, *ibid.*, 773.
39. Lynch, *op.cit.*, 304.
40. *Ibid.*, 306.
41. Caffery to Secretary of State, 9 Feb. 1946, 851.51/2–949 FRUS, 1946, vol. 5, Washington 1969, 413.

# 9   Conclusions: the reconstruction of the state

1. *Le Monde*, 20 Dec. 1944.
2. *Gendarmerie nationale*, report *Synthèses*, 15 Nov. 1944 – 15 Dec. 1944, AN, 72AJ 384; CR Clermont-Ferrand, 1st *quinzaine*, Nov. 1944, AN, Fla 4021; CR Marseille, 1st *quinzaine*, Nov. 1944, AN, Fla 4023.
3. *Le Monde*, 28–9 Jan. 1945.
4. *Le Monde*, 1 Feb. 1945.
5. *Combat*, 26 Jan. 1945.
6. *Ibid.*
7. *Combat*, 3 Feb. 1945. See also, *Le Monde*, 4–5 Feb. 1945.
8. *Le Monde*, 1 Feb. 1945; *Le Monde*, 2 Feb. 1945.
9. CR Dijon, 16–28 Feb. 1945, AN, Fla 4021; CR Marseille, 2e *quinzaine*, Feb. 1945, AN, Fla 4023.
10. See Annexe I in *Gendarmerie nationale* report *Synthèses*, 15 Jan. 1945 – 15 Feb. 1945; 15 Feb. 1945 – 15 March 1945, 15 March 1945 – 15 April 1945, AN, 72AJ 384.
11. See Fauvet, *op.cit.*, 150; B. D. Graham, *The French Socialists and Tripartisme, 1944–47* (1965), 66.
12. See CR Marseille, 1st *quinzaine*, March 1945, AN, Fla 4023; prefect Marne, 1–31 March 1945, AN, Flc III 1222; prefect Bouches-du-Rhône, 15 March 1945 – 16 April 1945, AN, Flc III 1210; prefect Isère, 15 March 1945 – 15 April 1945, AN, Flc III 1219.

13. *Gendarmerie nationale* report, *Synthèses*, Annexe I, 15 Nov. 1944 – 15 Dec. 1944, AN, 72AJ 384.
14. CR Clermont, 16 Oct. 1944, AN, Fla 4021; Wright, *op.cit.*, 67.
15. CR Nancy, 15–31 March 1945, AN, Fla 4024; *Contrôles techniques*, 1st *quinzaine*, Jan. 1945, AN, F7 14936.
16. Quoted in Kramer, *op.cit.*, 229.
17. Figures on recruitment, A. Kriegel, *Les Communistes Français*, *op.cit.*, 13 and 82, footnote 6; Fauvet, *op.cit.*, 154; Rieber, *op.cit.*, 156. Robrieux, vol. 2, 95, has a useful footnote, distinguishing between *cartes expédiées* to the federation, and those signed up: he gives, 1937, 325,453 for former, and 791,373 in 1945.
18. See prefect Cantal 1 Jan. 1945 – 15 Feb. 1945, AN, Flc III 1211; Kriegel, *op.cit.*, 77.
19. See Graham, *op.cit.*, and Kramer, *op.cit.*, 244.
20. See n. 13 (this chapter).
21. See n. 10 (this chapter).
22. Graham, *op.cit.*
23. Quoted in Kramer, *op.cit.*, 250.
24. See R. E. M. Irving, *The Christian Democratic Parties of Western Europe* (1979).
25. For example, 15 Jan. 1945 – 15 Feb. 1945, seven meetings; 15 Feb. 1945 – 15 March 1945, 29; 15 March 1945 – 15 April 1945, 40.
26. *Gendarmerie nationale* report *Synthèses*, 15 March 1945 – 15 April 1945, AN, 72 AJ 384.
27. Kramer, *op.cit.*, 280, 281.
28. Graham. *op.cit.*, 64.
29. See Wright, *op.cit.*, 76.
30. *Le Monde*, 5 May 1945.
31. See Graham, *op.cit.*, 67; Kramer, *op.cit.*, 280; CR Nancy, 15–28 Feb. 1945, 1–15 March 1945, AN, Fla 4024; prefect Rhône, 15 Feb. 1945 – 15 March 1945, AN, Flc III 1225; CR Dijon 1–15 Jan. 1945, AN, Fla 4021.
32. See CR Nancy, 15–30 April 1945, AN, Fla 4024; prefect Charente-Maritime, 10 April 1945 – 10 May 1945, AN, Flc III 1213; CR Nancy, 1–15 May 1945, AN, Fla 4024; *Le Monde*, 6–7 May 1945.
33. *Le Monde*, 25 April 1945, 28 April 1945, 1 May 1945.
34. *Combat*, 3 May 1945, 15 May 1945; *L'Aurore*, 1 May 1945; Kramer, *op.cit.*, 187.
35. For figures and analysis, see *Année Politique*, *op.cit.*, 200–4, 491.
36. Quoted in *Le Monde*, 1 May 1945.
37. *Le Populaire*, 4 May 1945; see also, Graham, *op.cit.*, 70.
38. In Michel and Mirkine-Guétzevitch, *op.cit.*, 216.
39. P. Novick, *The Resistance Versus Vichy*, Columbia, 1968, 52–3.
40. de Gaulle, *Mémoires de Guerre*, *op.cit.*, vol. 2, 213.
41. Quoted in Rioux, *op.cit.*, 52.
42. Madjarian, *op.cit.*, 213–14.
43. Novick, *op.cit.*, 82.
44. For figures see Novick, *op.cit.*, and R. Aron, *Histoire de l'Epuration vol. 1: Le Monde des Affaires* (Paris, 1974), 44–53; and *Des Prisons Clandestines aux Tribunaux d'Exception*, September 1944–June 1949 (Paris, 1969).
45. Novick, *op.cit.*, 159.
46. See, for example, Flandin's trial preparation, PRO, FO 371, 49139.
47. Comment by Speaight, 17 Jan. 1945, on Duff Cooper to FO, no. 11, 4 Jan. 1945, PRO, FO 371, 49139; see also Duff Cooper to FO, no. 338, 22 March 1945, PRO, FO 371, 49140, Embassy to FO, 20 Dec. 1944, PRO, FO 371, 42014.
48. Wright, *op.cit.*, 51.
49. Interview, 2 Feb. 1945, quoted in Kramer, *op.cit.*, Appendix II, 400, 403.

50. Kramer, *op.cit.*, 300
51. For details, see Graham, *op.cit.*
52. de Gaulle, *op.cit.*, 124.
53. Kramer, *op.cit.*, 268.
54. Quoted in *Combat*, 1 Feb. 1945.
55. *Le Monde*, 28 Feb. 1945; *Combat*, 6 Feb. 1945.
56. Prefect Rhône, 15 Jan. 1945 – 15 Feb. 1945, AN, Flc III 1225.
57. For comment see *Combat*, 6 Feb. 1945, 9 Feb. 1945, 3 March 1945.
58. See *Année Politique*, *op.cit.*, 442–51, for de Gaulle's speech; summary of speech and debate, 135–8.
59. For details of the press see Pickles, *op.cit.*, and *Année Politique*, *op.cit.*, 138–42.
60. CR Nancy, 1–15 Feb. 1945, AN, Fla 4024.
61. Prefect Jura, 10 March 1945, AN, Flc III 1219.
62. See n. 10 (this chapter) (Annexe II).
63. See Madjarian, *op.cit.*, 238–9.
64. J. Lacouture, *P. Mendès-France* (Paris, 1981), 155.
65. *Ibid.*, 158.
66. See, for example, Gridley's report on the French economy, 7 Feb. 1945, PRO, FO 371, 49130.
67. Lacouture, *op.cit.*, 164.
68. R. O. Paxton, *Vichy France, Old Guard and New Order, 1940–1944* (1972), 336.
69. Lacouture, *op.cit.*, 166.
70. Quoted in Lynch, *op.cit.*
71. Lacouture, *op.cit.*, 167.
72. *Journal Officiel*, 1945, no. 37, 30 March 1945, 957.
73. Lynch, *op.cit.*, 227.
74. Lacouture, *op.cit.*, 168–70.
75. Madjarian, *op.cit.*, part 3, chapter 2.
76. *Ibid.*, 181 and *Journal Officiel*, 1944, no. 81, 13 Dec. 1944, 507.
77. Gridley Report, 7 Feb. 1945, PRO, FO 371, 49130.
78. P. Hervé, *La Libération Trahie* (Paris, 1945), 12.

# Bibliography

## Archives

BRITAIN

*Public Record Office:*
War Cabinet Minutes and Memoranda, CAB 65/66
War Cabinet, Chiefs of Staff Committee, CAB 79/80
War Cabinet, Combined Chiefs of Staff Committee, CAB 88
Various Ministers and Official Files, CAB 118
Prime Minister's Office, PREM 3/4
Foreign Office, General Correspondence, FO 371
Political Warfare Executive, FO 898
Avon Papers, FO 954
SHAEF Papers, WO 219
War Office Papers, WO 202/220
21st Army Group War Diaries, WO 171

UNITED STATES

*United States National Archives*
*Modern Military Division:*
SHAEF ABC file, SHAEF G4 file, SHAEF G5 file, SHAEF G5 Ops branch, SHAEF
   Secretary of General Staff file.
*Department of War:*
WD Combined Chiefs of Staff/Joint Chiefs of Staff; WD Civil Affairs Division; WD
   OPD file; OSS Historical file group 226; OSS Documents, group 1 France, R and A
   France; OSS 'Survey of underground movements'.
*Department of State Division:*
State Decimal File (740, 851 etc.); Matthews-Hickerson file – record group 59.

FRANCE

*Archives Nationales:*
*Commissariat à l'Intérieur de Londres (sept. 1941 – juin 1943)*
*Délégation à Londres du Commissariat à l'Intérieur d'Alger (juin 1943 – août 1944)*
*Service Central des Commissariats de la République (1945–7)*
*Rapports des préfets depuis la Libération (1944–6)*
*Cabinet du Ministre de l'Intérieur (1944–7)*

72 AJ series

*Fonds d'Astier de la Vigerie*

*Fonds Cochet*
*Fonds Frenay*

*Institut d'Histoire du Temps Présent*:
Collected *témoignages*

*Association pour la Création d'un Musée de la Résistance*:
*Fonds Tollet*

NOTE:
In the following sections, the bibliography refers only to material which has been
found particularly useful in this study.
CHDGM and RHDGM refer respectively to the *Comité d'Histoire de la Deuxième Guerre
Mondiale* and the *Revue d'Histoire de la Deuxième Guerre Mondiale*.

## American memoirs, papers and official histories

Acheson, D., *Present at the Creation: My Years in the State Department* (New York, 1969)
Alsop, S. and Braden, T., *Sub Rosa* (New York, 1946)
Arnold, H., *Global Mission* (New York, 1949)
Blum, J. M., *From the Morgenthau Diaries: Years of War 1941–1945* (Boston, 1967)
Blumenson, M., *The Patton Papers* (Boston, 1972)
Brinton, C., 'Letters from Liberated France', *French Historical Studies 2 (1)* Spring 1961
Bullitt, O. H., *For the President: Personal and Secret; Correspondence Between Franklin D.
    Roosevelt and William C. Bullitt* (Boston, 1972)
Butcher, H. C., *My Three Years With Eisenhower* (New York, 1946)
Byrnes, J., *Speaking Frankly* (New York/London, 1947)
Campbell, T. M. and Herring, G. C., *The Diaries of Edward R. Stettinius Jr. 1943–46*
    (New York, 1975)
Chandler, A. D. (ed.), *The Papers of Dwight David Eisenhower: The War Years*, 5 vols
    (Baltimore, 1970)
Coles, H. L. and Weinberg, A. K., *Civil Affairs: Soldiers Become Governors* (Washington,
    1964)
Conn, S. and Fairchild, B., *The U.S. Army in World War II: The Western Hemisphere*
    (Washington, 1960)
Eisenhower Foundation (foreword by O. N. Bradley), *D-Day: the Normandy Invasion in
    Retrospect* (Lawrence, 1971)
Eisenhower, D. D., *Dear General: Eisenhower's Wartime Letters to Marshall* (Baltimore,
    1971)
——*Crusade in Europe* (1948)
Freedman, M. (ed.), *Roosevelt and Frankfurter: Their Correspondence* (1967)
Hassett, W. D., *Off the Record with FDR* (1960)
Hull, C., *The Memoirs of Cordell Hull*, 2 vols (New York, 1948)
Israel, F. L., *The Diaries of Breckenridge Long* (Lincoln, Nebraska, 1966)
Kimball, N. F., *Roosevelt and Churchill: The Complete Correspondence* (Princeton, 1984)
Langer, W. L., *Our Vichy Gamble* (New York, 1947)
Leahy, W. D., *I Was There* (New York, 1950)
Lowenheim, F. L., et. al., *Roosevelt and Churchill: Their Secret Wartime Correspondence*
    (New York, 1975)
Maginnis, J. J., *Military Government Journal* (Boston, 1975)
Marshall, G. C., *The Winning of the War in Europe and the Pacific—the Biennial Report of
    the Chief of Staff of the U.S. Army*, 1 July 1943 – 30 June 1945 (New York, 1945)
Morgan, W., *OSS and I* (New York, 1947)

Murphy, R., *Diplomat Among Warriors* (New York, 1964)
Notter, H., *Post-War Foreign Policy Preparation 1939–1945* (Washington, 1949)
Patton, G., *War As I Knew It* (Boston, 1947)
Pogue, F. C., *Supreme Command* (Washington, 1946)
Roosevelt, F. D., *Franklin D. Roosevelt Papers* (New York, 1959)
Roosevelt, E. (ed.), *Roosevelt Letters* (1952)
Roosevelt, E. and Lash, J. P., *F.D.R.: The Personal Letters, 1928 – 1945* (2nd edn) (New York, 1970)
Rosenman, S. I., *The Public Papers and Addresses of Franklin D. Roosevelt* (New York, 1950)
——*Working with Roosevelt* (New York, 1972)
Sherwood, R. F., *Roosevelt and Hopkins* (New York, 1951)
——*The White House Papers of Harry L. Hopkins: An Intimate History*, 2 vols (New York, 1949)
Smith, R. H., *OSS: The Secret History of America's First Central Intelligence Agency* (Berkley, 1972)
Stimson, H. L. and Bundy, McG., *On Active Service in Peace and War* (New York, 1947)
US Army, *War Reports of Generals Marshall, Arnold and King* (Philadelphia, 1947)
US State Dept. *Foreign Relations of the United States (FRUS)* (Washington, yearly)
USSR Ministry of Foreign Affairs, *Russia: Correspondence Between the Chairman of the Council of Ministers of the USSR and the President of the USA and the Prime Minister of Great Britain during the Great Patriotic War of 1941–45*, 2 vols (Moscow, 1957)

## British memoirs, papers and official histories

BBC War Correspondents, *War Report* (1946)
Beesley, P., *Very Special Intelligence* (1977)
Berlin, I., *Washington Despatches* (1981)
Cadogan, Sir A. (ed. D. Dilks), *The Diaries of Sir Alexander Cadogan* (1971)
Churchill, W. S., *Closing the Ring* (1951)
——*The Grand Alliance* (1950)
——*The Hinge of Fate* (1950)
——*Triumph and Tragedy* (1953)
——*Secret Session Speeches* (1946)
Donnison, F., *Civil Affairs and Military Government, North-West Europe, 1944–1946* (1961)
Duff Cooper, A. D., *Old Men Forget* (1953)
Eade, C. (ed.), *The War Speeches of Winston Churchill* (1965)
Eden, Sir A., *The Eden Memoirs* (1965)
Foot, M. R. D., *SOE in France* (1966)
Halifax, Viscount, *Fullness of Days* (1957)
Harvey, O. (ed. Harvey, S.), *War Diaries 1941–1945* (1978)
Hamilton-Hill, D., *SOE Assignment* (1973)
Lockhart, B., *Comes the Reckoning* (1948)
Macmillan, H., *The Blast of War* (1967)
——*War Diaries: Politics and the War in the Mediterranean; Jan. 1943 – May 1945* (1984)
Marshall, B., *The White Rabbit* (1952)
Nicolson, N. (ed.), *The Diaries of Harold Nicolson*, vol. 2 (1967)
Rennell of Rodd, Lord, *British Military Administration of Occupied Territories in Africa during the Years 1941–1947* (1948)
Sweet-Escott, B., *Baker Street Irregular* (1965)
Wilson, Lord General, Maitland H., *Eight Years Overseas* (1950)
Woodward, Sir L., *British Foreign Policy and the Second World War* (1962)

# French and German memoirs, papers and official histories

Abetz, O., *Histoire d'une Politique Franco–Allemande, 1930–1950: Mémoires d'un Ambassadeur* (Paris, 1953)
Aboulker, M., *Alger et ses Complots* (Paris, 1945)
Alphand, H., *L'Etonnement d'Être: Journal, 1939–1973* (Paris, 1977)
Assemblée Consultative Provisoire, *Journal Officiel de la République Française*, Alger, 1943–4, (Paris, 1944–5)
Auphan, P., 'Mes dialogues de guerre avec M. Teitgen', *Ecrits de Paris, mai* (1973)
Baufre, Gen., *La Revanche de 1945* (Paris, 1966)
Béthouart, A., *Cinq Années d'Espérance* (Paris, 1966)
Bidault, G., *D'Une Résistance à L'Autre* (Paris, 1965)
Billoux, F., *Quand Nous Étions Ministres* (Paris, 1972)
Bloch, J., *La France en Armes* (Paris, 1946)
——*Le Vent Souffle sur L'Histoire* (Paris, 1959)
Bloch, M., *The Strange Defeat* (trans.) (1949)
Blum, L., *À L'Échelle Humaine* (Paris, 1945)
——*Oeuvre: 1940–1945* (Paris, 1955)
Boislambert, H., *Les Fers de L'Espoir* (Paris, 1973)
Bourdet, C., *L'Aventure Incertaine* (Paris, 1975)
Cassin, R., *Les Hommes Partis de Rien* (Paris, 1975)
Catroux, Gen. G., *Dans la Bataille de la Méditerranée: Egypte–Levante, Afrique du Nord, 1940–44* (Paris, 1949)
Ceretti, G., *À L'Ombre des Deux T., 40 Ans Avec P. Togliatti et M. Thorez* (Paris, 1973)
Cerf-Ferrière, R., *L'Assemblée Consultative vue de Mon Banc, nov. 1943 – juillet 1944* (Paris, 1974)
Chauvel, J., *Commentaires, 1. De Vienne à Alger, 1938–1944* (Paris, 1971)
Closon, F. L., *Commissaire de la République du Général de Gaulle: Lille, septembre 1944 – mars 1946* (Paris, 1980)
——*Le Temps des Passions* (Paris, 1974)
Cogniot, G., *Parti Pris*, 2 vols (Paris, 1976)
Coulet, F., *Le Vertu des Temps Difficiles* (Paris, 1967)
Darlan, A., *L'Amiral Darlan Parle . . . .* (Paris, 1952)
D'Astier, E., *Les Dieux et les Hommes* (Paris, 1952)
——*Seven Times, Seven Days* (trans.) (1958)
——*De La Chute à la Libération de Paris, 25 Aôut 1944* (Paris, 1965)
Davidson, J., *Correspondant à Washington: Ce Que Je n'ai Jamais Câblé* (Paris, 1954)
De Gaulle, C., *Mémoires de Guerre*, vols 1–3 (Paris, 1954–1959)
——*War Memoirs, Unity, 1942–1944* (trans.) (1959)
——*Discours de Guerre*, 2 vols (Paris, 1070)
——*Lettres, Notes et Carnets* (Paris, 1980)
De Lattre, J., *History of the First French Army* (trans.) (1952)
——*Reconquérir: Ecrits, 1944–1945* (Paris, 1985)
Duclos, J., *Mémoires* vol. 3 (Paris, 1968)
Farge, E., *Rebelles, Soldats, Citoyens* (Paris, 1946)
Fourcade, M-M., *L'Arche de Noé*, vols 1–2 (Paris, 1971)
Frenay, H., *La Nuit Finira* (Paris, 1973)
Giuraud, H., *Un Seul But, La Victoire* (Paris, 1949)
Gombault, C., *Un Journal, Une Aventure* (Paris, 1982)
Groussard, G. A., *Service Secret, 1940–45* (Paris, 1964)
Herriot, E., *Épisodes: 1940–1944* (Paris, 1950)

Hervé, P., *La Libération Trahie* (Paris, 1946)
Leclerc, Gen. F., *La 2ème D. B.* (Paris, 1955)
Marty, A., *L'Affaire Marty* (Paris, 1955)
Massigli, R., *Une Comédie des Erreurs, 1943–1956* (Paris, 1978)
Mendès-France, P., *Liberté, Liberté Chérie* (Paris, 1977)
Monnet, J. *Mémoires* (Paris, 1976)
Passy, Col., *Souvenirs*, vols. 1–2 (Monaco, 1947), vol. 3 (Paris, 1951)
——*Missions Secrètes en France* (Paris, 1951)
Pedroncini, G., 'Journal de René Mayer', *Revue d'Histoire de la Deuxième Guerre Mondiale* 29, Jan. 1983
Pétain, Maréchal P., *Paroles aux Français* (Lyon, 1941)
Rémy, Col., *10 Ans Avec de Gaulle* (Paris, 1971)
Reynaud, P., *Mémoires* (Paris, 1960, 1963)
Schuman, M., *Un Certain 18 Juin* (Paris, 1980)
Spaak, P. H., *The Continuing Battle* (trans.) (1971)

## Biographies

Ambrose, S.E., *The Supreme Commander: The War Years of General Dwight D. Eisenhower* (New York, 1969)
——*Eisenhower*, 2 vols (1985)
Bellush, B., *He walked Alone: A Biography of John G. Winant* (The Hague, 1968)
Birkenhead, Earl of, *The Life of Lord Halifax* (1965)
Bohanan, R. D., *Dwight D. Eisenhower: A Selected Bibliography* (Abilene, 1981)
Burns, J. M., *Roosevelt, The Soldier of Freedom, 1940–1945* (New York, 1970)
Carlton, D., *Anthony Eden* (1981)
Childs, M. W., *Eisenhower: Captive Hero* (1959)
Current, R. N., *Secretary Stimson: A Study in Statecraft* (Brunswick, 1954)
Devine, R. A., *Eisenhower and the Cold War* (1981)
Donovan, R. J., *Eisenhower: The Inside Story* (New York, 1956)
Fisher, N., *Harold Macmillan: A Biography* (New York, 1982)
Funk, A., *Charles de Gaulle: The Crucial Years* (Oklahoma, 1959)
Gorce, P-M de la, *De Gaulle Entre Deux Mondes* (Paris, 1964)
Gilbert, M., *Winston S. Churchill: vol. 6, 1939–1941* (1983)
Gunter, J., *Eisenhower: The Man and The Symbol* (1952)
Hatch, A., *General Eisenhower: A Biography* (1946)
McCawn, K., *America's Man of Destiny: An Intimate Biography of General Eisenhower* (1952)
Lacouture, J. P., *P. Mendès-France* (Paris, 1981)
Anon., *Pétain: Contributions à un dossier* (Paris, 1978)
Morison, E. E., *Turmoil and Traditions: a Study of the Life and Times of H. L. Stimson* (Princeton, 1947)
Macridis, R. C., *De Gaulle: Implacable Ally* (New York/London, 1966)
Mengin, R., *De Gaulle à Londres* (Paris, 1965)
Muselier, E., *De Gaulle contre le Gaullisme* (Paris, 1946)
Pogue, F. C., *George C. Marshall* (1964)
——*George C. Marshall: Organiser of the Victory* (New York, 1973)
Robrieux, P., *M. Thorez, Vie Secrète et Vie Publique* (Paris, 1975)
Sampson, A., *Macmillan: A Study in Ambiguity* (1967)
Schoenbrun, D., *The Three Lives of Charles de Gaulle* (1965)
Sixsmith, E. K. G., *Eisenhower as Military Commander* (1973)
Summersby, K., *Eisenhower was my Boss* (1949)
Tesson, P., *De Gaulle et La Révolution Manquée* (Paris, 1965)

Touchard, J., *La Gaullisme, 1940–1969* (Paris, 1978)
Tournoux, J. R., *Pétain and de Gaulle* (trans.) (1966)
Warner, G., *Pierre Laval and the Eclipse of France* (1968)
Werth, A., *De Gaulle: A Political Biography* (New York, 1965)

## American politics and foreign policy

Alcorn, R. H., *No Bugles for Spies: tales of the OSS* (New York, 1962; London, 1977)
——*No Banners, No Bands* (New York, 1965)
Bishop, J., *FDR's Last Year* (1974)
Blumenson, M., *The US Army in WW2: Breakout and Pursuit*, Office of the Chief of
   Military History (Dept. of the Army, 1961)
——*Duel for France* (New York, 1963)
Buchanan, A. R., *The United States and World War II*, 2 vols, (New York, 1964)
——(ed.), *The United States 2nd World War II: Military and Diplomatic Documents* (South
   Carolina, 1972)
Cave-Brown, A., *The Secret War Report of the OSS* (New York, 1976)
Cooper, C., *The Lost Crusade. America in Vietnam* (New York, 1970)
Drachman, E. R., *The United States Policy Towards Vietnam 1940–45* (New York, 1970)
Fifield, R. H., *Americans in Southeast Asia* (New York, 1973)
Fulbright, J. W., *The Crippled Giant: American Foreign Policy and its Domestic
   Consequences* (New York, 1972)
Gaddis, J. L., *The United States and the Origins of the Cold War, 1941–1947* (New York,
   1972)
Gardner, L. C., *Architects of Illusion. Men and Ideas in American Foreign Policy, 1941–1949*
   (Chicago, 1970)
Greenfield, K. R., *American Strategy in World War II: A Reconsideration* (Baltimore, 1963)
Harris Smith, R., *OSS: The Secret History of America's First Central Intelligence Agency*
   (New York, 1973)
Hess, G. R., 'Franklin Roosevelt and Indo-China', *Journal of American History* 59 (1972)
Kolko, G., *The Politics of War* (New York, 1968)
——and Kolko, J., *The Limits of Power* (New York, 1972)
MacInnes, D. *Military Government Journal: Normandy to Berlin* (Univ. of Mass. Press,
   1971)
Pogue, F. C., *European Theatre of Operations* (Washington Govt. Printing Office, 1954)
Simpson, B. M., 'The Navy and US/French relations 1942–1944' (Ph.D, Fletcher School
   of Law and Diplomacy, Tuts. Unviersity, 1968)
Smith, Bradley F., *The Shadow Warriors: OSS and the Origins of the CIA* (1983)
Stuart, G. H., *The Department of State: A History of its Organisation, Procedure and
   Personnel* (New York, 1949)
Viorst, *Hostile Allies: FDR and Charles de Gaulle* (New York, 1965)
Warner, G., 'From Teheran to Yalta, Reflections on FDR's foreign policy', *International
   Affairs* 3 (1967)
Welles, S., *The Time for Decision* (New York, 1944); *Where are we heading?* (New York,
   1946)
Wilmot, C., *The Struggle for Europe* (1952)

## British politics and foreign policy

Barker, E., *Churchill and Eden at War* (1978)
Bell, P. M. H., *A Certain Eventuality* (1974)
Buckmaster, M. J., *Specially Employed: the Story of British Aid to the French Patriots of
   Resistance* (1952

——*They Fought Alone* (1958)

Bybelezer, H. M., 'British Policy Towards General de Gaulle and the Free French Movement. June 1940 – November 1942' (Ph.D, Cambridge, 1979)

Cairns, J., 'Great Britain and the Fall of France: a Study in Allied disunity', *Journal of Modern History 27* (1955)

Cointet, J-P. 'Les Relations Entre de Gaulle et le Gouvernement Britannique durant la seconde Guerre Mondiale', *Revue Historique 268 (2)* (1982)

Cookridge, E. H., *Inside SOE—Story of Special Operations in Western Europe 1940–1945* (1965)

Deacon, R., *A History of the British Secret Service* (1969)

Deakin, F. W., 'Great Britain and the European Resistance Movements', in *European Resistance Movements 2* (1964)

Fuller, J. O., *German Penetration of SOE; France 1941–1944* (1975)

Gates, E. M., *End of the Affair, the Collapse of the Anglo-French Alliance, 1939–40* (Berkeley, 1981)

Gaunson, A. B., 'To end a mandate: Sir Edward Spears and the Anglo-French collision in the Levant: 1941–1945' (Ph.D. thesis, Hull, 1981)

Gifford, P. and Louis, W. R., *France and Britain in Africa* (1971)

Horne, A., *To Lose a Battle: France 1940* (1959)

Howard, M., *Special Operations* (1955)

Kersaudy, F., *Churchill and De Gaulle* (1981)

Montague, R., 'France, England and the Arab States', *International Affairs 25* (July 1949)

Rothwell, V., *Britain and the Cold War, 1941–1947* (1982)

Stafford, D., *Britain and European Resistance 1940–1945* (1980)

——'The Detonator Concept: British Strategy, SOE and European Resistance after the Fall of France' in *Journal of Cont. Hist. 10(2)*, 1975

Roskill, S. W., *Churchill and the Admirals* (1977)

Thomas, R. T., *Britain and Vichy* (1979)

Williams, J., *The Ides of May: The Defeat of France May–June 1940* (1968)

Young, J. W., 'The Labour Government's policy towards France, 1945–51' (Ph.D. thesis Cambridge, 1982)

## Inter-Allied politics and diplomacy

Beam, J-C., 'The Intelligence Background of Operation Torch', *Parameters 13* (1983)

Butler, J. R. M., *Grand Strategy* (1957)

Callender, H., *Preface to Peace* (1944)

CHDGM, *La guerre en Méditerranée (comité d'Histoire de la 2e guerre mondiale, colloquium 1969* (Paris, 1971)

De Belot, R., *The Struggle for the Mediterranean 1939–1945* (trans.) (Princeton, 1951)

Dallin, D. J., *The Big Three: U.S., Britain, Russia* (Yale, 1945)

Duroselle, J-B., 'Le conflit stratégique Anglo-Américain de juin 1940 à juin 1944', *RHMC* July–Sept. 1963

Egglestone, G. T., *Roosevelt, Churchill and World War II Opposition: A Revisionist Biography* (Conn., 1979)

Ehrman, J., *Grand Strategy*, vol. 5 Aug 1943 – Sept. 1944, *U.K. Military History Series: History of 2nd World War* (1956)

Feis, H., *Churchill–Roosevelt–Stalin* (Princeton, 1957)

Fischer, L., *The Road to Yalta: Soviet Foreign Relations 1941–45* (New York, 1972)

Funk, A., (ed.), *Politics and Strategy in the Second World War* (Kansas, 1976)

——*The politics of Torch: the Allied Landings and the Algiers Putsch* (Kansas, 1974)

Gun, N. E., *Les secrets des archives américaines: Pétain, Laval, de Gaulle* (Paris, 1979)

Harris, C. R. S., *Allied Military Administration of Italy, 1943–1945* (1957)
Harris, D. E., *The Diplomacy of the Second Front, America, Britain, Russia and the Normandy Landings* (Ph.D. thesis, University of California Santa Barbara, 1969)
Howard, M., *Grand Strategy* (1969)
Hurstfield, J., *America and the French Nation, 1939–1945* (N. Carolina, 1986)
Iriye, A., *Cold War in Asia* (New Jersey, 1974)
Kimball, W., *Churchill and Roosevelt* (1980)
La Feber, W., *America, Russia and the Cold War* (New York, 1967)
——'Roosevelt, Churchill and Indochina, 1942–1945', *American Historical Review 80* (1975)
Lash, J. P., *Churchill and Roosevelt, 1939–1941* (new York, 1976)
Latreille, A., *La Seconde Guerre Mondiale* (Paris, 1967)
Launay, J. de, *Secret Diplomacy of World War 2* (New York, 1963)
Medicott, W. N., *The Economic Blockade* (1959)
Michel, H., *La Deuxième Guerre mondiale*, 2 vols (Paris, 1968)
Pendar, K., *Adventure in Diplomacy, the Emergence of General de Gaulle in North Africa* (1968)
Reynolds, D., *The Creation of the Anglo-American Alliance, 1937–41* (1982)
Sainsbury, K., *The North African Landings 1942* (1976)
Sainteny, J., *Face à Ho Chi Minh* (Paris, 1970)
Sabbatier, Gen. G., *Le Destin d'Indochine: Souvenirs et Documents 1941–1951* (Paris, 1952)
Sharp, A., *The Wartime Alliance and the Zonal Division of Germany* (1975)
Stettinius, E. R., *Roosevelt and the Russians. The Yalta Conference* (New York, 1949)
Stoler, M. A., *The Politics of the Second Front* (Westport, Conn. 1977)
Vidalen, C. J., '*Anglais et Américains dans la guerre de l'ouest*', RHDGM 14, avril, 1954
Viénot, A. P., 'The Levant Dispute: the French Case', *London Quarterly of World Affairs* 9(3), Oct. 1945
Waites, N., *Troubled Neighbours* (1971)
White, D. S., *Seeds of Discord – De Gaulle Free France and the Allies* (New York, 1964)
Williams, A., *Britain and France in the Middle East and North Africa 1914–1967* (1968)

## French Resistance

Amouroux, H., *La grande histoire des Français sous l'Occupation*, 7 vols (Paris, 1976–1985)
Aragon, C. de, *Résistance sans Héroïsme* (Paris, 1977)
Baudot, M., '*La Résistance face aux problemes de répression et d'épuration*', RHDGM 8, Jan. 1971
Bédarida, R., *et.al.*, 'Aspects de la Résistance Française', RHDGM 61, Jan. 1966
——R. and F., *Témoignage Chrétien 1941–44: Les armes de l'esprit* (Paris, 1977)
Calmette, A , *L'OCM, l'Organisation Civile et Militaire* (Paris, 1961)
Choury, M., *Tous bandits d'honneur* (Paris, 1956)
——*Les Cheminots dans la Bataille du Rail* (Paris, 1970)
Dainville, A. de, *L'ORA, la Résistance de l'Armée/Guerre, 1939–1945* (Paris, 1974)
Ehrlich, B., *Resistance France, 1940–45* (1965)
Foot, M. R. D., *Resistance. An Analysis of European Resistance to Nazism, 1940–65* (1976)
Gazagnaure, L., *Le Peuple, héros de la Résistance* (Paris, 1971)
Granet, M., *Ceux de la Résistance (1940–1944)* (Paris, 1964)
Hawes, S. and White, R., *Resistance in Europe: 1939–45* (1975)
Kedward, H., *Resistance in Vichy France* (1978)
Kedward, R. and Austin, R. (eds) *Vichy France and the Resistance: Culture and Ideology* (1985)
Lecoeur, A., *Le Partisan* (Paris, 1965)
Lefranc, G., *Les Expériences Syndicales en France: 1939–1950* (Paris, 1950)

Lefranc, P., *Le Vent de la Liberté* (Paris, 1976)
Luirard, M., 'Courrier français du T. C.', *Cahiers d'Histoire 14.2* (1969)
Montaron, G., *Quoi qu'il en Coûte* (Paris, 1975)
Michel, H., *Histoire de la Résistance* (Paris, 1950)
——and Mirkine-Guétzevitch, B., *Les Idées Politiques et Sociales de la Résistance* (Paris, 1954)
——*Les Courants de Pensée de la Résistance* (Paris, 1962)
——*The Shadow War: The Resistance in Europe* (trans.) (1975)
Noguères, H., *Histoire de la Résistance en France*, 5 vols (Paris, 1967–1981)
RHDGM, '*Les maquis dans la Libération de la France* (numéro spécial)', 55, 1964
——'*Aspects de la Résistance Française*' (numéro spécial), 99, 1975
Rousseau, M., '*La répression dans le Nord de 1940 à 1944*', *Revue de Nord 51*, 203, 1969
Seghers, P., *La Résistance et ses Poètes* (Paris, 1974)
Tillon, C., *Les FTP–Témoignage pour servir à l'Histoire de la Résistance* (Paris, 1962)
——*Les FTP–La Guérilla en France* (Paris, 1966)
——*On Chantait Rouge* (Paris, 1977)
UFF (eds.), *Les Femmes dans la Résistance*, colloquium 1975 (Paris, 1977)
Veillon, D., *Le Franc–Tireur, un journal clandestin, un Mouvement de Résistance, 1940–1944* (Paris, 1977)
Vistel, A., *La Nuit sans Ombre* (Paris, 1970)

## French political forces

Aron, R., *The Vichy Regime 1940–44* (1958)
Auphan, G., *Histoire Elémentaire de Vichy* (Paris, 1971)
Austin, R., 'Propaganda and Public Opinion in Vichy France, the Department of Hérault 1940–1944', *European Studies Review* (October 1983)
Azéma, J-P., *De Munich à la Libération, 1938–1944* (Paris, 1979)
Baudot, M., *L'Opinion Publique sous l'Occupation* (Paris, 1960)
Bellanger, C., *Presse clandestine 1940–44* (Paris, 1961)
Bourderon, R. et.al., *Le PCF Étapes et Problèmes, 1920–1972* (Paris, 1981)
Brissaud, A., *La Dernière Année: Vichy 1943–1944* (Paris, 1964)
Buton, P., '*Le PCF, l'Armée et le Pouvoir*', *Communismes 3*, 1983
Chapsal, J., *La Vie Politique en France depuis 1940* (Paris, 1966)
Cohen, W. R., *Rulers of Empire: The French Colonial Service in Africa* (Stanford, 1971)
Cointet, J. P., *La France Libre* (Paris, 1975)
Cottier, G., *De la Résistance à la Révolution* (Neuchâtel, 1945)
Courtois, S., *Le PCF dans la Guerre* (Paris, 1980)
Crémieux, F. and Estager, J., *Sur le Parti 1939–40*, (Paris, 1983)
Danan, Y-M., *La Vie Politique à Alger de 1940 à 1944* (Paris, 1963)
Dank, M., *The French Against the French* (1978)
Bellescize, D. de, *Les Neuf Sages de la Résistance. Le Comité Général d'Études dans la clandestinité* (Paris, 1979)
Debû-Bridel, *De Gaulle et le CNR* (Paris, 1978)
Jonchay, R. de, *Les Communistes et la Résistance* (Paris, 1970)
Duclos, J. and Joannes, V. (eds), *Le Parti Communiste Français dans la Résistance* (Paris, 1967)
Durand, Y., *Vichy 1940–1944* (Paris, 1972)
Fauvet, J., *Histoire du PCF* (Paris, 1977)
Gaucher, R., *Histoire Secrète du PCF* (Paris, 1974)
Gelly, J-F., '*Le PCF et l'Unité Organique: 1934–1938*', *Le Mouvement Social 121* (Dec. 1982)
Gillois, A., *Histoire Secrète des Français à Londres* (Paris, 1975)

Graham, B. D., *The French Socialists and Tripartisme, 1945–47* (1965)

Halls, W. D., *The Youth of Vichy France* (1981)

Hostache, R., *Le Conseil National de la Résistance* (Paris, 1958)

——*De Gaulle 1944* (Paris, 1978)

Hytier, A. D., *Two Years of French Foreign Policy: Vichy, 1940–1942* (trans.) (Westport, 1974)

Irving, R. E. M., *The Christian Democratic Parties of Western Europe* (1979)

Kaspi, A., *La Mission Jean Monnet à Alger, mars-octobre 1943* (Paris, 1971)

Kedward, R., 'Behind the Polemics: French Communists and the Resistance' in Hawes, S. and White, R. (eds), *Resistance in Europe 1939–1945* (1975)

Kriegel, A., *Communismes au Miroir Français* (Paris, 1974)

Laborie, P., *Résistants, Vichyssois et Autres, l'évoulution de l'Opinion et des Comportements dans le Lot de 1939 à 1944* (Paris, 1980)

Lacretelle, C., *Sur les murs de Paris 1940–44* (Paris, 1959)

Lecoeur, A., *Le PCF et la Résistance: août 1939–juin 1941* (Paris, 1968)

Marrus, M. and Paxton, R., *Vichy France and the Jews* (New York, 1981)

Mast, Gen. C., *Histoire d'une Rébellion: Alger. 8. nov. 1942* (Paris, 1969)

Mayer, D., *Les Socialistes dans la Résistance* (Paris, 1968)

Michel, H., *Histoire de la France Libre* (Paris, 1972)

——'Une Histoire du PCF', *RHDGM 65*, Jan. 1967

Morton, D., 'The Free French Movement' in Toynbee A. and V. (eds), *Survey of International Affairs 1939–1946 4*, 'Hitler's Europe' (1954)

Nordmann, J-T., *Histoire des Radicaux 1820–1973* (Paris, 1974)

Ordion, P., *Tout Commence à Alger (1940–1944)* (Paris, 1972)

Ory, P., *Les Collaborateurs 1940–1945* (Paris, 1977)

——(ed.), *La France Allemande (1933–45)* (Paris, 1977)

Paxton, R., *Parades and Politics at Vichy* (Princeton, 1966)

——*Vichy France: Old Guard and New Order 1940–44* (New York, 1972)

Planchais, J., *Une Histoire Politque de l'Armée vol. 2 1940–1967* (Paris, 1967)

Queille, P., *Histoire diplomatique de Vichy* (Paris, 1976)

Rieber, A. J., *Stalin and the French Communist Party* (New York, 1962)

Rossel, A. (ed.), *La Guerre en Magazine (1940–44)* (Paris, 1977)

Rossi, A., *Les Cahiers du Bolchevisme Pendant la Campagne, 1939–1940* (Paris, 1951)

——*La Guerre des Papillons* (Paris, 1954)

——*Les Communistes Français pendant la drôle de Guerre, 1939–1940* (Paris, 1972)

Sadoun, M., *Les Socialistes sous l'Occupation, Résistance et Collaboration* (Paris, 1982)

——'Les Socialistes ont-ils été Résistants?,' *Histoire 55*, 1983

Simmonds, J., 'The French Communist Party and the beginnings of Resistance: September 1939–June 1941', *European Studies Review 11*, 1981

Stead, J. P., *Second Bureau* (1959)

Sweets, J., *The Politics of Resistance in France, 1940–1944* (Illinois, 1976)

Tollet, A., *La Classe ouvrière dans la Résistance* (Paris, 1969)

UNIR, *Histoire du PCF vol. 2* (Paris, 1962)

Vidal-Naquet, P., 'VIngt-cinq ans de politique communiste' (*Le Monde 22 dec.* 1965)

Willard, G., *De Munich à Vichy: La Drôle de Guerre* (Paris, 1969)

——*La Gestapo contre le Parti Communiste* (Paris, 1984)

——Joannes, V., Hincker, F., and Elleinstein, J., *De la Guerre à la Libération: France de 1939 à 1945* (Paris, 1972)

## Resistance/Liberation: specific areas

Baudot, M., *La Libération de Paris* (Paris, 1966)

——*La Libération de la Bretagne* (Paris, 1972)

——*Libération de la Normandie* (Paris, 1974)

Becamp, P., *La Libération de Bordeaux* (Paris, 1974)

Belfied, E., *Normandie Été 1944* (Paris, 1966)

Bertaux, P., *Libération de Toulouse et de sa Region* (Paris, 1973)

Blumenson, M., 'Politics and the Military in the Liberation of Paris', *The Yale Review* (2), Dec. 1960

Bonard, C., *Marseille, Batailles des Seigneurs* (Geneva, 1972)

Bourderon, R., *Libération du Languedoc méditerranéen* (Paris, 1974)

Bulletin Municipal, *Édité par la ville de Toulouse, no. sp. consacré à la Libération*, Oct. 1944

Chaudier, A., *Limoges 1944–1947: Capitale du Maquis* (Paris–Limoges) 1980

Collins, L. and Lapierre, D., *Is Paris Burning?* (1965)

Crémieux, F., *La Vérité sur la Libération de Paris* (Paris, 1971)

Crosia, *Marseilles: 1944 Victoire française* (Lyon–Paris, 1954)

Dansette, A., *Histoire de la Libération de Paris* (Paris, 1946)

Defromont-Leschevin, A., 'Le Mouvement FTPF dans le Valenciennois', *Revue du Nord 51* (203), 1969

Dejonghe, E., 'Aspects du régime d'occupation dans le Nord et le Pas-de-Calais durant la seconde guerre Mondiale', *Revue du Nord 53* (209), 1971

——(ed.), *Actes du Colloque de l'Université de Lille III tenu les 2 et 3 Novembre 1974 sur la Libération du Nord et du Pas-de-Calais 1944–7*, *Revue du Nord* (special number 226–7), 1975

——and Laurent, D., *Libération du Nord et du Pas-de-Calais* (Paris, 1974)

Denis, H., *Le Comité Parisien de la Libération* (Paris, 1963)

Dreyfus, P., *Vercors, Citadelle de Liberté* (Paris, 1969)

Durand, Y. and Vivier, R., *Libération des Pays de Loire* (Paris, 1974)

États-Généraux, *États Généraux des CDL de la Zone Sud à Avignon les 7–8 Oct. 1944* (Avignon, 1944)

Gambieux, Gen., *La Libération de la Corse* (Paris, 1974)

Goubert, M., 'Une "République Rouge" à Toulouse à la Libération: Mythe ou réalité', *RHDGM 131* (1983)

Granet, E., *Sur les Barricades de Marseille* (Paris, 1947)

Grandval, G. and Colin, A., *La Libération de l'Est de la France* (Paris, 1974)

Guicheteau, G., *Marseille 1943, la fin du Vieux Port* (Paris, 1973)

Guingouin, G., *Quatre Ans de Lutte Sur le Sol Limousin* (Paris, 1974)

Guiral, P., *Libération de Marseille* (Paris, 1974)

Lafierre, P. and Collins, L., *Is Paris Burning?* (1965)

Leroux, R., 'Le Combat de St Marcel' (18 June 1944), *RHDGM 55*, 1964; 64, 1966

L'Huillier, F., *Libération de l'Alsace* (Paris, 1975)

Ingrand, H., *Libération de l'Auvergne* (Paris, 1974)

Massiet, R., *La Préparation de l'Insurrection et la Bataille de Paris* (Paris, 1945)

Mesliand, C., 'La Libération de Marseille', *Cah. Hist. Inst. Maurice Thorez*, 36–37, 1974

Michel, H., *La Libération de Paris* (Paris, 1980)

Négis, A., *Marseille sous l'Occupation 1940–1944* (Paris, 1944)

Panicacci, J. L., 'Le Comité Départemental de Libération des Alpes–Maritimes (1944–1947)', *RHDGM 32*, 1982

Parrotin, A., *Le Temps des Maquis: Histoire de la Résistance en Creuse* (Limoges, 1981)

La Picirella, J., *Témoignages sur le Vercors* (Lyon, 1969); 'La Préfecture de police dans la Libération de Paris', *Liaisons* (special number Paris, *juin–juillet* 1974)

Roland, M., 'La Libération de Lille 2 et 3 Sept 1944', *Revue du Nord 51* (203), 1969

Rol-Tanguy (ed.), *La Libération de Paris* (Paris, 1964)

Romans-Petit, *Les Maquis de l'Ain* (Paris, 1974)

Rude, F., 'Le Dialogue Vercors-Algers', *RHDGM 49*, Jan. 1963

——*Libération de Lyon et de sa Région* (Paris, 1974)

Sauvageot, A., *Marseille dans la Tourmente* (Paris, 1949)
Thornton, W., 'Politics and the military in the Liberation of Paris', *Yale Review*, winter 1961)
Université de Toulouse, *La Libération dans le Midi de la France: colloque* (Toulouse, 1986)
Villate, *'La bataille de Paris (19–25 août) vue du PC. Ile de France'*, *RHDGM 30* (1958)

## The Liberation and beyond

Aron, R., *De Gaulle Before Paris: the Liberation of France June–Aug 1944* (1962)
——*Histoire de l'Épuration* (Paris, 1968)
——*Histoire de la Libération de la France juin 1944–mai 1945* (Paris, 1968)
Ballard, J., *'Souvenirs d'août 1944'*, *Cahiers du Sud* (Oct–Dec. 1944)
Bellanger, C., Michel, H., Lévy, C., *Histoire Générale de la Presse Française de 1940 á 1958* (Paris, 1975)
Bourderon, R., *'La situation de la France au Printemps 1944'*, *Cahiers d'Histoire de l'Instit. M. Thorez, 8–9, 1974*
——*'Colloque Int. de Paris: La Libération de la France'*, *Cahiers d'Histoire de l'Institut M. Thorez 24, 1978*
Brouillet, R., *'Le Général de Gaulle et la Libération de la France'*, *Espoir 9, 1975*
Calmette, A., *'Les équipes Jeburgh dans la bataille de France'*, *RHDGM 61*
Cazaux, Y., *Journal Secret de la Libération* (Paris, 1975)
Symposium of CHDGM (1974), *La Libération de la France* (Paris, 1976)
Debré, M., *'Un grand mouvement préfectoral'*, *Les Cahiers Politiques, XV14 1946 Fév-Mars*
——and Teitgen, P-H., *'Lettre à RHDGM'*, *90, avril 1973*
Deporte, A. W., *De Gaulle's Foreign Policy 1944–1946* (Cambridge, Mass., and 1968)
Dougherty, J. J., *The Politics of Wartime Aid: American Economic Assistance to France and French North Africa, 1940–1946* (Westport, 1978)
Easton, S. L., *The Twilight of European Colonisation: A Political Analysis* (1961)
Elgey, G., *Histoire de la 4e République, la République des Illusions 1945–51* (Paris, 1965)
Foulon, C-L., *'Les Commissaires de la République,'* Thèse de doc. Institut d'Études Politiques (Paris, 1973)
——*Le Pouvoir en Province à la Libération: les Commissaires de la République, 1943–1946* (Paris, 1975)
Le Goyel, Col, *'Libération de la France, l'unification des Forces Armées'*, *Revue Historique des Armées 1 (4), 1974*
Gouberville (Cue de), *'Les missions militaires de liaison dans la Libération'*, *Revue Historique de l'Armée 4 (1969)*
Guilloux, L., *Salido suivi de O.K. Joe!* (Paris, 1976)
Hoffmann, S., *In Search of France* (New York, 1965)
Hostache, R., *'Le Général de Gaulle et les Communistes à la libération'*, *Espoir 9, 1975*
Karnour, S., *Vietnam, a History* (New York, 1983)
Kaspi, A., *'La Libération de la France'*, *Rev. d'Hist. Mod. et Cont.* (1978)
Kramer, S., 'The Provisional Republic, the collapse of the French Resistance Front and the origin of post-war politics' (PhD thesis, Princeton University, 1971)
——*'La Stratégie Socialiste à la Libération'*, *RHDGM 98, 1975*
Kriegel-Valrimont, M., *La Libération: les Archives du COMAC mai–août 1944* (Paris, 1964)
Laborie, P., 'Opinion et Représentations: La Libération et l'image de la Résistance', *RHDGM 131* (1983)
Lacouture, J., *'L'Anniversaire de la Libération de Paris. Une operation conjugée, une operation contestée'*, *Le Monde* (24–25 août 1965)
Lacroix-Riz, A., *'Un ministre communiste et les salaires: A. Croziat'*, *Le Mouvement Social 123* (avril–juin 1983)
Latreille, A., *De Gaulle, La Libération et l'Église Catholique* (Paris, 1978)

Lévy, C., *La Libération: Remise en Ordre ou Révolution?* (Paris, 1974)
Lynch, F. M. B., 'The political and economic reconstruction of France, 1944–1947, in the international context' (Ph.D. UMIST, 1981)
Madjarian, G., *Conflits, Pouvoirs et Société à la Libération* (Paris, 1968)
——*La Question Coloniale et la Politique du PCF 1944–47* (Paris, 1977)
McCauley, M. (ed.), *Communist Power in Europe 1944–1949* (1979)
Milward, A. S., *The New Order and the French Economy* (1970)
——*The Reconstruction of Western Europe 1945–1951* (1984)
Mordal, J. de, *La Bataille de France* (Paris, 1964)
Noguères, L., *La Haute Cour de la Libération* (Paris, 1965)
Novick, P., *The Resistance versus Vichy. The Purge of Collaborators in Liberated France* (Columbia, 1968)
*L'Observateur,* 'Huit Ans Après' (special number 3, *année no.* 119, 21 Aug. 1952, no. 120, 28 Aug. 1952)
Parodi, A., Article in *Le Figaro,* 19 Aug. 1964
Porter, G., *Vietnam—A History in Documents* (New York, 1981)
Pickles, D., *France between the Republics* (1946)
Pilleul, G. (ed.), *Le Général de Gaulle et l'Indochine 1940–1946 (colloque)* (Paris, 1982)
Rioux, J. P., *La France de la 4e République* (Paris, 1980)
Sainteny, J., *Face à Ho Chi Minh* (Paris, 1970)
Sauvy, A., *La Vie économique des Français de 1939 à 1945* (Paris, 1978)
Sérant, P., *Les Vaincus de la Libération* (Paris, 1964)
Vigneras, M., *Rearming the French.* Dept. of the Army Office of Military History (Washington, 1958)
Villon, P., 'Juin–Août 1944', *La Démocratie Nouvelle* (Nov. 1964)
Yacono, X., *Les Etapes de la décolonisation Française* (Paris, 1971)
——*Histoire de la Colonisation Française* (Paris, 1973)

# Index